Scrap Cities

Joyful Modern Architecture-Inspired Quilts

Cathy Perlmutter

ISBN-13: 978-0-9799932-5-1
ISBN-10: 0-9799932-5-3
Published by: Uncommon Page Press
1129 Stratford Avenue
South Pasadena CA
Printed in the United States of America

Questions? Comments? Suggestions? Did you make
something from this book? I would love to hear from you!
Cathy Perlmutter
EMAIL: cathy.perlmutter@gmail.com
WEBSITE: cathyperlmutter.com
ETSY SHOP: https://www.etsy.com/shop/CathyPStudio
BLOG: gefiltequilt.com
FACEBOOK: Cathy Perlmutter
INSTAGRAM: @cathy.perlmutter
YOUTUBE: https://www.youtube.com/@cathyperlmutter1122

This is not a licensed product. I am not affiliated or associated
with any buildings that inspired the artwork in this book.

All photos are by the author, except where
otherwise credited.

**Profound gratitude to my pattern testers for their time,
patience, thought, creativity and rigor!**
Especially members of the Israel Quilters Association, for
bringing their own unique artistic gifts to class. Special thanks
to Flora Cohen and Gail Solomon, for efforts above and
beyond! Thanks to Gail, Margaret Finnegan and Elizabeth
Fieux for sharing their wonderful photos with me.

For my city kids, Riva, Liz, Eli, and Abe, and my Canarsie
husband, Alan.

Table of Contents

3

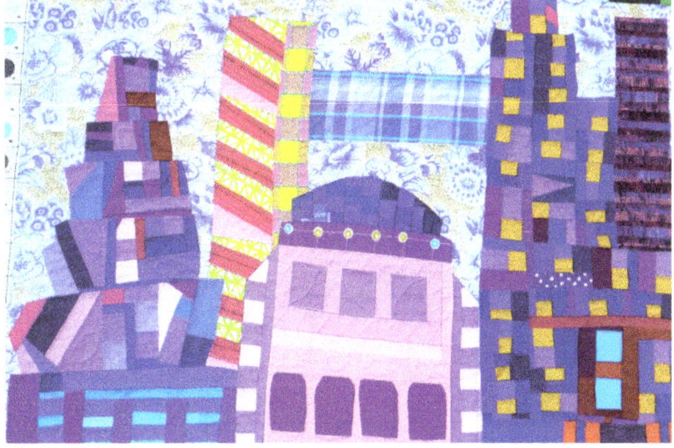

An Accidental Journey Begins...

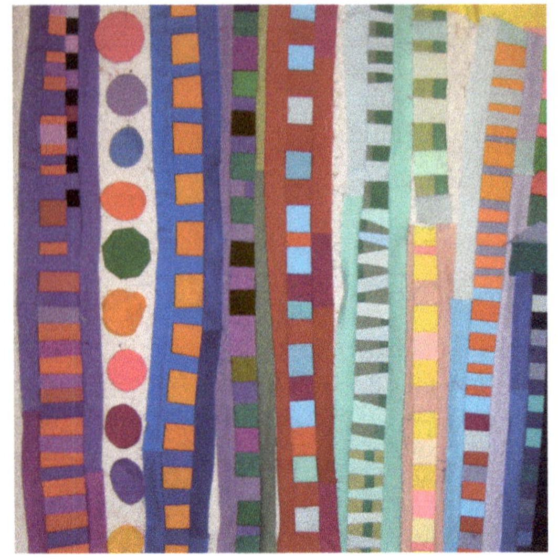

I've lived in or near big cities all my life, born in Queens, New York, raised in a Boston suburb, and as an adult in New York, Washington DC, Tokyo, and for the past 30 years, Los Angeles. Walking around cities has always been one of my great joys.

So maybe it was inevitable that I'd make cityscape quilts – but this journey started completely by accident.

In 2018, I was in the mood to make something modern, and I hit on the idea of ladders. So I made some funky improv ladders from solids. On my design wall, aligned at the top (left) they did look a bit like ladders. (I threw in some circles for contrast.)

Then I tried offsetting the tops. And a miracle occurred – the ladders turned into skyscrapers!

I ran with it! I made a whole bunch of improv ladders with plenty of irregularities. Then I made ladder wedges, short at one end and wider at the other, and sewed those together into an arch.

When I placed the arch above the buildings, it made me think of New York's iconic Chrysler Building spire. And when I added colorful circles (plus a few triangles) over the arch, they became diverse peoples' heads!

And that is how I accidentally made a quilt celebrating the glorious diversity that is New York City, in its people as well as its buildings! I was so happy with this surprise ending!

I quilted the area with under the arch with triangles and arcs, also inspired by the Chrysler Building. And I vowed to myself to make an **intentional** New York City quilt. But first, by complete coincidence, we had to leave town....

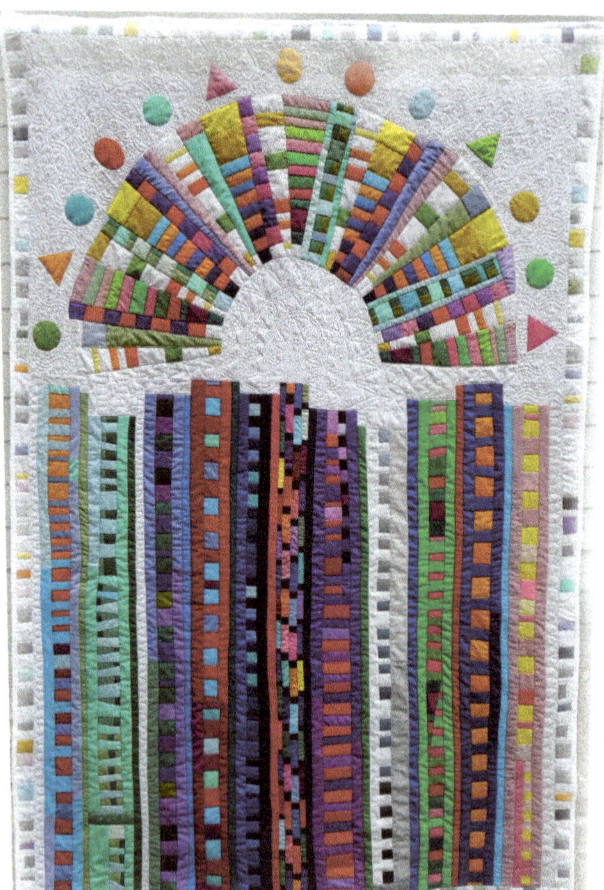

Accidental New York, 50" x 74"

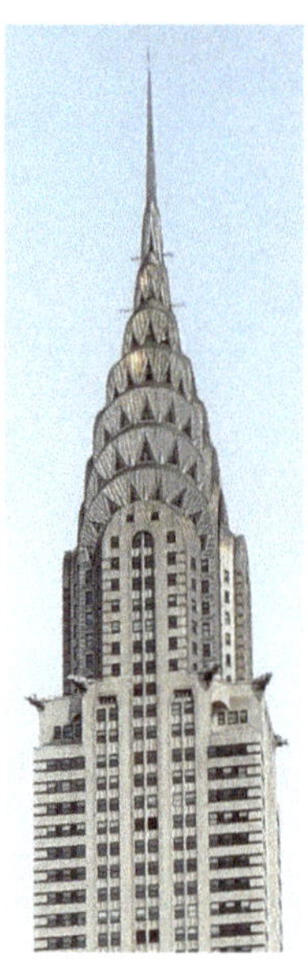

Chrysler Building

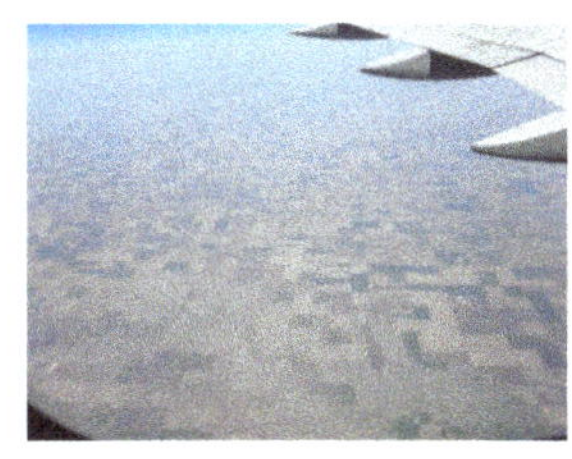

April 28, 2018. We traveled from Los Angeles to spend three weeks in New York City for my husband's work. Six hours later, we arrived at our new residence on the 29th floor of a midtown hotel. The apartment was tiny, but the view was staggering! (Nothing like the view from the ground floor living room of a Greenwich Village apartment, where I lived in the 1980s!)

Lessons Over Manhattan

I ran to the windows and started taking pictures! I saw a forest of shapes, patterns and shadows, some regular, but many highly irregular and asymmetric. Often, even within the same building, different sections were wildly different and unpredictable!

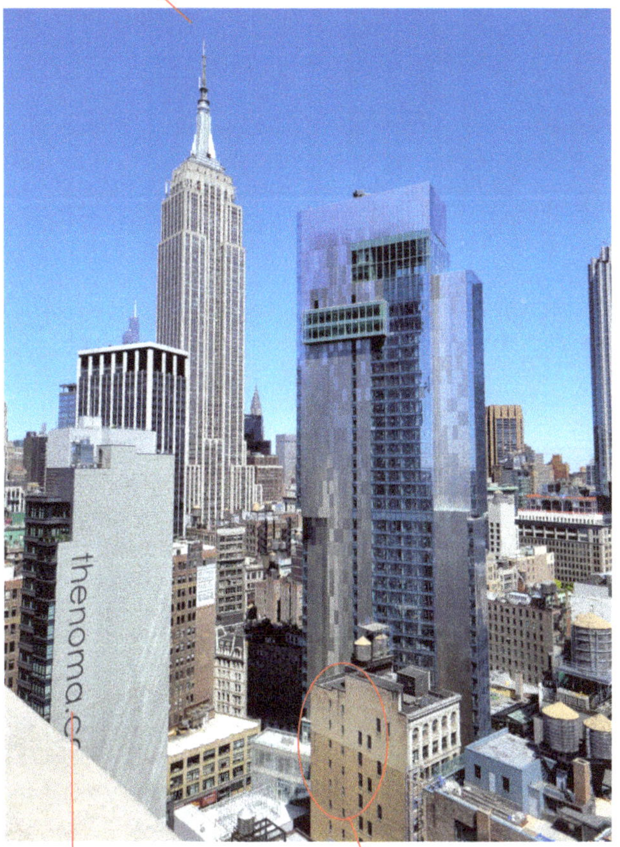

Large lettering, like this massive web address!

Off-balance placement of windows

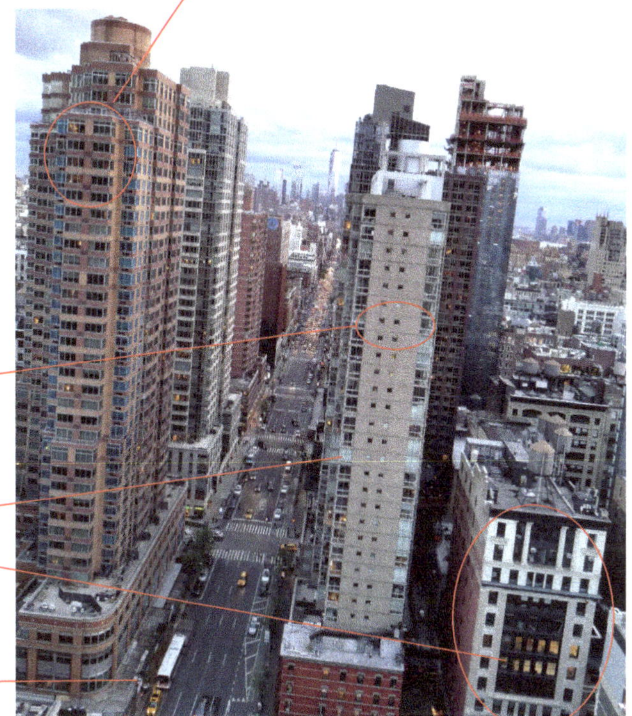

Random, subtle changes in shade – caused by weathering, renovation, or maybe the architect's whimsy?

More off-kilter patterns

Lights or dark windows unpredictably placed

Road running up the middle inspired the composition of 'Scrap City 1', on top of p. 7.

So much randomness!

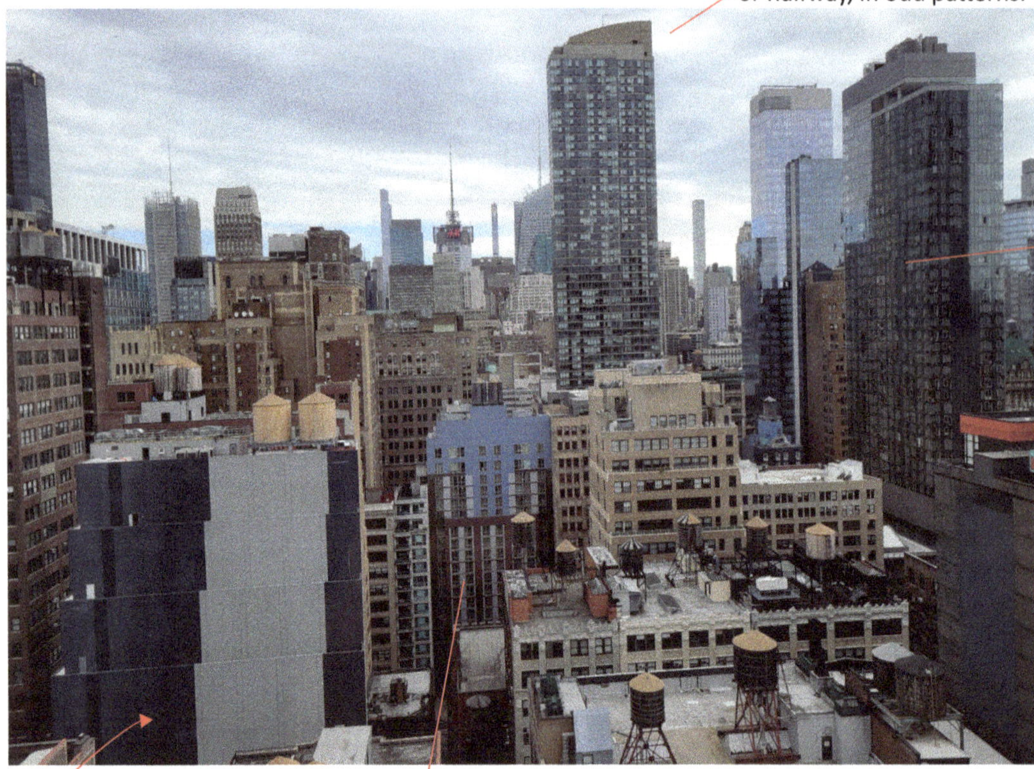

Puzzling: It has no windows at all on its back side! It's a classic wedding cake stack (p. 36), but with off-balance colors.

Check out the blue, brown and white building, with unusual color layout!

So many broken patterns! So many vertical, horizontal and diagonal lines!

Grids upon different grids, upon different grids!

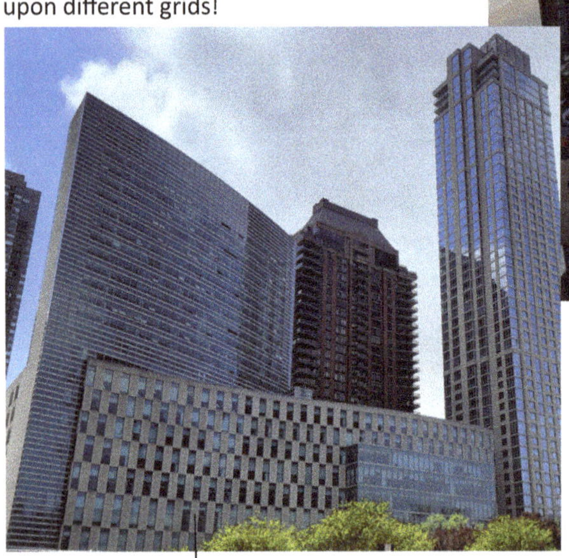

Bargello! See p. 22

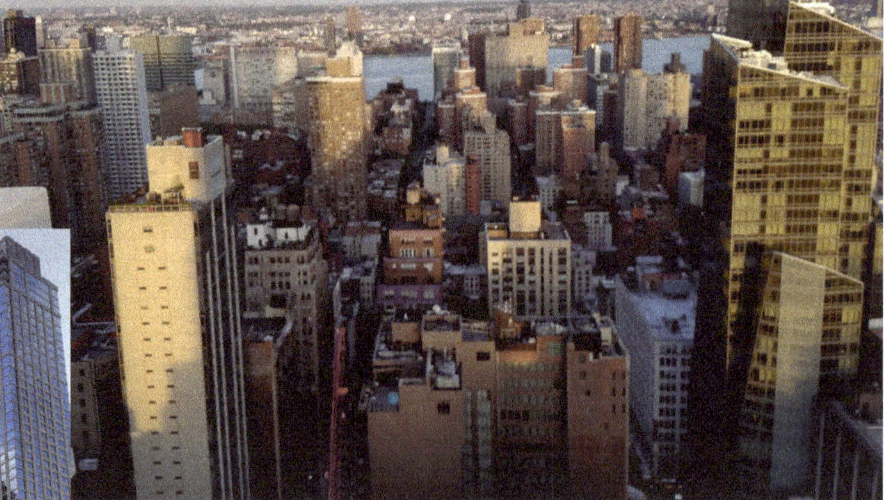

Surprising shadows!

After three weeks, we returned home, and I started making intentional buildings!

Medium to Large Cityscapes

Scrap City 1   48" x 43"

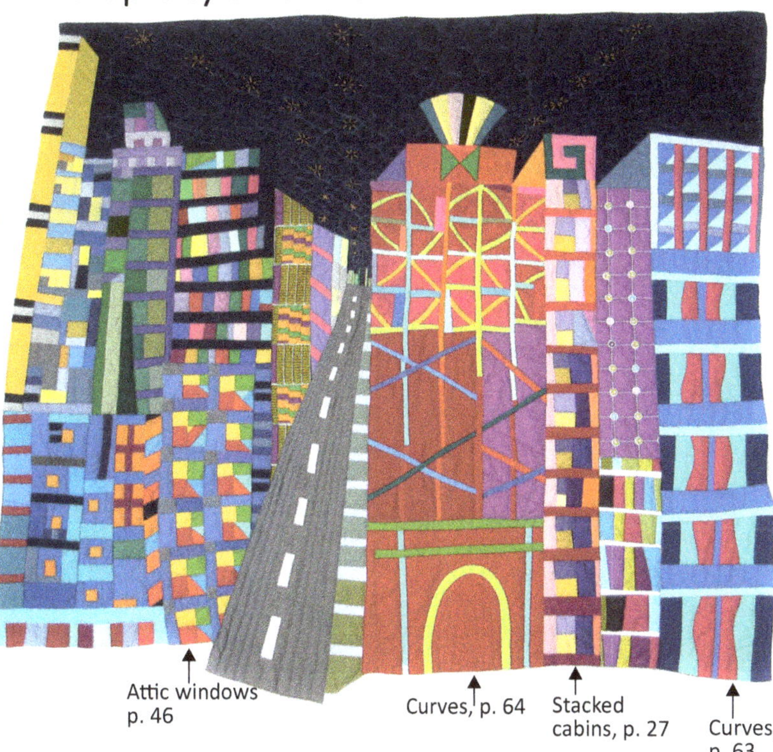

Scrap City 2   57" x 75"

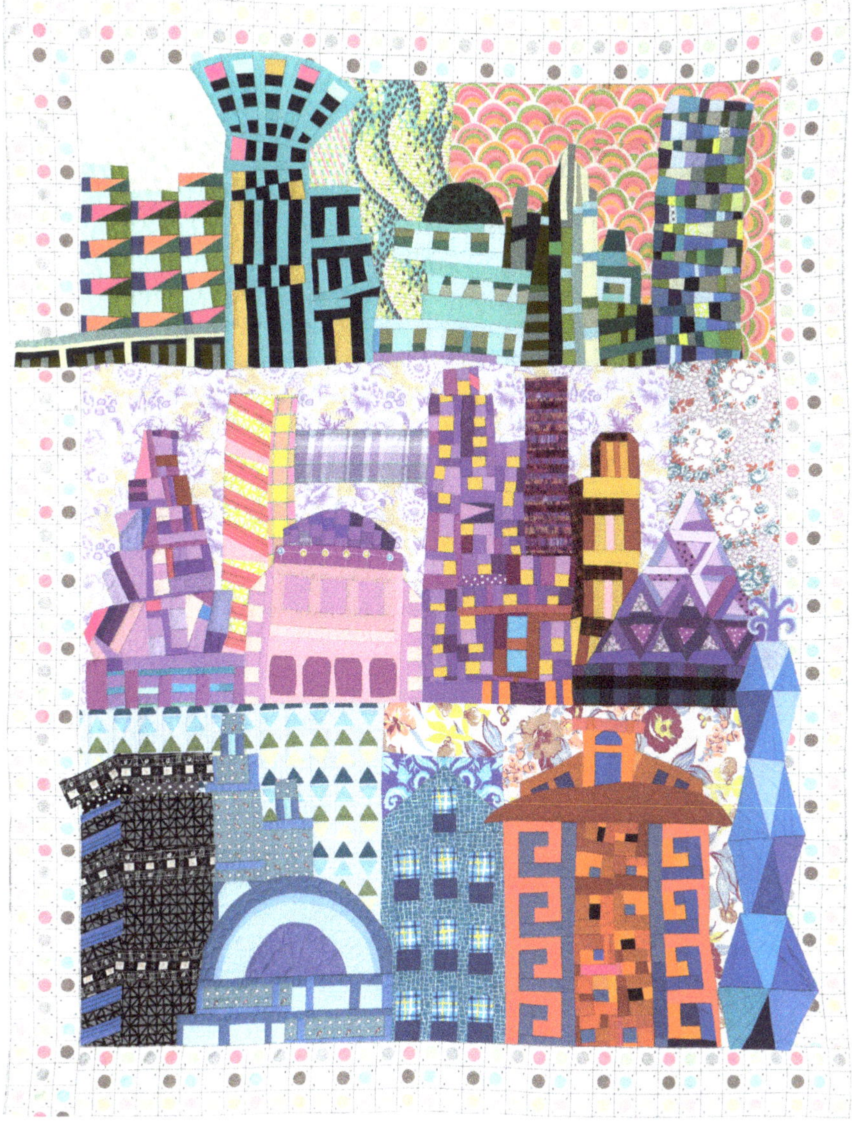

Left, any one of these rows by itself could be a wallhanging.

Top row. Emerald City: Far left, a half-square triangle building (p. 50); several wedge buildings (p. 29); and a domed building that's the ancestor of the Emerald Observatory (p. 38).

Amethyst City: Wedding cake piecing, far left (p. 36); a purple pileup (with yellow windows, p. 43); and far right, a Pei-inspired pyramid (p. 54).

Sapphire City: Airport tower, far left (a different version is on p. 14); a bandshell; a townhouse (p. 35); an orange Greek key mansion (p. 32); and a triangle tower (p. 59).

I Love Los Angeles 1   61" x 61"

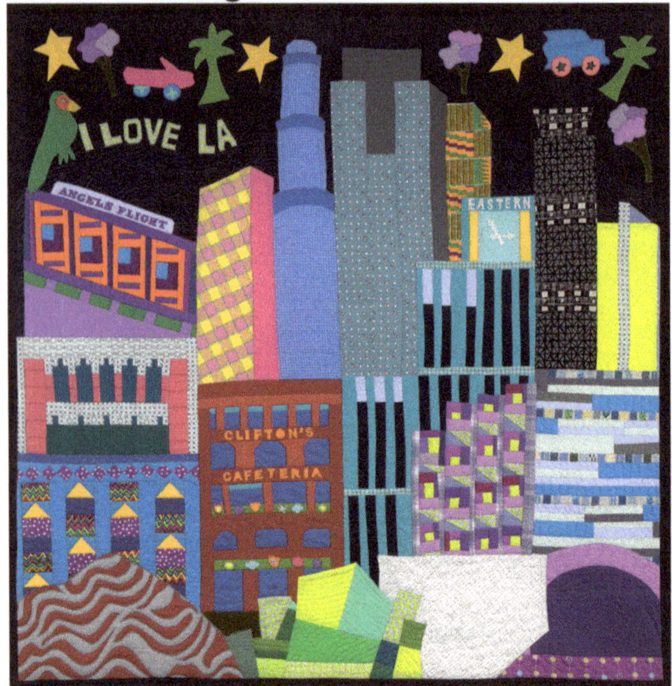

Color Block New York   72" x 72".

Each building has its own background. The pattern is in my book, "Quilted New York, Celebrate the City in Color and Fabric," 2022.

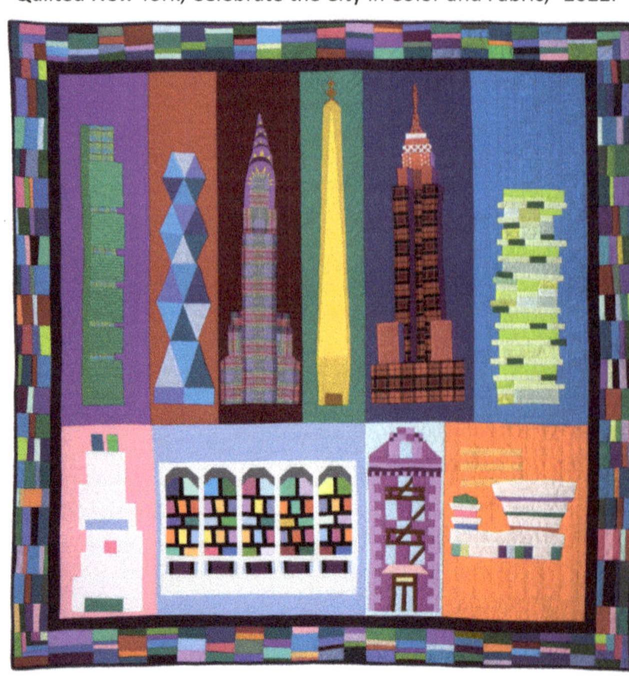

I Love Los Angeles 2

55" x 60"

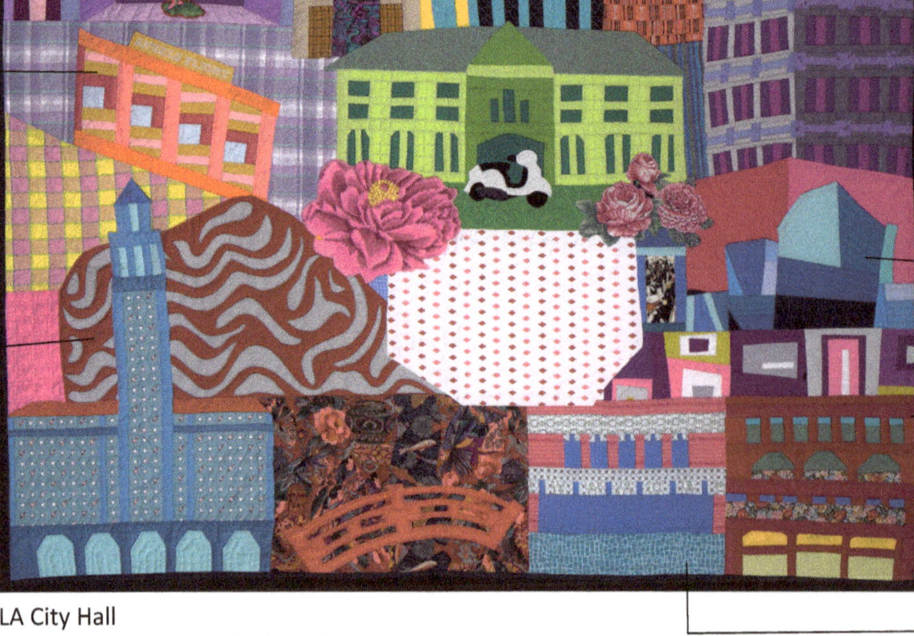

LAX's Theme Building

Pasadena Red Cross Building

Greek Theater

Angel's Flight cable car

Peterson Automotive Museum

LA City Hall
Squares-in-corners arched windows, p. 82.

Hotel Bargello, p. 22. To its immediate left is my version of the Capitol Records building. Then, the teal Eastern Building with its unique crown-like smokestack.

Disney Hall, in blues

Clifton's Cafeteria w/squares in the corners arched windows, p. 82

Mayan Theater. The white shape above it was inspired by the Broad Museum. In lime green above that is Tournament House.

Irene's Chicago

All the buildings (and sculptures, sailboats, etc.) on this commissioned quilt were requested by the client, based on the Chicago of her childhood.

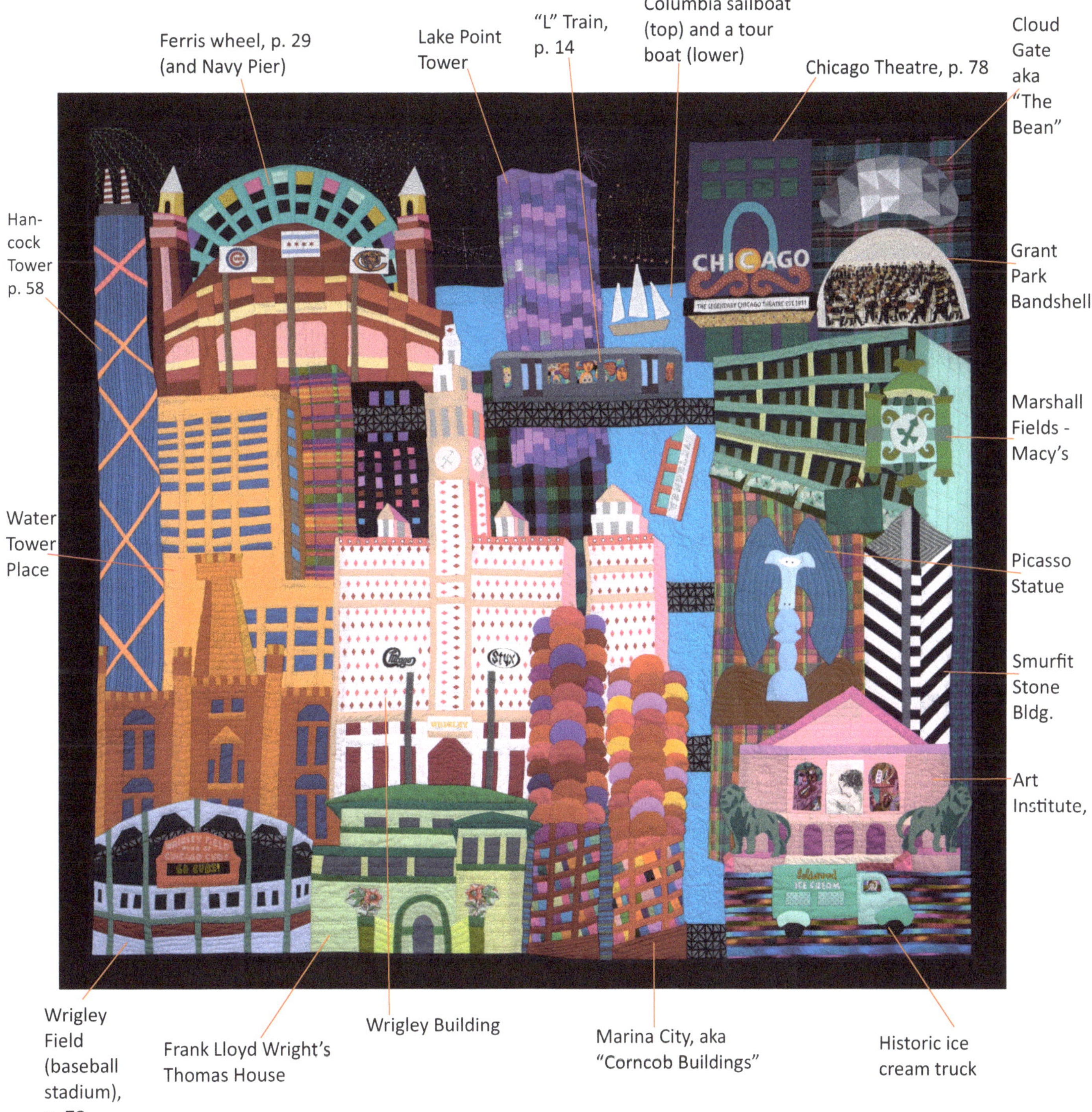

Ferris wheel, p. 29 (and Navy Pier)

Lake Point Tower

"L" Train, p. 14

Columbia sailboat (top) and a tour boat (lower)

Chicago Theatre, p. 78

Cloud Gate aka "The Bean"

Hancock Tower p. 58

Grant Park Bandshell

Water Tower Place

Marshall Fields - Macy's

Picasso Statue

Smurfit Stone Bldg.

Art Institute,

Wrigley Field (baseball stadium), p. 78

Frank Lloyd Wright's Thomas House

Wrigley Building

Marina City, aka "Corncob Buildings"

Historic ice cream truck

Nonsense Town

65" x 71"

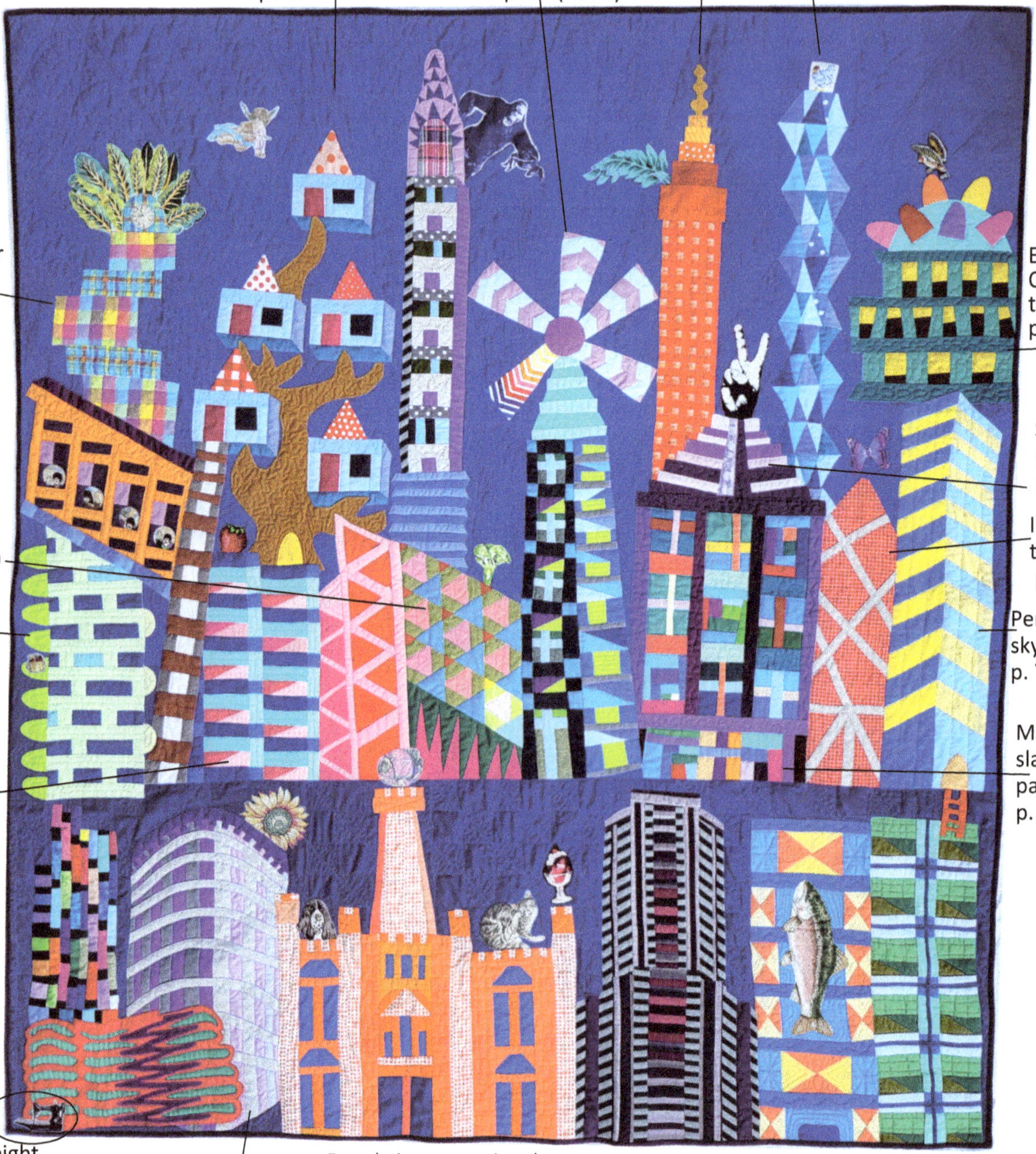

Treehouse hotel, p. 48

Windmill, p. 29 & p. 87 (stairs)

Orange wedding cake stack, p. 36

Isosceles triangles, p. 59

Zigzag tower p. 43

Emerald Observatory p. 40

Starry wall or glass ceiling, p. 60

Step pyramid p. 90

Bargello & balconies, p. 24.

Irregular triangles p. 57

Half square rectangle building #1, p. 53

Perspective skyscraper, p. 74

Modern slashed panes, p. 80

Featherweight sewing machine!

Curved bias, appliquéd p. 64

Foundation paper pieced windows, p. 83

Stripes with perspective, p. 70-71

Reverse applique door, p. 81

Half-square rectangle building #2, p. 51

See also

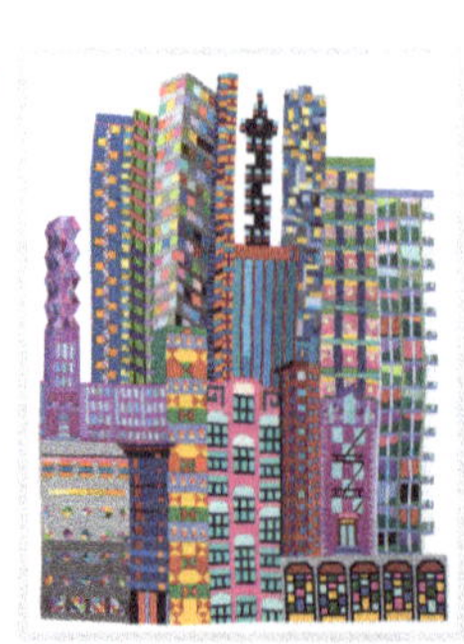

Room 2913 (New York City) Large photo is on the cover.

Beach Houses See p. 86 for a larger photo.

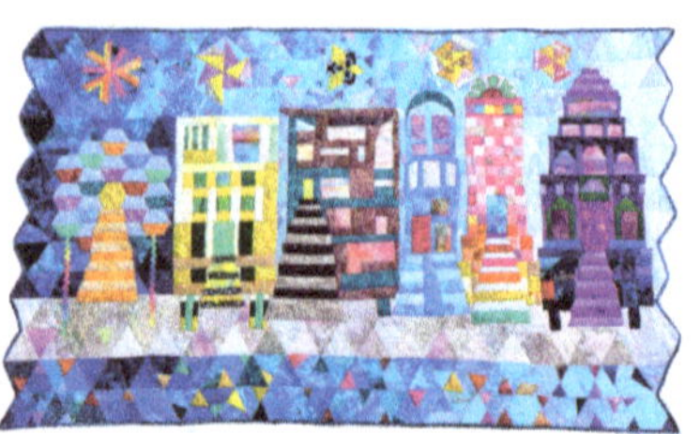

Small Projects and Student Work

Most of these were made by quilters who took my cityscape classes.

1 - 6 buildings – Make a tote bag, pillow, or small wall quilt.

7+ buildings – Big wall or bed quilt.

Principles of construction for a small or large quilt start in Part X, p. 91.

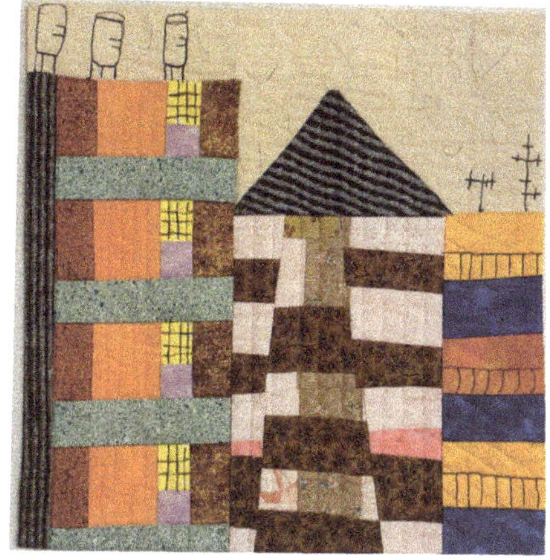

Above, wallhanging by Shoshi Rimer Roof details are machine-embroidered.

Tote bag
by Flora Cohen

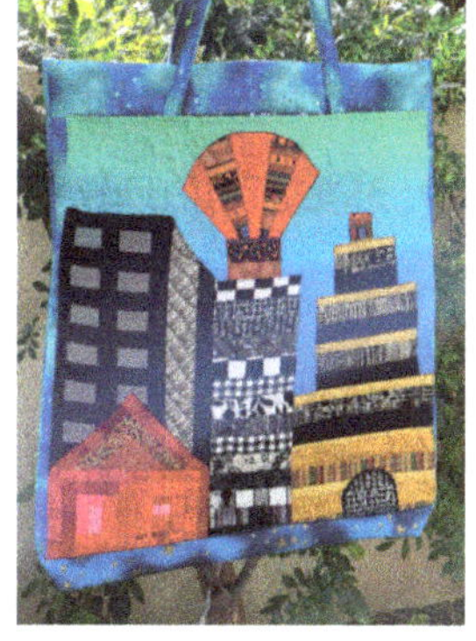

Below, on the reverse side of Flora's tote, the yellow checkered building is also a cellphone pocket!

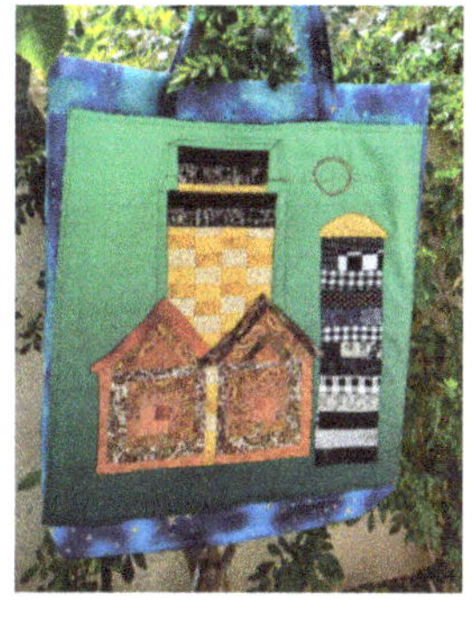

Wallhangings

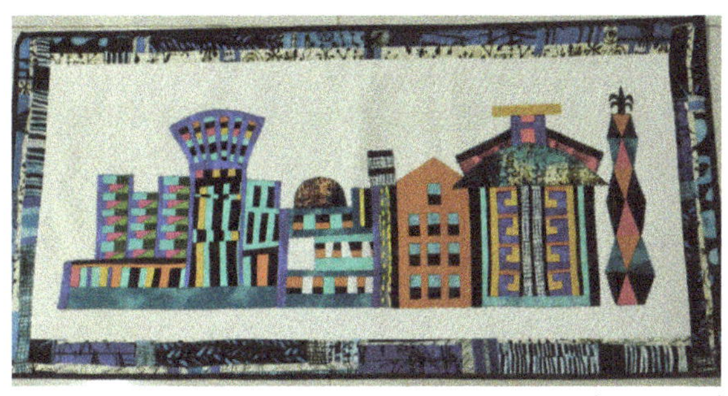

Clara Zuriel

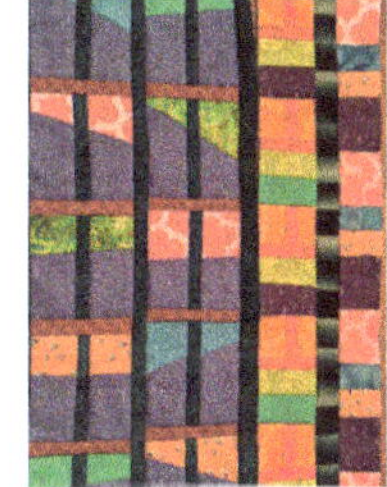

Left, Malki Lapidus' version of the building on p. 19.

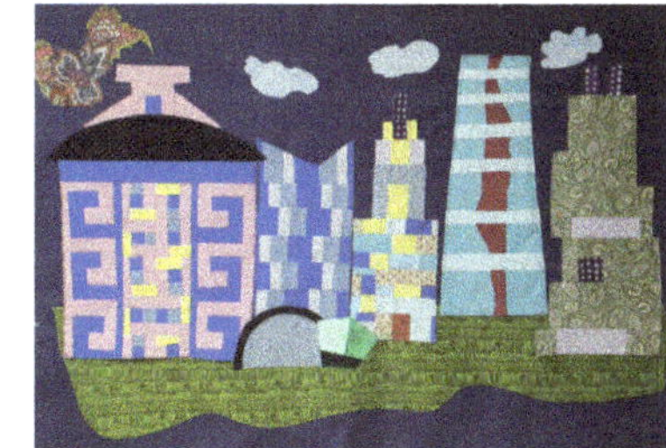

Left, 'City Street' by Nurit Caine

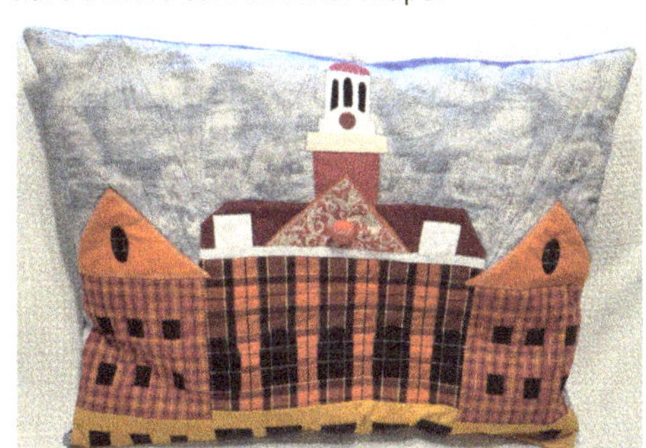

Above, Rivka Hamdani's 'Tel Aviv Central,' inspired by the mishmash of architectural styles in that city's busiest district.

Pillows

Author-made pillows: A skyscraper, right, and college dorm, below (also on p. 80). If building's outline is rectangular like the skyscraper, just add sides and a back; the pillow will be building-shaped! If the building has an uneven outline, like below, put it on a square, rectangular, or circular background/sky fabric. The pillow will have a more conventional shape.

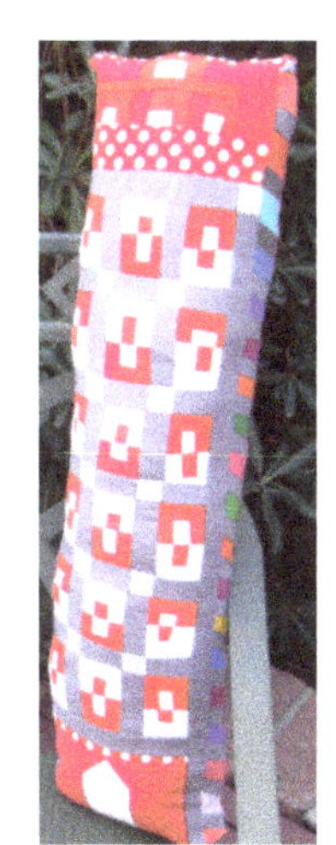

Baby quilt in progress

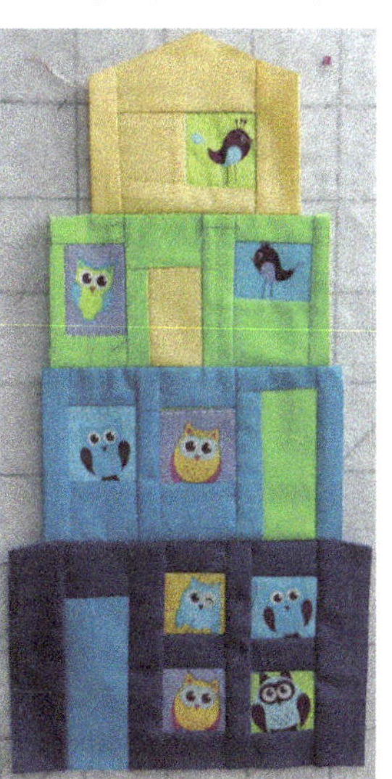

Yaffa Yassaf used bright colors, and fussy-cut cute characters to put in windows.

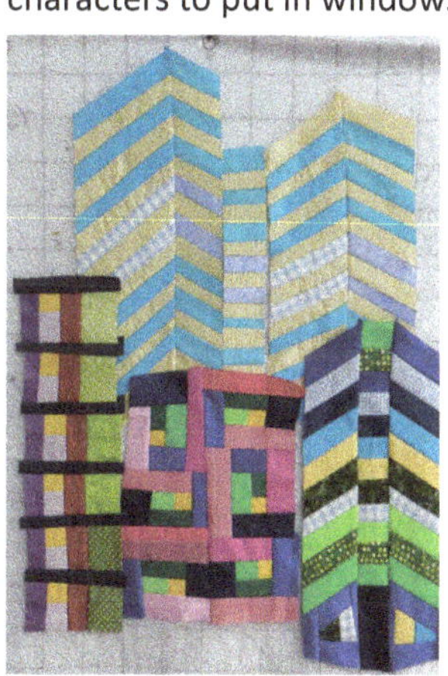

Overview

Part I and II introduce this cityscape process.

In Parts III-VIII, there are two kinds of chapters: Buildings and Ideas. Building chapters have complete directions. Idea chapters introduce key concepts, like 'Attic Windows,' but only have directions for that part of the process; apply the ideas to your constructions.

Part IX provides guidance for creating your own buildings, whether fantasy or inspired by real structures (or both!)

The final stage, putting the buildings into a quilt, is covered in Section X.

The buildings in this book are:

– Mostly **pieced**.

– Mostly **fun**, not fussy. I don't do Y seams.

– Many can be done **improv**. Follow my measurements, or make up your own (or do both!)

– NOT strictly realistic, but with plenty of opportunities for "**realistic randomness.**"

– Some buildings incorporate artist's perspective, to pop the scene into 3-D.

– With my unusual piecing approach, most edges are turned to the back **during** construction.

– A few buildings require raw-edge fusible appliqué, especially for tiny and/or curvy areas, like spires.

– Finished buildings are pieced or appliquéd in position – whichever's easiest!

The process goes like this:

1 Make several buildings that appeal to you. Start in Part III, 'Easy Improvisable Buildings with Even Edges'. That will warm you up for more advanced buildings. See box on the right.

2 Create your own buildings. Part IX has information you can use to design windows, doors, roofs and stairs for the building of your dreams!

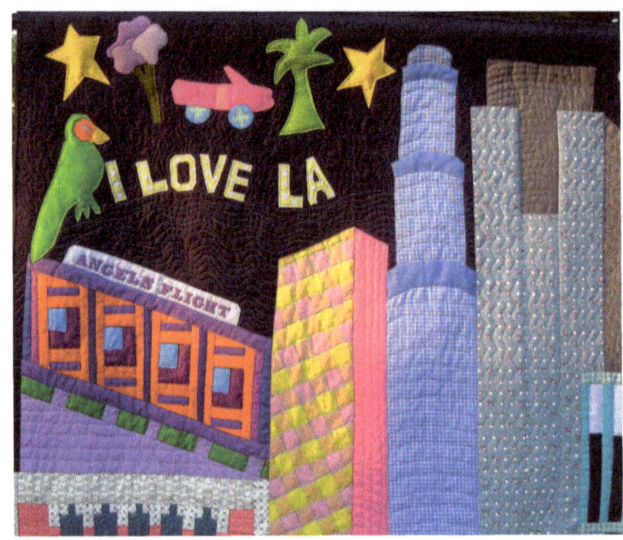

3 Audition arrangements and backgrounds. With 2+ buildings, start auditioning layouts. Also test different background fabrics. Part X explains how.

4 Piece and appliqué everything in place. Appliqué is explained on pp. 17-18, and appliquéing buildings to a large quilt is in Part X.

Find Your Buildings, Easiest to Most Challenging

Find buildings you will enjoy making in:

Part III, Easy improvisable buidings with even edges Only thrilling techniques, like the Hotel Bargello and a Seminole-pieced tower.

Part IV, Uneven stacked structures Uneven seamed edges can require stitch-ripping to turn under. Instead, I turn edges **during** piecing, to make the building stronger, hide thread ends, and avoid ripping. This easy and intuitive method is fully explained in every project that uses it.

Part V, Attic Windows-based buildings

Part VI, Triangle-based buildings

Part VII, Buildings with curves

Part VIII, Perspective Small touches have a big impact. These buildings approximate one-, two-, or three-point perspective.

Part IX, Create Your Own Design a fantasy building, or interpret a building you love. Includes techniques for windows, doors, roofs, and stairs.

You Will Need:

Fabric

Amount For most buildings, a fat-quarter of the main fabric is enough. Each will also require window fabric (usually a little less than the main fabric.) You probably have what you need for one building in your stash. You are more likely to need to shop for larger pieces to serve as background/sky.

Type In the examples on the right, solids and prints are on the left, and batiks on the right. In general:
– Solids create a modern look.
– Prints add so much texture and fun! And they can also instantly create the illusion of hundreds of windows!
– Batiks create a different mood, like watercolor art.

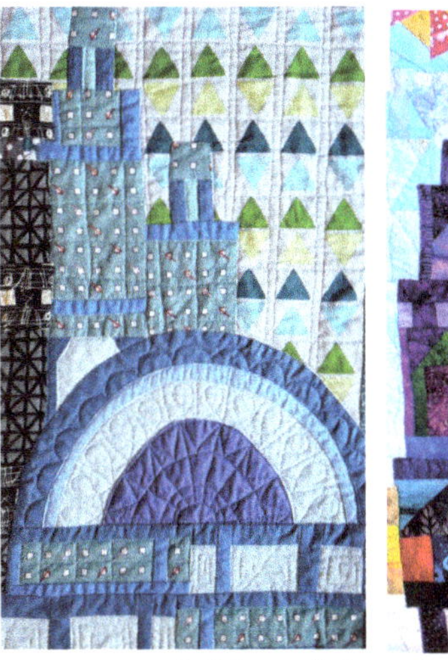
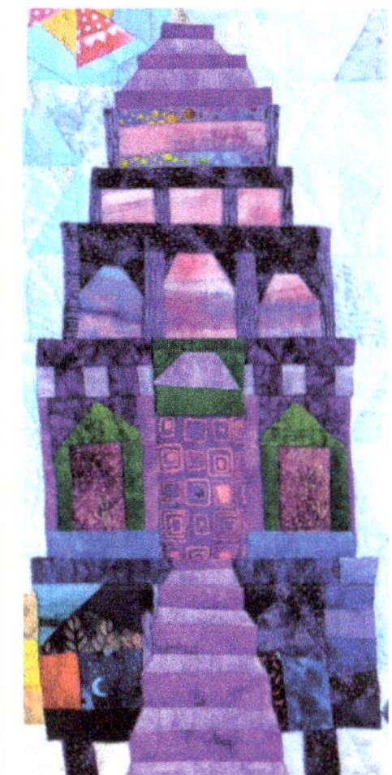

Solids + prints   Batiks

Supplies

– **The Usual** Zigzag-capable sewing machine + Rotary cutter, ruler & mat + iron + seam ripper + sharp scissors

– **Sharp awl** Also known as a stiletto. To tuck in flaps as you machine piece or appliqué. A pointed seam ripper works, too. Here's my favorite awl:

– **Temporary glue sticks** or **stitchers' glue pens** Pens have a narrow tip, which is less messy. (Brands include June Tailor, Fons & Porter). Washable school glue sticks are wider, messier, less expensive, and do the job just as well.

– **Open-toe sewing foot** For machine appliqué.

Optional but helpful items

– **Tear-away stabilizer** (or clean lightweight paper). Can be helpful for appliqué.

– **Invisible monofilament thread** and/or **thread that matches each building**, for appliqué.

– **Freezer paper** A roll from the supermarket, or 8.5" x 11" sheets. To shape curved pieces.

– **Paper-backed fusible web** For details like spires.

– **Appliqué press sheet** or **parchment paper** To keep ironing surface clean when working with fusible web.

Let Print Fabrics Do (a lot of) the Work!

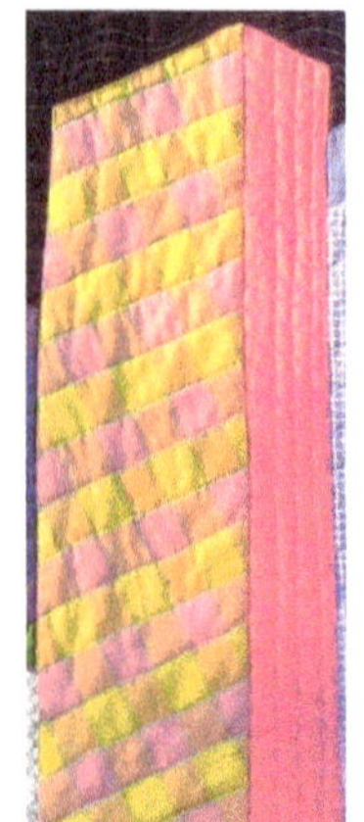

For a quilt with a modern, abstract look (like "Room 2913" on the cover), use mostly solids. For a richer look, toss in plaids, stripes, geometrics, and novelty prints. Viewers will have as much fun looking at the details, as you had finding the fabric!

Prints are especially useful for windows that are too small/too many/too boring to piece! On the left is a quilt shop plaid that instantly created almost 100 windows! I cut the plaid on an angle for perspective. (Learn about this in Part VIII.)

On the near right, inspired by the Los Angeles hotel on the far right, I combined solids with the print below depicting striped beach chairs. Cut close, they look like Venetian blinds!

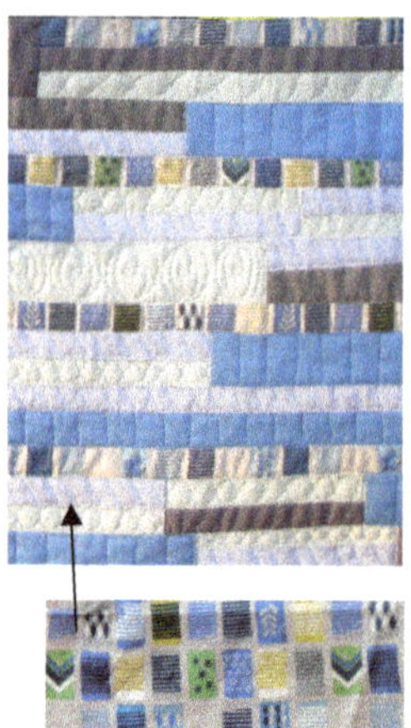

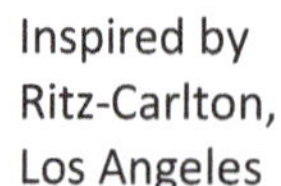
Inspired by Ritz-Carlton, Los Angeles

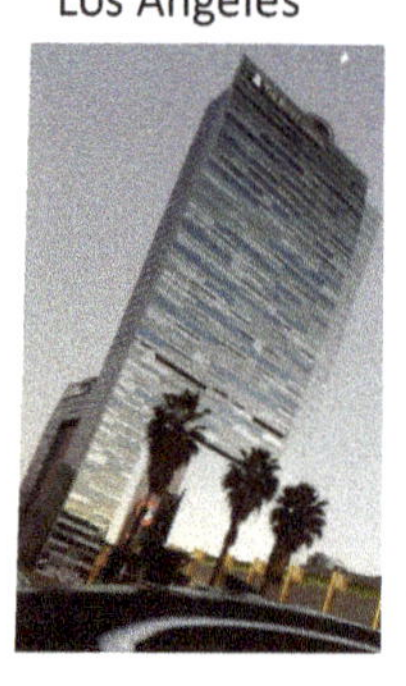

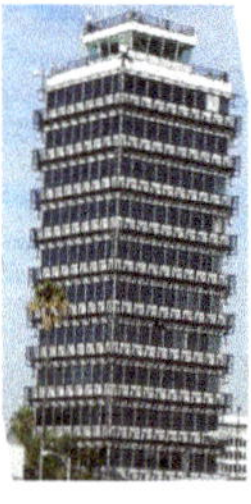

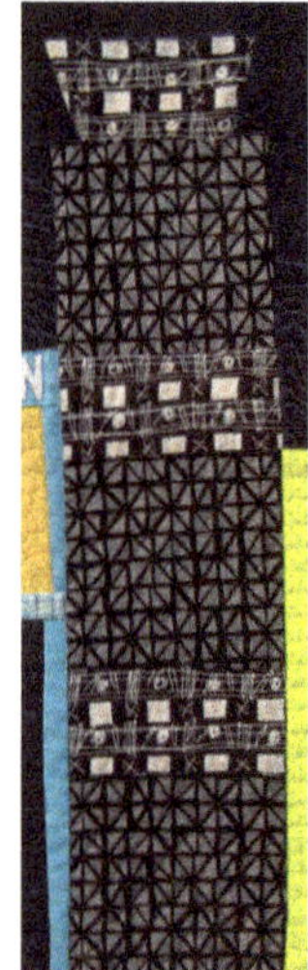

Near left is my version of one of Los Angeles Airport's control towers, which, as you see in the far left photo, is black, white and grey. I built it with a quilt shop fabric (grey with black x's), and one of my husband's old shirts (black with white rectangles). Shirts can be a great source of stripes and plaids!

Right, the gold fantasy building is an unpieced African print. The big blue building was inspired by LA's Gas Company Tower; it's a print of little white boxes, some containing red check marks. I've used this whimsical fabric for several different buildings, including the 'bowl' in the first photo on the previous page.

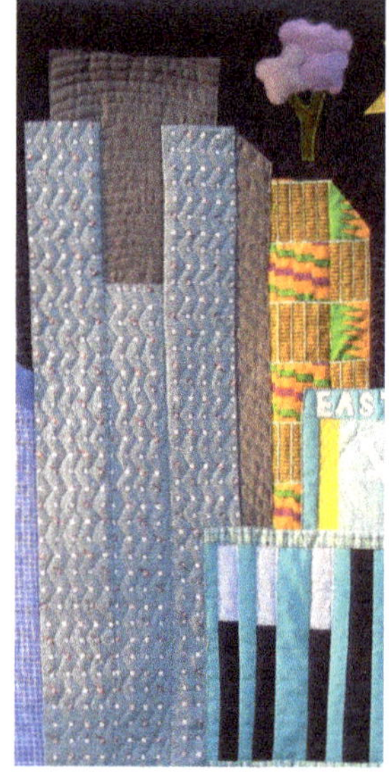

Novelty Fabric Details

The client who commissioned my Chicago quilt (p. 9) felt the trains were too empty. So I filled them with passengers (far right). The three details below, from my "Nonsense Town" quilt, were added as a last step. I backed each fabric character or object with fusible web; cut close around it; and pressed them in place.

Last, I stitched over the outlines with matching or invisible thread. Details in this quilt (p. 10) include a cat, dog, fish, chicken, angel, kale, cabbage, King Kong, giant hand, and more!

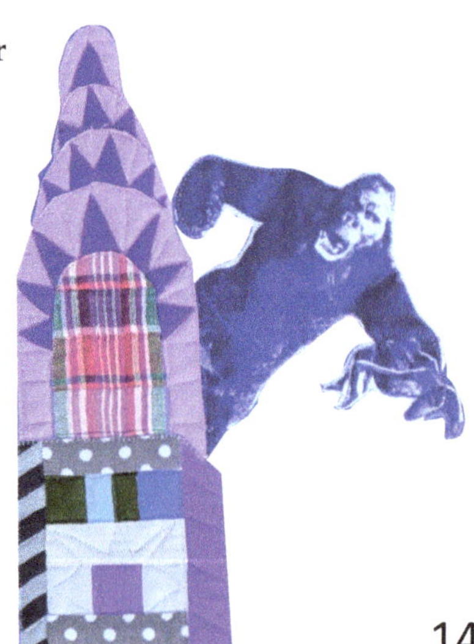

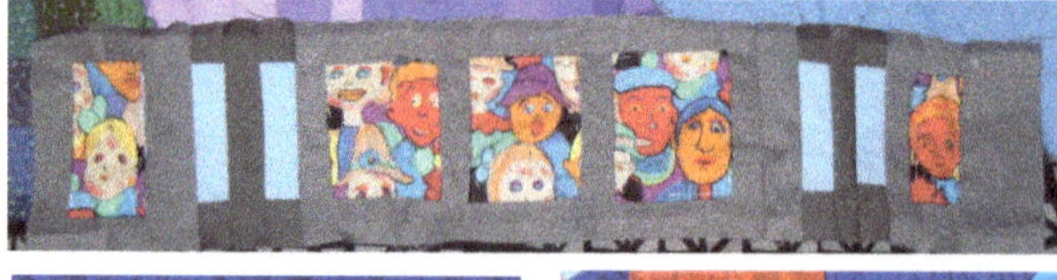

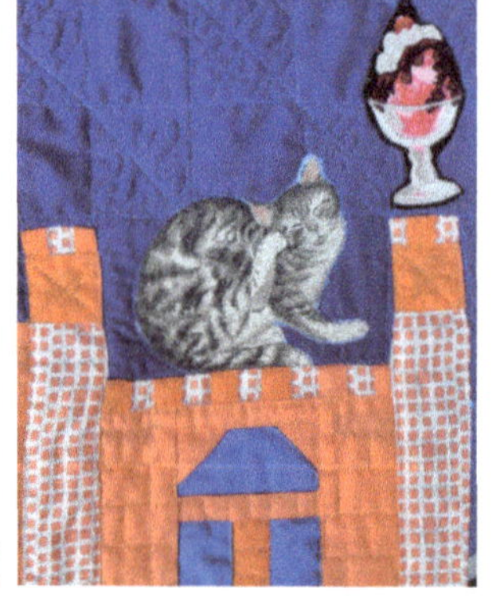

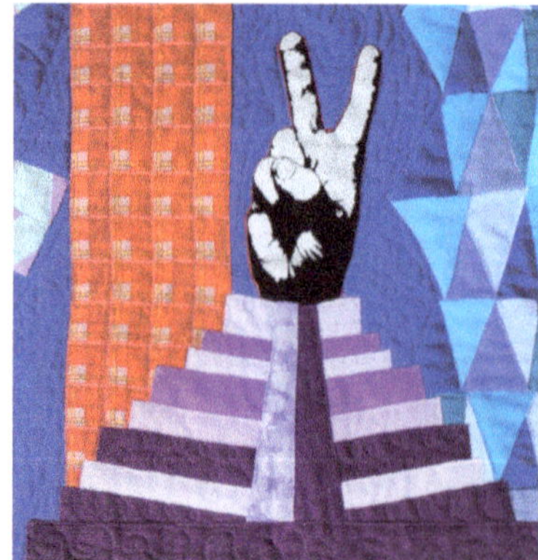

The Joy of Realistic Randomness

One of the most surprising things I learned from making cityscapes is that often, the more you interrupt a building's patterns, the more realistic and interesting the building becomes. I call this "realistic randomness."

An example on the near right is a tenement made for my "Quilted New York" book. Down its right vertical side – edge B – there's a strict pattern of alternating darks and lights.

But on its left side, Edge A, I improvised, interrupting the pattern in multiple ways.

Based on that, I designed the second townhouse with measurements for readers to follow. The edgings on both sides, C and D, are perfectly predictable.

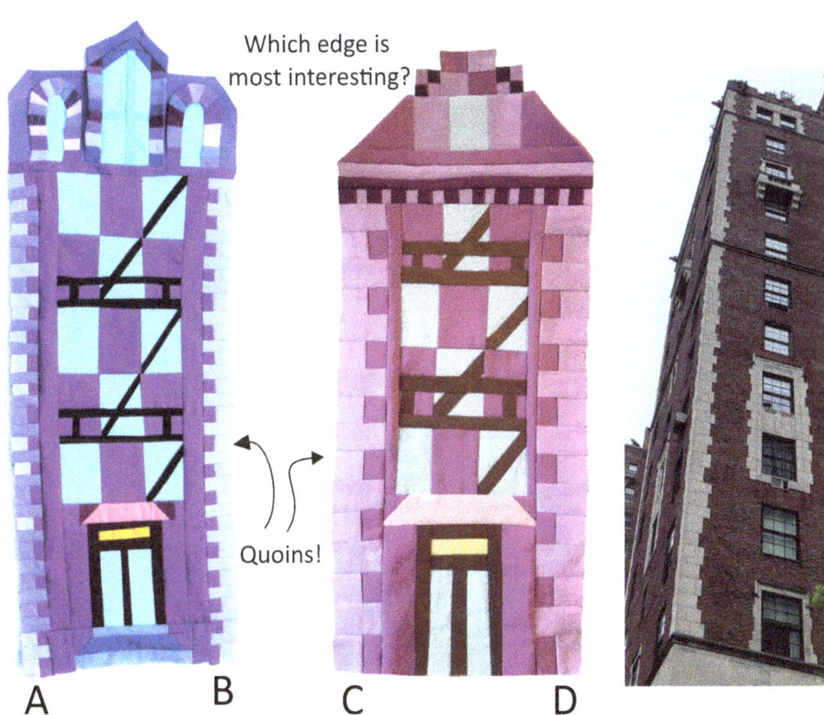

So which of these four edges is the most intriguing? I bet you chose A, the irregular one. Your brain tries to figure it out. Also, broken patterns abound on real buildings, whether by design, weathering, shadows, reflections, renovations, or maybe the whims/exhaustion of the masons! Look at the corner brickwork in the photo above, far right, and on the windows on the right (both NYC buildings). The brickwork patterns are inexplicably interrupted in even more ways than I dared in my townhouse!

One more thing I've learned from these projects: Decorative brickwork in a buildings' corner has a name – it's called a "quoin." You may need this for Scrabble or Wordle one day!?

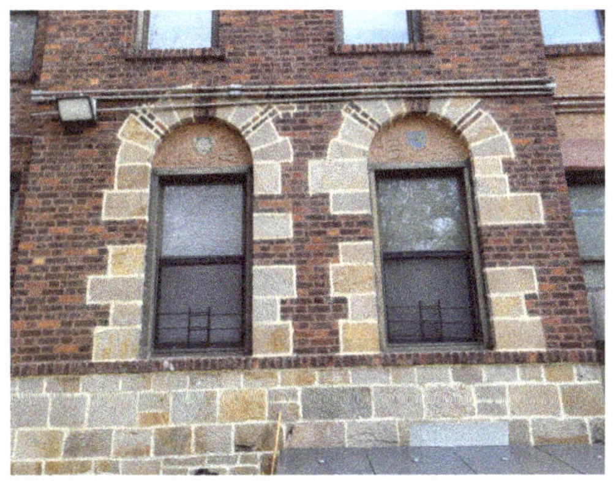

It's because of this phenomenon that I encourage you to improvise. It will make your buildings more realistic! Plus it's fun!

Consider Color

Real American city buildings tend to have dull, limited palettes (unlike, say, Copenhagen, a color feast). But if you place a bunch of white, brown, and grey buildings next to each other, they may weld into an amorphous blob. That's my reason for often going fanciful. For each building, I choose a main hue, and use light, medium, and dark shades of it. For its windows, I choose a different color and/or value. But quilters who've taken my classes have figured out ways to make a monochrome palette work! Right, Israeli artist Flora Cohen went with mostly golds and browns on her cityscape - yet it's easy to tell her buildings apart because of dark outlines, or background between them.

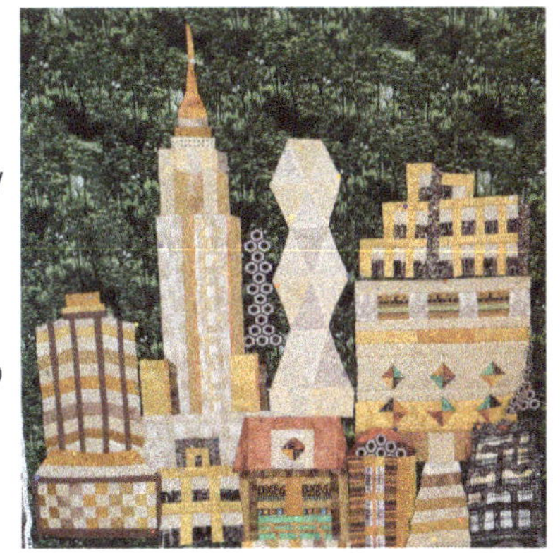

So follow your muse, but whether you choose fantasy or realistic colors, ALWAYS audition your arrangements from a distance. Then you'll know you have to do something more to separate them or define their outlines better.

More Starting Thoughts

As you start making buildings – from patterns in this book, or ones you invent – think about these things. No need to decide immediately, just keep them in mind!

Do you want a sunny side?

If two sides of a building are on view, a lighter and darker side will enhance the sense of depth.

If we were aiming for strict realism, we might choose one side that the light is coming from, and be consistent with all the buildings in the scene. But this rule was made to be broken!

When I started out, I blithely shattered the rule constantly. The funniest example is in this photo of one side of my second LA quilt (p. 8).

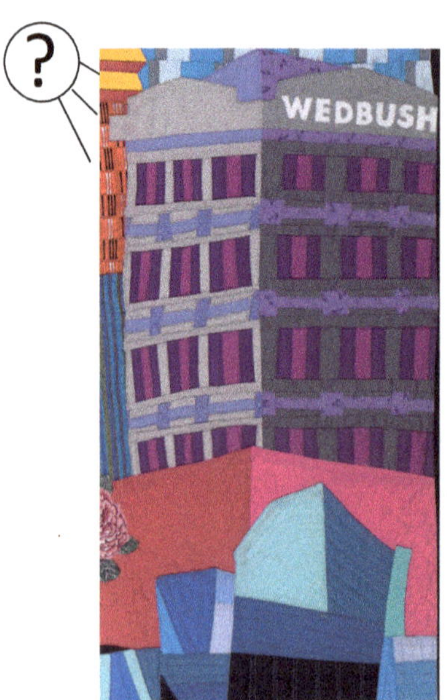

On the top building, the light comes from the left.

In the pink middle building, the right side is lighter.

On bottom (that's a blue Disney Hall), the light side returns to the left!

I didn't notice this for at least a year, and probably never would have if I hadn't started writing this book. Once I saw it, it bugged me. But over time, I've grown to like it. In fact, I could argue that this mistake makes the scene better, because there's a stronger contrast between the light pink, and the darker shades above and below it! If they'd all been the same dark value, they might have run together!

So **you** decide about consistency! Look at your placement from a distance to make sure buildings don't run together, and then choose where lights and darks go!

What's the likeliest background (sky) color or value?

I'm usually not sure until late in the process. From experience, I know it's likely my sky will be very dark, as in most of the quilts on pp. 8-10. I don't want the buildings to meld with the sky. So I avoid extremely dark fabric for most building's sides and top (it's fine for inside areas like windows).

But if by chance I do make a building that's the same value and/or color as the sky, I can always put things around it to differentiate it.

On the right, from my Chicago quilt, the black building with pink and purple windows on the lower middle is similar to the sky. But I surrounded it with lighter buildings.

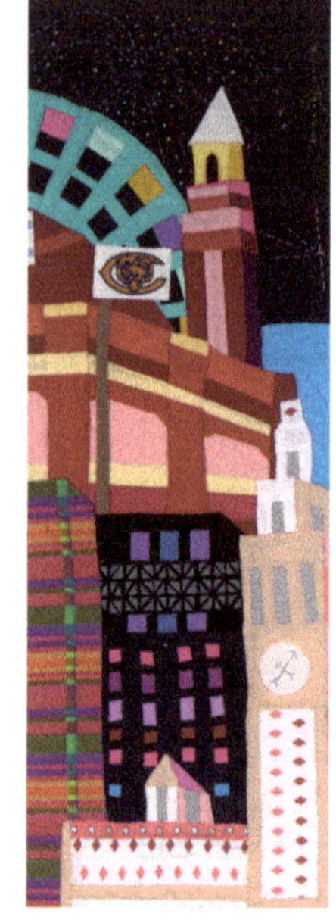

Do you want a vanishing point (or two?)

After reading Section VIII on perspective, I hope you'll try it. It's fine to have some flat buildings , and others with 1, 2, and/or 3 point perspective. Mix it up! Blame Picasso! Be on the lookout for opportunities to strengthen perspective, and maybe even create a vanishing point; perspective evokes a delightful vertiginous feeling for viewers, that they're falling into the scene!

Google "interesting architecture," followed by the city's name!

In my own smallish city, I had to go online to discover fantastic buildings I'd never noticed! Then I could drive over there, park the car, and take all the pictures I need!

And speaking of photos, see p. 79 for guidance on using photos you find online.

Appliqué Guide

When, where, and how

The projects in this book require appliqué in two situations:

– Around most buildings. For fastening turned edges to the background or to other buildings when piecing is not possible.

– Around small or curved raw-edge details. I put fusible web on back, and sew around with machine appliqué, using a medium-tight zigzag.

Choices

– Hand appliqué. Disadvantage: It's slow. Advantage: It's slow, so you can easily tuck flaps under as you stitch. See stitches in diagram, right.

– Machine appliqué. Much faster – but that's also a disadvantage. Once in the machine, it's more challenging to tuck flaps under, so do cleanup work in advance. Suggestions below will help.

Prepare for machine appliqué

– Clean up the building. Turn back, trim and/or glue back every protruding flap/thread you find, so they can't be seen from the front. Use a glue stick. (A spritz with water can loosen this glue later if it becomes necessary.)

– Have a sharp awl handy. No matter how good a job you do in cleanup, you'll spot more flaps and threads that poke out as they approach the presser foot. A sharp awl (aka stiletto) is the best way to tuck things under at the last minute. See mine in the 'Supplies' list on p. 13.

– Try to love "invisible" monofilament thread. Clear for light color fabrics, smoke for dark. It's a time-saver, and looks like hand-stitching. But plenty of people hate it – it is like sewing with hair. If you dislike it, use a thin neutral thread, or matching shades for each building.

– Improve visibility. Install an open-toe foot in your machine. I wear a magnifying headgear.

– Do a tension test. Do it before you start, and again when you change thread, fabric, or stitch. You don't want bobbin thread to show on top; you do want to see if stabilizer will help. See p. 18.

Machine Appliqué Stitches

On the right side of the diagram below.

– Zigzag My favorite for turned-edge appliqué, usually medium wide (1.5 - 3), medium tight (1-2). Most of the stitch lies on the appliqué (the grey building below). It swings just barely into the background. I use invisible or matching thread. A multi-step zigzag is another option, and a little more secure than a regular zigzag. For raw-edge fusible-backed details, I go to a tighter zigzag, close to a satin-stitch.

– Machine blind hem or blanket stitch Medium-width, great for turned edges. Its straight stitches go in the "background," parallel to the building's edges; then the needle swings intermittently to take a deep bite into the grey appliqué.

Whichever machine-stitch I use, I always start and end with a few tiny back-and-forth straight stitches.

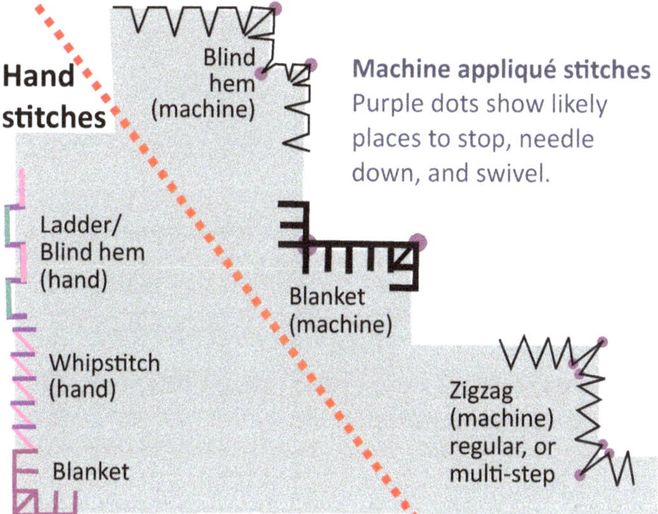

Hand Appliqué Stitches

On the left side of the diagram above.

– Ladder/blind hem. Pink is where needle travels below the surface of the appliqué. Purple is where the needle emerges and the thread shows. Then the needle dives and travels downward, under the opposite side (green). That side may be the background fabric, or it may be a different building. Needle comes up again (purple) and dives back into the other side, travelling inside the fold (pink). Repeat!

– Whipstitch Purple is where thread is above the surface. Pink is where it dives down beneath the surface, then comes up so you can do another whipstitch.

– Blanket A hand blanket stitch is a little complicated, especially turning corners. There are lots of tutorials online to guide you through and around corners!

(continued)

Test-Stitch a Sample

Making a sample is good idea if you're doing hand appliqué, and it's a must for machine appliqué.

Ideally, use the same fabrics and layers as in the building or element you want to appliqué. (If there's fusible in some of those pieces, apply fusible to your samples, too).

If the edges you plan to sew are folded under, fold under all the edges of the building fabric sample.

Then go around it with different stitches, widths, and lengths. See what you like best. If you can't get the tension right, and stitches are bunching up your fabric, it's time to consider a stabilizer.

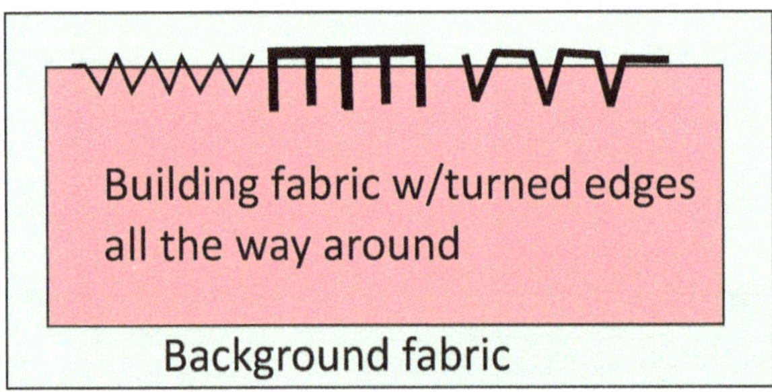

Make samples to test stitches, thread, and tension. Also, practice stitching around tricky shapes!

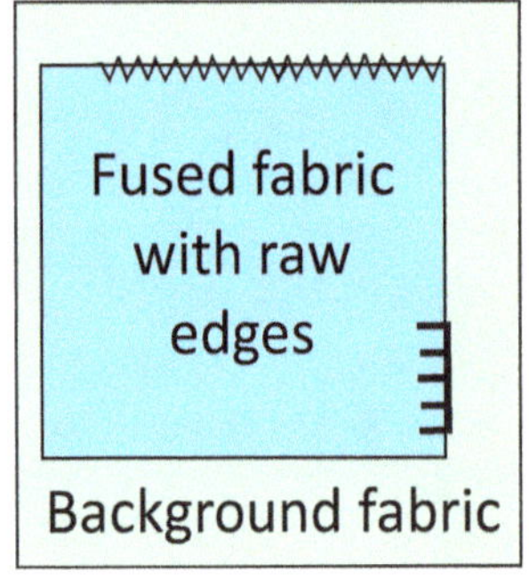

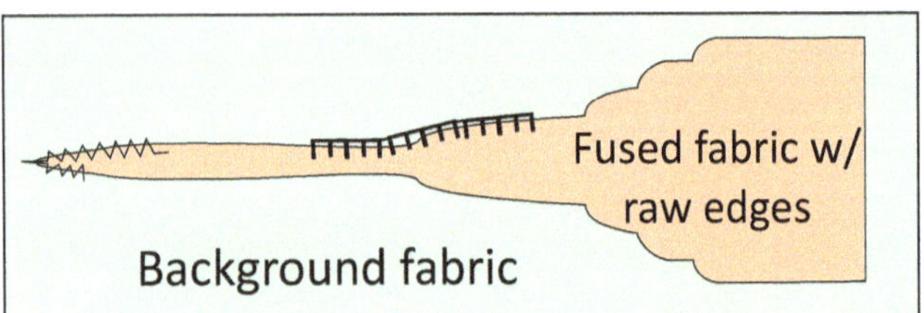

Stabilizer 101 for Quilters

Machine embroiderers use stabilizers to prevent fabric from distorting or collapsing when covered with hundreds of stitches. But stabilizers can also help quilters with machine appliqué.

Sewing stores sell sheets or rolls of "tear-away" stabilizer – it's not expensive. But sometimes, when I run out, or need a large piece, I use clean newsprint – a lifetime supply cost me $6 at the packing store.

Any lightweight paper is third choice, of it's clean and tears out easily. I've used printer paper when desperate, but test it first to make sure it doesn't rip out stitches, and that any printing on it won't run onto your fabric if it accidentally gets wet.

Put the stabilizer (yellow here) on back of your fabric samples, and then test all the stitches, tension, threads, etc. again.

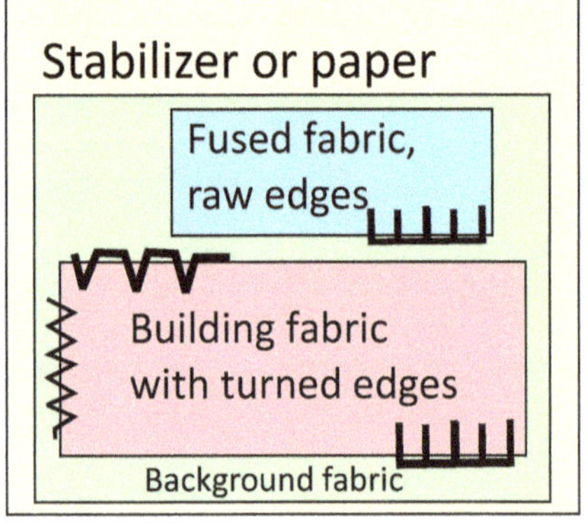

Once I know the stabilizer helps, and ripping it out won't also rip stitches, I cut a piece the length of the area that needs appliqué stitches, and pin it underneath.

Occasionally, stabilizer is needed behind an entire large building's outline, when sewing the building to the background. Yes, it's awkward to sew with a big sheet on the back, but you get used to it!

And if your stabilizer isn't big enough to cover the outline, add pieces as you go – just be diligent about checking the back often, so you know when you're about to sew into a no-stabilizer zone!

When removing the stabilizer, you may not be able to get every molecule out (especially if you used copy paper), but that's okay with me, as long as the remaining bits are tiny.

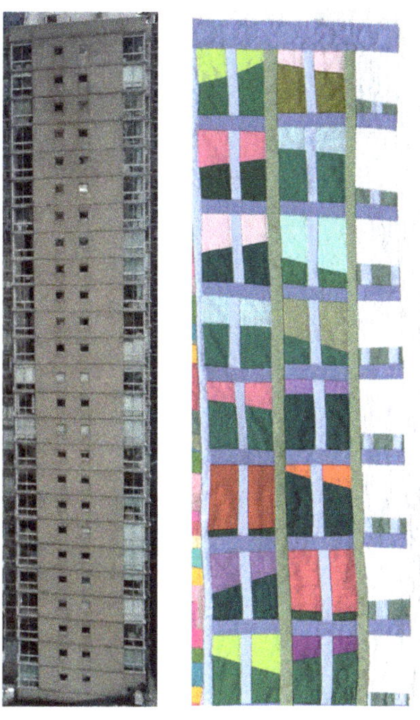

Flip & Split Condo Tower

This fantasy structure (in the cover quilt), was inspired by a midtown NYC tower just outside our hotel room. All the windows had white curtains. I turned them into colorful window shades. Balconies on the right are optional – the real building didn't have them. Wait until you choose your quilt's sky/background color to add them because each has "air" above it!

1 For a six-story building, cut twelve 4" squares to represent the glass in each window's lower area.

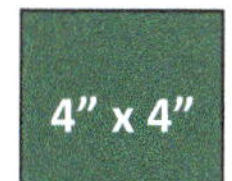

2 For each window's vertical panes: Cut strips 1" wide x about 48" long - it need not be continuous. Cut that piece down to twelve 4" pieces (one per window).

3 Prepare 12 shades from assorted colors. Cut pieces a little wider than the windows (approx. 4.5") by a slightly shorter height (3.5" or less). The top and two side edges should be cut square; vary the angles along their bottom edge.

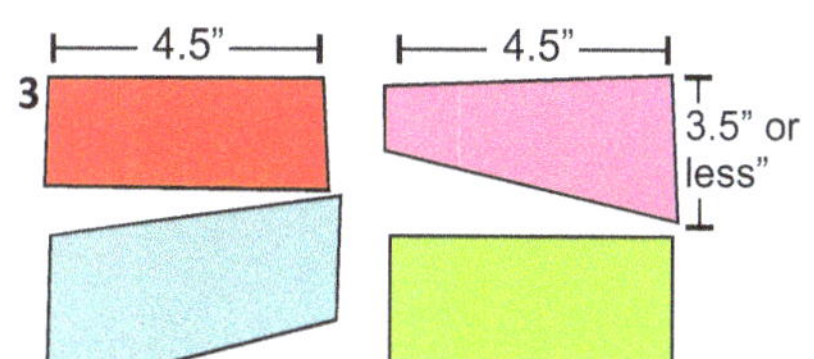

4 Press the bottom edge of each shade back 1/4" to the wrong side.

5 Place a shade (with fold), on a square. Slide up and down til you like the position, and the shade covers all of the window above the fold.

6 Holding the seam allowance in position, fold the top part down so you can see the fold's crease. Pin. Stitch the crease.

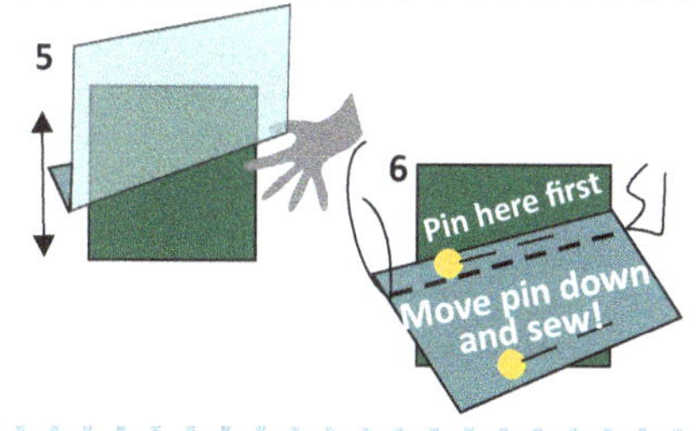

7 Trim away the back fabric, leaving about 1/4".

8 Fold up and press one more time.

9 Use a ruler to trim the unit down to a 4" square.

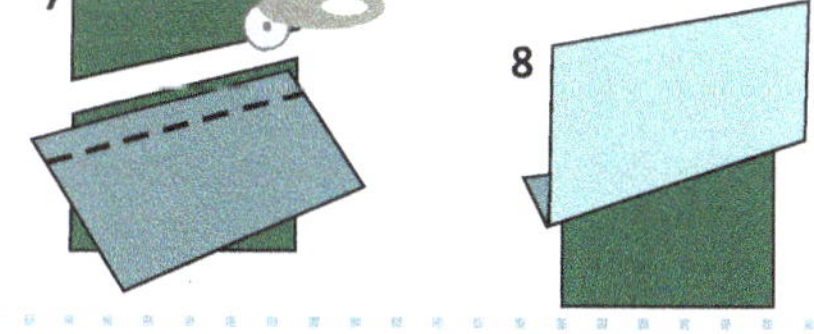

10 Cut in half vertically. Use a ruler to cut at exactly 2" across, or, for a wonkier look, guesstimate.

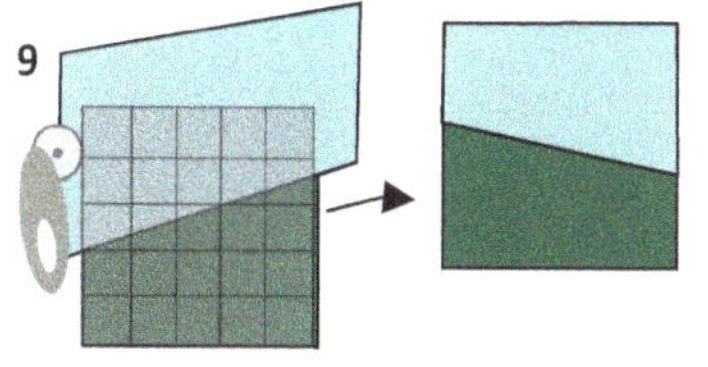

11 Sew a 4" x 1" pane strip to the right side of the left window half. Sew right window half to the other side of the pane. Press seam allowances under the strip. Trim so top and bottom strip ends are even with the window. Now each window is about 4" wide (again!)

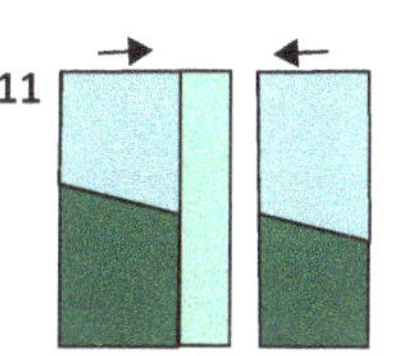

Six stories finishes at about 26" x 8.5" without balconies (10.5" width with them). Each story adds ~ 4.25" in height.

Fabric

Window glass. For 6 stories, twelve 4" x 4" pieces. Fat-quarter or 1/4 yard.

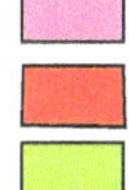

Window shade scraps, in 6+ colors. Twelve pieces, each at least 4.5" x 3.5"

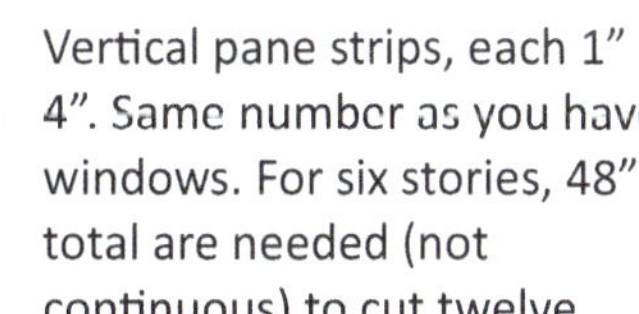

Vertical pane strips, each 1" x 4". Same number as you have windows. For six stories, 48" total are needed (not continuous) to cut twelve.

Floor dividers, 1" x 4". Same number as windows. For six stories, 48" total (not continuous) to cut twelve. Roof option: one more 2" x 12". Exact length will depend on your building's width.

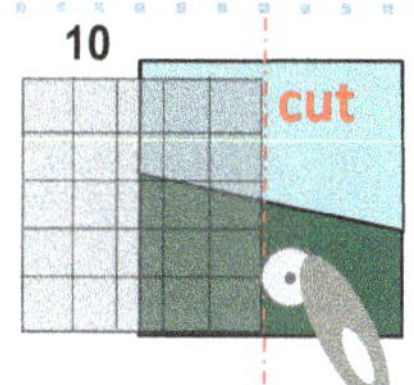

Side and middle strips: Two strips 1" x your finished building height. Plus a third, similar color strip, cut 1" x your building height. Can all be the same.

For balconies, see next page.

(continued)

12 For floor dividers, use 1" strips. Length: Your windows' average width (4" here). Cut as many as you have windows. (For 6 windows, start with a 24" x 1" divider strip; for 12, start with a 48" x 1 strip, but it needn't be continuous.)

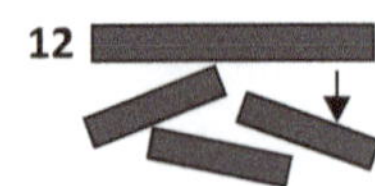

13 Sew one strip to each window's bottom edge. You can chain sew the units through the machine.

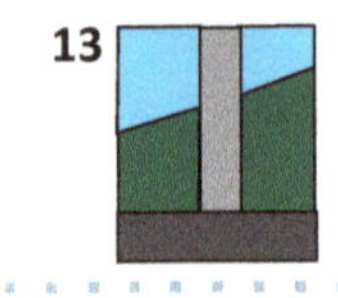

14 Arrange windows in two vertical columns, and check that adjoining blocks don't repeat the same shade fabric (unless you want them to match!)

15 Turn rows sideways (or just THINK of them sideways!), and chain sew. Starting in the upper left of diagram 15, flip the Column B Row 2 window (red shade), good side down, on top of Column B, row 1 window (yellow shade) Sew, joining the back of the pink shade area on 2 to the bottom edge of the floor divider along the bottom of the Column B Row 1 piece.

Without cutting threads, flip Column A Row 2 piece (pink shade) onto Column A row 1 piece (blue). You are joining the red shade's top edge to the bottom of the floor divider in row 1. Send through machine, then cut threads.

Lay the pieces back in position, with the two columns still attached by threads. Flip the Row 3 pieces onto the bottom edge of the row 2 pieces, and sew. Cut threads only after every two seams, column B followed by column A.

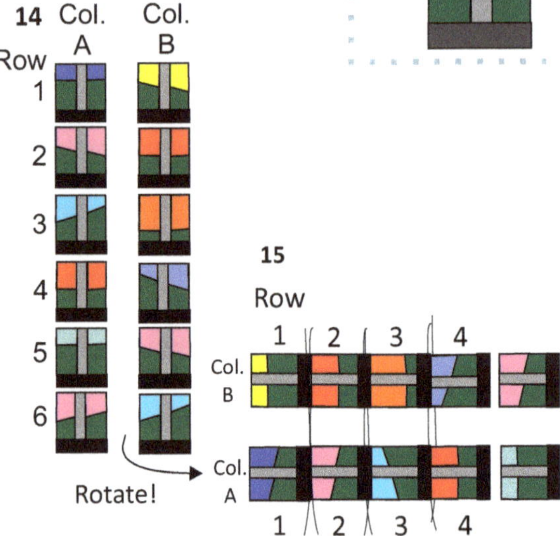

16 Press seam allowances under the floor dividers. Cut threads apart.

17 Measure column height. Six stories totals about 26". Cut three vertical strips, 1" X 26" (or your column height) from one color, or two similar colors. It's okay to piece these strips – buildings in the real world have all kinds of weathering and construction variations!

18 Choose one of the three strips to be the vertical center. Sew each column of windows to the sides of that strip. Sew the remaining vertical strips to the right and left sides of the building.

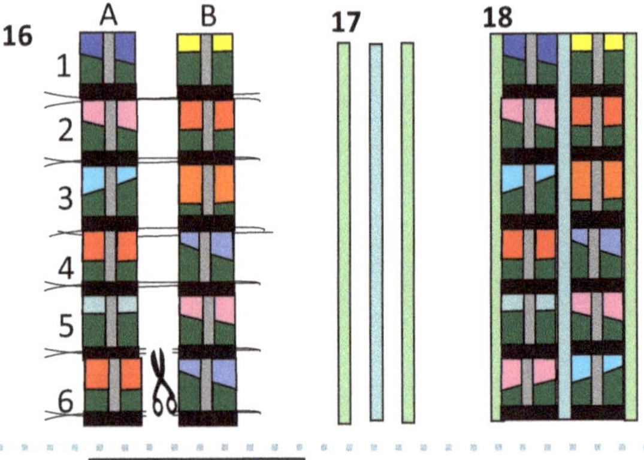

19 If you don't want balconies, you can add a roof now. Cut a strip 2" high by the width of your building and stitch in place. This can be your finished building, or...

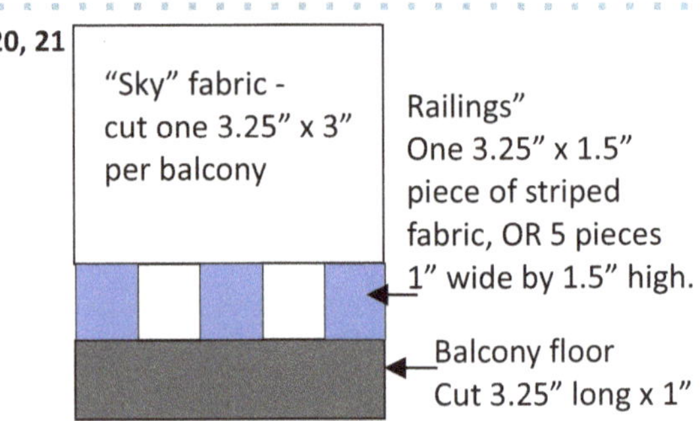

Add Balconies

20 Balconies can be added to one or both sides of the building. **You may have to wait until you choose your background/sky color.**

21 Each complete balcony (with railing and floor) should be at the same height as each window + floor in the main building. The balconies' floors should line up with floor dividers in the main building.

So, for each balcony's floor, I used the same width dark grey floor dividers strips, each cut 1" high, by 3.25" across. I strip-pieced railings for the balconies, from three dark and two "sky" (light) strips, each 1" wide x 1.5" high. Faster: Use a striped fabric, and cross-cut the entire railing unit, with stripes running vertically, to 3.25" x 1.5".

22 If you want the roof to cover the balconies (so the wealthy penthouse tenants don't get rained on), measure the entire building's width and use that to cut the roof strip and sew it on.

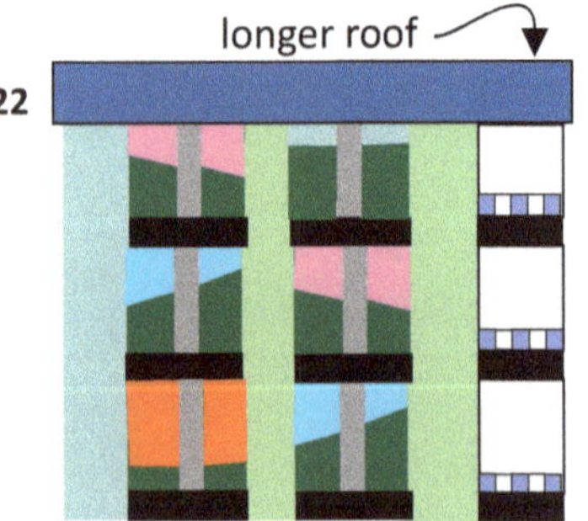

Seminole Stripe Tower

Florida Native Americans developed this piecing method for clothing embellishment. Ironically, it's great for depicting structures built mostly by invading Europeans! (Of course, Iroquois helped construct iconic NYC skyscrapers!). The three columns were inspired by many buildings – like the one on the upper right – with completely different-looking sections squashed together!

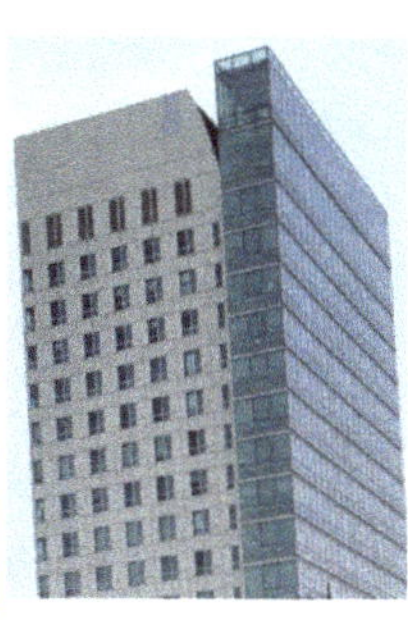

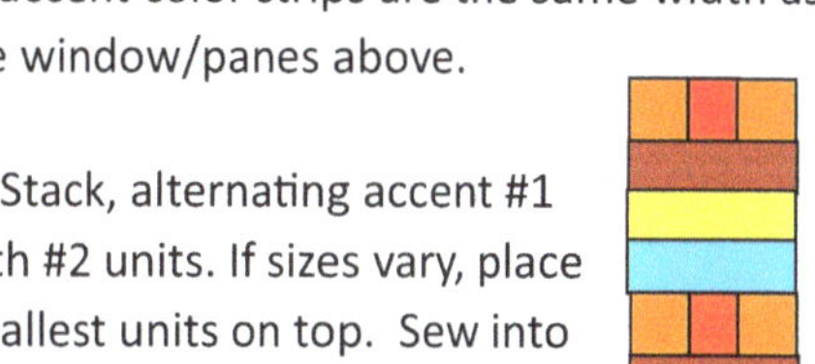

Size: 10 stories are approx. 45" x 4.25"

Fabric

Less than a fat-quarter or quarter-yard of:

- Window "glass"
- Window "pane" (2nd color is just for diagrams
- Accent color 1
- Accent color 2
- Accent color 3
- Stripe, buy or make

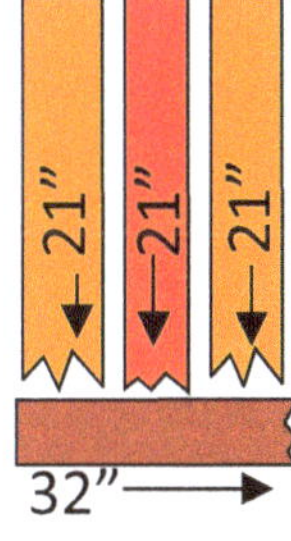

1 Cut:

– Two window glass strips, 1.25" x 21"

– One pane strip, 1"x 21"

– Another pane strip, 1" x 32"

(The 32" needn't be continuous; it will be cut to smaller pieces. Diagrams show this strip in brown, but you can use the same pane fabric as before.

32"

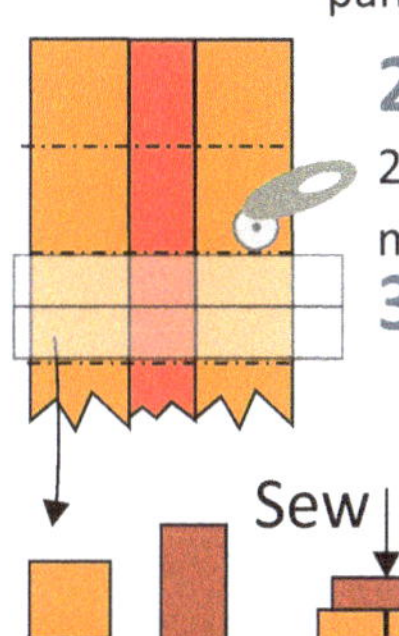

2 Sew a window strip to each side of the 21" pane strip. Press seam allowances to middle strip. Total width is about 2.5"

3 Slice across at 2" intervals.

Sew

4 Flip 3-part units, good side down, onto the right edge of the longer pane strip, good side up. Sew the 3-part units to the long strip, with a little space (~1/2") between.

5 Press seam allowances under each lower pane strip. Cut apart so each bottom strip is same width as the unit above it.

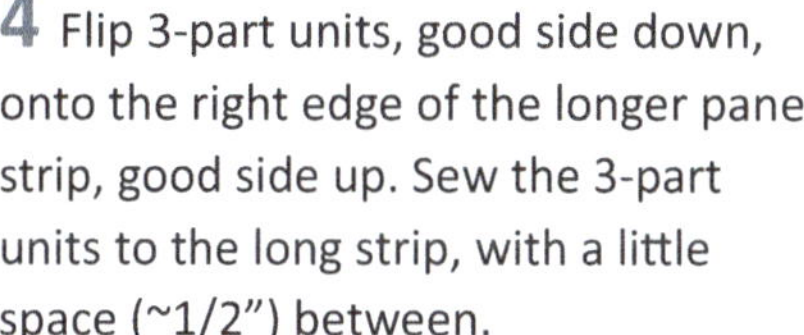

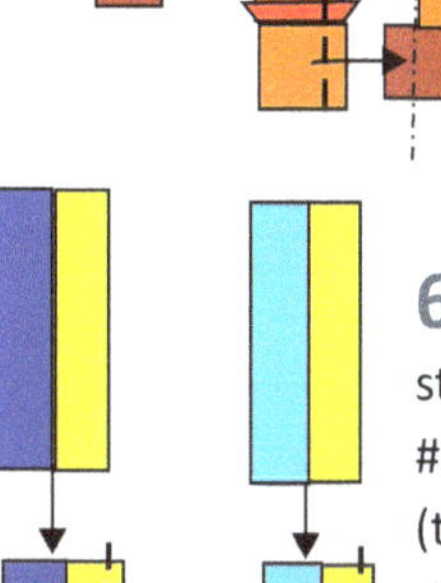

6 Cut two accent color #1 (yellow) strips 1.5" x 16". Cut one accent color #2 (navy) and one accent color #3 (turquoise) strip to 1.5" x 16". Sew two strip sets: One with accent colors #1 and #2, the other with accent colors #1 and #3.

7 Sew window units to accent strip sets. Half will have color #2, half will have #3.

8 Press seam allowances down. Cut apart so accent color strips are the same width as the window/panes above.

9 Stack, alternating accent #1 with #2 units. If sizes vary, place smallest units on top. Sew into a tower.

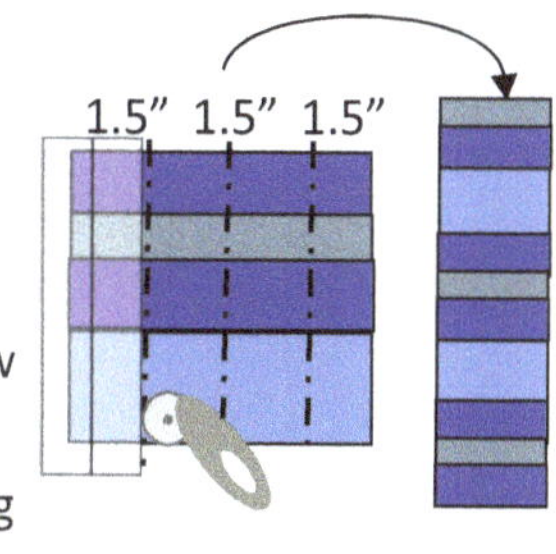

10 My skyscraper has a central column of blues. Use a printed stripe, or make a stripe. I made mine from dark solids. Cut four 15" long strips horizontally – vary widths from 1", up to 1.5". Sew together. Cut into 1.5" wide columns. Stack to create a repeating pattern, far right.

1.5" 1.5" 1.5"

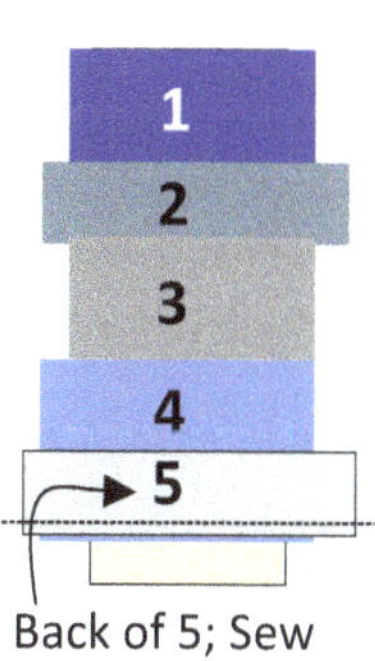

11 Or, for a more random look, string piece (sew and flip) pieces onto a 1.5" wide strip of paper cut to the height of your first window column from Step 9. Start at the top. Place piece 1 good side up. Flip piece 2 on it, good side down. Open piece 2 and press. Continue till you reach the desired height. Trim to 1.5" wide.

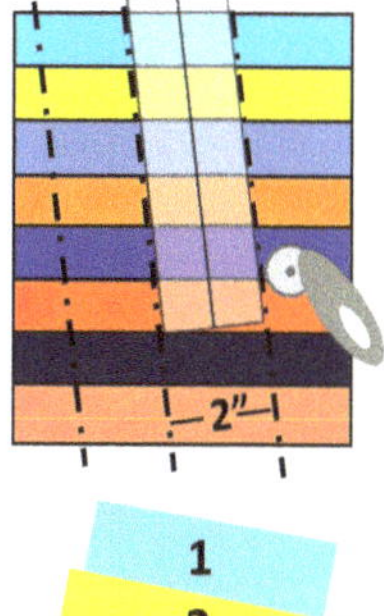

Back of 5; Sew and press open.

12 For the bright column on the far right, one option is to use the same technique as in step 11 – but place the ruler on a slight angle, to create a little perspective.

13 Or, string piece it like in Step 11, onto a 2" wide piece of paper. Here, set the strips pointing slightly down on the lower left. (This is just a taste of perspective - lots more is coming.) Trim edges even.

14 Join the three vertical columns. Press all outside edges in 1/4". You're done!

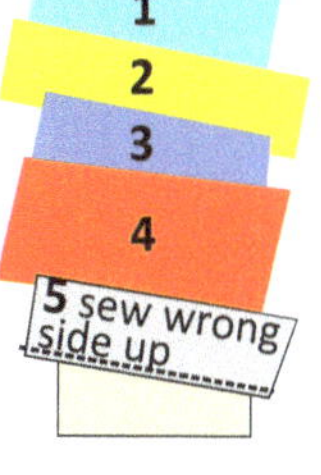

The Hotel Bargello

Bargello is a fun quilting technique combining strip piecing with offsetting. Plenty of buildings scream "bargello" at me! My favorite is Los Angeles' Hotel Indigo, far right. Once you start looking, you'll see bargello everywhere!

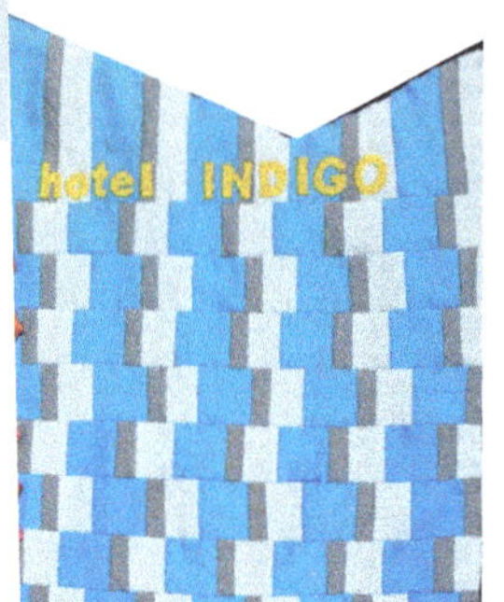

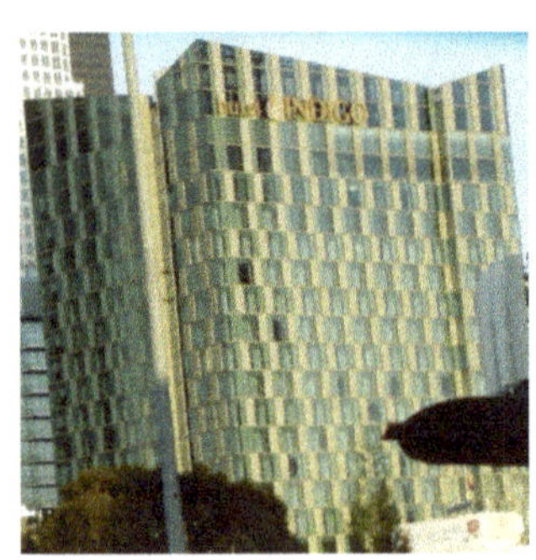

Size approx. 16" x 18"

Fabric

Less than a fat-quarter of:

Window "glass"

Window "pane"

Accent color

1 **Cut:**
– Five strips of window glass (dark blue) fabric, 2" wide x 18". **(Strips 1 in the diagram below)**
– Four strips of window pane (medium grey) fabric, 1" wide x 18". **(Strips 2 in the diagram)**
– Four strips of accent color (light blue) fabric, 1.5" wide x 18". **(Strips 3 in the diagram)**

2 Lay out as shown. Join any way you like. I space them into groups of 3, numbered (in my head) as shown. Then, I chain sew:

Flip the first piece 2 on the left (grey) face down, onto the first piece 1 (dark blue, furthest left), and send through machine. Without cutting threads, flip the **next** piece 2, face down, onto the **next** piece 1 - and sew. Keep going so you have a connected chain of four pairs.

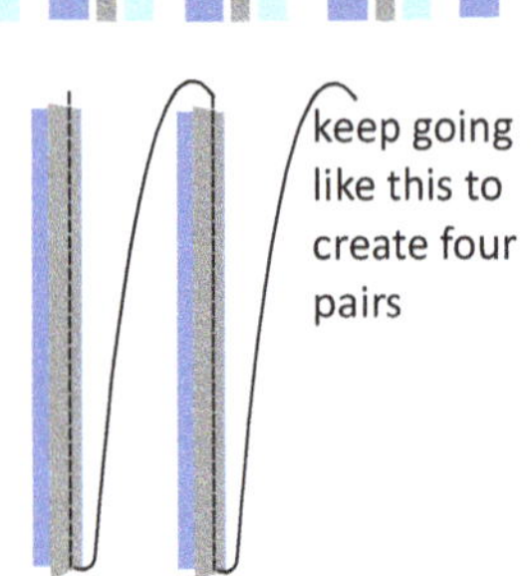

3 Press seams (choose a direction, right or left, and stick with it). Cut threads, lay everything out in order again.

4 Chain sew again. This time, flip each strip 3 onto the right edge of each 2, and sew. When you've done all four, press seam allowances in the same direction as before.

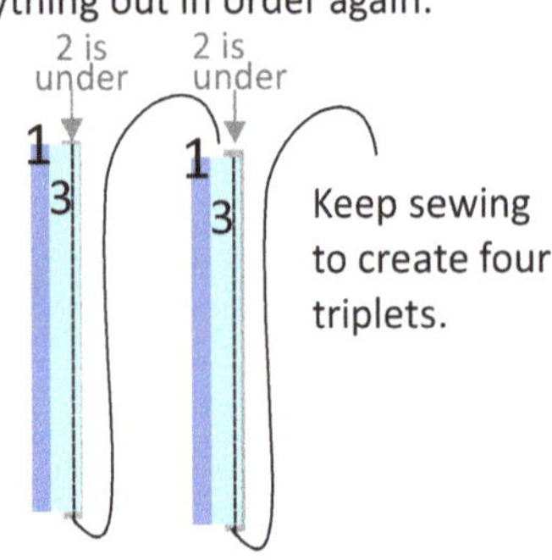

5 Cut apart and lay out in order again. Now you have four triplets and a single on the far right.

6 Sew the first two triplets together, and then the second two triplets together, creating two groups of six.

7 Join the groups of six, and add the remaining strip on the far right. Press in same direction as earlier seams.

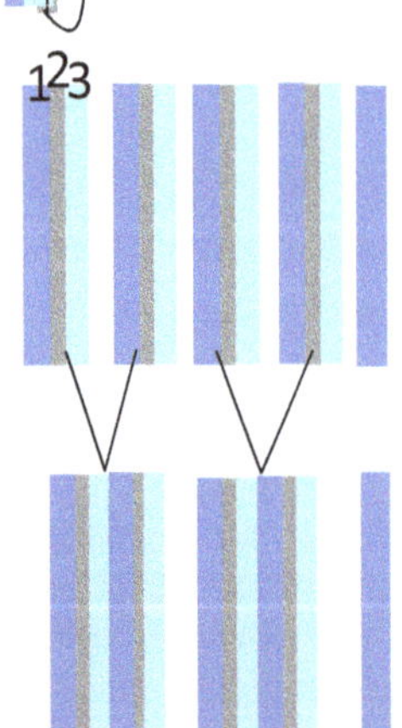

8 Use rotary cutter and ruler to cut the set apart at 2" intervals, starting at the bottom. Leave the top 4" (or however much is leftover).

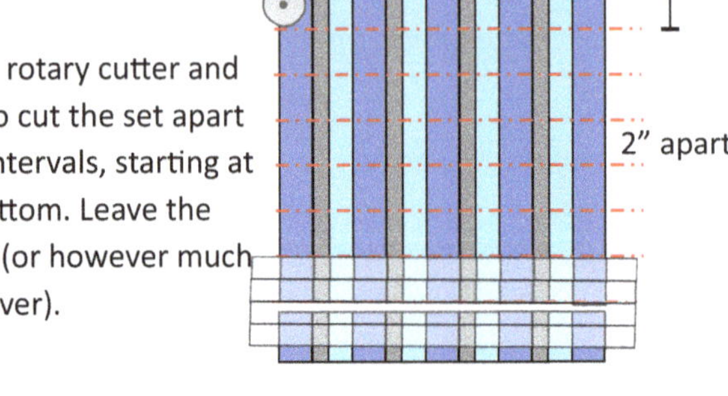

9 Option: Cut top edge into a wedge, like the hotel in the photo above. The top right and left corners stay the same 18" height; the low point is on the seam, about 2" down from the top.

10 Shift every other strip a bit to the right, so each window glass piece (dark blue) sits PARTIALLY on the same color piece below it.

11 Sew strips together, maintaining shifts. I turn everything sideways. Chain sew the middle six strips into pairs: Flip each piece 2 (which is lower) onto each 1 (higher), maintaining the offset. Pin and sew.

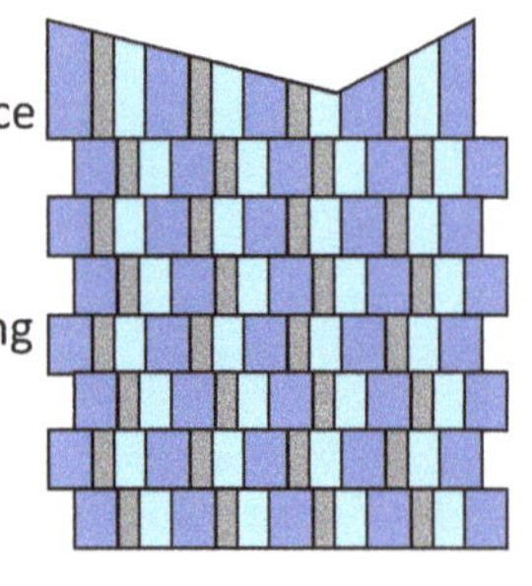

12 Do all three pairs shown. Press all new seam allowances in the same direction (toward top or bottom of the building – pick a direction and stick with it.)

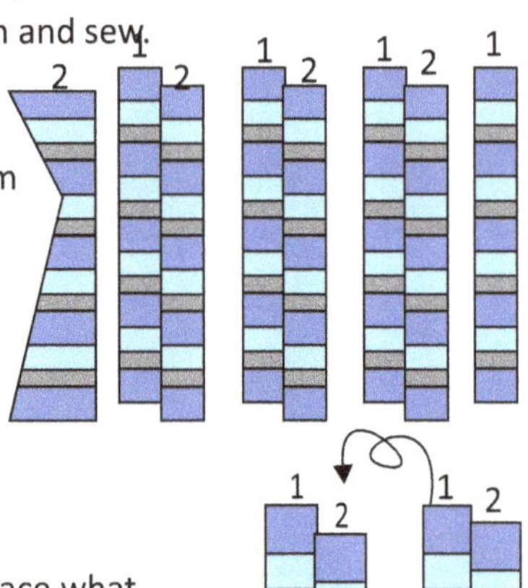

13 Cut threads and replace what you've sewn in the lineup. Now each higher piece 1 (which has a 2 sewn to its right side) must be flipped and sewn onto the lower 2 piece **in the pair to its left** - but that means the strip 1 on top will hide the beginning of the underlying #2 piece!

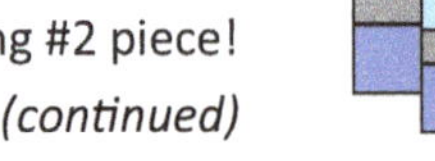

(continued)

There are a couple of ways to handle this. One is to flip the strips you're joining to their reverse side – but I find that confusing. Here's what I do that confuses me less!

14 The diagram shows the back of a 1+2 pair (grey because it's the back), flipped onto the 1+2 pair to its left. Raw right edges are aligned. On the back of grey strip 1 on the far right, I put a mark or a pin where the underlying 2 piece begins. Bring up threads and sew down from there. (No need to backstitch).

15 At the bottom, you can clearly see a where to stop (Where the strip 1 on top ends. It's okay if you sew off the end onto 2, however – nothing terrible will happen.)

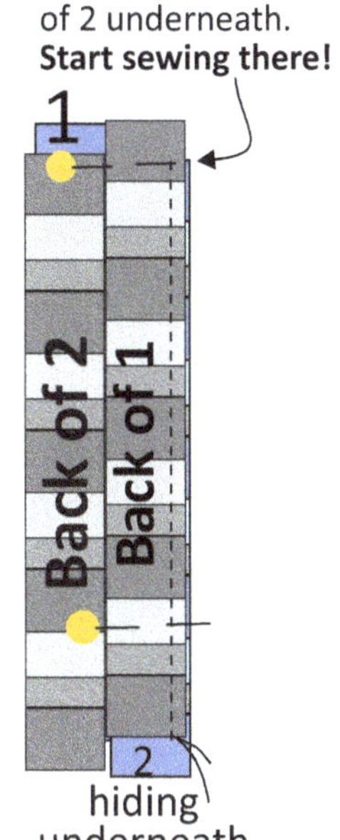

16 Sew the remaining seams this way. Here's what it will look like when you join the roof to the pair on its right. Again, start at the top where the underlying piece (in this case the roof) starts.

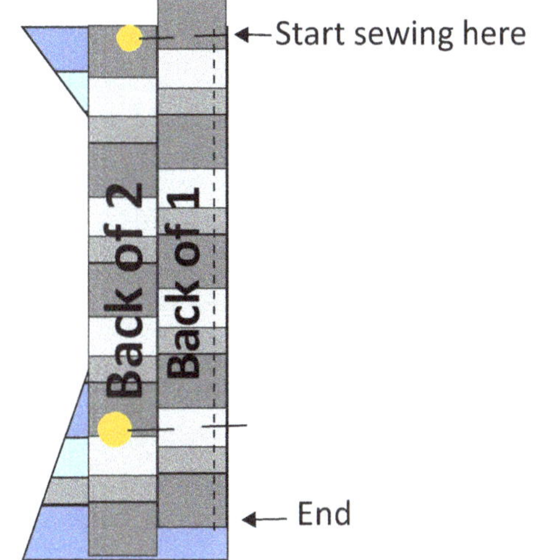

17 Trim sides even (on the red dotted line).

18 Press all edges under 1/4". If you angled the roof, you will have to release a few stitches from the seam where the lowest point lies.

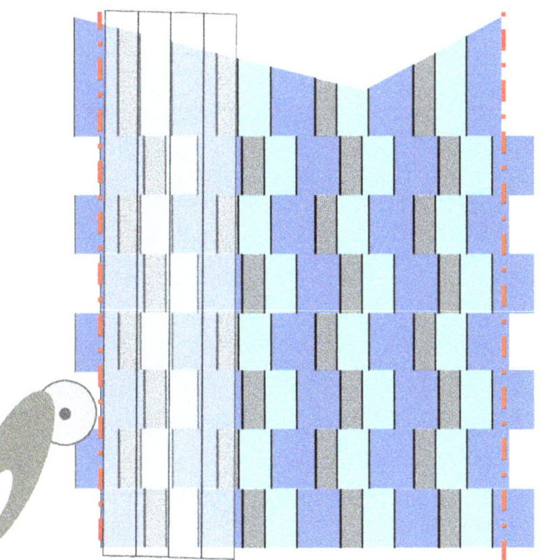

Bargello + Balconies Tower

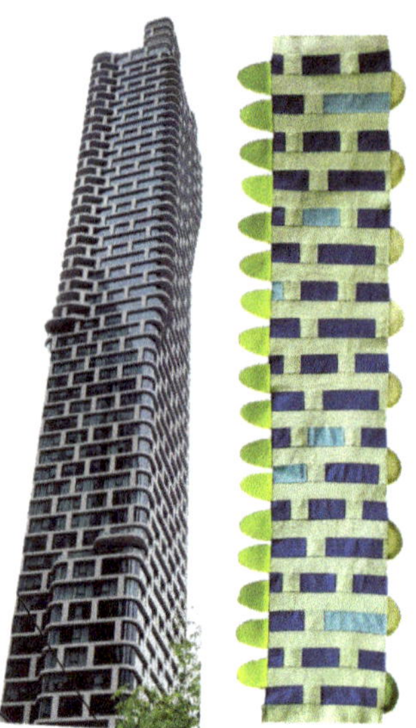

Also crying "bargello" is the ARO building, NYC's 67th tallest building. Along with offset windows, it has a thick white exoskeleton, which forms curved balconies. Part of this tower wound up in my 'Nonsense Town' quilt on p. 10.

1 Cut:
– **Four light (green) strips 1.5"x 16"** Light vertical bars
– **Ten light (green) strips 1.5" x 16"** Light horizontals
– **Two dark (navy) strips 4.25" x 16"; and two 2.5" x 16"** Windows

2 Match each light vertical strip to a dark window strip, and sew them into pairs, always placing dark strips on the right. Join pairs into 2 groups of 4. Sew the middle seam. Press all seam allowances behind the lighter strips.

3 Cut set apart at 1.5" intervals. You should wind up with about 10 horizontal strips.

4 On design wall or desk, flip every other strip upside-down, and alternate with a 16" framing strips. Don't sew yet.

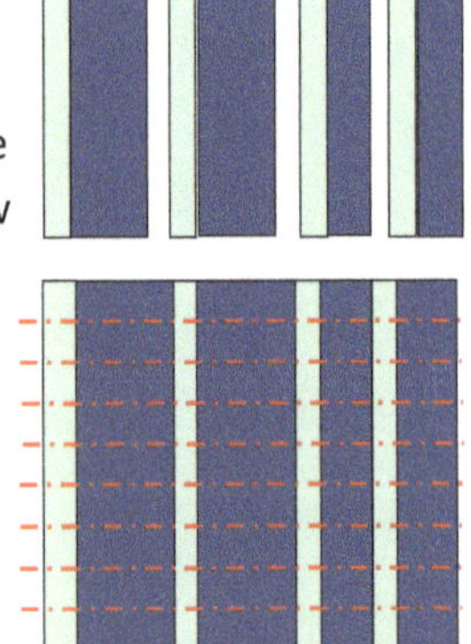

5 Day or night, city buildings' windows are light or dark in unpredictable patterns. So let's switch out a few dark windows for light ones. Use a seam ripper to randomly remove about five dark windows, measure them, and replace them with same-size strips of a lighter fabric. I used light blue.

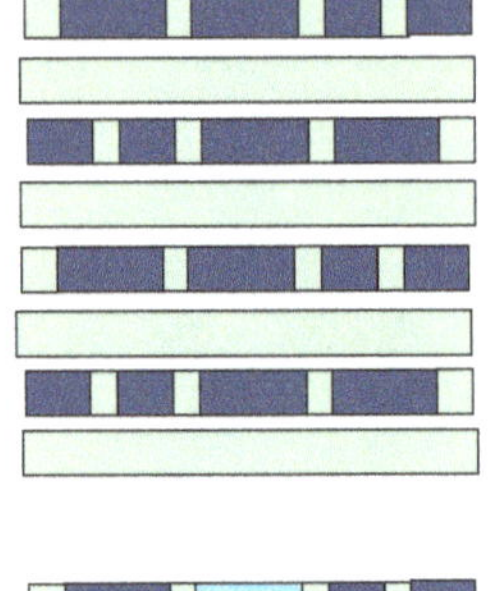

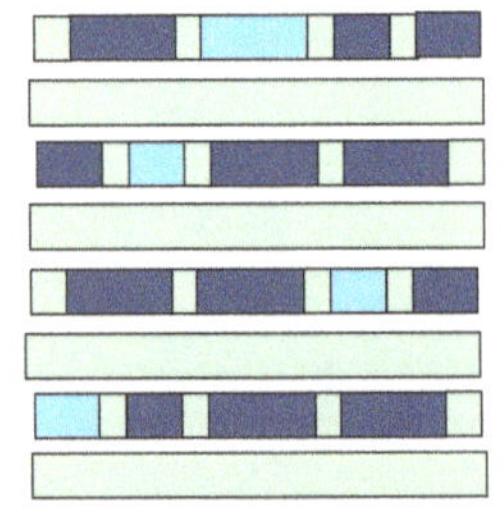

Finished approx. 8" x 34" for tall option, 16" x 20 for short one.

Fabric

Most windows. 1/4 yard or fat-quarter

Exoskeleton. 1/4 yard or fat-quarter

A few windows. Scraps.

Porches & ledges. Fat-quarter. Use a color close to or the same as the exoskeleton.

Also helpful, for balconies only:
– Spray starch or sizing;
– Clean cardstock (like from a file folder).

6 Join rows into pairs, then groups of four, and so on. Send through machine with the back of the pieced side on top, so you can see earlier seam allowances and make sure they stay turned correctly. Press horizontal allowances under the long, lighter pieces.

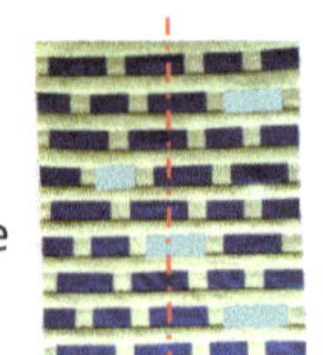

Keep the building this way if you need something low.

Or, for a tall, narrow skyscraper, fold in half to find the vertical center. Cut the piece down that center (red line above). Stack half on top of the other, and sew them together.

You can stop here – unless you want curved ledges and balconies like those in the inspiration building.

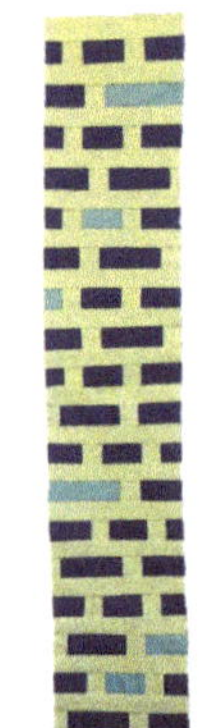

Curvy ledges and balconies

For balconies, I added half circles to one side, and longer half-ovals to the other. Full size pressing templates are on p. 26. The ovals finish at 4" x 1.5" (they'll ultimately be cut in half vertically into two 2" pieces). Circles finish at 2" across (and then are cut into 1" pieces).

7 Print p. 26 on cardstock, freezer paper, or if you don't have those, regular paper. Do the red box size check – if the size isn't right, adjust printer settings to "print actual size".

8 Cut out shapes. If you printed on regular paper, trace around shapes onto cardstock (like a file folder.) Cardstock and freezer paper templates can be reused about three times, so you can probably get with just one printout.

9 My building is 18 stories (I count each window row + one solid floor divider row as one story), so I need 9 fabric half circles (cut from 5 full circles), and 17 fabric half ovals (The bottom floor doesn't have a balcony).

My technique is familiar to both appliquérs and English Paper Piecers – turn-under appliqué, with a boost from spray starch or sizing.

10 Place a cardstock oval on fabric. Cut fabric about 1/4" bigger. Repeat to make 9 ovals.

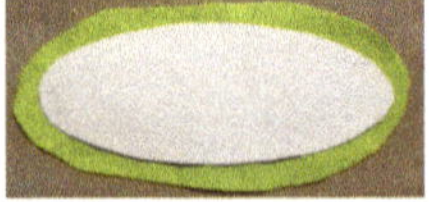

(continued)

11 Spray oval with starch. Or, spray a little starch into a shallow bowl or lid, then roll oval in it (illustrated in step 15 below). Press edges inward. Press until it's dry. Remove template and press again.

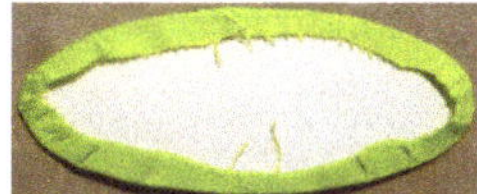

12 Fold in half to find and press a light crease down the center.

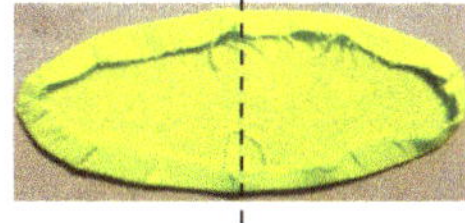

13 Open and cut in half.

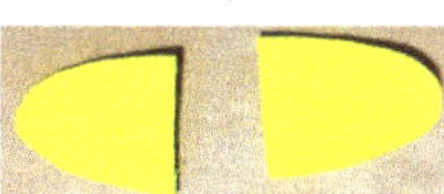

14 Circles can be made the same way. I didn't need to cut cardstock circles because I own a set of Karen Kay Buckley's "Perfect Circles," made from heat-resistant plastic, shown on the right. The process is the same as with cardstock.

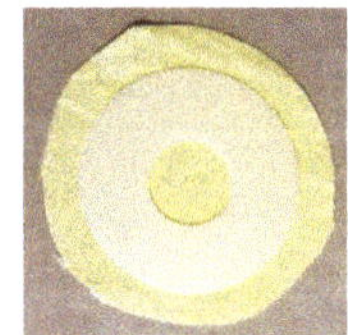

Distributing creases evenly on circles is a bit more challenging than ovals. After cutting fabric about 1/4" larger than template, do a long hand-basting stitch just inside the fabric's raw edges. Draw the thread up, so the fabric is tight around the cardstock (or plastic) template); tie a big knot to hold it.

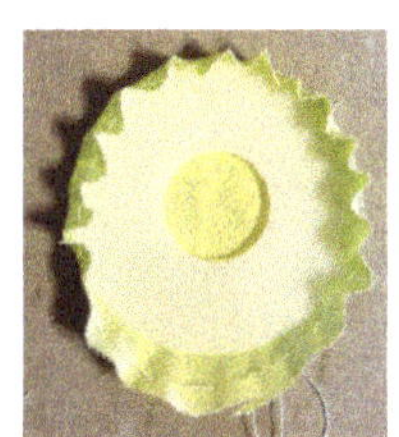

15 Again, spray starch or sizing onto the back; or into a shallow saucer or lid. Some people then use a small paintbrush to paint the outer edges; I find it faster to roll the edges in the shallow puddle as shown. Wait a few seconds for it to spread. Press well until it's dry.

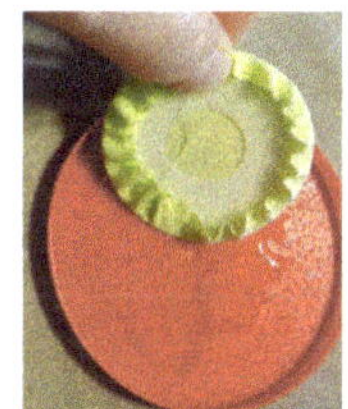

16 Remove template and press well again.

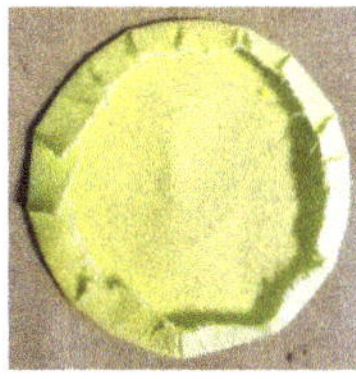

17 Fold in half to find the center. Press lightly, then open and cut along that line.

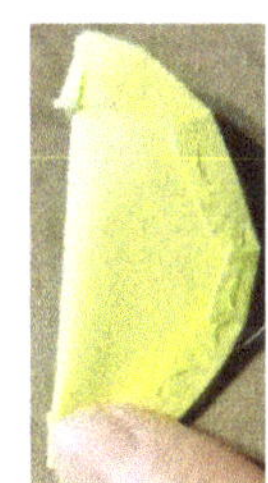

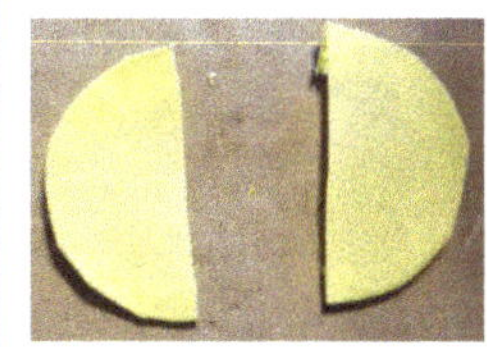

18 When you have enough half-circles for every other floor (nine for the building above,) pin them on one side.

I center them over every other seam, always between a (light) sashing strip on the left, and a window on the right.

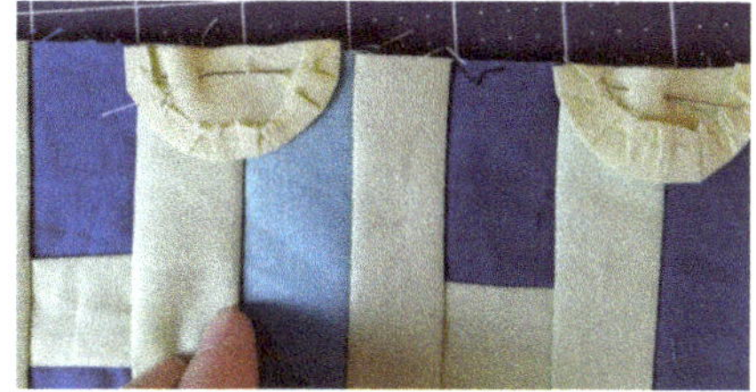

19 Sew each in place, with a 1/4" seam allowance. Instead of cutting threads at the end of each circle, just pull the units forwards, to sew the next half

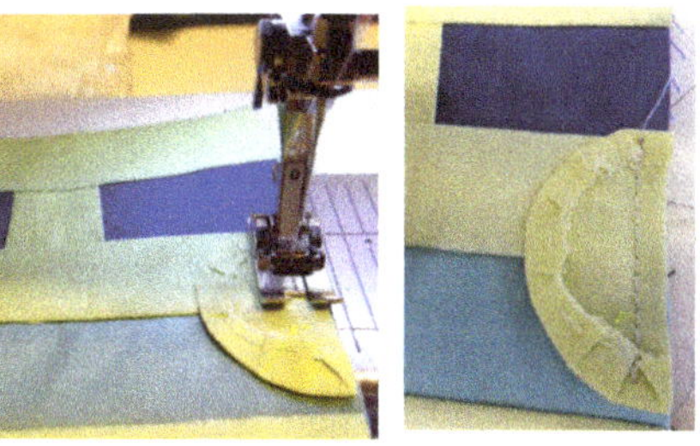

20 Trim connecting threads. Press all shut, then flip each circle outward, and press seam allowance back under the building.

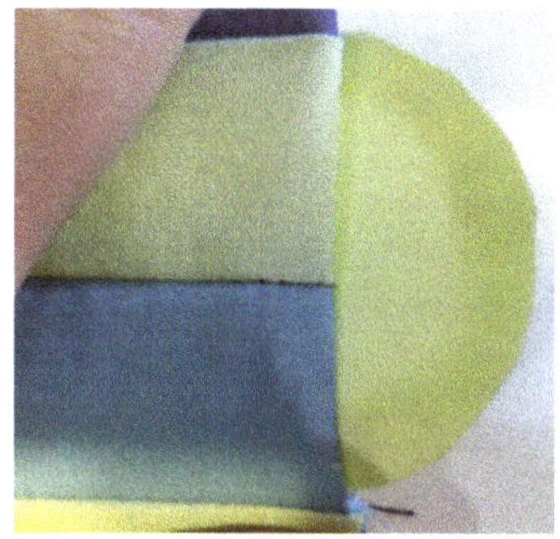

21 Repeat this procedure with all half-ovals. They go on each floor. Pin in place first. I lined up each oval's bottom edge with the bottom of each horizontal strip.

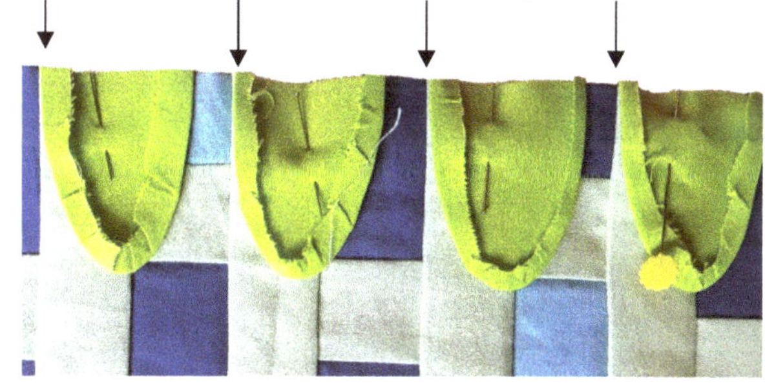

22 Chain sew, as before.

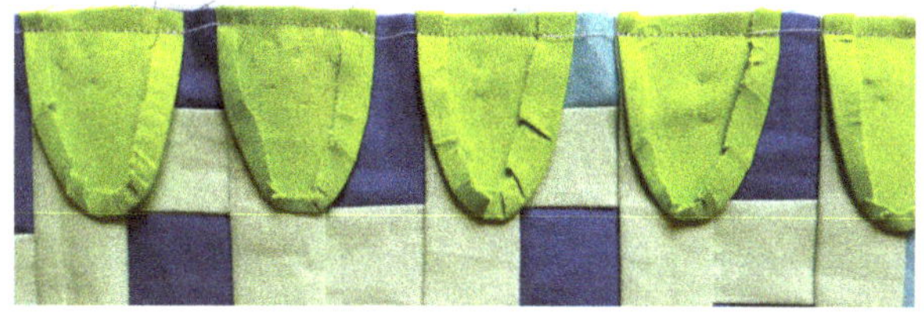

23 Last, trim threads connecting pieces, then press the half ovals outward, with the seam allowances pressed back under the building. Press remaining raw edges on top back 1/4".

(Templates are on next page)

Full size templates for Bargello & Balconies Building

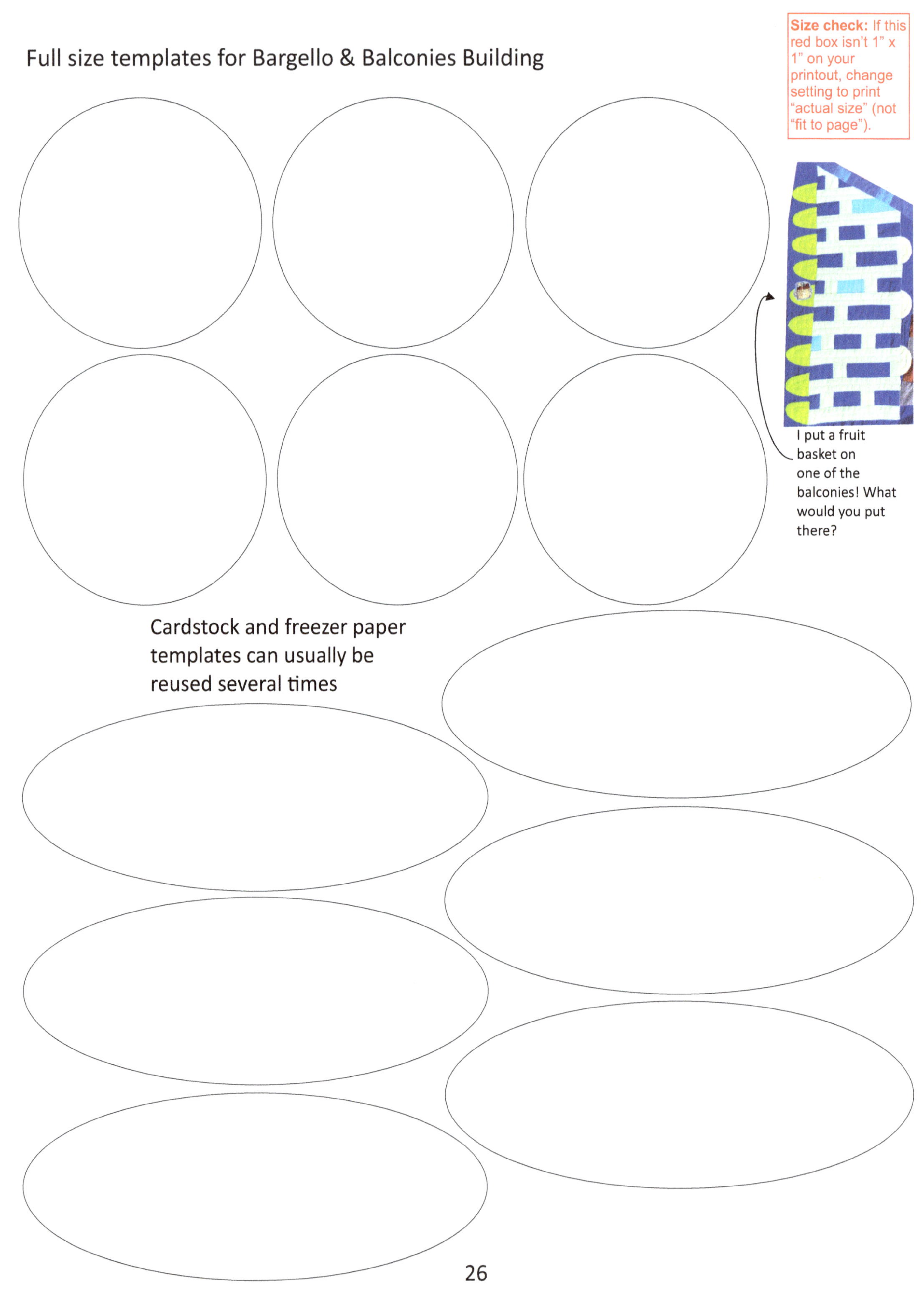

I put a fruit basket on one of the balconies! What would you put there?

Cardstock and freezer paper templates can usually be reused several times

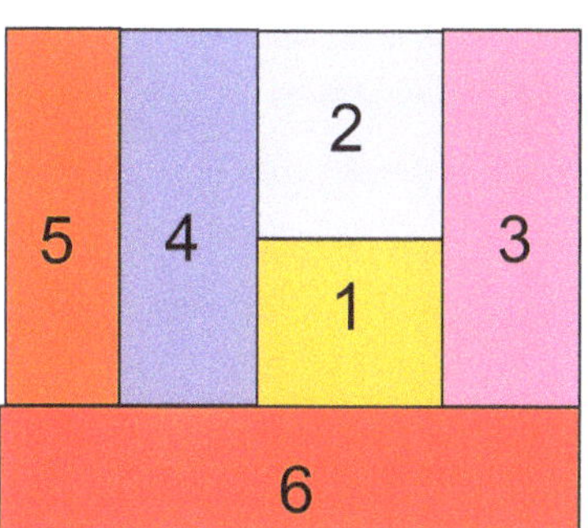

Stacked Super-Tall Cabins

Super-tall, super-slender super-luxury buildings have caught on around the world. Maximum real estate on minimum land makes money! Engineering advances allow them to stand up to wind and earthquakes. On the left are three that overlook the Central Park reservoir in NYC.

The fantasy stacked apartments on the right are log cabin blocks. To maximize modernity, improv cut the pieces with scissors. If they vary in size and value, place the smallest, lightest cabins higher up, for perspective. This building wound up in 'Scrap City 1', on p. 7.

Squat alternative: Use multiple log cabins to build a low, wide building, like in the diagram on bottom of this page.

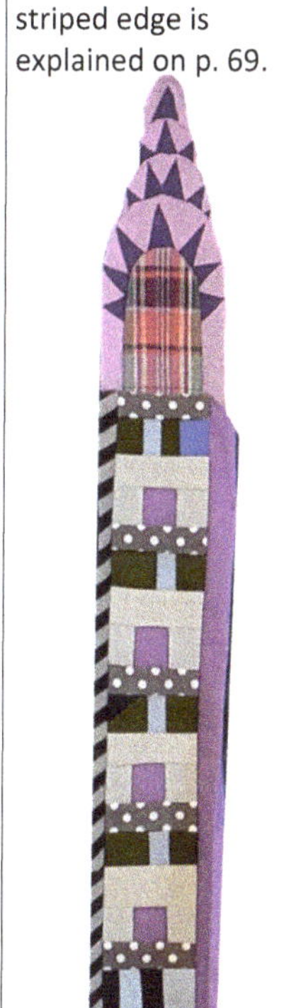

Frankentower!

I grafted the head of something like NYC's Chrysler Building onto a tower of log cabins! The perspective striped edge is explained on p. 69.

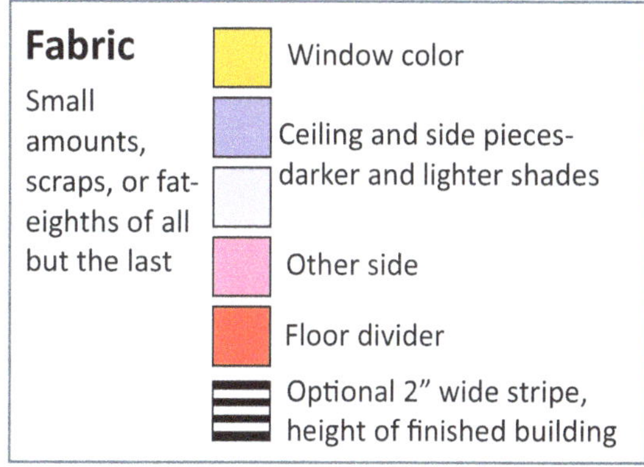

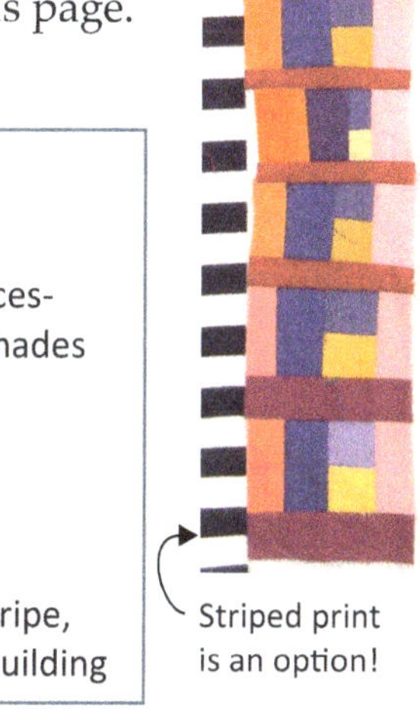

Fabric

Small amounts, scraps, or fat-eighths of all but the last

- Window color
- Ceiling and side pieces- darker and lighter shades
- Other side
- Floor divider
- Optional 2" wide stripe, height of finished building

1 Piece blocks like the one above (use this order, or change as desired!). Use any size you choose, but don't cut pieces less than 1" wide.

2 Stack cabins. If they're all a little different, for perspective, put smaller/lighter ones higher.

3 Option 1: Cut a printed stripe, and add it to one side (as on the upper right).

4 Option 2: Want something short and wide instead? Create several shorter columns. Separate them with vertical strips. You can wind up with something like the virtual building on the lower right (made in my graphics program), which looks a lot like the real Los Angeles hotel in the photo below, middle! Also the New York City building with log cabin windows, on the lower left.

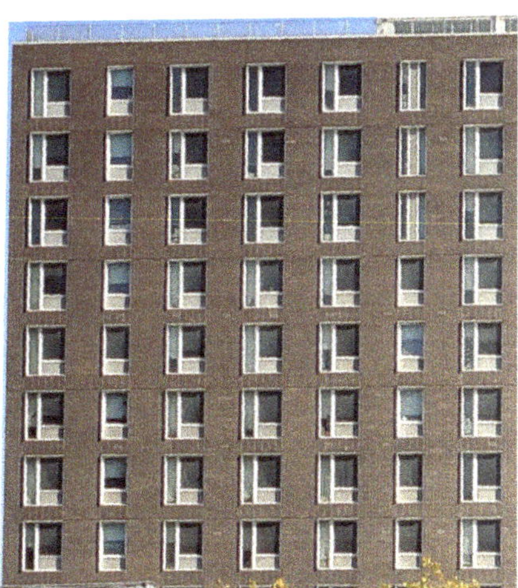

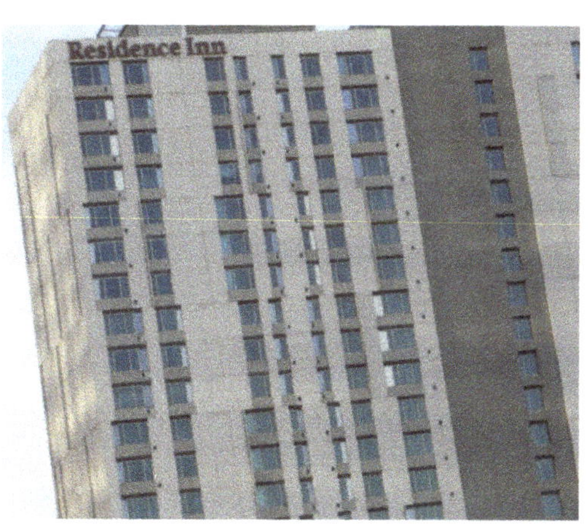

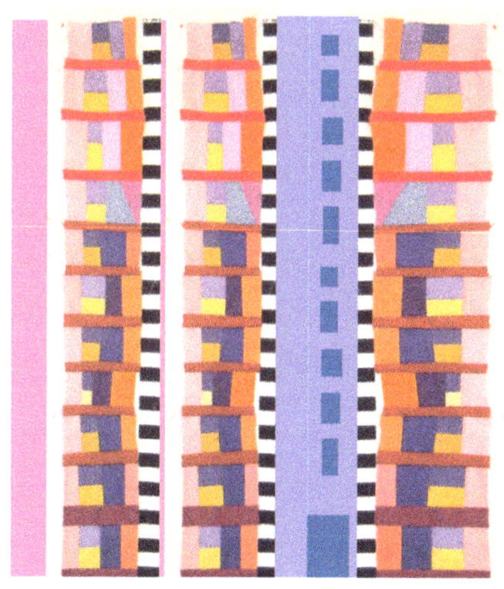

Stacked Clusters, Straight Edges

The fantasy structure below, right was inspired by French architect Jean Nouvel's condo building at 100 11th Ave., NYC, on the left. Its curved shell is made up of more than 1600 panes of glass, each tilted differently, to make the building glitter. I took the photo below in mid-day, but photos of the same building at dusk show the windows turn glorious shades of orange and gold!

My fabric version wound up on the top right of the cover quilt.

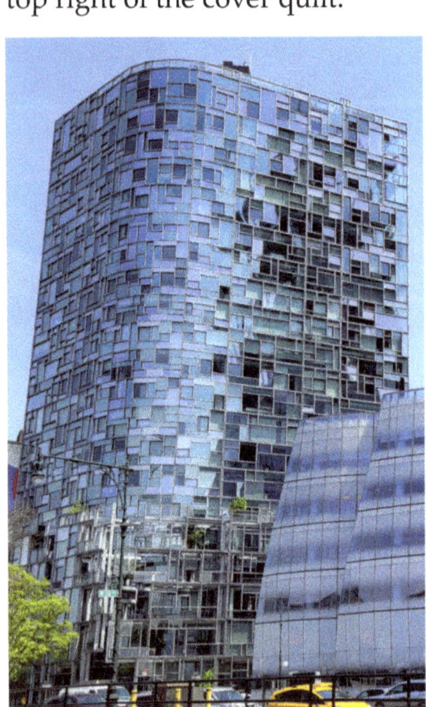

Author's Photo

1 Use scraps; or get a running start by cutting strips of each color between 1"-2" wide and about 10" long. (Some strips can be 1.25" wide, some 1.5", 1.75", etc.)

2 Start some blocks with the main "window" color, yellow or gold here. Surround with other colors in varying shades. Every block doesn't need every fabric; every main window doesn't have to be #1, or to be completely surrounded!

3 Arrange finished blocks. Blocks that have significantly smaller and/or lighter windows should go towards the top, for perspective.

4 Sew several blocks into rectangular subgroups, trimming extra. Join subgroups to make larger rectangles, trimming or adding individual strips as needed.

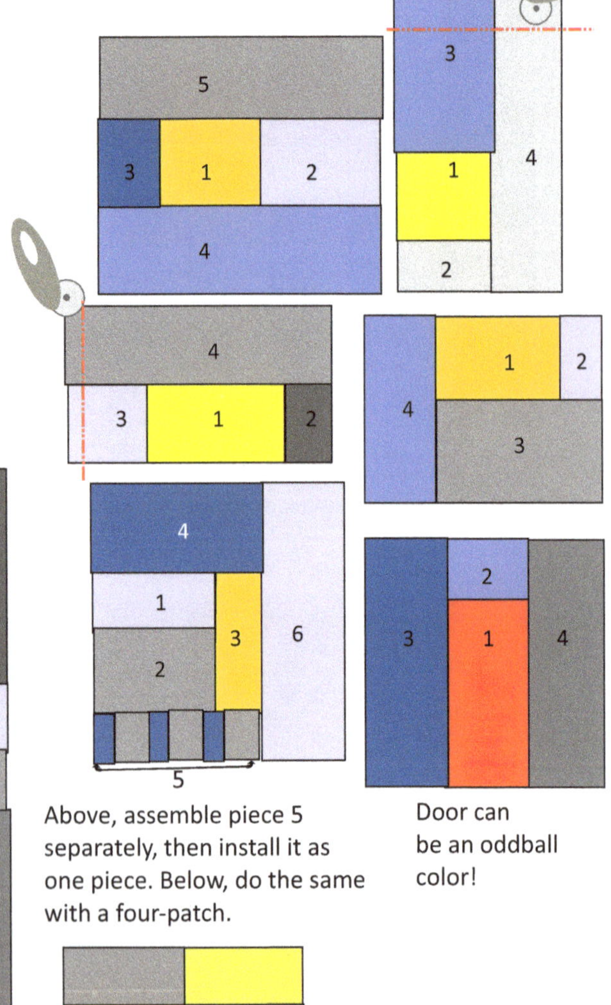

Above, assemble piece 5 separately, then install it as one piece. Below, do the same with a four-patch.

Door can be an oddball color!

Fabric

Use scraps or strips in at least three color families.

Window glass color: Scraps or strips of 2+ shades

Building Color 1: Two or more shades

Building Color 2: Two or more shades

Can be tall or squat!

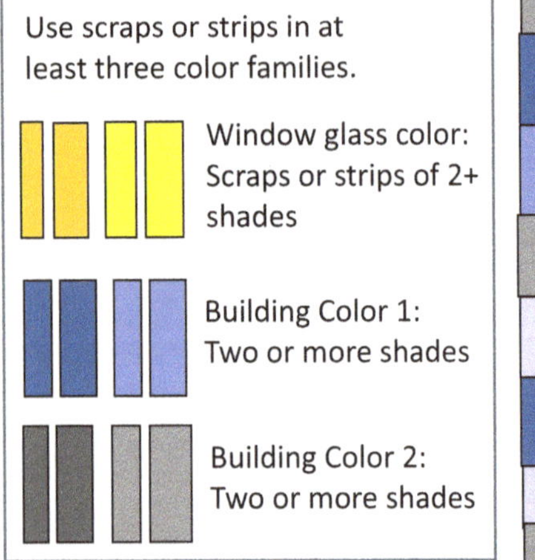

Wedges for Wheels, Windmills + More

The first 'building' I made using a wedge ruler was inspired by Chicago's Navy Pier Ferris Wheel, right. I cut too many, so I turned the leftovers into the fan-shaped penthouse on top of building **A** below. Building **C**, in the same row, has 18 wedges.

If you don't own a wedge ruler, make a template from the black outline on the lower right.

Ferris Wheel

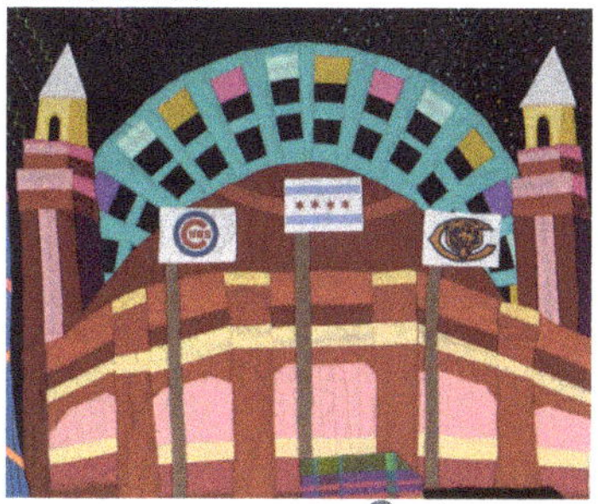

1 Make strip sets with sky color (navy) built in.

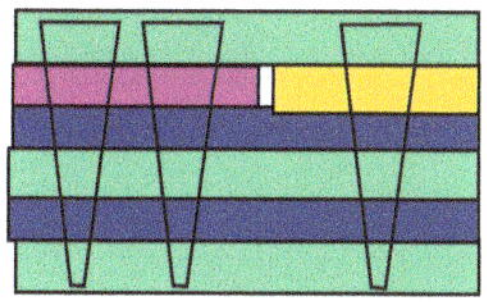

2 Cut plain spacer wedges

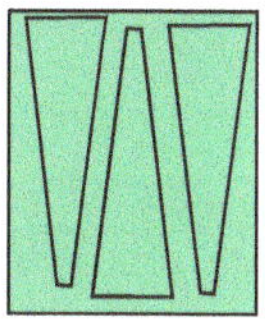

3 Alternate

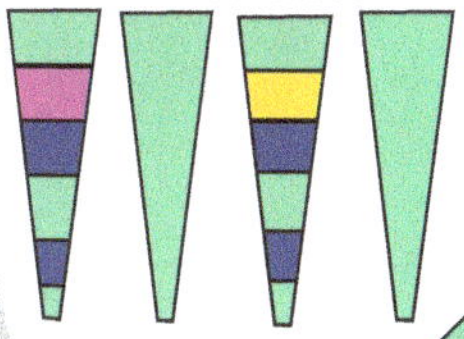

4 Sew

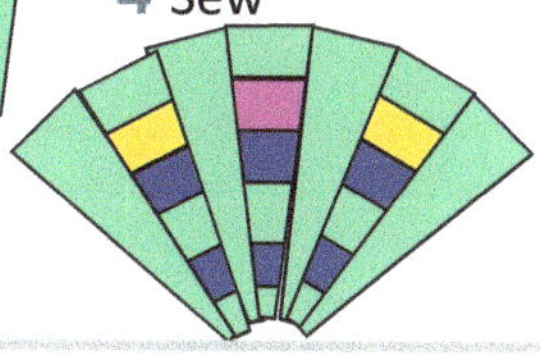

A Ferris wheel leftovers **B** Long scraps, wider at base **C** Directions below

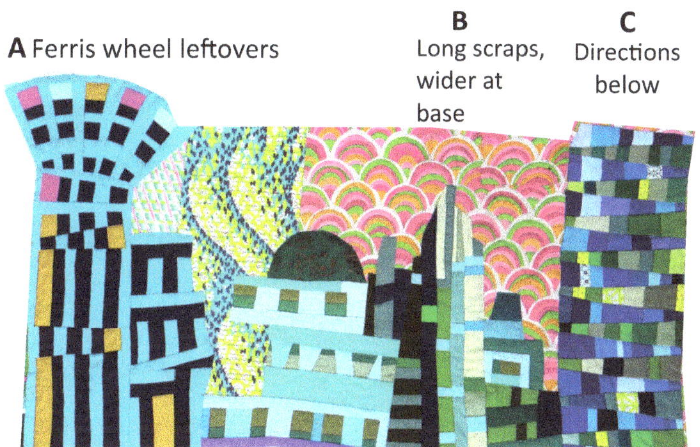

Windmill

To Make Building C

Method 1: Stitch and Flip

Trace wedge template on clean paper 18 times. Cut out. Stitch and flip scraps of fabric horizontally across each wedge. Cut fabric wedge out, following wedge's outline. Remove paper, press, and trim again if needed.

Method 2: Strip Piecing

Make two 20" strip sets, from two color families. Here, one is medium and dark blues; the other is light and medium greens. Vary strip widths 1" - 3". Finished height of strip sets should be about 7" for the template on this page.

Cut 9 wedges from each strip set. Flip wedge ruler each time to cut.

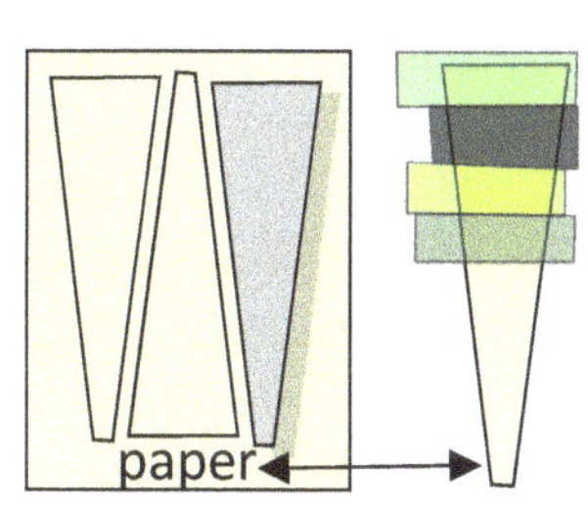

Finishing for both: Sew wedges in alternating directions. Press edges inward. Building will measure approx. 25" x 6.5".

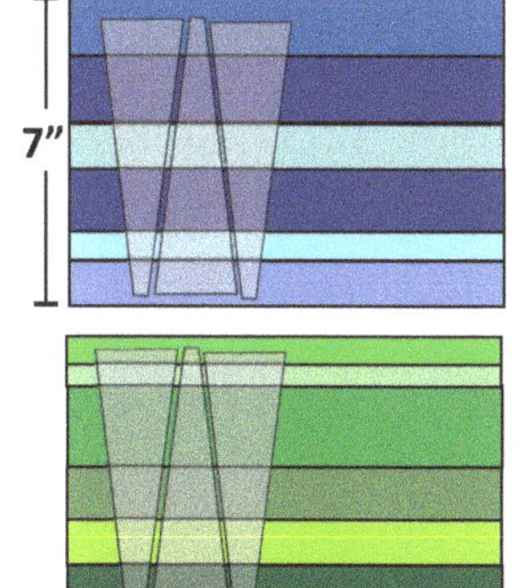

Each blade is made of two wedges, cut from a strip set at opposite angles, then stitched into pairs.

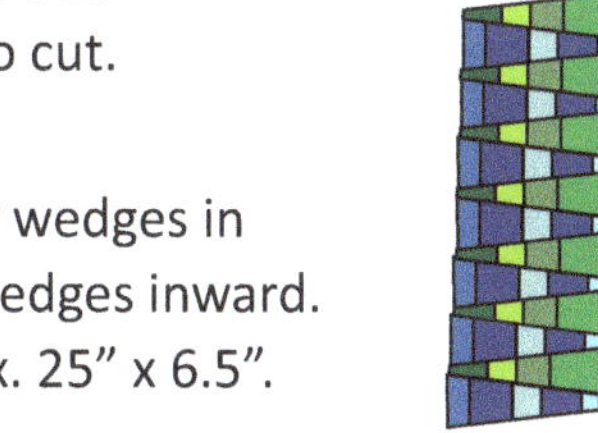

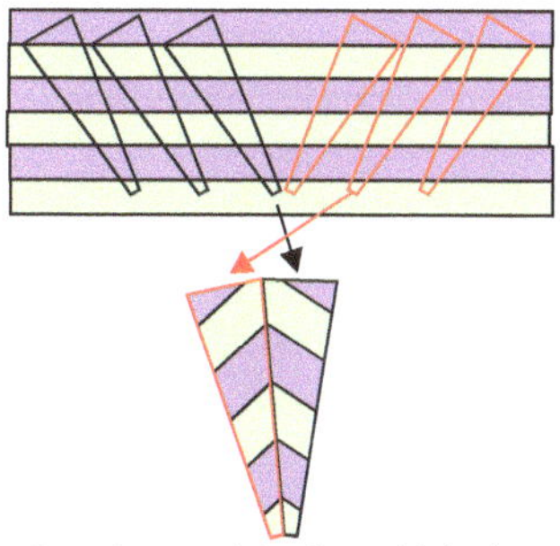

For the multicolored blade, I used a rainbow-striped fabric. I cut two wedges, one angled left and one angled right, the same way as above. I sewed them together the same way.

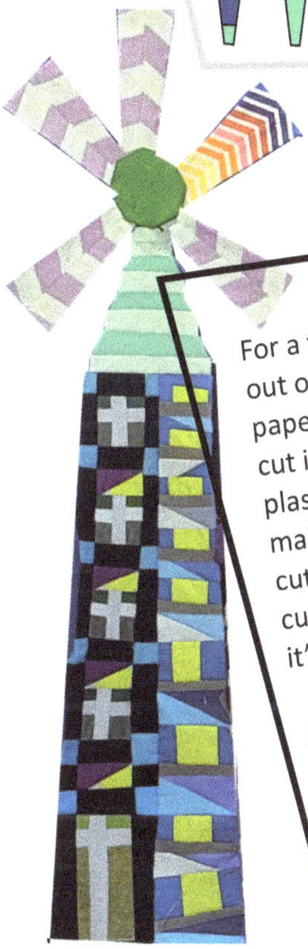

For a temporary wedge ruler, print out or trace this black outline on paper; glue paper to cardboard, and cut it out. Or trace it on template plastic. This is okay if you only are making a few wedges; but if you're cutting lots of them, an acrylic wedge-cutting ruler is a good investment — it's safer, easier, faster and more fun!

Size Check: The black outline should measure 6.5" high from center top to bottom. Check your printout. If the measurement is different, adjust print settings to "print to actual size."

Grey, Interrupted

Too many buildings are relentless grey, especially those in the mid-20th century style aptly called "Brutalism." At first glance, this appears to be one of them, NYC's Fifth Ave. Synagogue, built in 1958. The front is grey stone wall, with black cutout ovals.

Only from inside (and online) can you see that the windows have colorful, glowing stained glass stripes. They represent olive leaves, a biblical peace symbol! Not brutal at all! (See for yourself*)

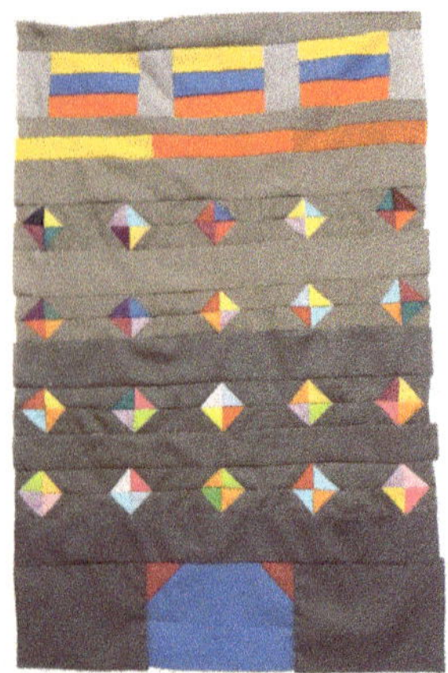

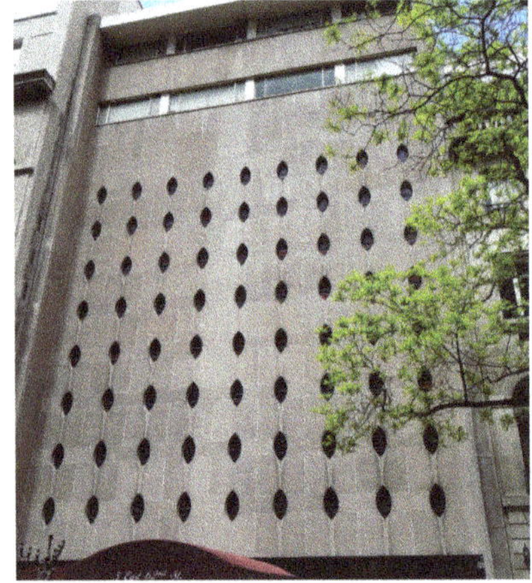

Class work by Haya Shafran

I made mine with an improv stitch-and-flip game. Light grey strips are highest, to signify the sun hitting the building's top.

If you replace the grey segments with bright colors, and double the size, it would make a delightful, non-brutal kid's quilt.

1 Cut 32 grey strips, 4.5" x 1.5" Cut all from the same grey; or half from light grey, half from dark. These are the "s" pieces in the diagram on the lower left. *(Improv: Cut any length strips, no less than 1.25" high.)*

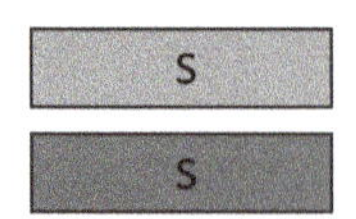

2 Cut 80 squares in assorted colors, each 1.5" x 1.5" *(Improv: same size as your strip height.)*
Place one square face down on one end, and stitch across the diagonal, as on the blue square. Repeat with a different color on the other end.
Option: Trim seam allowances to 1/4" from the seam, shown here on the pink end.

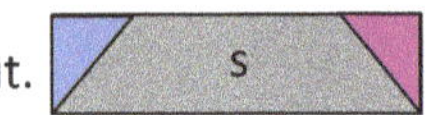

3 Press triangles up and out.

4 Make another unit with different color triangles. Lay out the pair on your design wall or table.

Make and pair up 30 more strips like this. The lighter grey strips will go high on the building, and dark grey low.

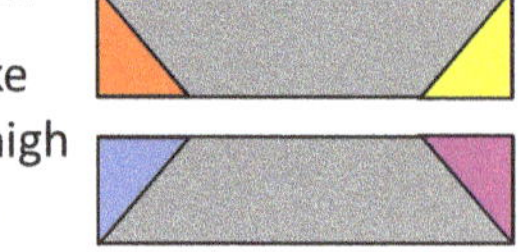

Finished size 20.5" x 28.5"
Fabric

- Building color 1: Fat-quarter (or 1/2 yard if you want only one shade)
- Building color 2: Fat-quarter in a darker shade
- Top windows. Use 1, 2, or 3 shades. Scraps or 2.5" x 44" strips of three fabrics.
- Enough scraps to cut 80 pieces, each at least 1.5" square. It's fine to repeat colors!
- Top window, and door - 14" x 1.5" strip, plus a 6.5" x 4.5" rectangle
- Awning- Two 2" squares

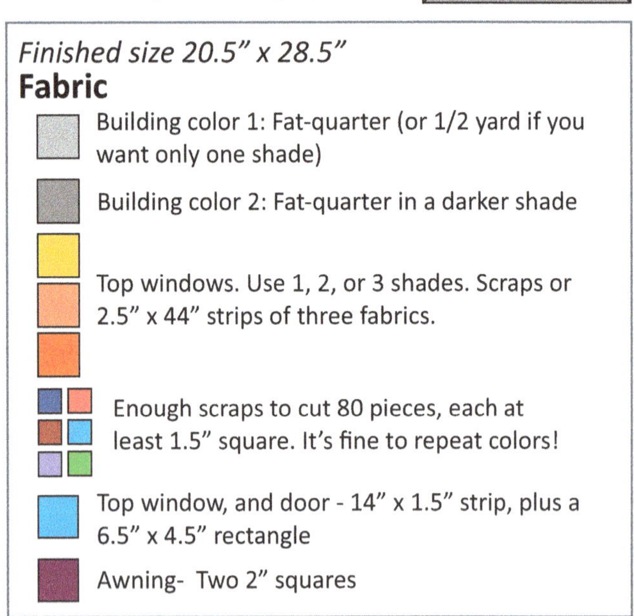

*See the windows at https://tilesinnewyork.blogspot.com/2016/05/mid-twentieth-century-synagogues-in.html.

5 Lay out rows as below, so where four colored triangles meet forms a square on point. I'm calling these diamonds. There are 4 rows, with 3 finished diamonds per row, plus a half-diamond on the far right and left ends.

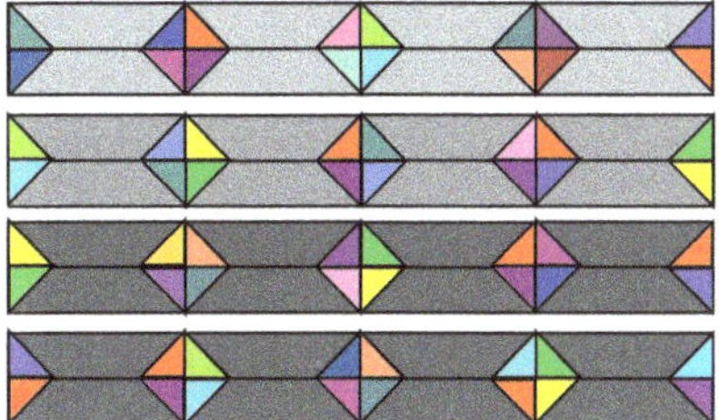

6 To complete the end half-diamonds, you need 16 half-square triangles that are half grey, half assorted colors (four are circled in the diagram below.)

Make them by **A**, cutting one grey square and one colored square the same size as your earlier squares (1.5" x 1.5"). **B**, Place face to face, sew, corner to corner. **C**, Cut seam allowance on one side back to 1/4". **D**, press open. Place in position at each strip end.

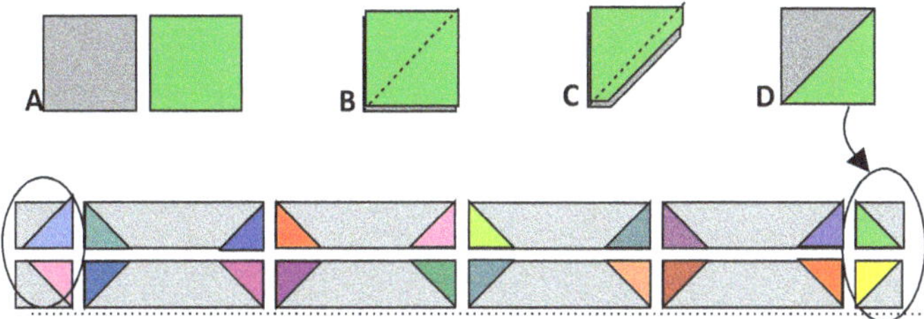

7 Chain sew each top square or strip to its partner square or strip on bottom. The row then looks like this:

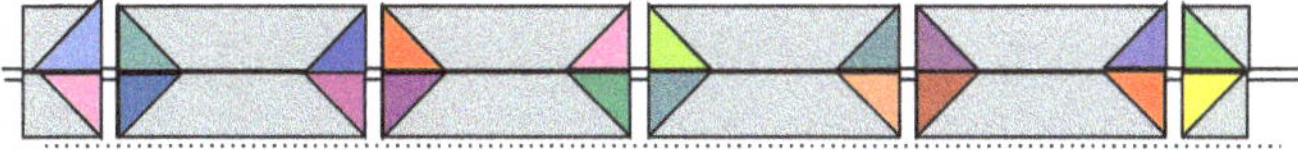

8 Sew the short vertical seams between pairs.

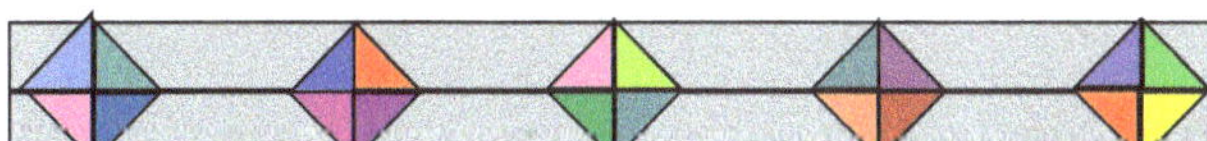

9 Measure finished strips. They should be 18.5" x 2.5"; if yours differ, use your measurement.

10 Cut three dark grey strips 18.5" (or your Step 9 measurement) x 2.5". These are **a**, **b** and **c** in the diagram. Cut two more LIGHT grey strips the same size. These are **d** and **e**.

Cut two additional LIGHT grey strips to the same width (18.5") – but only 1.5" high. They'll be **f** and **g**. Lay out all units as in the diagram.

11 For the narrow window in section **h**, I made a three-part strip of light, medium, and dark orange/gold. Cut each fabric to 6.5" x 1.5" (If your building is a different width, divide your total by 3 and add seam allowances).

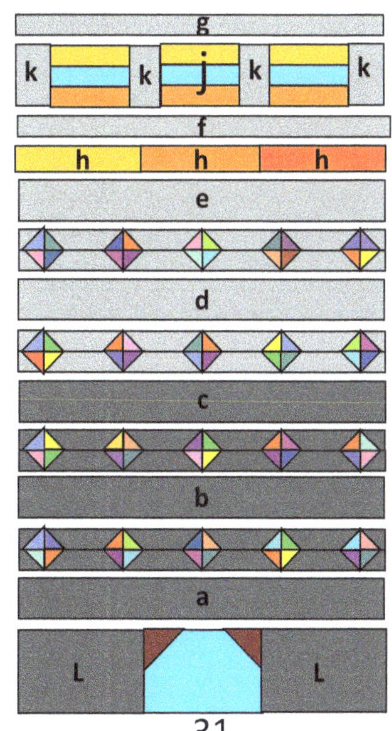

12 For top long windows (area j), cut three strips: two orange strips to 14" x 1.5", and a blue strip the same size. Join like this.

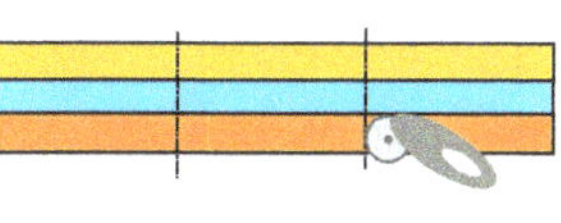

13 Cut crosswise at 4.5" intervals to create three "**j**" units.

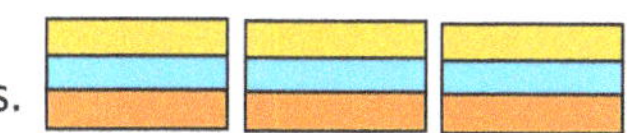

14 Cut four grey rectangles to alternate with the strips, to 2" wide x 3.5" high (or the height of your 3-strip set).

If your building's width is different, adjust rectangles' sizes. Sew in place.

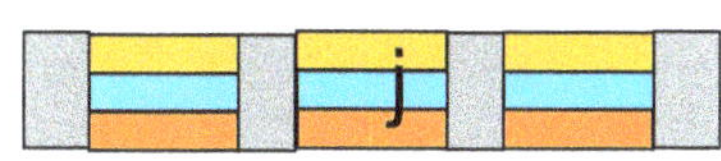

15 Add light strip **g** above this unit - it's the roof (not shown).

16 Make a ground floor. Cut two dark grey rectangles and one blue one 6.5" x 4.5". *(Improv: Adjust to your building's width).*

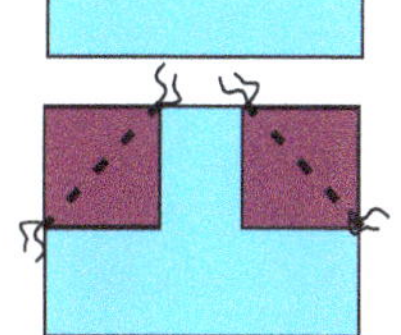

17 Cut two awning squares 2" x 2". Sew one in the blue rectangles' upper left corner, and one in the upper right, both on the diagonal.

18 Press bottom square points up.

19 Sew the blue piece between the two grey L rectangles. Place at the base of the building.

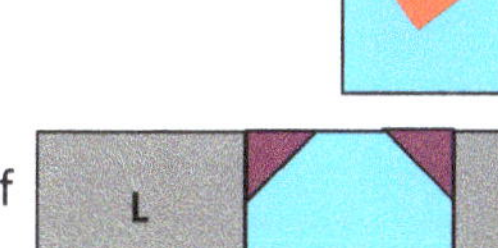

20 There are 14 rows to join. I rotate the layout so the bottom edge is on the right. Then chain sew the rows into 7 pairs, beginning on the right/bottom.

– Flip doorway row (with two **L**'s) onto row **a**. Sew. Don't cut any threads until step 21.
– Flip the lowest diamond row onto strip **b**. Sew.
– Sew the second diamond row from the bottom onto strip **c**.
– Sew the third diamond row from the bottom onto strip **d**.
– Sew top diamond row onto **e**.
– Sew **h** row onto **f**.
– Sew **jk** row onto **g**.

21 Cut threads, press seams under unpieced strips, and lay everything back in place.

22 Join pairs into four groups of 4 (plus a pair).

23 Repeat to sew the last seams.

24 Press remaining horizontal seam allowances under the unpieced strips.

25 Because it's a simple rectangle, this building can easily be pieced to another building; or easily appliquéd after turning outer edges 1/4" under.

Keys to the (Greek) Mansion

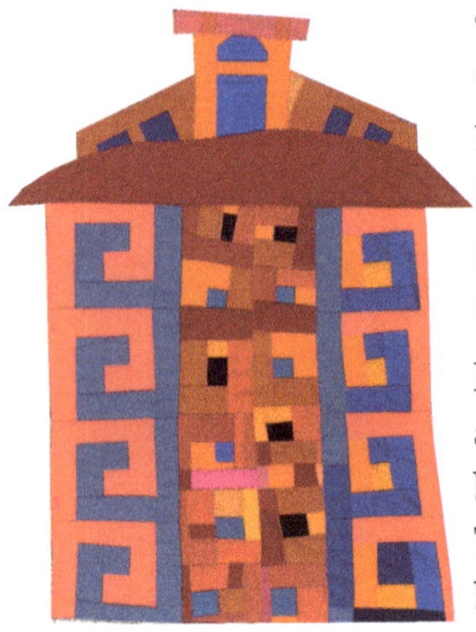

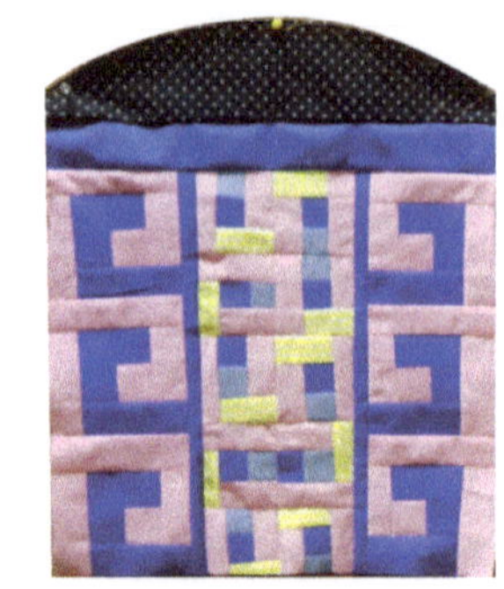

The curled motif in this fantasy building is called a "meander" or "Greek key." Ancient Greeks invented it – but so did the Chinese, Egyptians, Romans and others! Straight out of the human unconscious, it adorns objects and buildings around the world! As a quilter, I see it as a combination of a Log Cabin and Snail's Trail block.

My orange version is on the left, and one of my students, artist Nurit Cain, made the pink one above, right. The building has six "key" blocks. Those patterns are on p. 34. The central area has 12 log cabin blocks – that pattern is below, left. But you can also easily improvise both of these blocks, if you prefer!

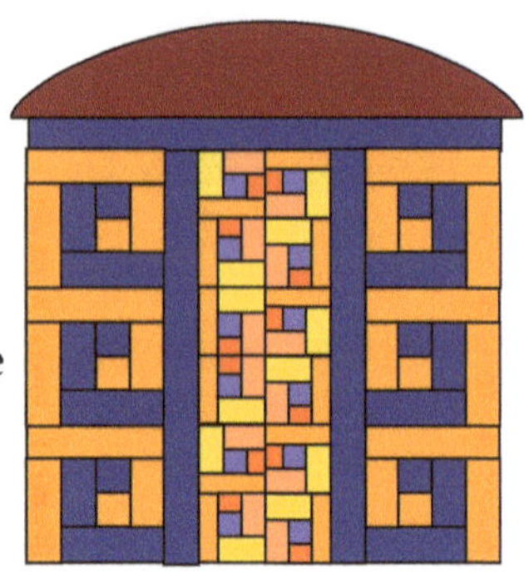

Log Cabin block: Make 12

5 Cut 1.25" x 2.75"	**2** Cut 1.25" x 1.25" — **1** Cut 1.25" x 1.25" — **3** Cut 1.25" x 2"
	4 Cut 1.25" x 2"

Make the 'Key' blocks

1 Refer to the key block patterns on p. 34.

– From dark key color, cut 1.75" strips, that add up to about 60" (not continuous – we'll subcut as we go).
– From light key background color, cut 1.75" strips that add up to about 86" (not continuous).

2 Cut two 11" pieces off each color strip. Sew together.

3 Cut joined strips apart at 1.75" intervals. Cut six. These are the starting pairs.

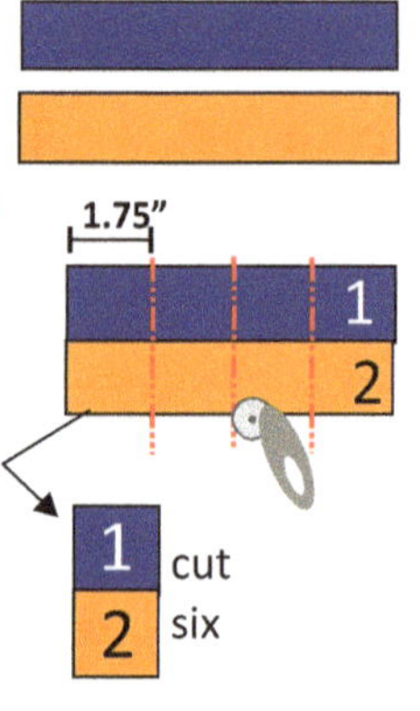

Size approx. 16" x 16"

Fabric

Key color. 1/4 yard, fat-quarter, or 60" x 1.75"

Key block's background color. 1/4 yard, fat-quarter, or 86" x 1.75"

Log cabin block central color, fat-eighth or 1.25" x 15"

Log cabin block background colors, 1.25" x 80" total. Use same background as in key blocks, or an assortment of colors for a scrappier look.

Roof 16" x 3.5"

Supplies
-Freezer paper
-Ironing fluid, like spray starch

4 Let's do the left key block first. You already joined 1 and 2. Following the sizes on the pattern, cut piece three to 1.75" x 3" and add it to the left side. (*Improvisers: Cut piece three to the height of your 1 + 2 unit.*)

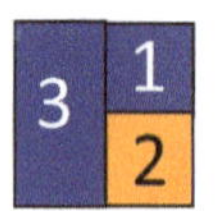

5 Cut piece four to the size on the pattern, 1.75" x 3" (*or the height of your unit so far*). Sew it to the right side.

6 Sew piece five to the bottom. Keep adding through piece seven. Pieces six and seven are narrower than the others, but don't cut them back now – add them at their current 1.75" width, and trim as needed after the next step.

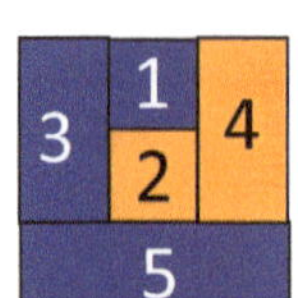

7 Make three left blocks this way. Then make the right hand blocks. You should have created enough starting pairs in step 3 for all six.

8 Each block should be 5" x 5". If yours needs trimming. cut through pieces six and seven (rather than four and five).

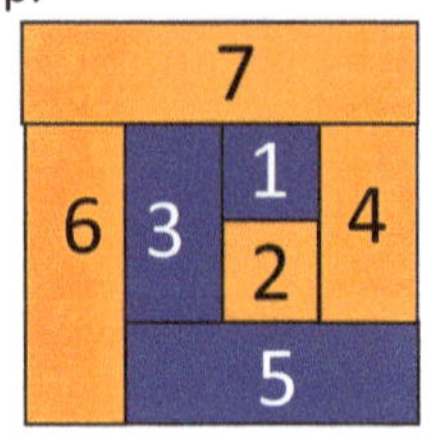

Make the Log Cabin blocks

9 There are 12 regular log cabin blocks in the center of the mansion. Cut strips of darker log cabin fabric to 1.25" x 15". The full-size pattern is above, left.

10 Cut surrounding fabric scraps to a total of 1.25" x 80". (You can reuse the key block background color).

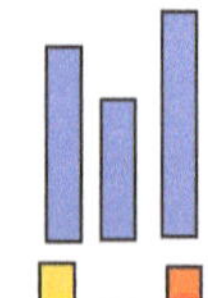

(continued)

11 From strips, cut 15" of dark and 15" of light. Subcut 12, each at 1.25" intervals. These will be starter units for all log cabin squares. (*Improvisers: Cut squares 1 and 2 to similar sizes and sew*).

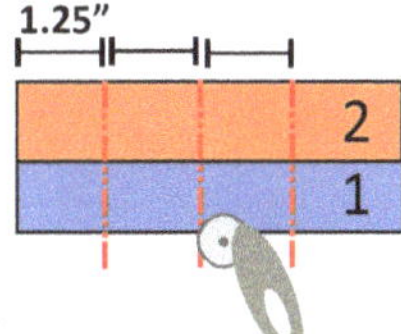

12 Make 12 log cabin blocks. They should wind up 2.75" square. (*Improvisers*: Trim each finished log cabin to half the size of your key blocks **plus** .25".)

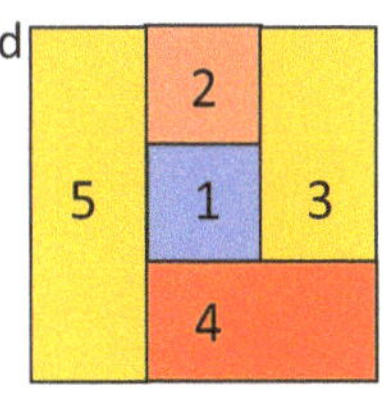

13 Sew the 12 regular log cabin blocks together like this, in two columns of six.

14 Measure the height and add dark strips from your key fabric to each side. The strips are 1.5" wide x 12.5" with my measurements (but use your total!)

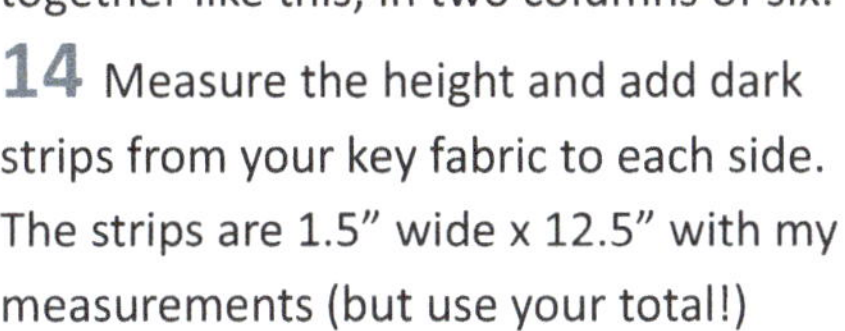

15 Sew the three left key blocks on top of each other, and the three right key blocks on top of each other.

16 Sew each column of key blocks to the outside of the dark side strips.

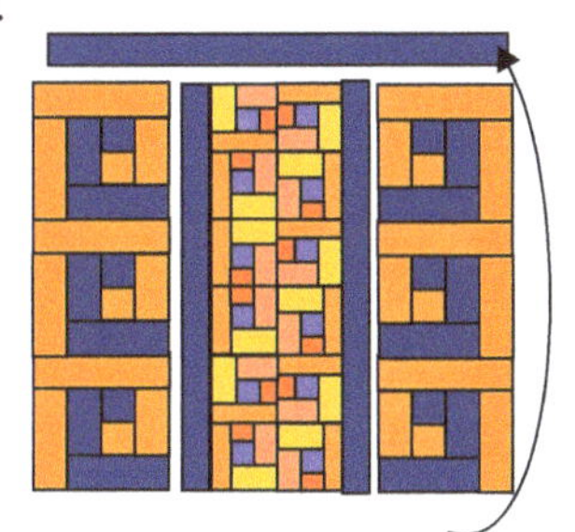

17 Measure across the top – it should be about 14.5". Cut a dark key fabric strip 1.5" wide x that measurement. Sew to the top.

18 Press sides back 1/4".

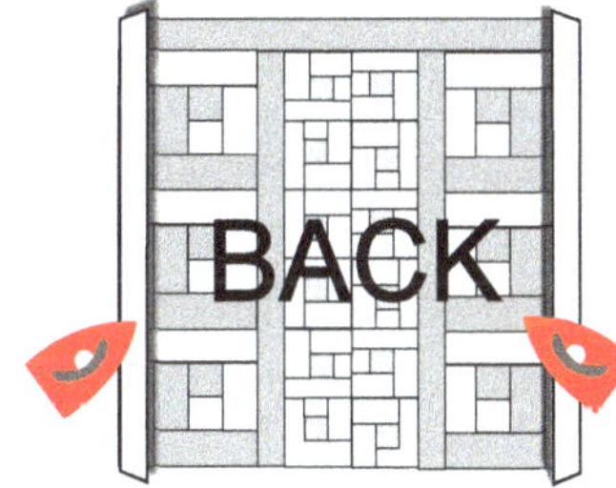

Make the roof

19 Print and cut out the half-oval pattern on the next page. Cut out a 16" x 3.5" freezer paper strip and fold it in half, with waxy side inside.

Place dotted line on top of the freezer paper fold. Draw around it, onto the paper side of the freezer paper.

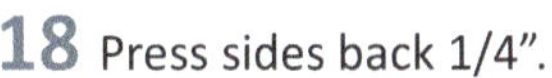

20 Cut folded freezer paper shape on the line, through both layers. Unfold.

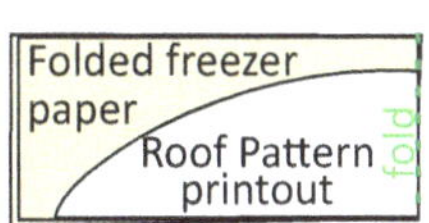

21 Press waxy side to roof fabric. Cut fabric a generous 1/4" beyond the top curved freezer paper edge.

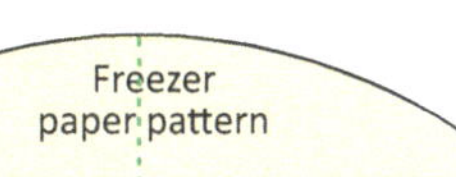

22 Press fabric raw edges to the back, along the freezer paper edge. (The bottom fabric edge is cut even with the freezer paper.) Painting a little spray starch or other ironing fluid on the edge will help it stay.

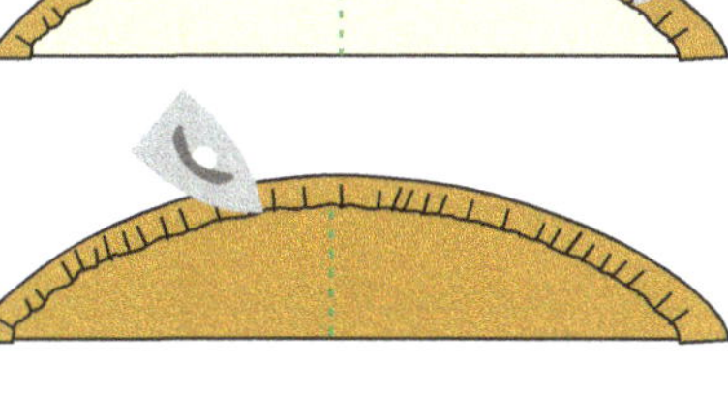

23 Peel out the freezer paper, and press the folded edge down one more time.

roof goes underneath!

23 Press the two side edges of the main body 1/4" to the back. Press well. (Marked "side flap" in the diagram.)

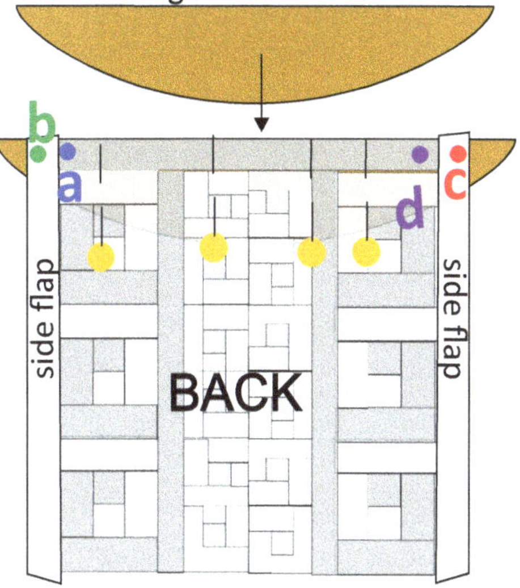

24 Place the roof good side up, curve lowest, as shown above. Place the top edge of the building, good side down, on top of it. Align top raw edges and pin. (My pins have yellow heads!) The roof will extend a bit on both sides.

25 Rotate pinned seam right. Pull up threads at the dot by the **a**. Backstitch over the fold to **b**, just before the fold. **You are sewing that flap shut**. Try not to oversew onto the roof (but a few stitches won't be a problem). Sew to **c**, **sealing that side's flap**. Backstitch and cut

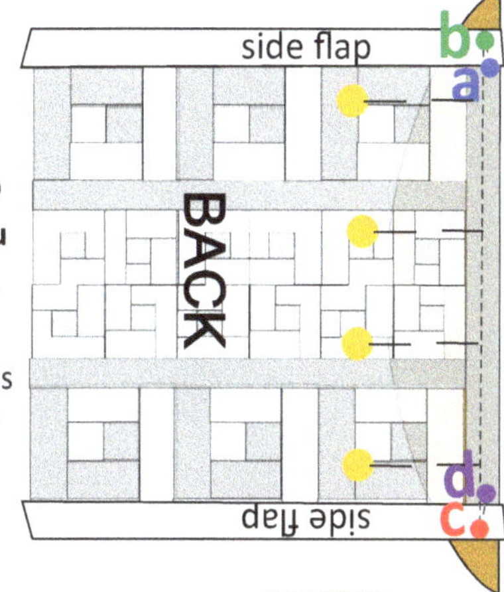

26 Press roof up, and press entire extended seam allowance up, too. This gives the roof a nice lift over the building.

Does it look done? Mine didn't, so I improv appliquéd some more shapes behind the top edge.

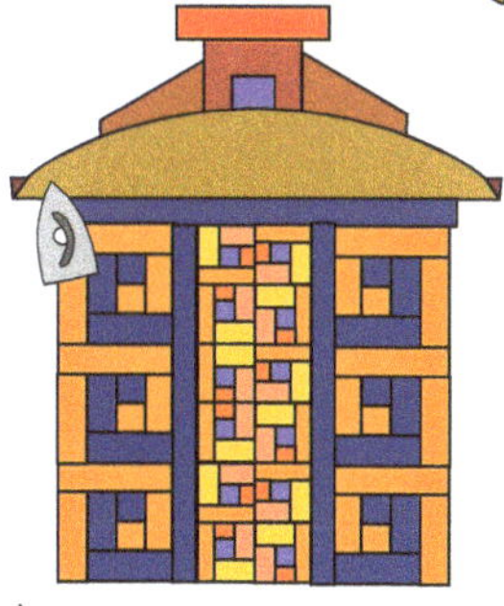

(patterns are on next page)

Right key block

Make 3. Trim to 5" square, trimming through pieces 6 and 7

7
Cut 5" x 1.25"

1
Cut 1.75" x 1.75"

6
Cut 1.25" x 4.25"

4
Cut 1.75" x 3"

3
Cut 1.75" x 3"

2
Cut 1.75" x 1.75"

5
Cut 1.75" x 4.25"

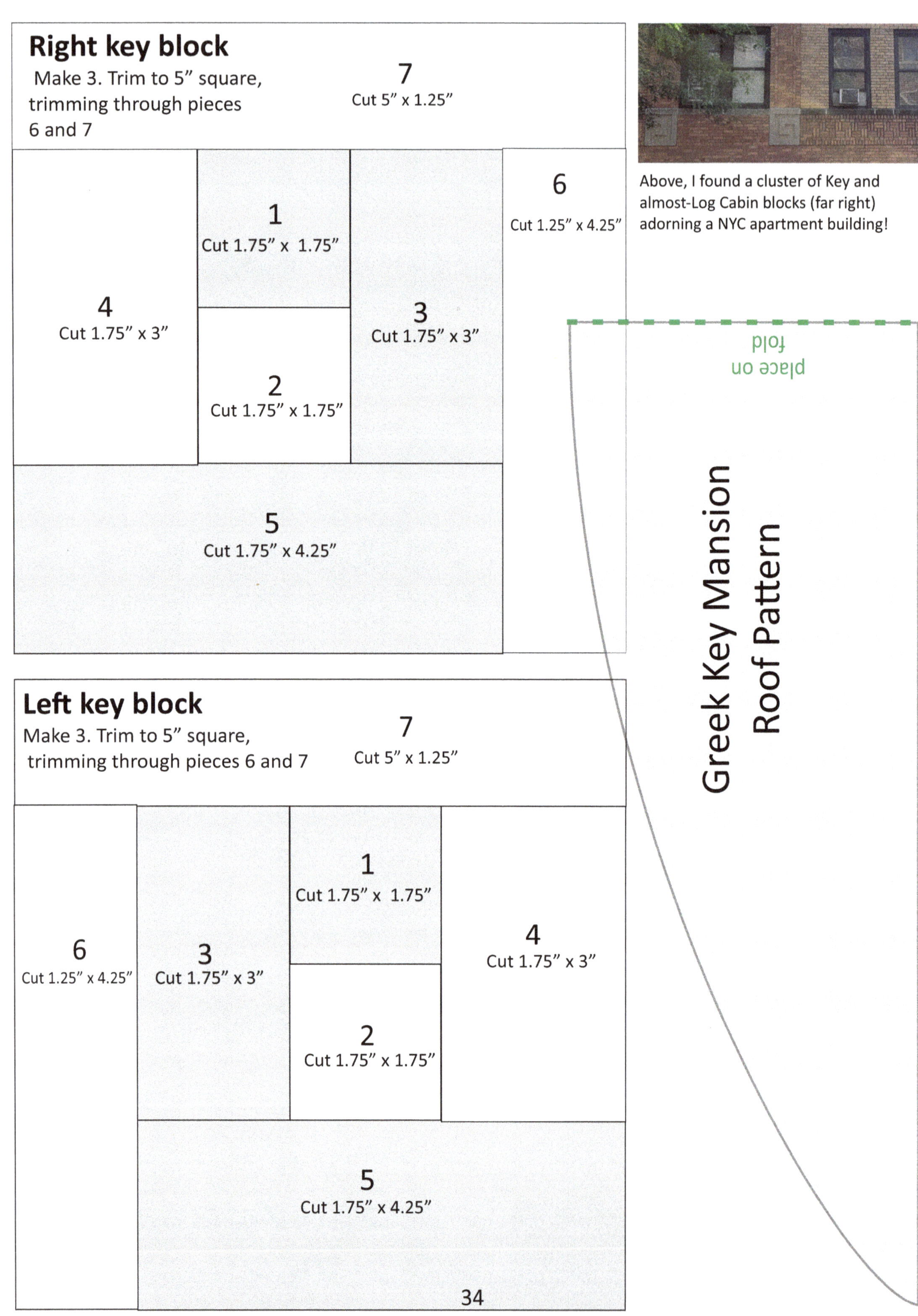

Above, I found a cluster of Key and almost-Log Cabin blocks (far right) adorning a NYC apartment building!

Left key block

Make 3. Trim to 5" square, trimming through pieces 6 and 7

7
Cut 5" x 1.25"

1
Cut 1.75" x 1.75"

6
Cut 1.25" x 4.25"

3
Cut 1.75" x 3"

4
Cut 1.75" x 3"

2
Cut 1.75" x 1.75"

5
Cut 1.75" x 4.25"

34

A Townhouse and the Pane of Windows

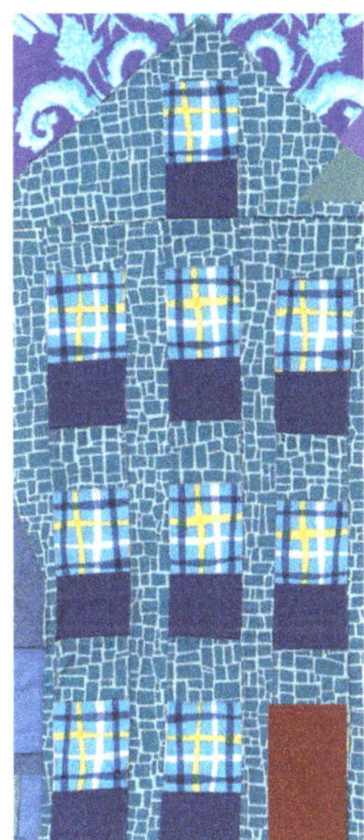

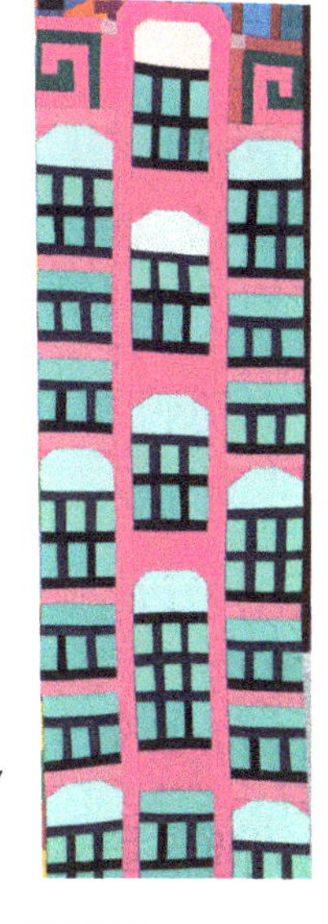

On right is one of my earliest buildings, which I like but is also a cautionary tale. I made the windows first, cutting turquoise rectangles to 1.5" x 2", which seemed reasonably small.
I added more windows, panes, arches, and pink building strips. Each addition caused the thing to grow, and grow, ultimately to 42" high! You can see the bubblegum overdose on the cover quilt. When I look at it, I (mentally) smack my forehead and say, "Dang, I shoulda made that building smaller!"

Eventually I learned to draw a full-size outline of the building **first,** and work **inward** to reduce window size and count (see p. 78).

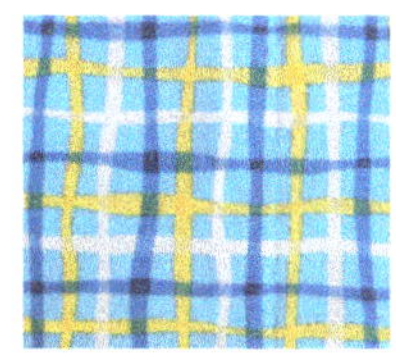

I also learned: Instead of trying to piece ultra-narrow panes, browse prints. Many have stripes narrower than you could piece. In the townhouse on the far left, windows are fussy-cut from the plaid print in the near left. (Or, embroider the panes, by hand or machine; or even quilt them in! See bottom of p. 80.)

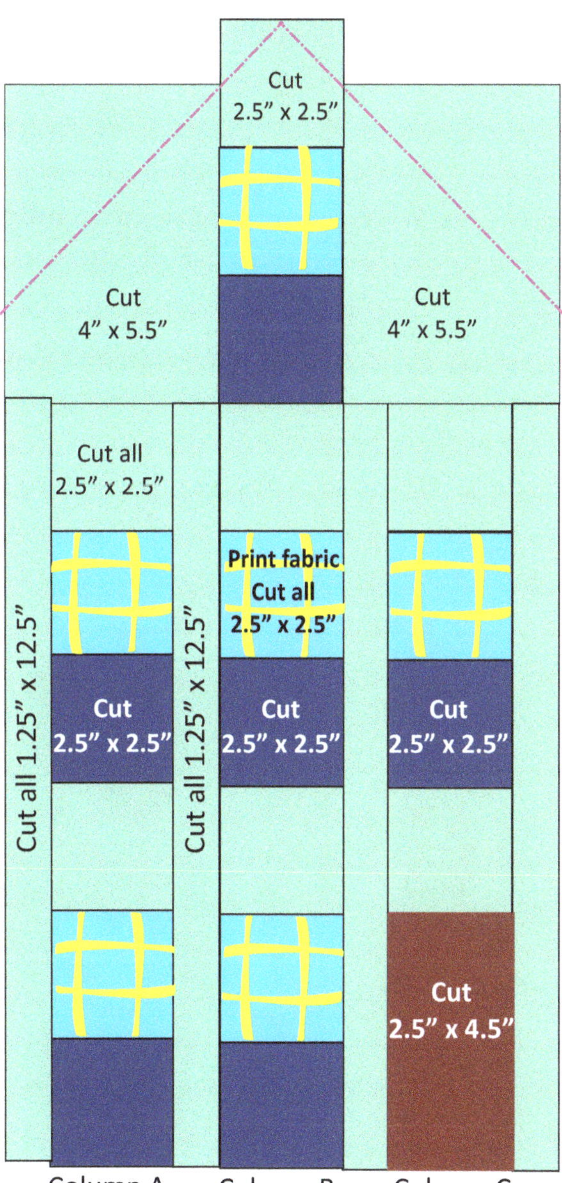

1 Cut all squares and rectangles to sizes listed in the chart below. Arrange as in the diagram.

2 Join all pieces within Columns A, B, and C together along their horizontal seam lines. Most are 2.5" x 2.5" squares (except the door in column C.)

3 Sew the narrow sashing strips to both sides of Column B.

4 Sew one narrow strip to the right of Column C, and another one to the left of Column A. Join those units to the middle unit.

5 Roof/Gable: Sew the middle column (three 2.5" x 2.5" squares) together, stacked. Sew large rectangles to the left and right side. Or, choose one of the roof options on pp. 84-85.

6 Sew this unit to the top of the main house.

7 Mark the center of the topmost square. With a rotary cutter, cut a 45 degree line from the center outward in both directions, on an angle, as shown.

8 Turn under the outside edges of the roof, now or later when you're ready to appliqué it in place.

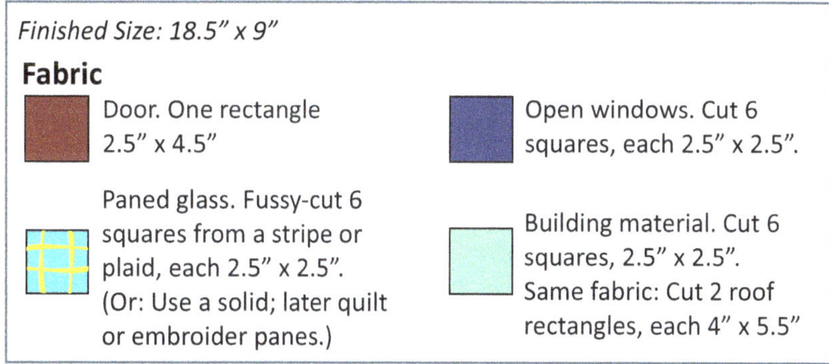

Finished Size: 18.5" x 9"
Fabric

Door. One rectangle 2.5" x 4.5"

Open windows. Cut 6 squares, each 2.5" x 2.5".

Paned glass. Fussy-cut 6 squares from a stripe or plaid, each 2.5" x 2.5". (Or: Use a solid; later quilt or embroider panes.)

Building material. Cut 6 squares, 2.5" x 2.5". Same fabric: Cut 2 roof rectangles, each 4" x 5.5"

Wedding Cake Stacks

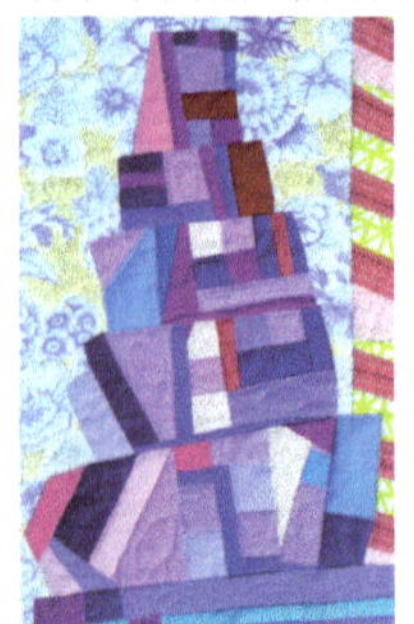

This section introduces my technique for turning edges as you build, for structures with uneven edges. "Wedding cake" buildings narrow on both sides as they rise. It's in all kinds of buildings, especially early 20th century buildings, like the Empire State and New Yorker Hotel (right). Before steel, tall buildings had to shrink as they rose to carry the extra weight. And setbacks at buildings' tops were mandated by New York City law circa 1916, because pedestrian access to sunshine was considered a public health priority!

You can piece each level, as above left (which wound up in 'Scrap City 2,' p. 7); or use a single fabrics for each level, as in the orange tower on the right. (It found a home in 'Nonsense Town,' p. 10). We'll revisit this same technique in a different way when we want to give a building a side in perspective, on p. 67.

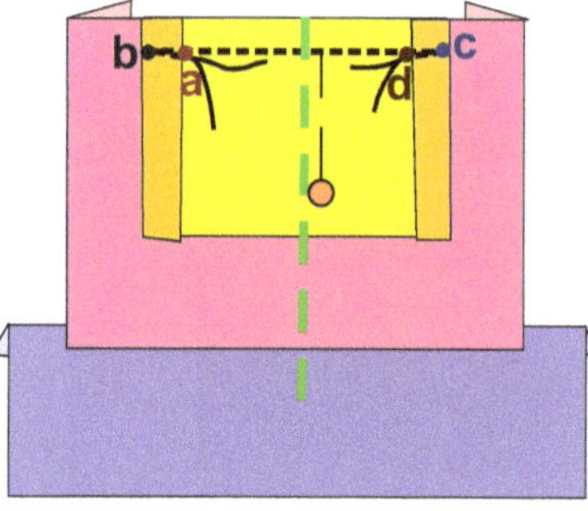

Above, 1930 New Yorker Hotel, with wedding cake setbacks on top. Right, Empire State Building, same era.

1 Make as many stories as you want. Make them narrower sizes as they rise.

2 On each story, press the two side edges back 1/4".

3 Fold and lightly pretss each in half (matching folded edges) to mark he vertical center of each. The green line represents these centers.

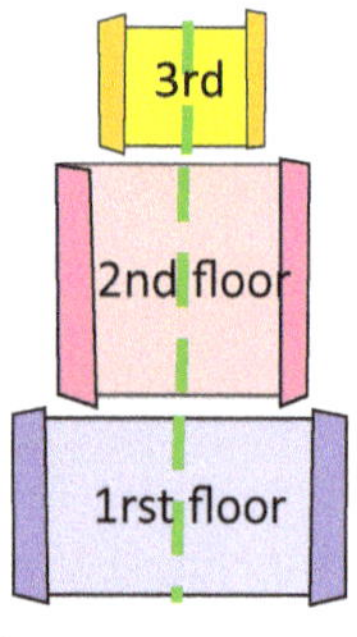

4 Place the first floor good side up on the table, and the second floor wrong side up on top of it. Match top edges, and centers. Pin. **The flaps are SHUT!**

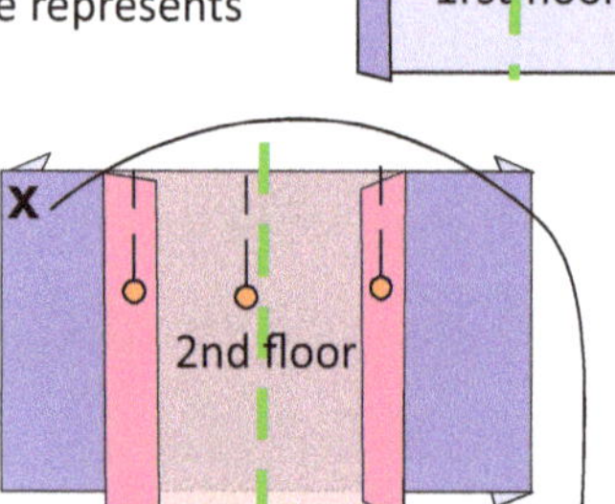

Rotate to sew!

5 Rotate everything clockwise so the pinned seam is along the right edge. You're still looking at the back of the second floor.

6 Bring up threads at the dot by the **a**. Backstitch over the pink flap sealing it shut. Stop at **b**, just below the fold. Sew forward, over the first and last flap, to **c**. (An **awl** helps the bottom flap go under the foot.) Backstitch to **d**. Cut threads. Backstitching secures the seam, and hides thread tails away from edges.

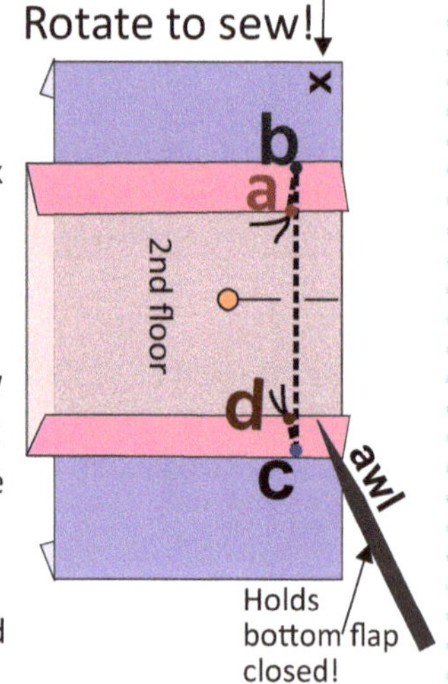

7 Press seam allowance, **including the extensions of the 1rst floor,** neatly down to the back 1/4". (Pressing with a bit of glue in the corners will hide flaps.

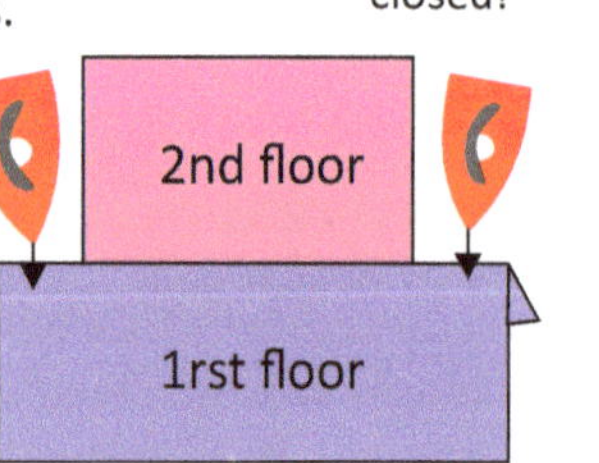

8 Add the next level. Pin, rotate, and sew as you did in steps 4-6: Bring up threads at **a**, backstitch to **b**, stitch straight to **c**, backstitch to **d**, then cut threads.

9 Press as you did in step 7.

10 Build as high as you want! Press all horizontal seam allowances (except the one along the bottom) downward, to the wider level. The arrow shows the pressing direction.

11 Press top edge back 1/4". If you didn't turn in the vertical sides of the bottom floor, do it now. You may need to press the bottom edge up, or not, depending where you place it.

The building is ready to be pieced or appliquéd to another, or hand or machine-appliquéd on the quilt.

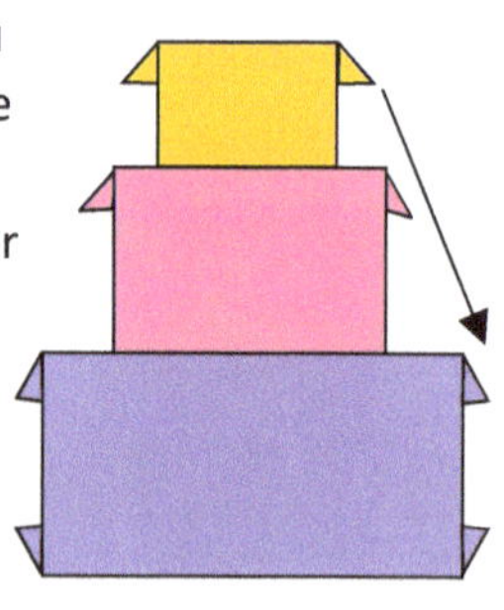

Fountain Stack

Need a fountain? Make a wedding cake stack as above. Press water-color fabric to a fusible web backing. Cut curls of water and tuck them under the levels. Fuse in position, then appliqué the fountain's turned edges to the building and the scene's background.

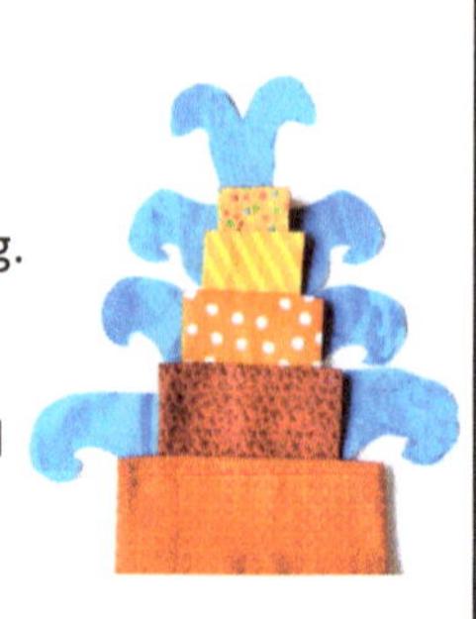

Crooked on One Side: Left-handed Tower of Arches

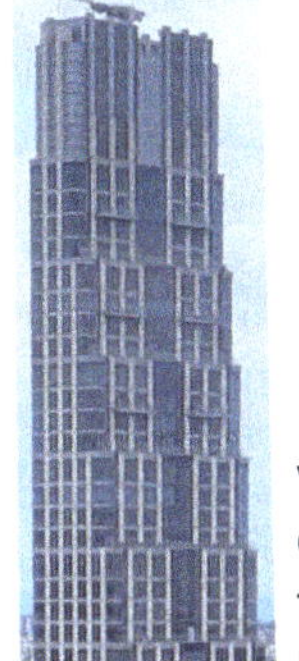

Some buildings are only crooked on one side, like this stepped NYC tower. This technique can also be used to join buildings with different heights (see box on the right).

1 Make levels any way you like. One piecing option: the left-handed tower of arches on the lower right of this page.

Or, use unpieced blocks, like a different solid color, or geometric print, on each level.

2 Press the uneven side edge back 1/4". Here, right edges will be uneven. [On level 1, it's optional to do this now – because only that piece will NOT be attached to a wider piece. You can press its far edge at the end.]

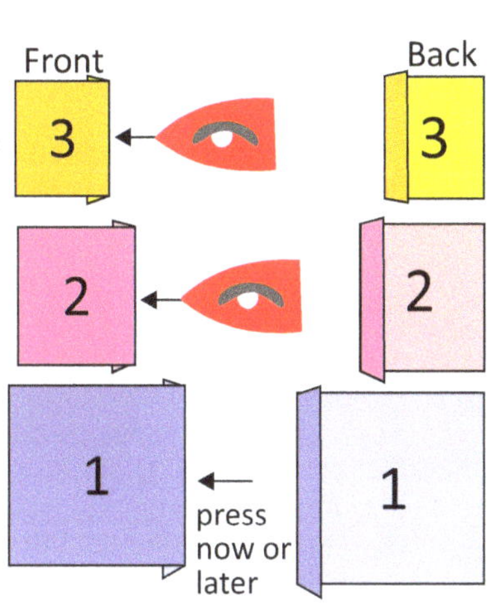

3 Flip level 2, face down, on level 1, face up. Align top and left edges. Pin with the flap on the right of level 2 closed.

4 Rotate pinned edge right. Start sewing at **a** – no need to backstitch, because there's no flap there, and ithe top edges are even. Sew, traveling over the closed flap, past **c**, to **b**. (As the presser foot approaches **c** and **b**, an awl helps the flap go under it, staying closed.) Backstitch to **c**. Cut threads.

5 Press extended seam allowances neatly downward under 1 (under the red irons in the drawing on the far right.)

6 Sew Level 3 to 2 the same way.

7 Last steps: Press the entire straight (left) edge of the building inward 1/4".

8 Press the right edge of level 1 inward 1/4" (if you didn't do it earlier). Press top edge of Level 3 to the back 1/4", and bottom edge upwards 1/4" (unless you know that will be the bottom of the quilt, or think that the bottom edge might wind up hidden behind other buildings.)

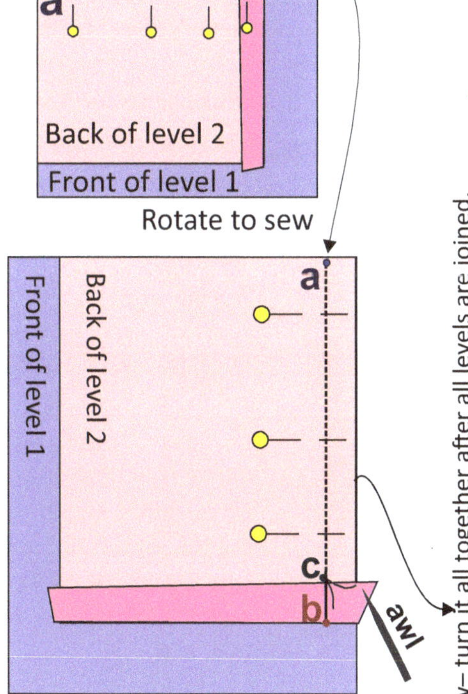

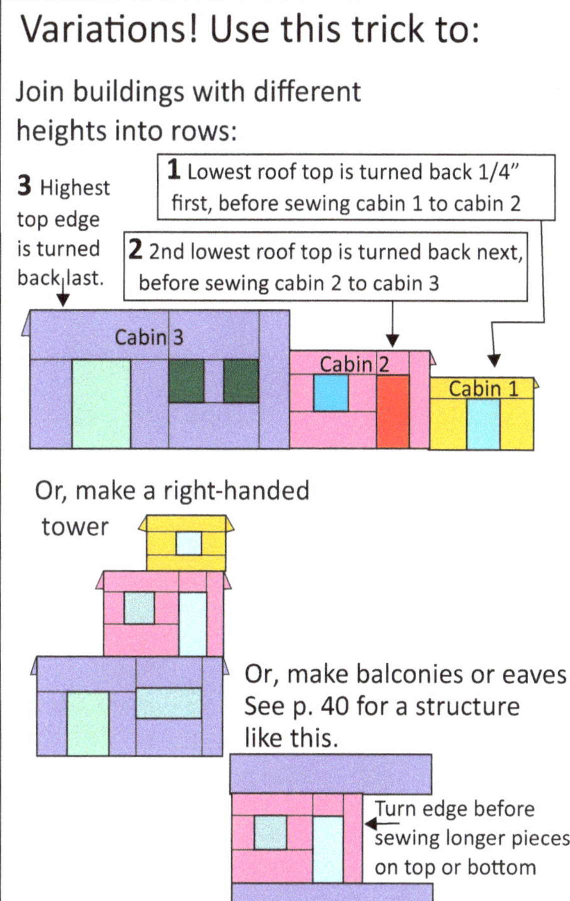

Result: Left-Handed Tower of Arches

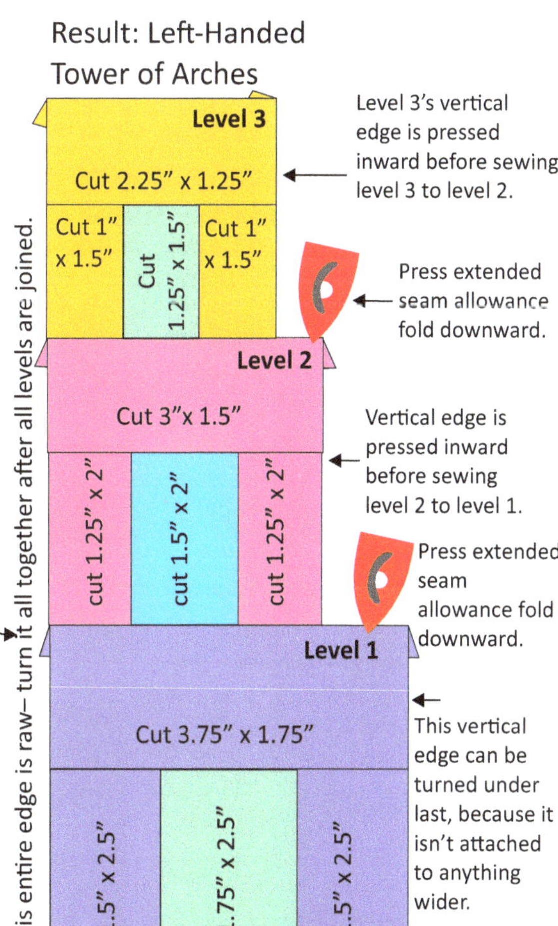

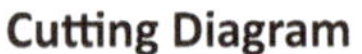

Above, Boston University's new computing & data science building

Above, Jersey City, NJ's Urby building. Right, 56 Leonard St., NYC. A pattern it inspired is in my "Quilted New York" book.

BUILDING
Zigzag Towers

Several US cities have zigzag buildings that locals nicknamed "Jenga"[TM], after the game in which you pull protruding blocks from a tower.

New York's is on the near left. Jersey City's Urby building, center left, is similar, as is Boston University's data science center, far left, and the "Independent" in Austin (not shown). Sections that overhang others without end supports are "cantilevered." As in architecture, they're a challenge in piecing and appliqué. They inspired the fantasy building on the right. Here, again, we'll make it easier by turning edges during piecing, so you don't have to rip seam ends afterwards.

Cutting Diagram

Top
3"x 3.5"

Level 5
5"x 3"

Level 4
6" x 2.25"

Level 3
6" x 3.75"

Level 2
7" x 2.5"

Level 1
7" x 5"

1 Cut three pieces from fabric 1 and three pieces from fabric 2 to the sizes shown here, for a 16" building.

2 On pieces 1-5, press both vertical side edges inward 1/4". Don't do this to the top piece.

3 Arrange. This arrangement has each piece offset differently on both sides. *Improv: Center some levels, or line up some edges; use previous two pages' Wedding Cake or Crooked- on-One side piecing for those floors.*

4 Flip level 2 face down on top edge of level 1. All side flaps are pressed in. Pin. Mark a dot at **b**, where the far left fold of the hidden (yellow) piece is; and at **a**, above the hidden flap's raw edge. The two dots should be about 1/4" apart.

You do NOT need to mark dots on the other end – at **c** and **d** – because you can see those spots as you sew – the fold at **c**, and 1/4" before that, where the flap ends, at **d**. I put those dots in the diagrams just for reference.

5 Rotate pinned edge right. Bring up threads at **a**, backstitch to **b**, sew down, over the closed flap (an awl will help you keep the flap shut), to **c**, then backstitch and cut threads at **d**.

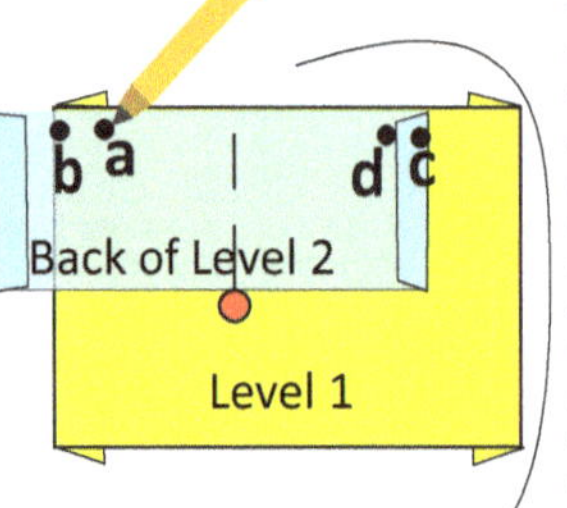

6 Open. Press seam allowances between 1 and 2 OPEN.
Why? If you press both flaps up, the yellow raw edge at **X** would stick up.

But if you press both flaps down, the blue raw edge of the upper story, at **Y**, would protrude downward. Thus the seam demands: Press me open!

7 Flip level 3 on top of 2. Mark dots at **a** and **b**, where the hidden (blue) layer's fold and flap end are. You do NOT have to mark **d** and **c** – this side will be up as you sew, so you can clearly see where level 3's right flap starts and ends.

8 As in Step 4, rotate and sew: Bring up threads at **a**, backstitch to **b**, sew to **c**, and backstitching to **d**. Press seam allowance open.

The building looks like this. All seam allowances are pressed open. Now we'll zag to the right.

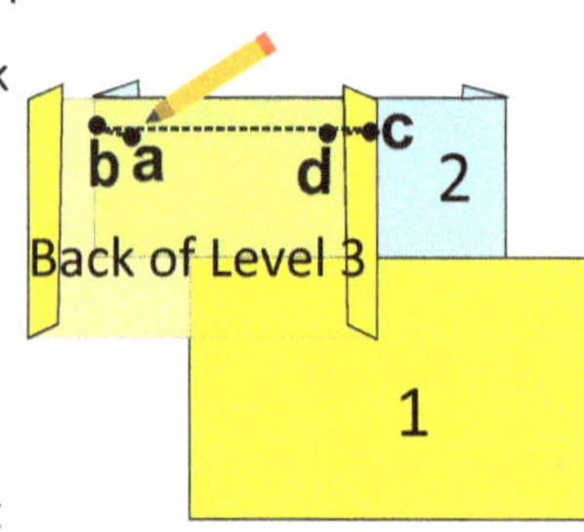

9 Flip level 4, good side down, on the right upper edge of 3. Don't mark **a** and **b**, – you can see those spots. DO mark dots where hidden level 3's right fold is (under **c**), and 1/4" before that, at **d**.

Rotate right and sew, pulling up threads at **a**, backstitching to **b**, sewing to **c**, backstitching to **d**.

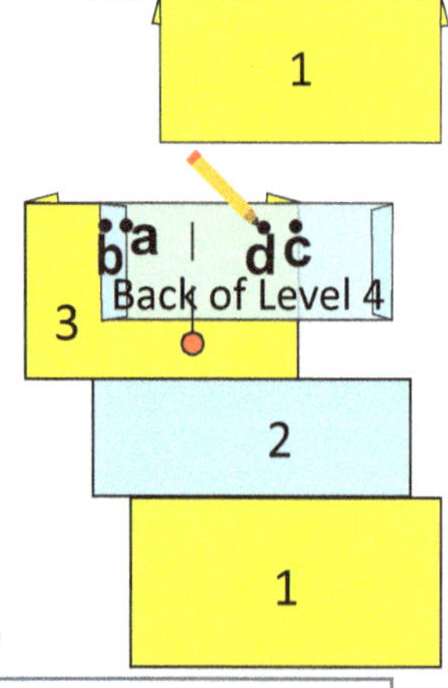

(continued)

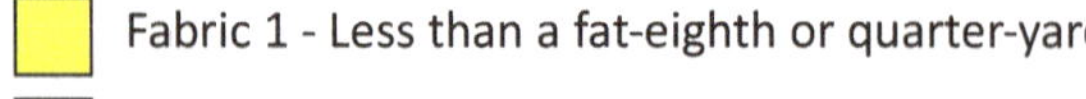

Fabric

Fabric 1 - Less than a fat-eighth or quarter-yard

Fabric 2 - Less than a fat-eighth or quarter-yard

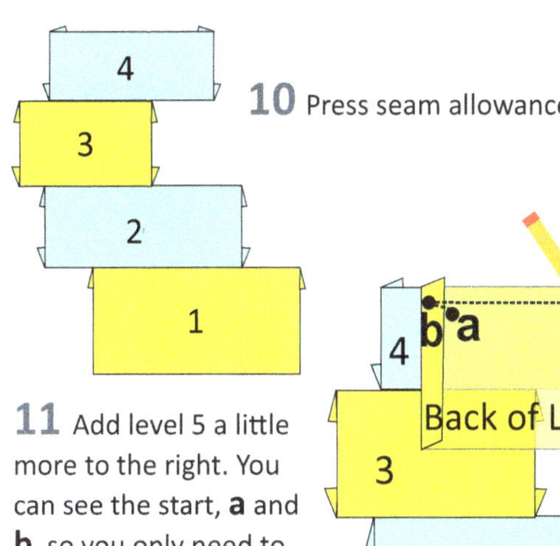

10 Press seam allowance open.

11 Add level 5 a little more to the right. You can see the start, **a** and **b**, so you only need to mark **d** and **c**, above the hidden right flap on level 4, where level 5's left flap begins and ends. Sew. Press seam allowance open.

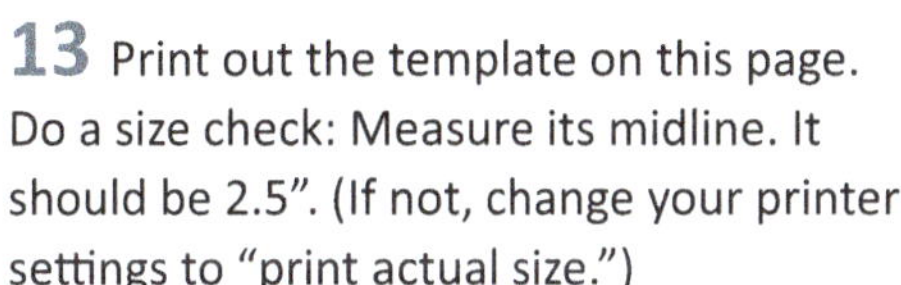

Top it off!

12 I topped off my building with an arch. The next steps are basically the same as for the Emerald Observatory dome on p. 42. The arch is centered on level 5, so we can use wedding cake piecing (p. 36).

13 Print out the template on this page. Do a size check: Measure its midline. It should be 2.5". (If not, change your printer settings to "print actual size.")

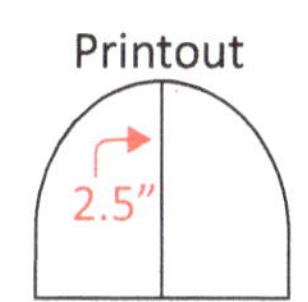

14 Use the paper version to trace and cut a freezer paper version. (No need to trace its midline).

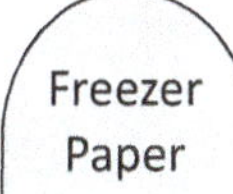

15 Cut arch fabric to at least 3.5" x 3". (You may have cut this piece in Step 1).

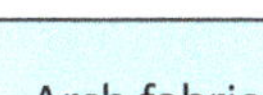

16 Press freezer paper pattern to the back of the dome fabric. Align the bottom edges.

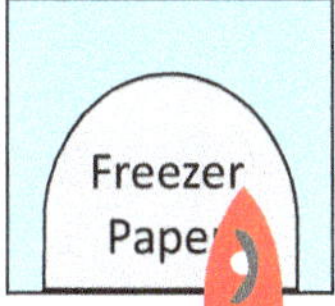

17 Cut out around the fabric to 1/4" beyond the freezer paper template.

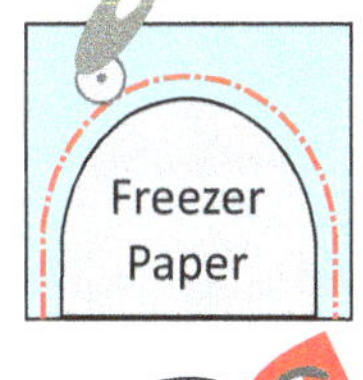

18 Press raw edges inward on the curved edge – leave the bottom flush with the template. A little starch or pressing fluid helps hold it.

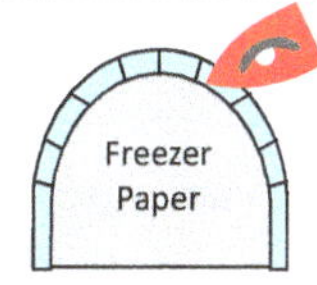

Full-size pattern for the arch on top of the zigzag tower

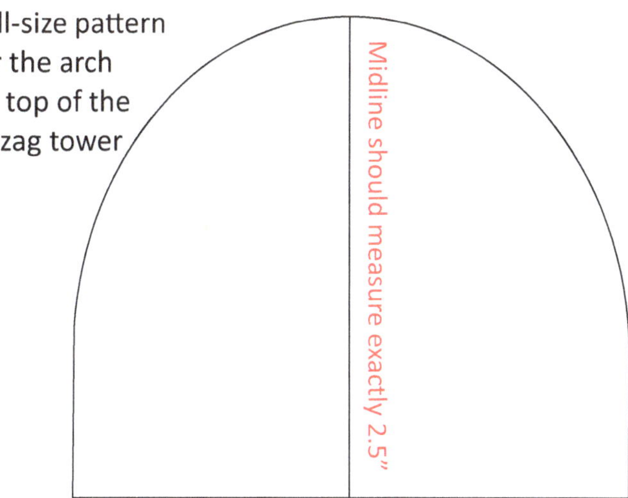

19 Peel out the freezer paper. Center the arch in the middle top of level 5, good side down. Piece 5's top raw edge extends upward.

20 Pin raw bottom edge of the arch to the center top of level 5. You can clearly see where to stop and start, so you don't need to mark these spots.

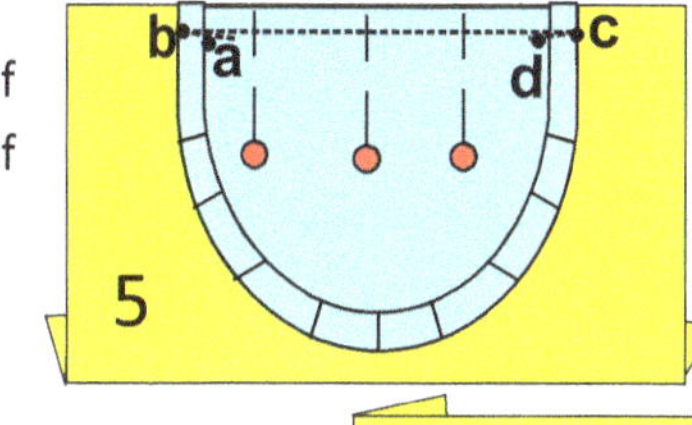

21 Rotate pinned seam to the right. Pull up threads at **a**, backstitch to **b**, sew down to **c**, backstitch to **d** and cut threads.

22 Press both seam allowances DOWN behind wider level 5.

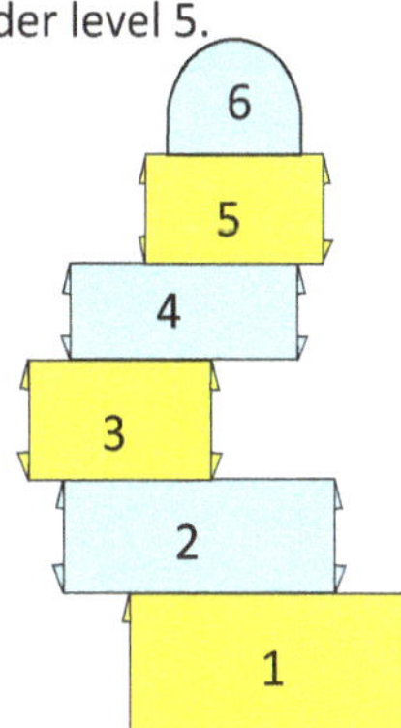

23 Your tower is finished! Or is it? I cut a clock from one novelty fabric, and Kaffe Fassett kale from another! I backed them with fusible web, and zigzag stitched the raw edges with invisible thread.
I quilted along seam and main plaid lines. This building is in 'Nonsense Town,' p. 10.

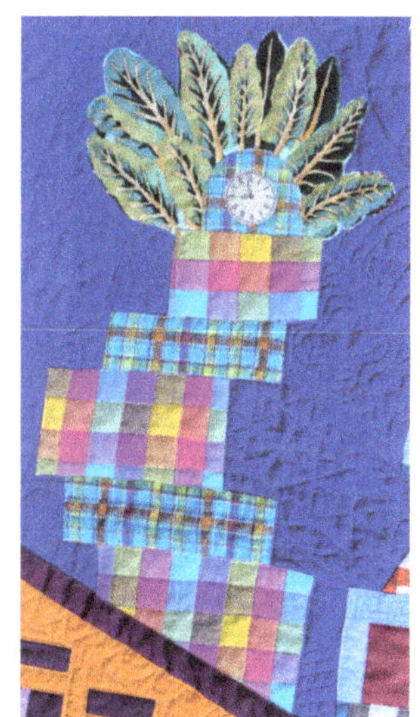

Emerald Observatory

Here's a building that's crooked on the left, and mostly straight elsewhere (except the dome.) It looks to me like a cross between a modern beach house and an astronomical observatory. I imagine the dome parting and a telescope emerging! I put the offsets on the left, but you could switch that to the right.

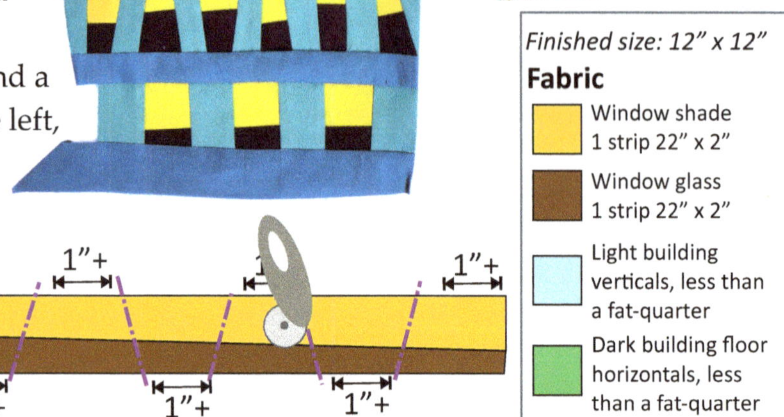

Solid version, left. Batik version, right. The left one is in 'Nonsense Town,' p. 10.

Finished size: 12" x 12"

Fabric

	Window shade 1 strip 22" x 2"
	Window glass 1 strip 22" x 2"
	Light building verticals, less than a fat-quarter
	Dark building floor horizontals, less than a fat-quarter
	Dome, 9" x 5"

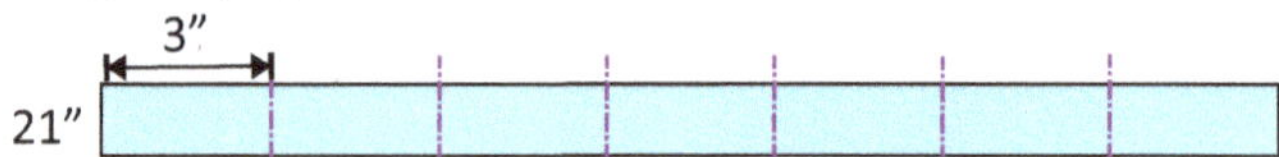

Wedges cut freehand, at gentle slants

1 Cut two strips to serve as window shades (top, gold here) and glass (bottom, brown). Cut a 22" strip from each that's 1" at one end and 2" at the other. Sew together as shown, and press seam allowances up under the window shades.

2 Cut apart as above. Start by cutting off a 1.5" piece, then a 2" piece, then 1.5" again, alternating until you have four 1.5" pieces and three 2" pieces. (Alternate cutting will make shade lengths vary.)

Last, freehand cut 6 wedge-shaped pieces with their narrowest edge 1" or more. as on the upper right.

All the two-part pieces you cut so far should be approximately 2.75" high, but if your measurement is different, use it, not mine, for the next couple of steps.

3 Sort units into three groups, by size and shape. For the 1.5" rectangle row, cut a building strip 2.75" *(or your windows' height)* x 7.5" long. Subcut that into five pieces, each 1.5" wide, and lay out as below, alternating with windows.

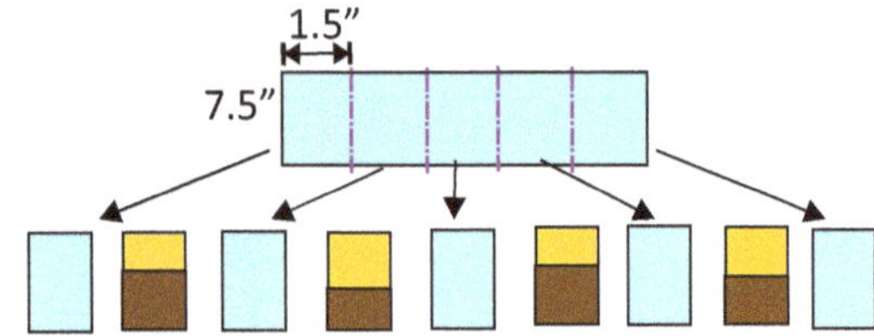

4 For the 2" rectangle window row, cut a building strip to 2.75" (or your pieces' height) x 8". Subcut that to four 2" x 2.75" pieces. Lay out as on the right.

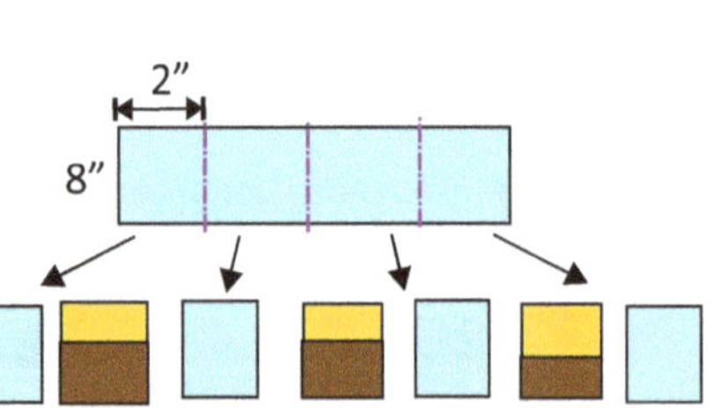

5 Sew each of the two rows together. I chain sew pieces into pairs first; join pairs into quartets; and so on until each row is complete.

6 Press seam allowances in to the center of the building material strips. They get a nice "lift." over the windows.

7 Trim top and bottom edges even.

Create the wedge row

8 Cut a strip of light building fabric 1.25" x 21". Cut that into 3" pieces *(or a bit longer than **your** two-part wedges' average height)*.

9 Lay out as below, alternating 3" segments (set vertically), with two-part wedges. Also alternate which side of the wedges (wider or narrower) is at the top.

Make sure the window shade color is always at the top (if you want the building to make logical sense, which is not mandatory!)

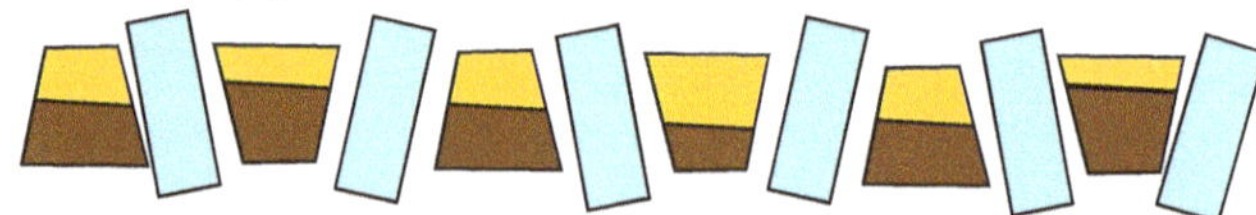

10 Joining gentle wedges like these is the same as joining rectangles: Place good sides together, sew down the right edge, open, press and add the next piece. Try to keep things in a straight line, but don't sweat uneven edges.

11 Trim the two side edges straight up and down, on the red dotted lines.

(continued)

12 Press seam allowances inward on each light building strip. Trim top and bottom edges even. It should now be 2.5" high, but any measurement works!

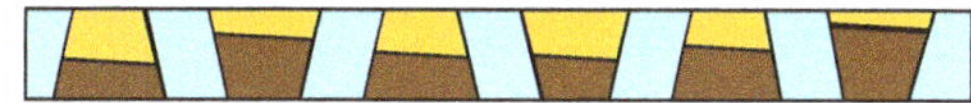

Add Floor Divider Strips

13 Cut dark building strip to top the wedge row. Cut to the same length x 1.25" high. Cut a second floor divider strip for the bottom that's the same length x 1.5" high.

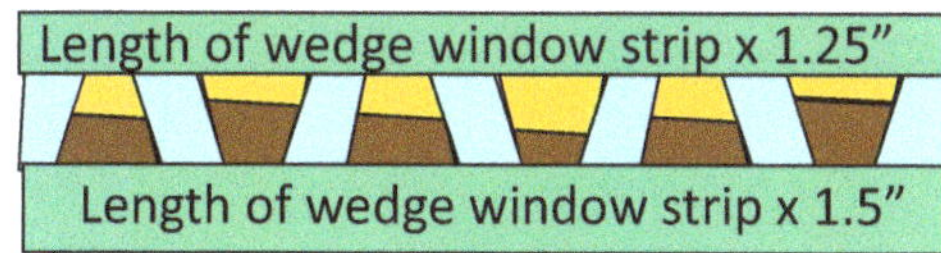

14 Sew strips to the wedge row, with the back of the wedge strip facing up at you, so you can keep seam allowances turned correctly.

15 Cut floor divider strip for the top. Measure pieced top row's length (mine is 9.25"). Add 1". Cut dark building fabric 1" longer, in this case 10.25" (or your length) x 1.25" high. This is the "top divider."

16 Fold the left edge of first window strip 1/4" to the back.

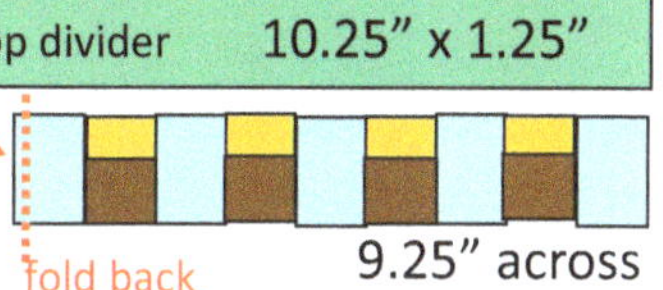

17 Flip pieced window strip, good side down, onto the front of the top divider. Match bottom and far right edges.

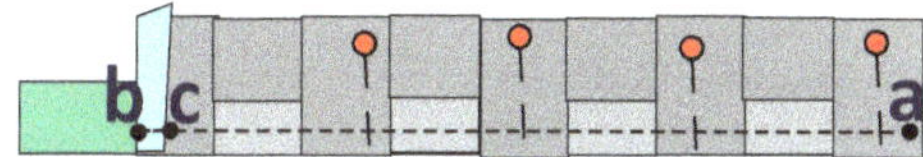

18 Hold back threads and start sewing at **a**, above right. (There's no flap there, so no need to backstitch there.) Sew to **b**, where the window row ends. Backstitch to **c** and cut threads there. Unfold and press seam allowances up.

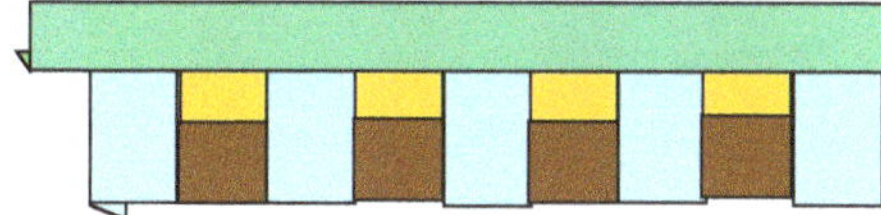

19 Flip this top unit, face down, onto the middle unit (wedge windows with dividers above and below.)

Bring up threads at **a**. Backstitch to **b**, where the fold is. Stitch to **c**.

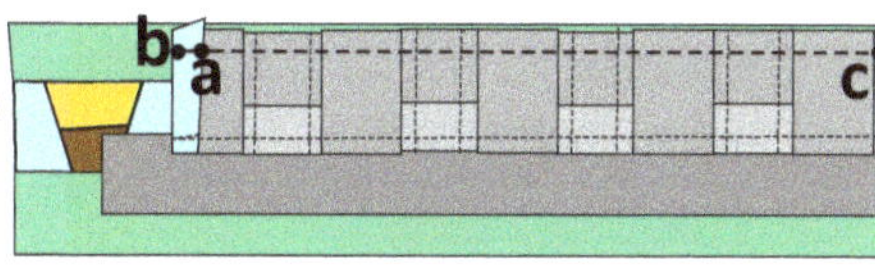

20 Press seam allowances down. Press left raw edge of wedge unit 1/4" to back (orange dotted line).

I dab glue under the top and bottom flaps first, press, then add more glue under vertical edge, and press it 1/4" to the back.

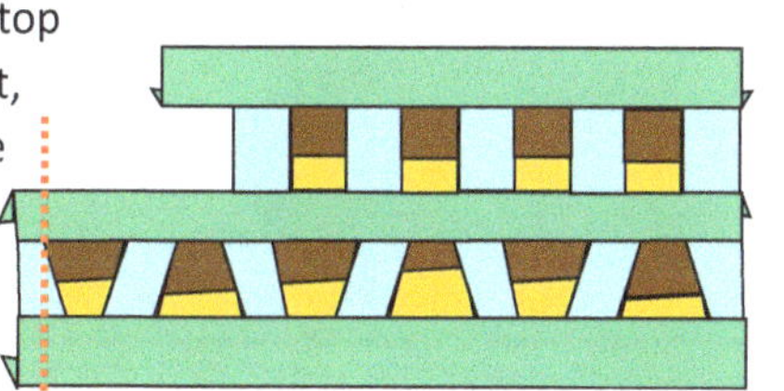

21 Measure lowest window row. It should be about 10.5", but use your measurement. Cut bottom strip 2" longer x 2" high. My measurements put this at 12.5" x 2".

22 Press far left edge 1/4" to the back.

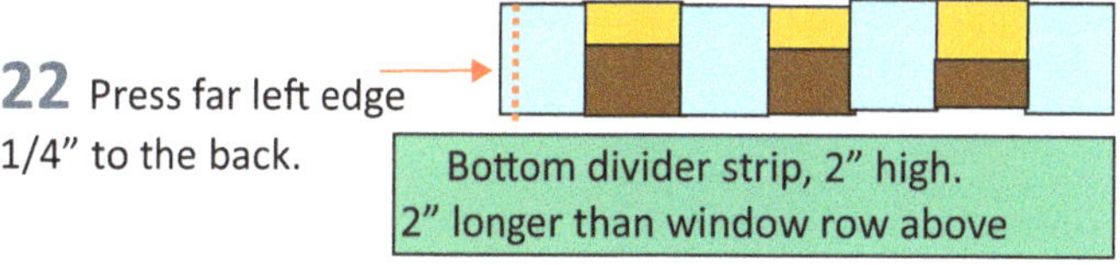

23 Flip the window row face down onto the lowest divider strip, face up. Match top and right edges.

Pin, then sew, starting at **a**, backstitching to **b**, ending at **c**. Open and press seam allowances down, behind the base strip.

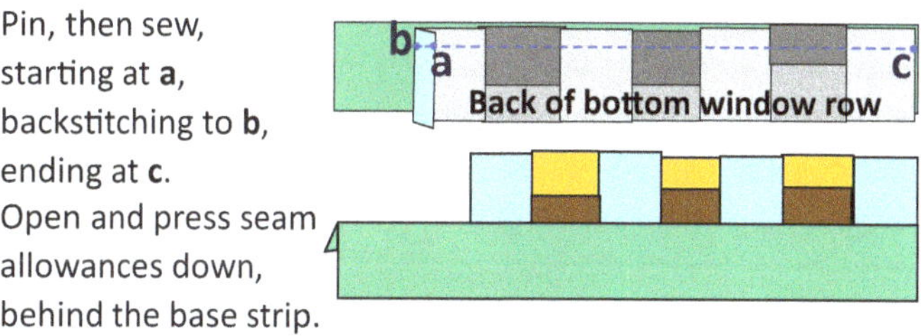

24 Flip the entire bottom unit, face down, onto the lower edge of the upper section. Match right and lower edges.

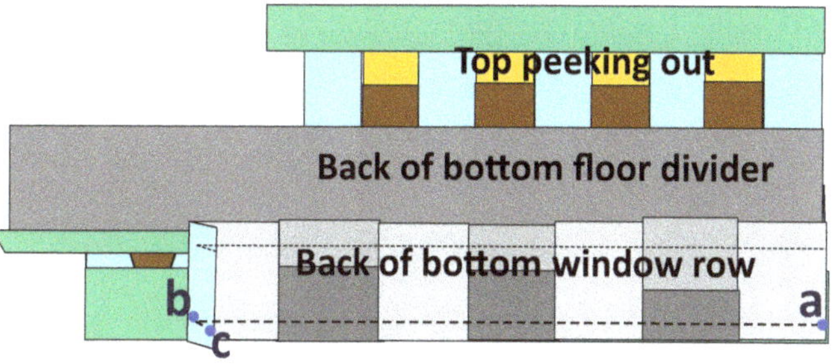

25 Sew from **a** to **b**, at the fold; backstitch to **c**. Unfold and press seam allowance up, under the longer strip.

26 Press top left edge of top strip up at an angle (orange line at A). Cut off fabric 1/4" from that crease (on red line). Press strip's bottom flap up, side flap in, then top flap down. Below left is a photo of that corner with edges pressed in.

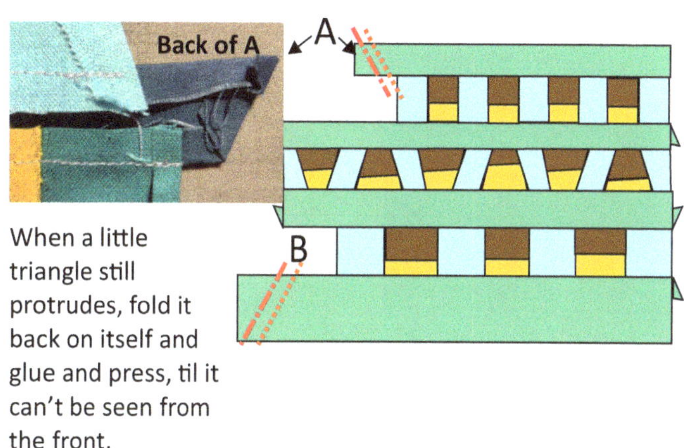

When a little triangle still protrudes, fold it back on itself and glue and press, til it can't be seen from the front.

27 Crease bottom floor divider on an angle (the orange line at B above). Cut off 1/4" out from that crease, on the red line and press edges inward the same way.

28 Press strip's top seam allowance down, bottom seam allowance up, and side seam allowance inward, gluing at the corners and pressing and gluing back any flaps that protrude.

(continued)

Add a dome (to this or any building!

29 **Print a circle** Print or photocopy this page and cut out the partial circle below. Do the size check in red. Trace the pattern onto freezer paper and go to step 2. (You do not need to trace the red line.)

Or locate a circle! Instead of this printout, you can use a plate or other round object (brown in the photo).

Lay freezer paper under the circle, and building on top. Slide circle around until its bottom edge is at least 1/4" below the building's top edge, and at least 1/2" within the building's sides. Draw around the circle onto the freezer paper.

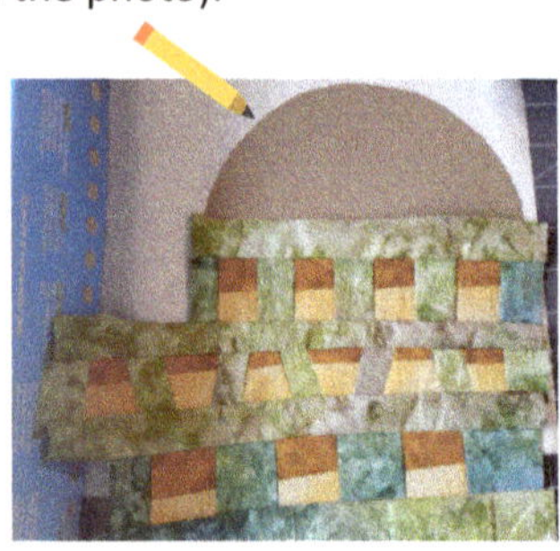

30 Here's the pattern on freezer paper. Cut it out.

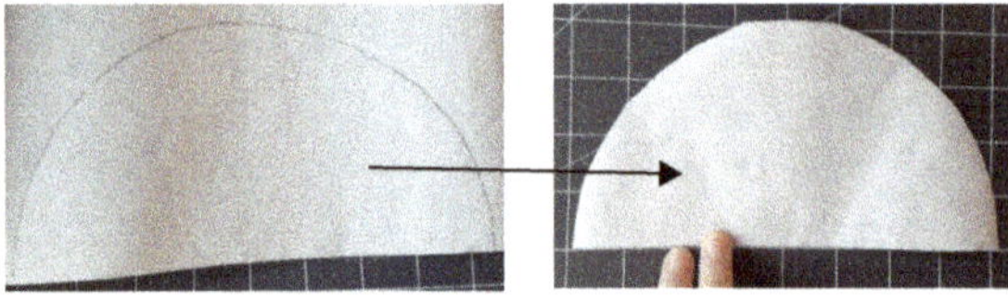

31 Press it to the back of dome fabric.

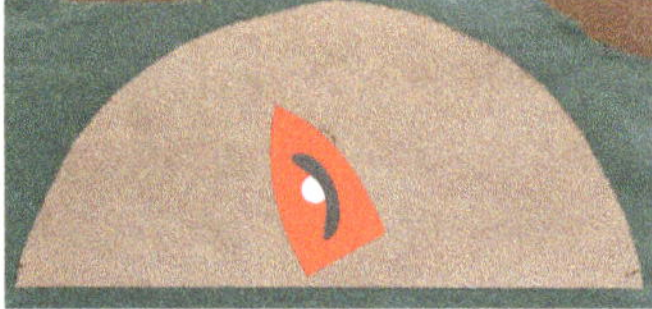

32 Trim fabric 1/4" out from the curved edge (on the dotted line). On bottom, trim fabric even with freezer paper edge.

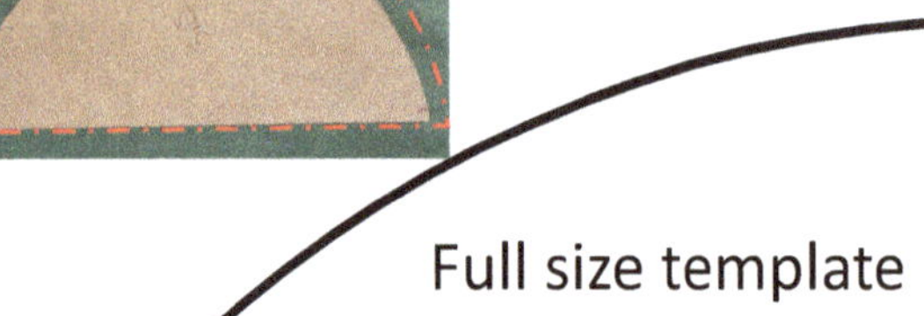

33 I like to paint the round edges with pressing fluid. Then press top edges down around the freezer paper. Leave bottom edge as is.

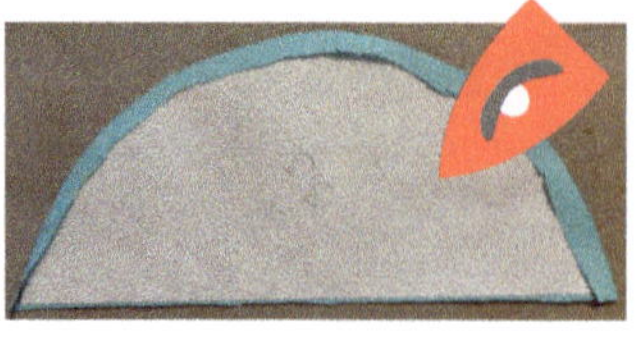

34 Peel out freezer paper. Pin to top edge of building. Dome's sides should be pressed in.

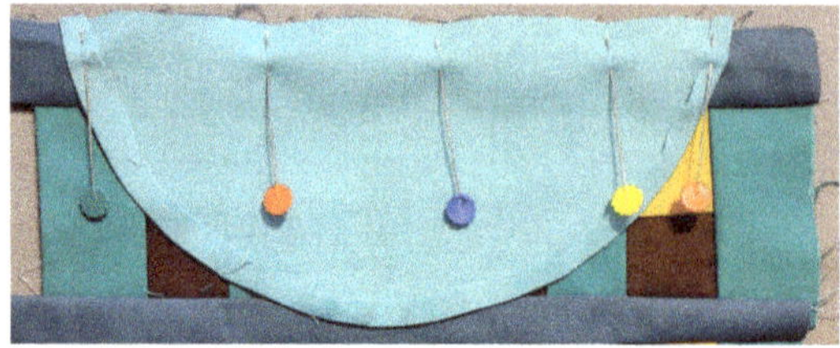

35 Bring up threads and start sewing at **a**, backstitch to **b**, sew to **c**, backstitch to **d**. You'll be stitching the dome's side flaps shut.

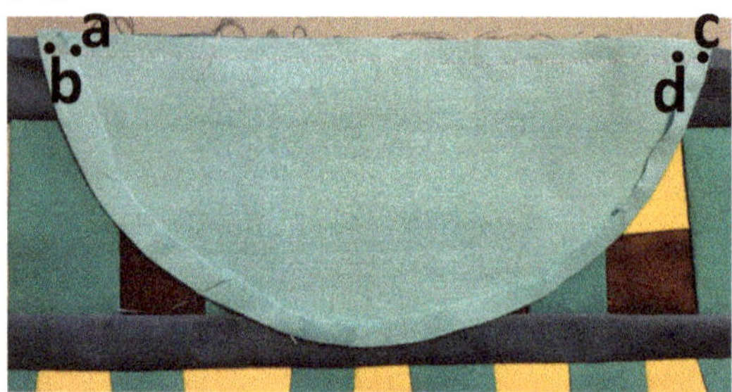

36 Press seam allowances down, including the extended edges of the building's top strip.

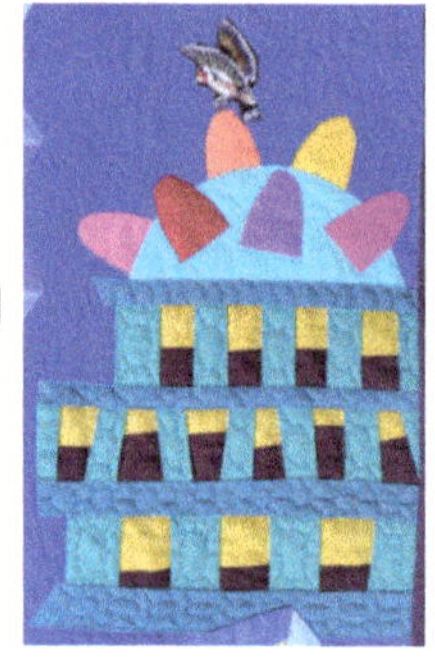

37 Last minute additions: Assorted gumdrops and a bird! A better view is on p. 92.

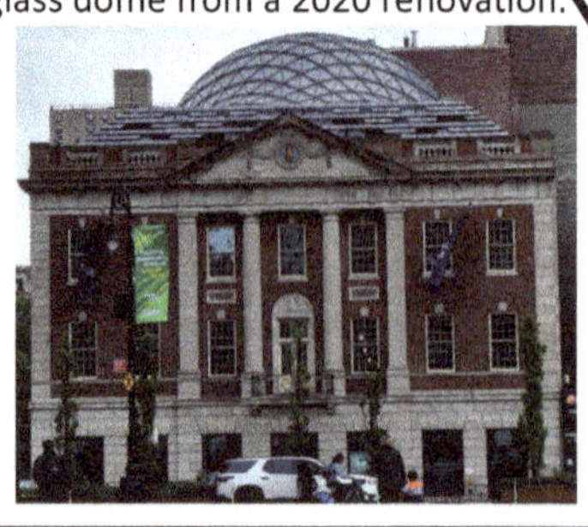

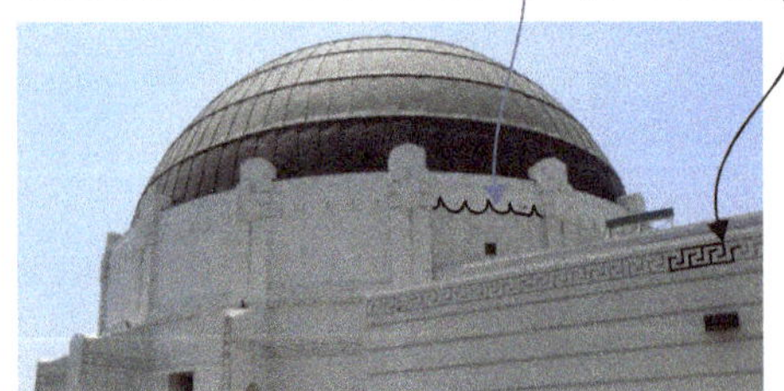

Full size template
for Emerald Observatory
roof dome

Below, quilting ideas from Los Angeles' Griffith Observatory. It has a gridded dome, curved trim, and a 'meander' (p. 32).

44 Union Sq. is a 1929 NYC building with a triangle-based glass dome from a 2020 renovation.

Clusters: Purple Pile-up

We'll use the previous techniques to make a building that is uneven on three (or more) sides. The building will tell you which edge to press in before sewing. (Spoiler: The shorter one!)

Start with about 30 improv log cabin blocks if you want the purple pileup in the lower left corner. The next diagram shows the same idea, but with only about a dozen blocks. Even simpler, consider using one fabric for each section – see box on the bottom of the next page. In that case, you'll only need five different fabrics total! The hotel in the photo might be done with much far fewer than 50 shades of grey (5-8 is good).

1 If you want to use log cabin blocks, begin with a long 1.5" light purple strip sewn to a 1.5" yellow strip. Cut apart at 1"-2" intervals. Add "logs" to sides in shades of the same color.

After finishing that batch, make a new batch, starting with narrower (1.25") or wider (1.75") strips. Varied sizes let you create perspective by placing the smallest ones in the furthest part of the building (usually the top.)

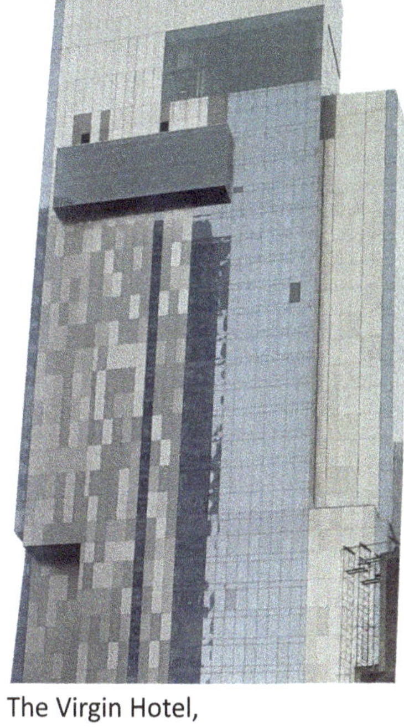

The Virgin Hotel,
1227 Broadway, NYC

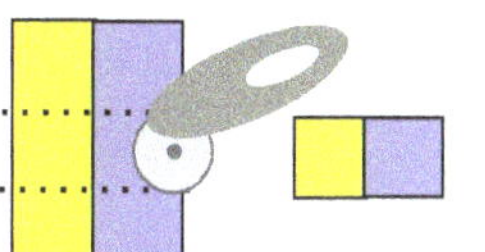 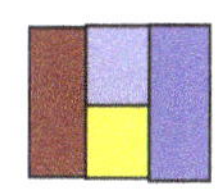 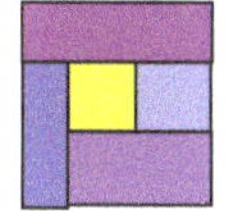 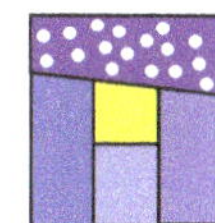

2 Cluster blocks into 5 rectangular groupings, and do a rough layout. The sections outlined below show how mine worked. Trim or add blocks, strips and/or rectangles as needed.

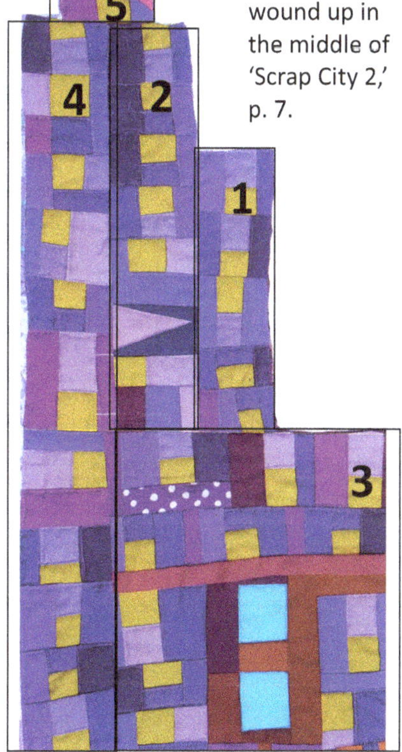

Single Block

This building wound up in the middle of 'Scrap City 2,' p. 7.

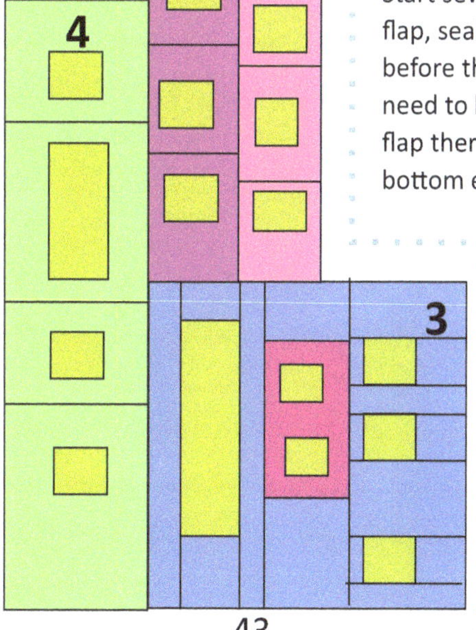

3 Assemble units 1 and 2. Press top edge of shorter piece one to the back 1/4". (We'll deal with the top of section 2 later.)
From here, diagrams won't show windows!

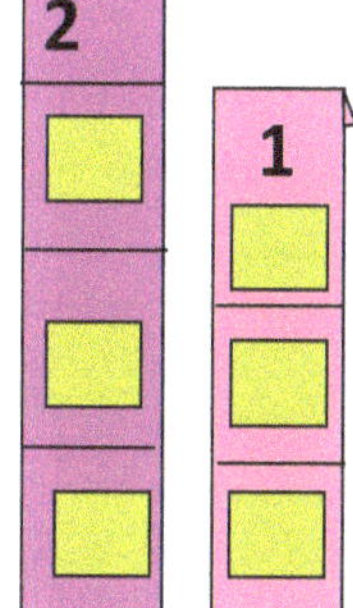

4 Flip column 1, good side down, onto the right edge of column 2, good side up. Pin.

Start sewing at **a**. Backstitch up over the flap, sealing it, to the dot under **b**, just before the fold. Sew down to **c**. There's need to backstitch at **c** because there's no flap there (and there's no flap because the bottom edges are even!)

5 Unfold and press seam allowance toward the longer/higher piece 2. Also neatly press the extended seam allowance on the upper right of piece 2, 1/4"to the left, as shown.

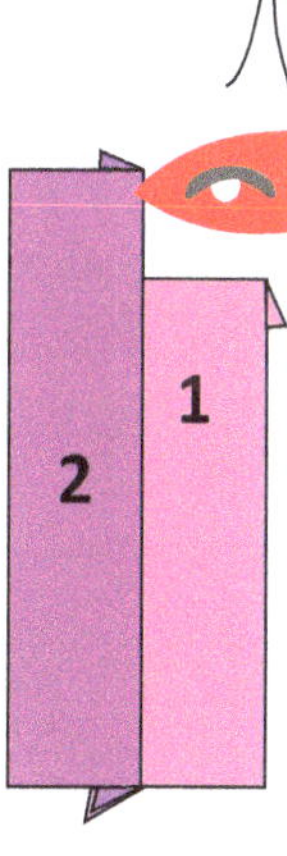

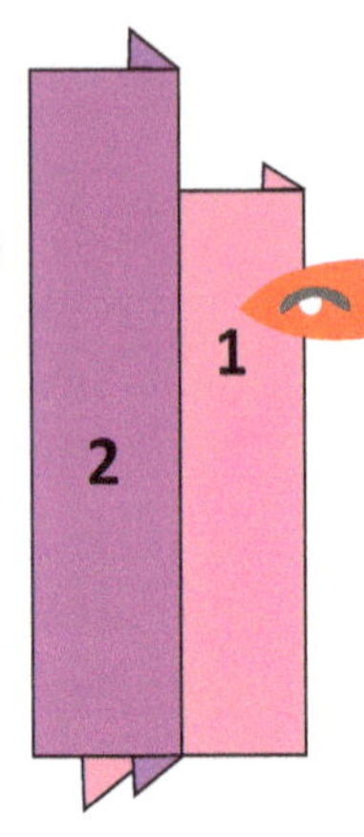

6 Press the right edge of piece 1 to the left 1/4", because we're about to attach its base to a piece that's wider and we want that edge finished.

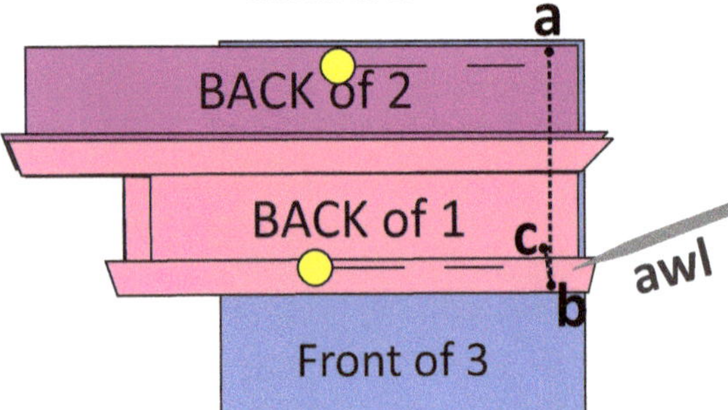

7 Flip unit 1/2 face down, onto unit 3 below it, which has its good side facing up. Align and pin top and left edges.

8 **Rotate** pinned seam right. Bring up threads and start sewing at **a**. Sew to **b**, at the fold. (An awl pushes flap down, so presser foot can travel up and over it). Stop, backstitch and cut thread at **c**.

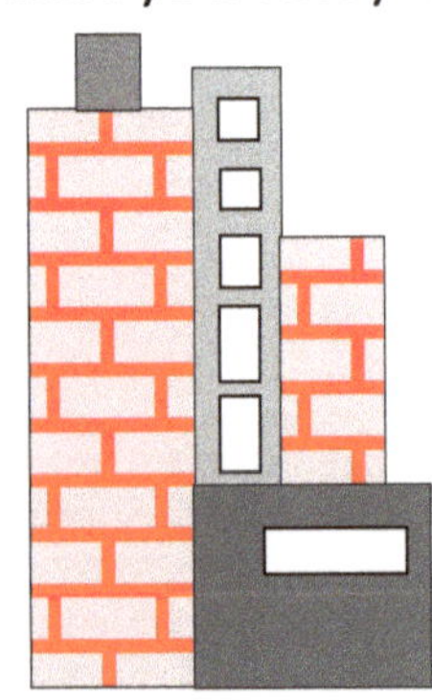

Option: Make a clustered building with a combination of prints and solids. Each section can be just 1 fabric that you fussy-cut.

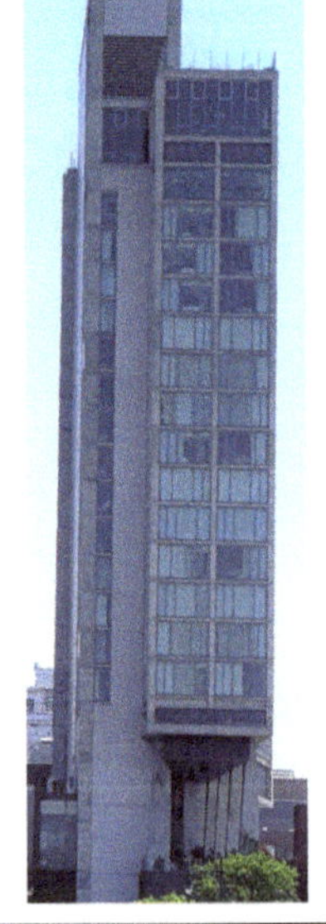

9 Press seam allowances down, including the extended area along the top of unit 3.

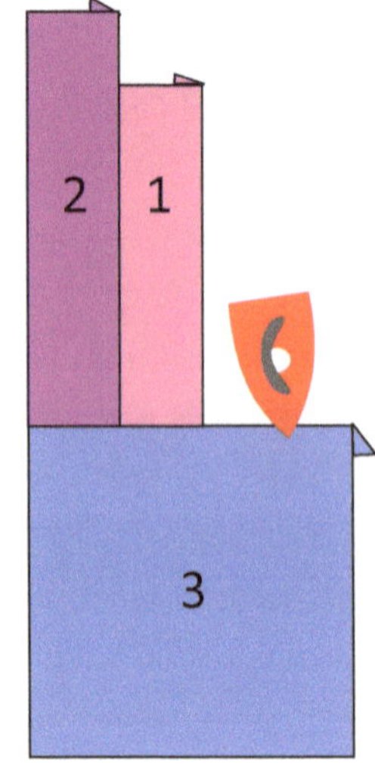

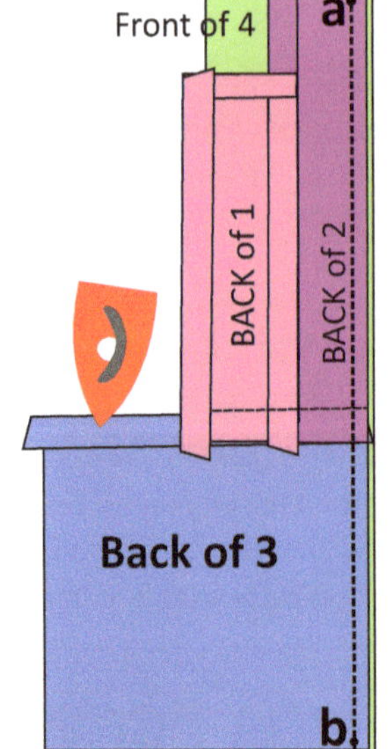

10 Flip unit 1/2/3, face down, onto the right edge of unit 4, which is face up. **Because unit 4 is the same height as 1/2/3, there's no need to fold back any edge in advance or to backstitch at a.** Simply sew from **a** to **b**. Open and press seam allowance either way!

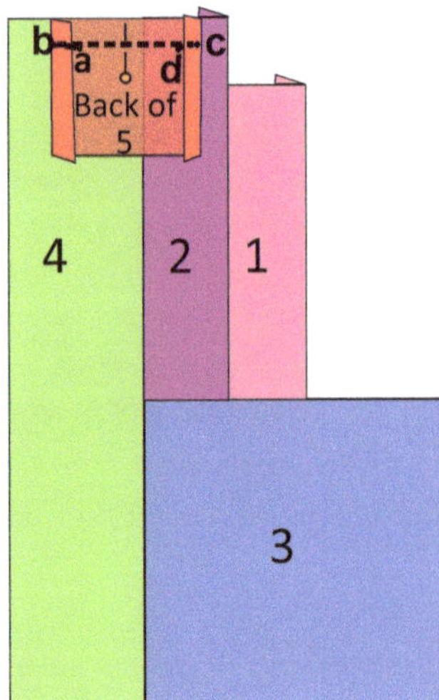

11 Wedding cake piece the topmost block. Press its vertical sides 1/4" to the back and pin in place. As you did in step 7, rotate the seam to the right. Sew, bringing up threads at **a**, backstitching to **b**, sewing straight down to **c**, and backstitching to **d**, where you cut threads.

12 Press seam allowances down to the lower levels, and also press down the extended areas on top of 2 and 4. Press the top quarter inch of block 5 downward, to prepare the top of the building for appliqué.

13 The left and bottom edges of pieces 4 and 3 can be turned now, or later if you're not sure whether you'll appliqué or piece this building to a background, or to another building.

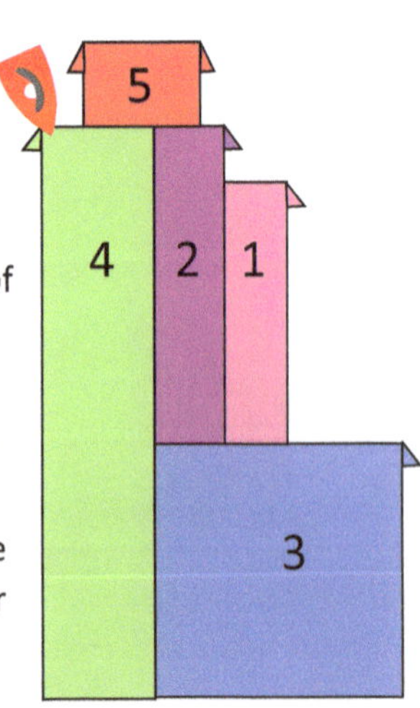

IDEAS
Peering Into Attic Windows

"Attic windows" is a traditional quilt block that creates the illusion of looking into a room or window. In real life, none of the buildings I photographed suggested attic windows to me – until I looked closely at my photos of this building under construction, taken from the very high roof of an adjacent building.

I finally saw attic windows in the wild! Because this is real-world perspective, each window is slightly different!

Look at the column on the far right of the unfinished building.

Towards the top, you can see ceilings, a bit of a right wall and a back wall. (I gave each a different color in the diagrams to make it clear). For the next 15 or so rooms down, the ceiling shortens and more of the back and right walls become visible.

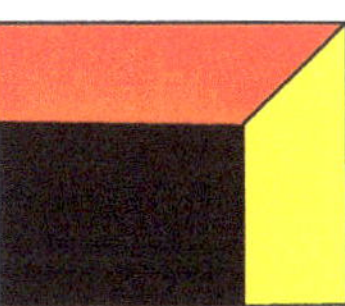

Next, at about my eye level, the ceilings dwindle away, and you can start to see the floors.

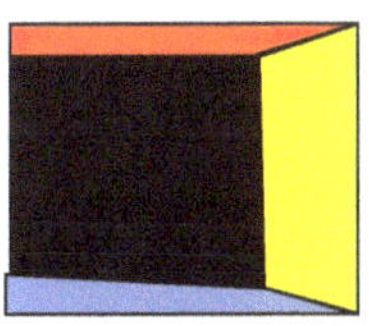

Moving down from there, the floors grow bigger and bigger, until you can't see the back walls at all.

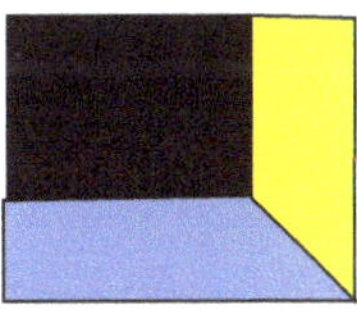

I made a drawing, doing my best to follow the rules of one-point perspective (p. 65.)

Creating and sewing this as a foundation paper piecing pattern was very tricky and took a very long time.

There had to be an easier way – something between the highly complex foundation piecing required to make every level different, and the very static attic windows in traditional quilts. That's what this section is about.

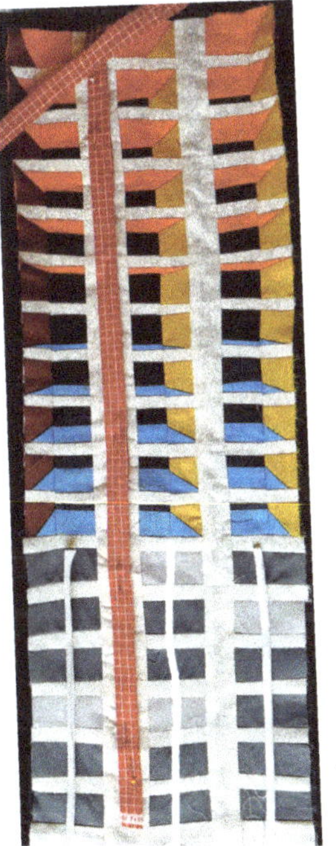

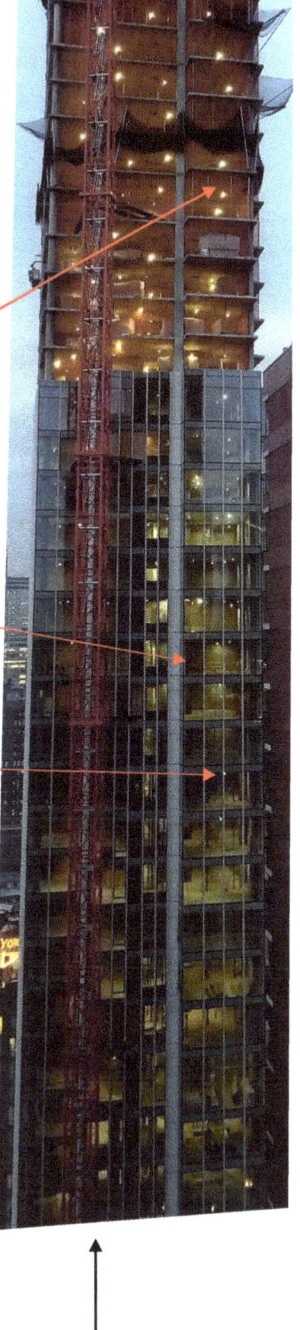

The grey boxes below the open rooms show where glass was installed.

45

Easier/Wilder Attic Windows

The traditional method, right, requires a y-seam (aka "mitering"). I don't enjoy it. The cheat technique below (which I did not invent) uses half-square triangles. Follow my measurements, or start with any size window square, and cut improv from there. The version on the left (in 'Scrap City 1,' p. 7) is a little wilder and more interesting, with a color shift, just for fun, explained beneath it.

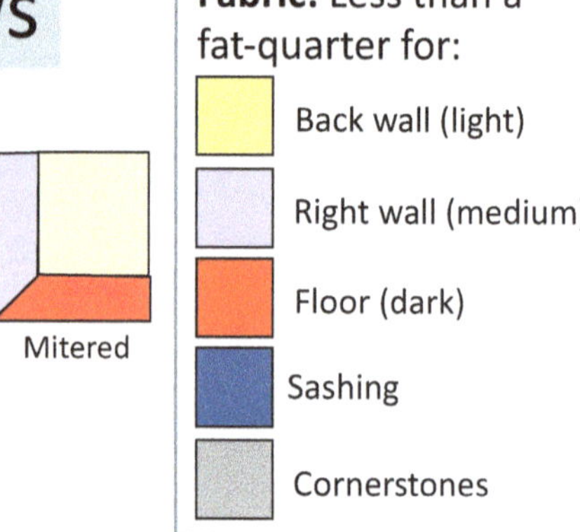
Mitered

Fabric: Less than a fat-quarter for:

- Back wall (light)
- Right wall (medium)
- Floor (dark)
- Sashing
- Cornerstones

Optional wild version: Match values (dark on bottom, medium on the right) but use different colors in the corner than those on the side and bottom.

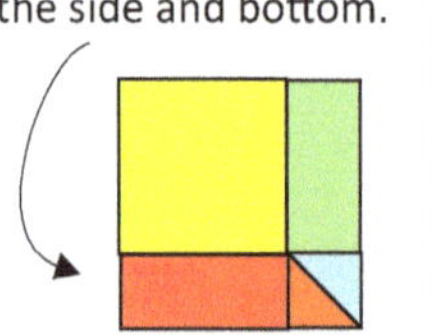

1 Cut ten 2.5" x 2.5" squares as windows. (Start with a 25" x 2.5" strip.) *Improv: Cut squares any size.*

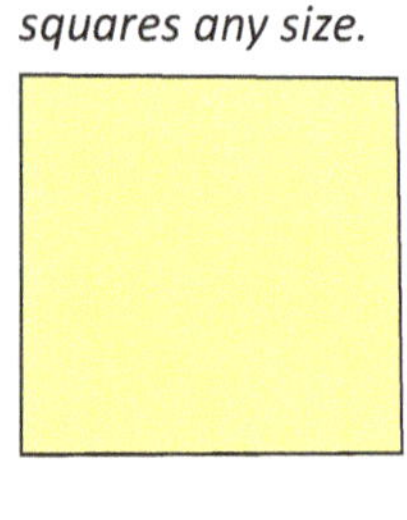

2 Cut 18" x 1.75" strip of medium color; and same size strip of dark. Subcut ten 1.75" x 1.75" squares. Place one of each right sides together. Mark diagonal. Sew. Chain sew all 10. *Improv: Cut any size narrower than your window squares, but don't go less than an inch.)*

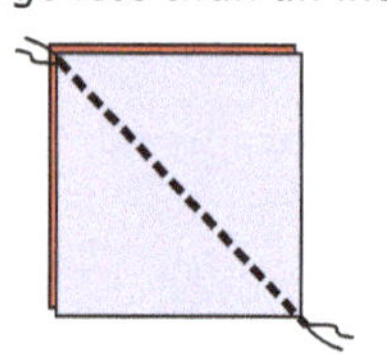

3 Cut off 1/4" from the seam on one side.

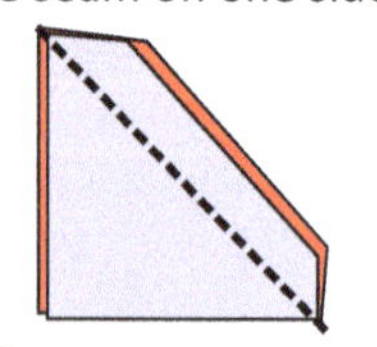

4 Open and press. Make 10.

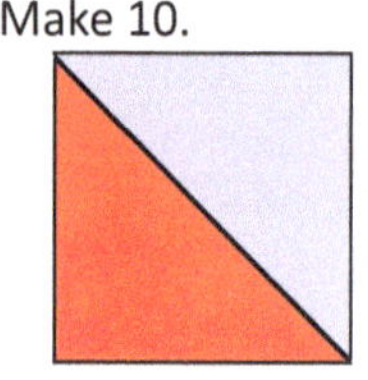

5 Cut medium and dark sashing strips 2.5" x 18". Subcut it into ten pieces, each 1.75" x 2.5". *Improv: Cut medium and dark strips same lengths as windows, same width as your half-square triangles' square.*

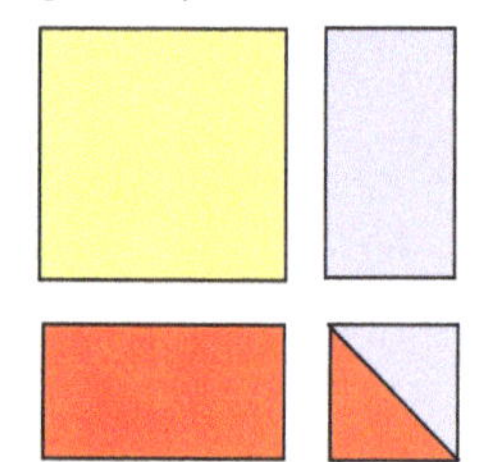

6 Sew medium vertical strip to one side of window.

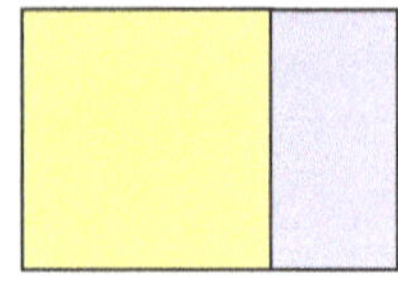

7 Sew dark horizontal strip to the diagonal square.

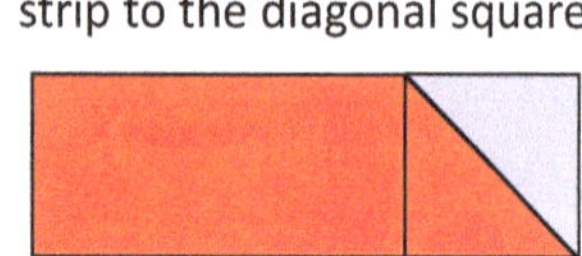

8 Sew top to bottom unit.

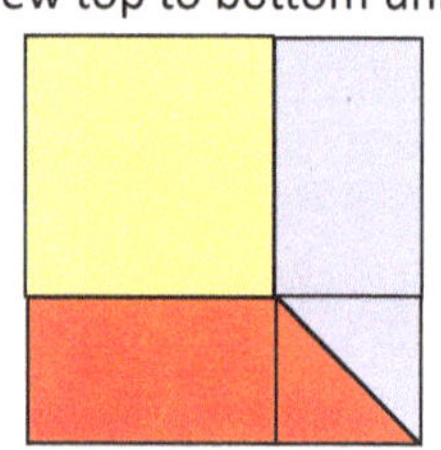

9 Sashing strips are dark blue in diagrams. Cut 25 pieces, 3.75" x 1.75" (Start with a 38" x 3.75" strip, cut into 1.75" pieces). *Improv: Choose sashing width – 1.75" is good – and cut a long strip. Subcut to match window widths while doing Step 11.*

10 Cut 15 cornerstones to sashing width (1.75" x 1.75"). *Improv: Cut as needed.*

11 Lay out pieces as in diagram. Sew top four windows in each column to sashing strips below them. *Improv: For perspective, group smallest units toward building's top. If blocks aren't the same width: Measure and cut horizontal sashing for each. Cut cornerstones same width as adjacent sashing strips. You will do some fudging.*

12 Once pieces are in columns, join rows into columns.

13 Chain sew pieces together so it looks like the diagram on the far right.

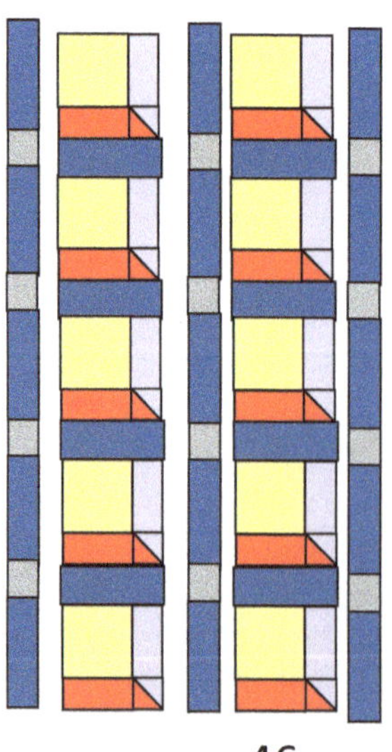

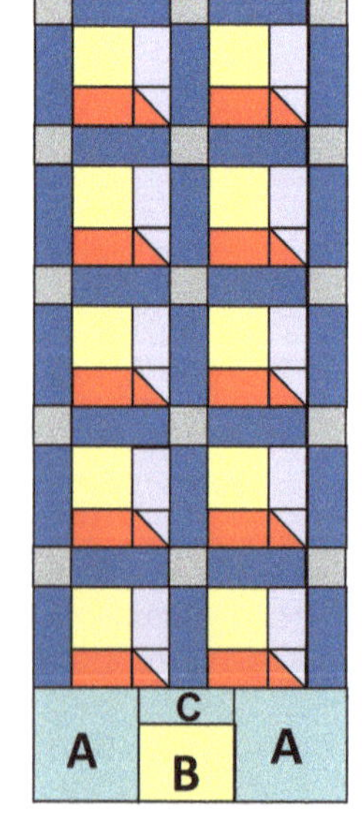

Option: Want a ground floor? If you followed the measurements above, cut
- Two A pieces, 3.75" x 4.5"
- One B piece, 4.25" x 3"
- One C piece 4.25" x 2"
Improv - Build a piece B + C doorway first, to any size you like. Measure and add what you need to both sides to match your upper building's width.
Extra credit: The door doesn't have to be centered!

Rotated Attic Windows Blocks

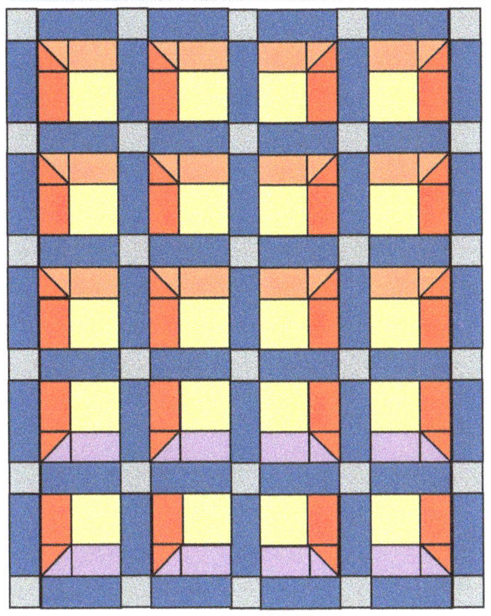

For more of a sense of realistic shifting perspective, use the same approach to attic windows blocks on the previous page, but make some of the blocks with ceilings (the top three floors), and some with floors (bottom rows.) Here, ceilings are medium value (orange color), and floors are also a medium value (lavender). All the blocks have back walls, which are all light (yellow); and all have one side wall, which is dark (red). The sashing is even darker, and the cornerstones are light. (They're well separated from the back walls, so those patches don't meld together).

Rotate the ceiling blocks so the ceilings are on top; rotate the floor blocks with the floors downward. Place as shown.

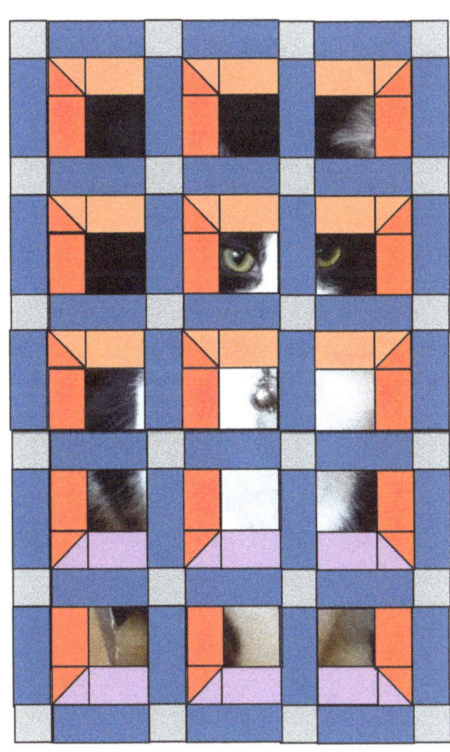

More ideas:

– Use a floral print for a back or side wall. It will look like wallpaper.

– Cut up a large panel portraying something interesting. Use a preprinted panel, or something you transfer to fabric— like this photo of my cat! Set it in the back wall spaces. Here I imagine a giant urban wild cat peering into an unfinished skyscraper, waiting for the rodents to come out of hiding!

Treehouse Hotel (using Attic Windows trick)

Use the easy attic windows trick on p. 46 to create boxy undersides! Make them improv (start with any size window), or follow my measurements to make 5.5" x 4" cabins plus 3.5" high triangle roofs.

If you're creating a child's quilt, they will want to move in here, and good news – I found tons of tree house hotels online! Sweden's was the most artistic, at (https://treehotel.se/en/.) Check out especially its cabin surrounded by 400 birdhouses!

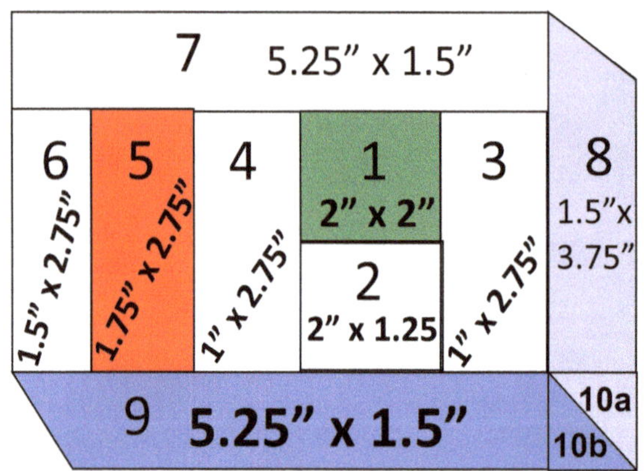

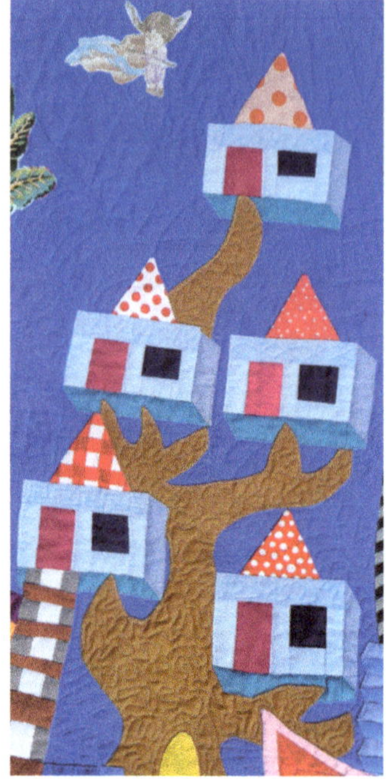

1 Make five cabins. As you add pieces 2, 3, and 4 around the window, press seam allowances away from piece 1.

2 Add 5, 6, and 7, pressing seam allowances away from 5 (the door).

3 Measure height and width of your unit, raw edge to raw edge, and write them down. With the plan above, it should be 5.25" x 3.75".

4 Press top raw edge of piece 7 1/4" back (green dotted line).

5 Cut piece 8 to the height you measured in step 2 (3.75" here), and a width of 1.5" (or improvise).

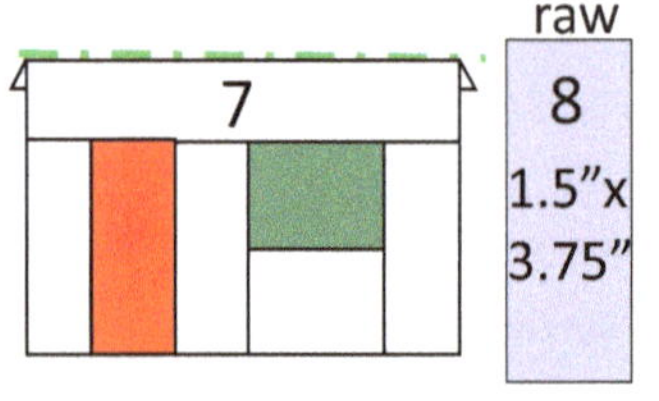

6 Flip main unit, face down, on piece 8, aligning left and bottom edges. Pin along the seam as shown.

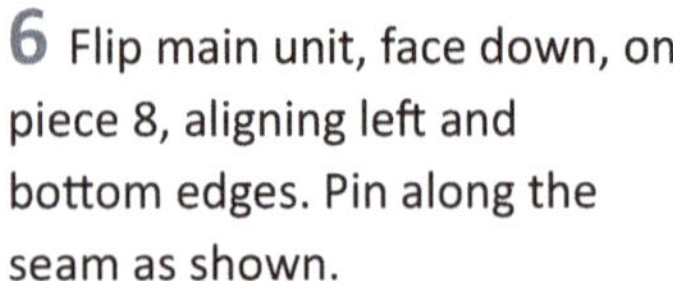

7 Rotate **a** to the upper right. Start at **a**, sew down, sealing the flap shut, and stop at **b**, just before the fold. Backstitch to **c**.

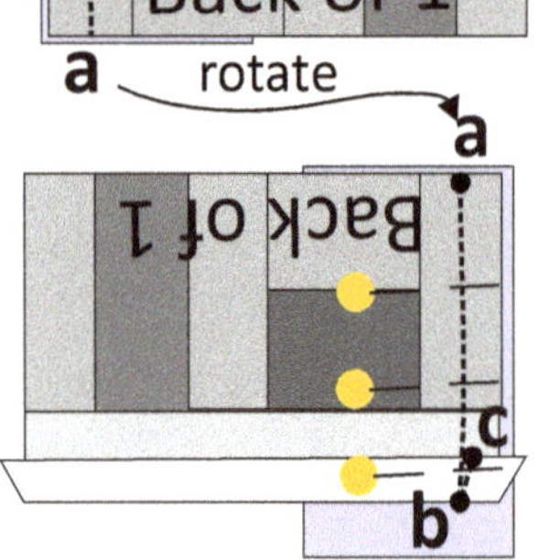

8 Press seam allowance left, under the main cabin. Fold top of 8 back at an angle (green line). If a tiny triangle pokes out on top, press and glue it back. The entire top edge is now folded backwards, first flat across, then angled on the far right.

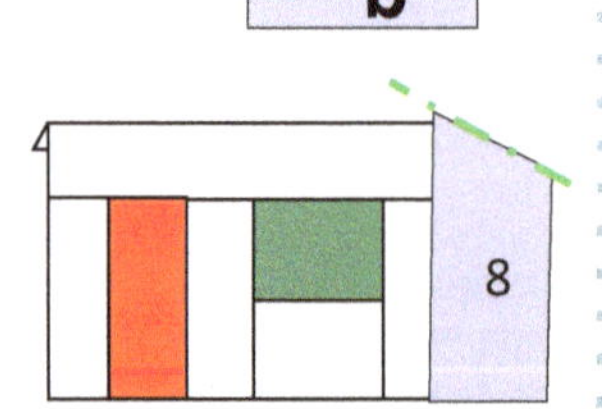

Fabric for treehouse with five cabins

Doors, 14" x 1.75"

Windows, 10" x 2"

Side pieces 8 and 10a
30" x 1.5" total

Bottom pieces 9 and 10b
35" x 1.5"

Building front, 74" x 2"(quarter-yard, fat-quarter, or fat-eighth)

Roof triangles: Five assorted scraps, each approx. 4.5" square

Lining for roof triangles
Approx 12" x 12"

Tree trunk,
11" x 16" (fat-quarter)

You will also need:
– Paper backed fusible web for tree trunk, about 17" square

9 Cornerstone: Cut two 1.5" squares (*Improvisers: use your piece 8's width*). One should be the same fabric as piece 8. The other should be noticeably darker, **a**. Sew face-to-face along the diagonal, **b**. Trim off half as in **c**, leaving a 1/4" seam allowance. Press pieces open, **d**, and seam allowances right.

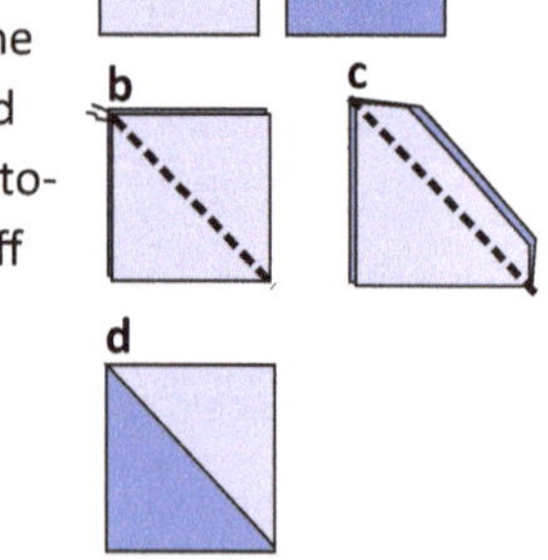

10 Cut piece 9 the same length as the cabin's width measured in step 3. (5.25" x 1.5")

11 Sew piece 9 to the left of the square (above). Press seam allowances right, under the square, which is piece 10.

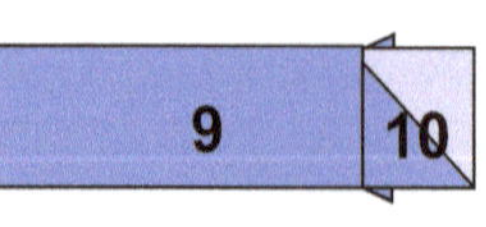

(continued)

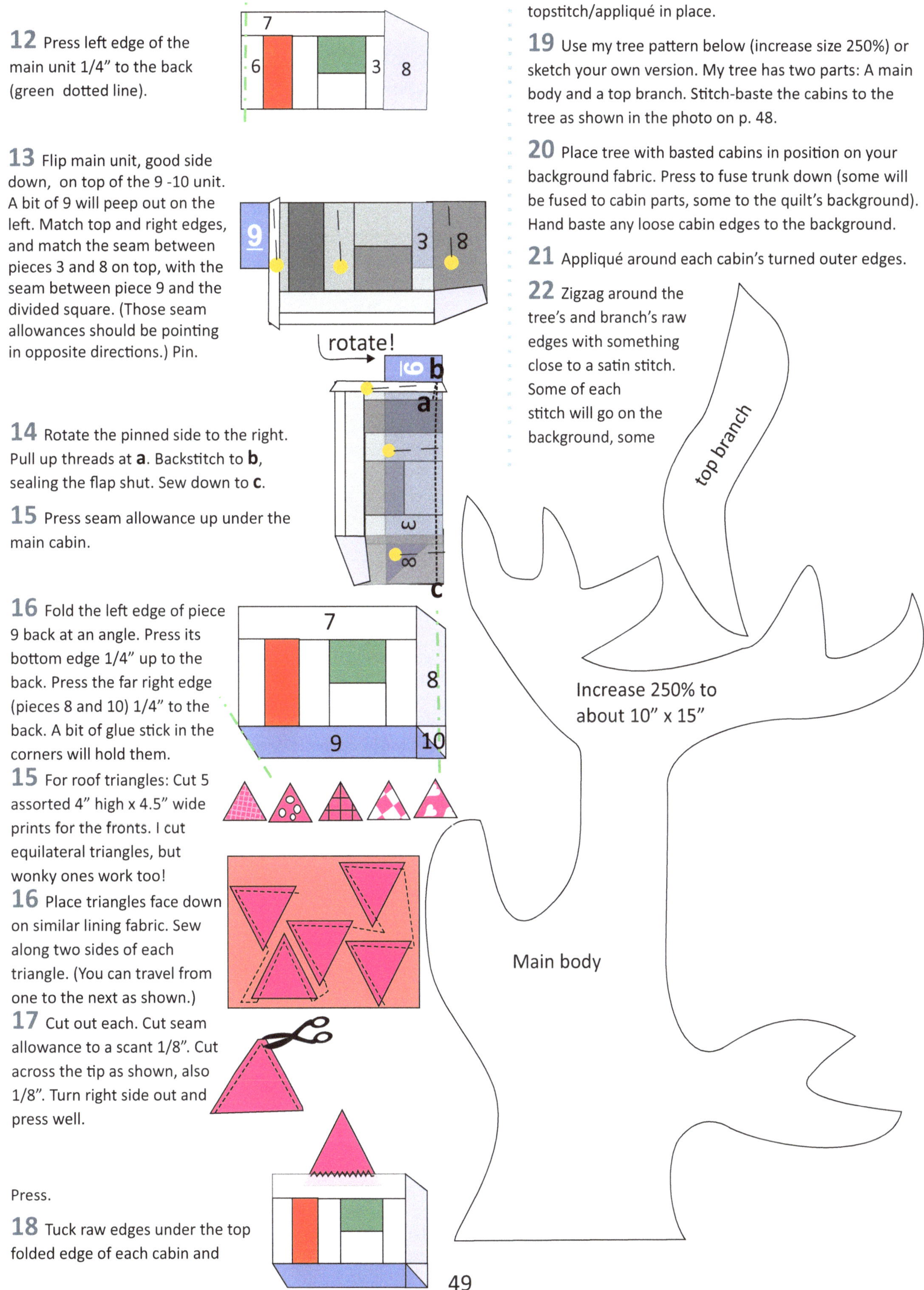

12 Press left edge of the main unit 1/4" to the back (green dotted line).

13 Flip main unit, good side down, on top of the 9 -10 unit. A bit of 9 will peep out on the left. Match top and right edges, and match the seam between pieces 3 and 8 on top, with the seam between piece 9 and the divided square. (Those seam allowances should be pointing in opposite directions.) Pin.

14 Rotate the pinned side to the right. Pull up threads at **a**. Backstitch to **b**, sealing the flap shut. Sew down to **c**.

15 Press seam allowance up under the main cabin.

16 Fold the left edge of piece 9 back at an angle. Press its bottom edge 1/4" up to the back. Press the far right edge (pieces 8 and 10) 1/4" to the back. A bit of glue stick in the corners will hold them.

15 For roof triangles: Cut 5 assorted 4" high x 4.5" wide prints for the fronts. I cut equilateral triangles, but wonky ones work too!

16 Place triangles face down on similar lining fabric. Sew along two sides of each triangle. (You can travel from one to the next as shown.)

17 Cut out each. Cut seam allowance to a scant 1/8". Cut across the tip as shown, also 1/8". Turn right side out and press well.

Press.

18 Tuck raw edges under the top folded edge of each cabin and topstitch/appliqué in place.

19 Use my tree pattern below (increase size 250%) or sketch your own version. My tree has two parts: A main body and a top branch. Stitch-baste the cabins to the tree as shown in the photo on p. 48.

20 Place tree with basted cabins in position on your background fabric. Press to fuse trunk down (some will be fused to cabin parts, some to the quilt's background). Hand baste any loose cabin edges to the background.

21 Appliqué around each cabin's turned outer edges.

22 Zigzag around the tree's and branch's raw edges with something close to a satin stitch. Some of each stitch will go on the background, some

Slanting Shadows:
Half-Rectangle Triangles

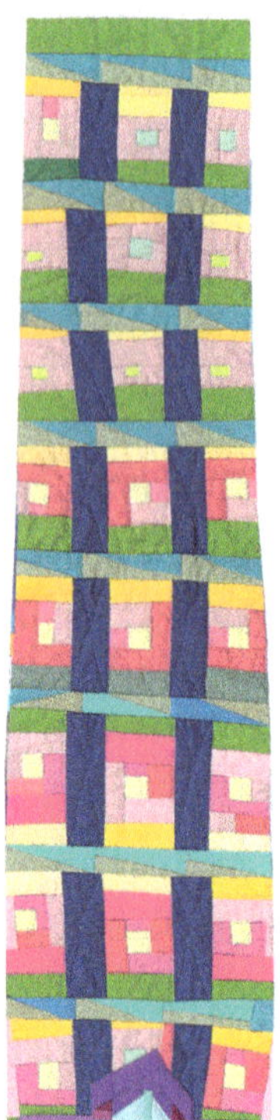

Photographers call Manhattan a "city of shadows," but of course that's true of all dense cities! Ledges, balconies, air conditioners, and entire buildings cast dramatic, massive, irregular shadows, most diagonal. They are multiplied and distorted by reflective windows, in ways that are challenging for artists to capture. Building sides in perspective also look diagonal. The techniques on these two pages are fun ways to create loads of diagonals inside rectangles.

1 Start with two rectangles, 2" x 4". Make one noticeably darker. I've put motifs on them to help you keep track of the action. Piece 1 has a red and yellow flower, Piece 2 has a white and gold star.

2 Imagine a line through both, from upper left to lower right. Flip piece 2 to its back. Now the line is going from upper right to lower left. Use a ruler to DRAW this line on the back (no need to draw any other lines).

3 Place piece 2 at an angle as shown. The underneath upper left corner of the pink piece is aligned with the back upper right corner of the blue piece. On the lower right, corners match.

4 Working from the back of Piece 2, sew 1/4" out from the dividing line, on both sides. (Don't sew on the dividing line!) A quarter-inch foot will help.

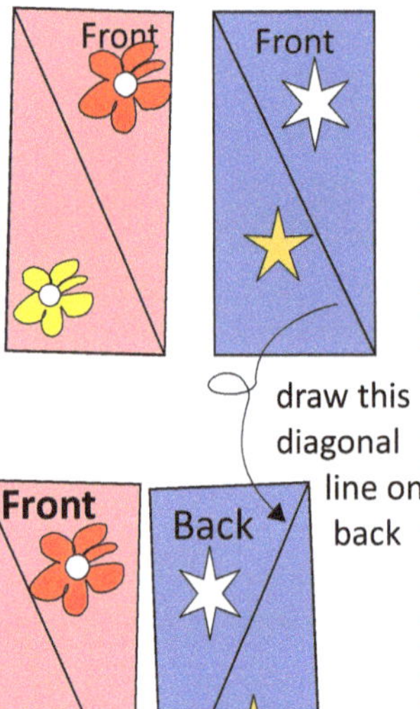

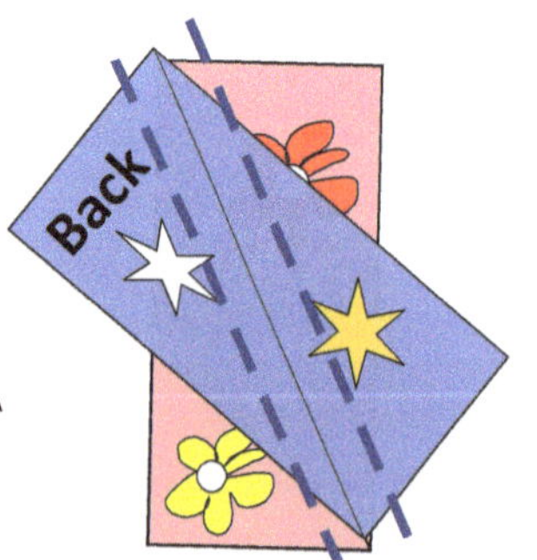

5 Cut along the diagonal you drew, through both levels.

6 Press open. Now your two rectangles look like this. Let's fix 'em.

7 Use a rotary cutter & ruler to chop off the weird protrusions at both ends (on the dotted line). Trim main piece to the largest rectangle possible – about 3.75" x 1.5".

Use it as is, or, If you want the diagonal to go all the way across the block with sharp points (which will make it substantially shorter), do the next step.

8 (Optional) Accurate full-length half-rectangle triangles, as in the diagram, are weird. If you want points to stay sharp, you must blunt them before sewing them to other pieces! This is not intuitive, but is easy once you get the idea.
Hold ruler as shown and cut off the top of the block, including the sharp tip of the lower left (blue) triangle. **Aim to put a tiny flat tip on the blue triangle, 1/8" across**. Then do the same thing to the pink tip on the other end. You'll also cutting off a substantial amount from each end, around 1/2"!

Here's what it should look like when properly trimmed. It will be about 3" wide instead of 3.75".

That's it! Now when you surround it with more pieces, the tips will become pointy again! It's magic! Again the alternative (if you stopped at Step 7) is a block that will look like the lower diagram when surrounded. I circled the difference. It's not a huge deal, and either one successfully creates an illusion of slanting shadows.

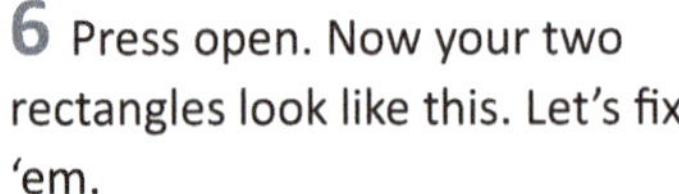

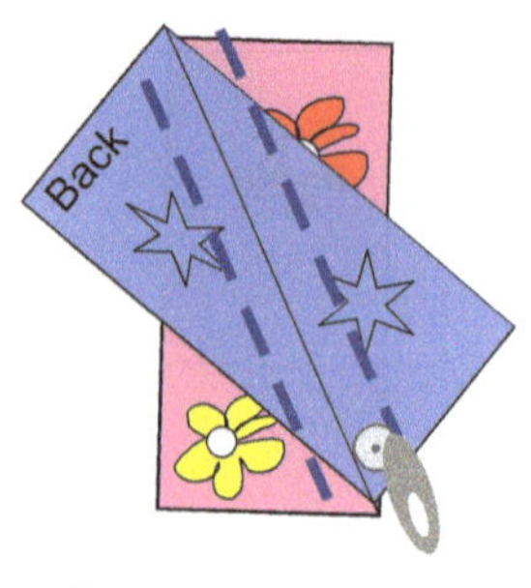

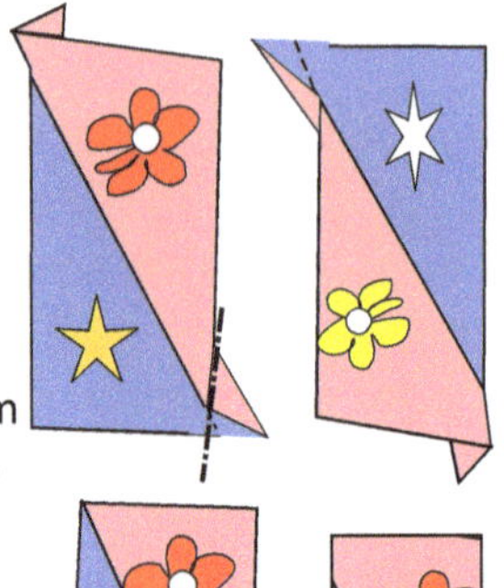

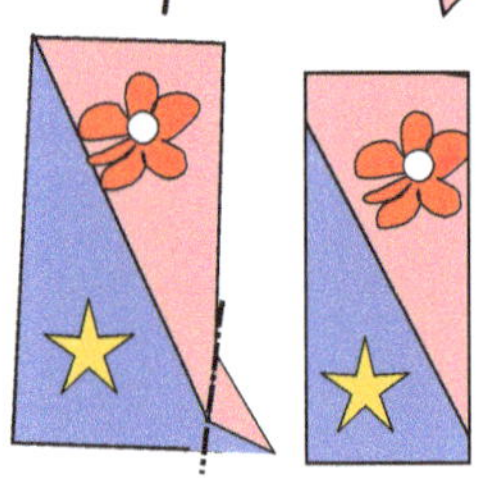

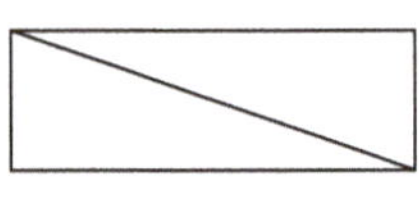

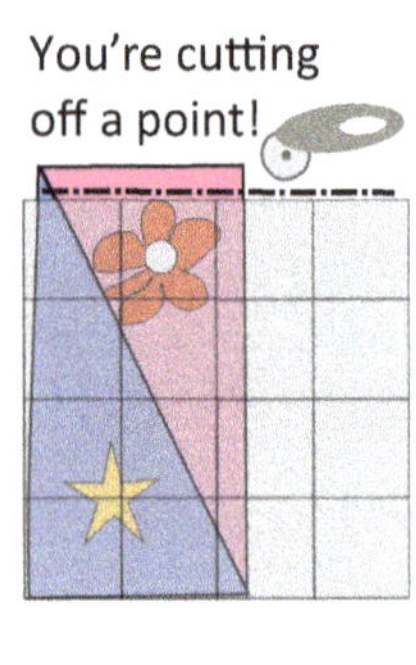

You're cutting off a point!

1/8"

1/8"

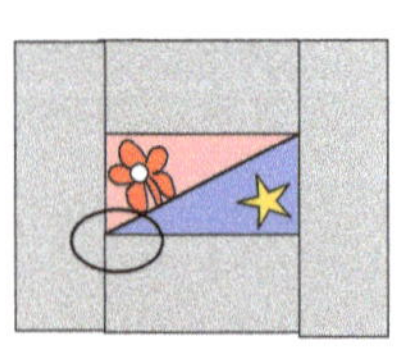

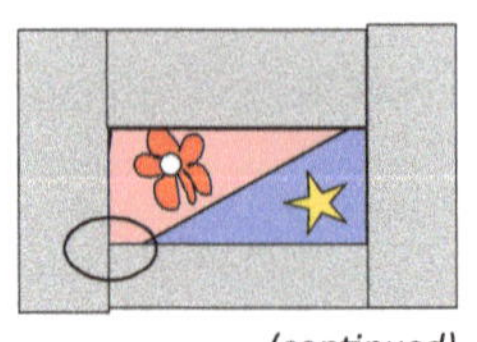

(continued)

Shade-Throwing Air Conditioner Building, with Half-Rectangle Triangles

Put the theory in the previous page into action. In this abstract building (and my mind), the turquoise strips are air conditioners. A sun is implied on the upper right, casting shadows that slant left beneath the air conditioners!

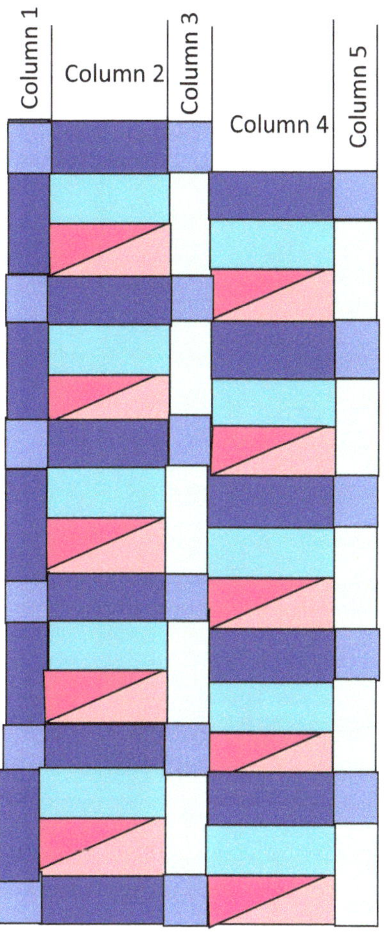

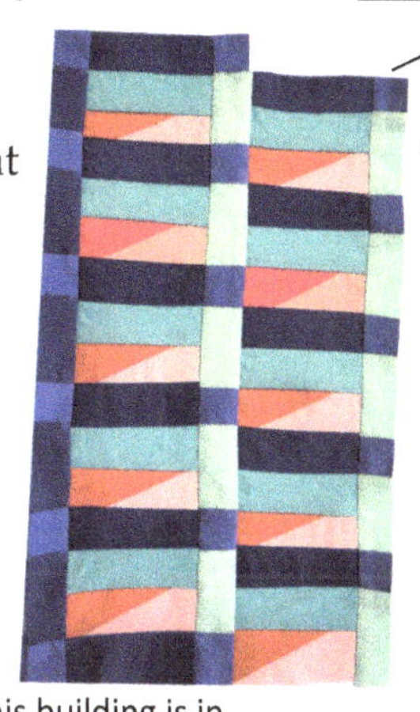

This building is in 'Nonsense Town,' p. 10

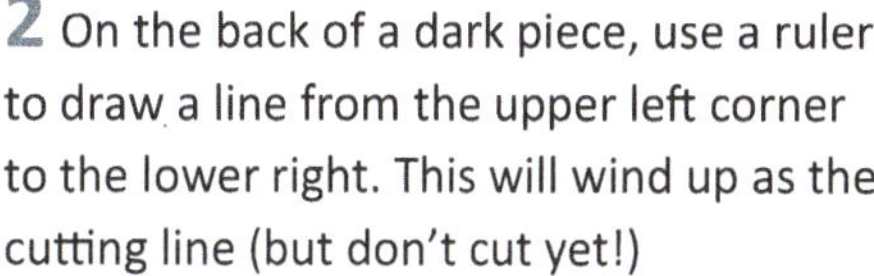

1 Cut 5 strips each of medium building color fabric (light pink) and dark building color fabric (dark pink) to 4" x 2.25" each.

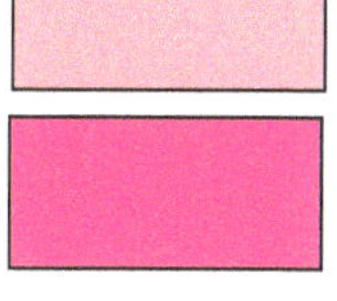

2 On the back of a dark piece, use a ruler to draw a line from the upper left corner to the lower right. This will wind up as the cutting line (but don't cut yet!)

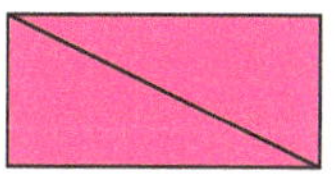

3 Draw two more lines, 1/4" out from the central line, on either side. These will be stitching lines. Repeat to mark all five dark pieces.

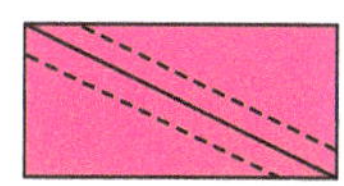

4 Place each dark piece on top of a light piece as shown, good sides together. Make sure the lighter pieces' upper left and lower right corners show (its opposite corners are hidden by the darker piece on top.) You can use a pin these together, but don't pin in the path of any of the three lines.

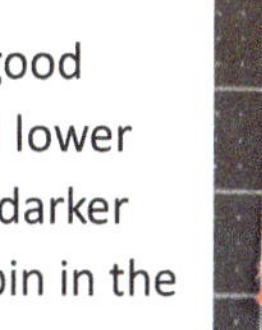

5 At the sewing machine, chain sew on all the drawn lines on the right of the cutting line.

Sew on the far right drawn line first.

After you finish sewing the line on the first pair, top, send the next pair through the machine, without cutting threads. (I'm only showing three, but you should sew all five this way.)

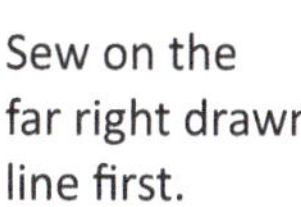

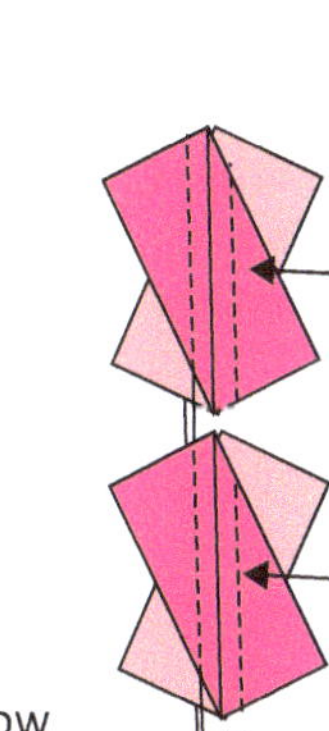

6 Take chain out of the sewing machine. Cut only the thread below the last pair. Rotate chain so the last pair is at the top. Chain sew the lines on the opposite side of the central line.

7 Use a ruler and rotary cutter to cut through the central line.

8 Press seam allowance under the darker side.

9 Use a ruler to trim each unit to 1.5" x 3.5". Try to take about the same amount off each end.

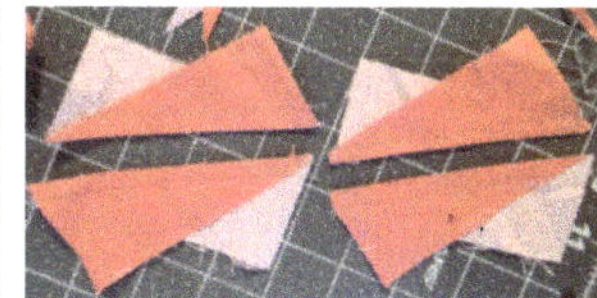

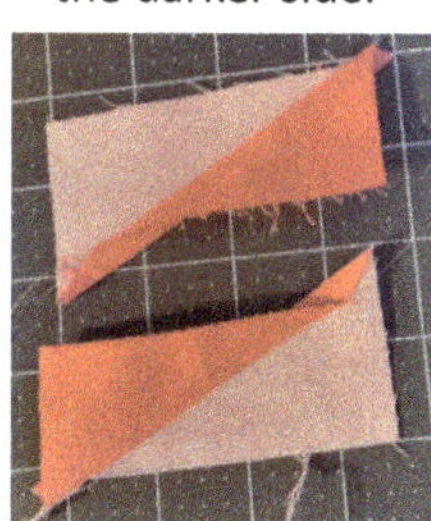

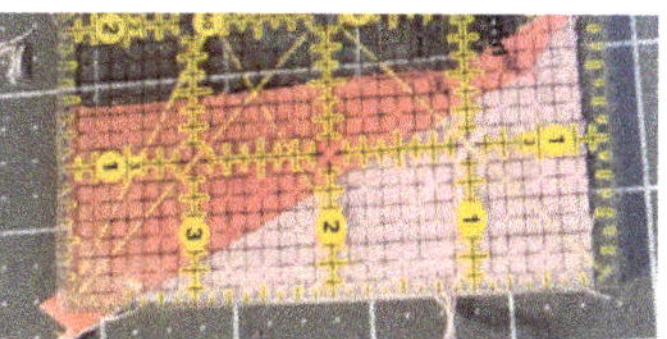

Finished size: Approx. 15" x 8.5"

Fabric

Cornerstones, about 26" x 1.5"(to be cut to seventeen 1.5" x 1.5"pieces)

Air conditioners, about 35" x 1.5" (to be cut to ten 3.5" x 1.5" pieces)

Light building color, about 25" x 1.5" (to be cut to ten 1.5" x 2.5"pieces)

Medium building color, 20" x 2.25" (to be cut to five 4" x 2.25" strips)

Shadow building color, 20" x 2.25" (to be cut to five 4" x 2.25" strips)

Darkest building color, one strip 40" x 1.5" (will be cut to eleven 3.5" x 1.5" horizontals;) and one strip 13" x 1.5" (to be cut to five 2.5" x 1.5" verticals)

(continued)

10 Cut remaining pieces to sizes in materials box on previous page. Lay pieces out – I do it on posterboard, so I can rotate it easily. All five short navy pieces go into col. 1. Rotate top to the far right, as in the diagram. We'll chain-sew columns 2 and 4 first, ignoring columns 1, 3 and 5 for now.

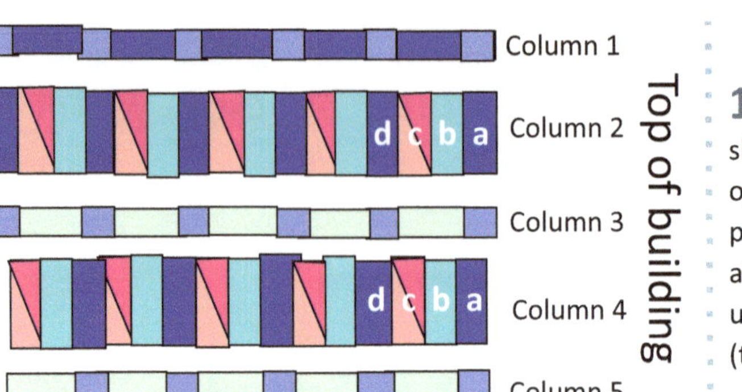

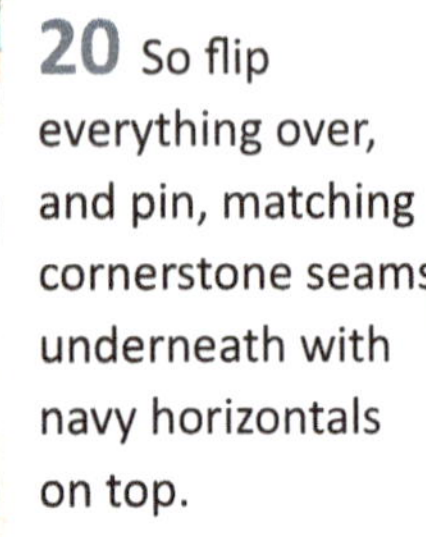

18 Press shut, then open, and press seam allowance under col. 1 (to the left).

11 Flip col. 2's piece **a** face down on **b** (good side up), and sew. Don't cut threads. Sew col. 4's piece **a** to its piece **b** the same way. Cut threads. Open and finger-press seam allowances toward piece **a**, the building's top.

12 Flip **ab** unit in column 2 on top of piece **c**. Sew. Repeat with column 4. Cut threads.

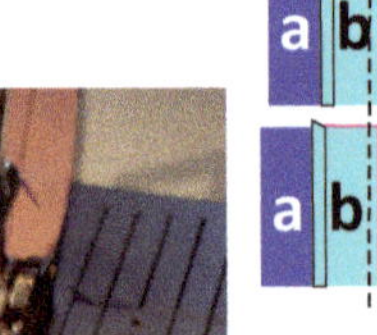

13 Open and finger-press seam allowances toward **a**. Join **abc** units to **d**'s. This will be trickier, because pink divided piece goes in seam-first. An awl will help you tuck the top seam allowance flap under the foot.

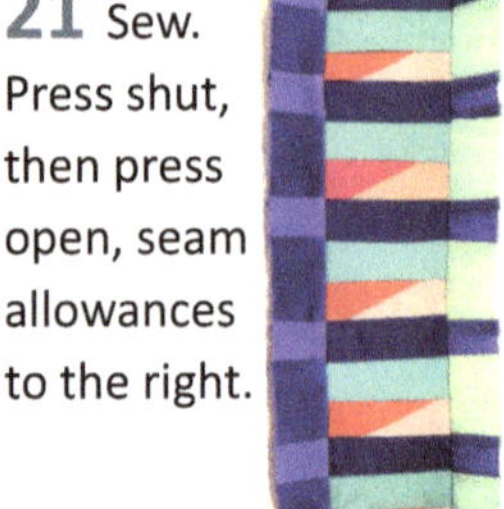
An awl helps

14 Keep going til you've completed both cols. 2 and 4. Press all seam allowances toward the building's top. They look like this. Set aside.

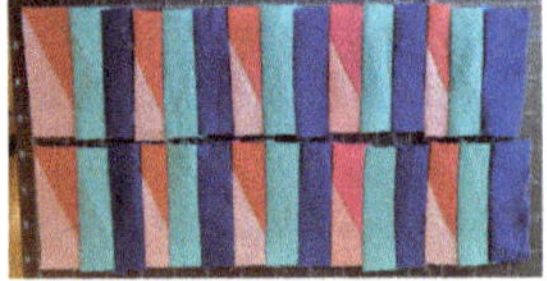

15 The pieces in cols. 1, 3 and 5 should still be in position, with the top of the building on the far right. We'll chain sew them like cols. 2 and 4.

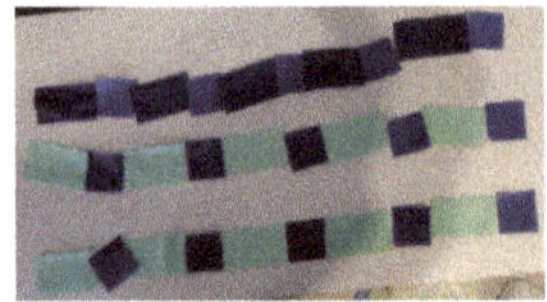

Start with the first piece on the right of col. 2 (a medium-blue cornerstone). Flip it onto the second piece (a short navy strip in col. 1.) Sew down the right edge. Without cutting threads, sew the far right cornerstone in column 3 to the neighboring light green strip; then do the same with column 5.

16 Sew until each column is finished. Now they look like this.

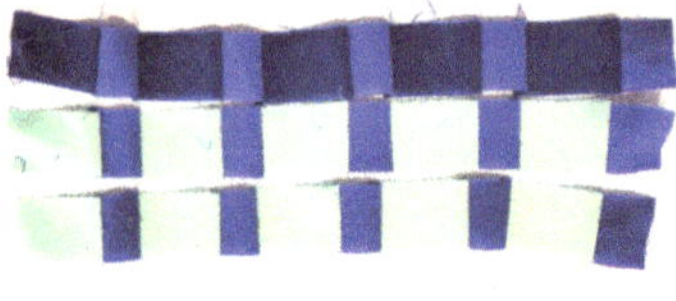

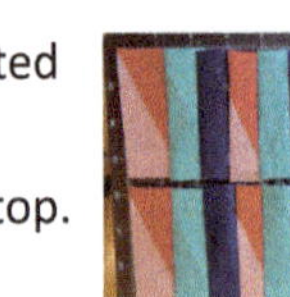

17 Place columns in position. On the left, col. 1 is next to col. 2. Flip col. 1 face down, on the left edge of col. 2, right. Match and pin col. 1's cornerstone seams with the seams above and below the navy horizontal strips in col. 2.

19 Flip col. 3 good side down onto col. 2. It looks like this, but will be easier to sew from the back of col. 2.

20 So flip everything over, and pin, matching cornerstone seams underneath with navy horizontals on top.

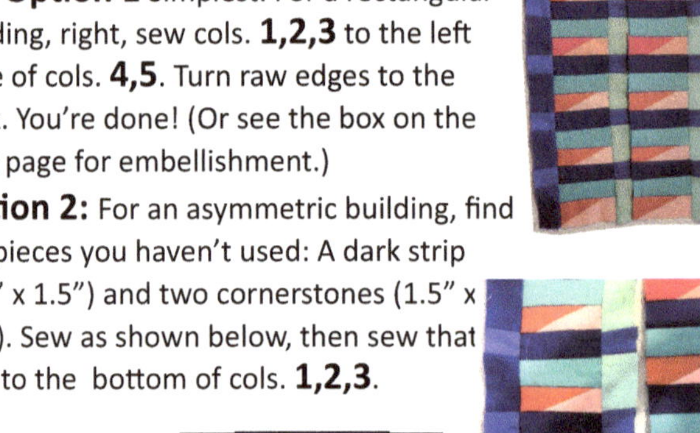

21 Sew. Press shut, then press open, seam allowances to the right.

22 Pin, then sew col. 5 to the right edge of col. 4.

23 **Option 1** Simplest. For a rectangular building, right, sew cols. **1,2,3** to the left edge of cols. **4,5**. Turn raw edges to the back. You're done! (Or see the box on the next page for embellishment.)

Option 2: For an asymmetric building, find the pieces you haven't used: A dark strip (3.5" x 1.5") and two cornerstones (1.5" x 1.5"). Sew as shown below, then sew that unit to the bottom of cols. **1,2,3**.

Cols. 1,2,3

Cols. 4,5

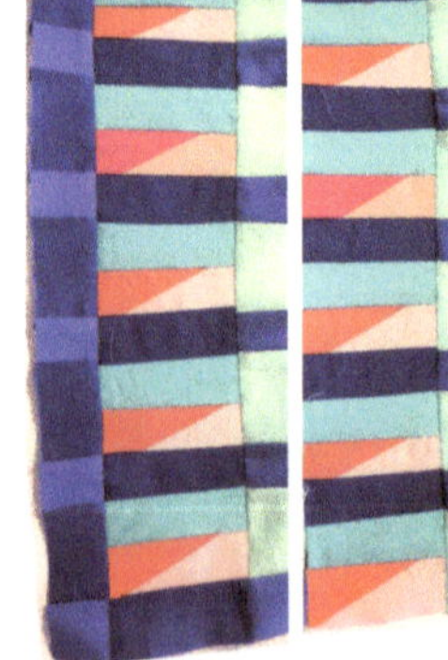

24 Don't sew the two units together yet! First press the top edge of lowest unit (cols. **4,5**), 1/4" to the back. (You don't have to press the top edge of cols **1,2,3** to the back yet – you can wait to the end to do that.)

(continued)

24 We'll match and pin the cornerstone seams on the far right of the cols. **1,2,3** unit, to the divided pink rectangles on the far left of the cols. **4,5** unit. The top of folded edge of cols. **4,5** will be one horizontal piece lower than the top edge of cols. **1,2,3** (under my hand in the photo).

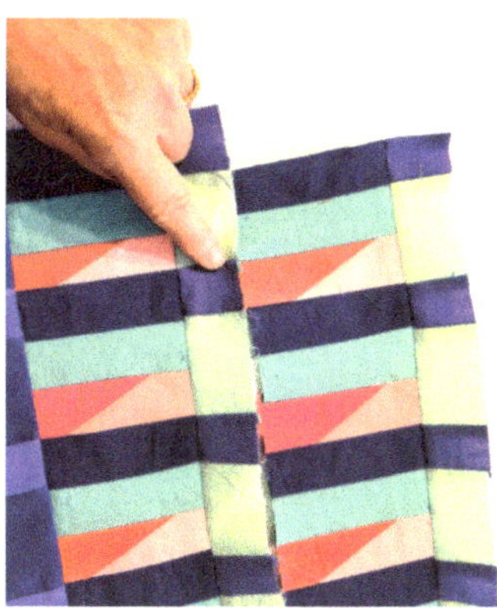

24 Flip **4,5** unit face down on the **1,2,3** unit as shown. Pin right edge, matching cornerstone seams (on bottom) with pink rectangle seams (on top).

25 Sew down the right edge. Start at **a**, just below the folded-back raw edge on top of **4,5**. Backstitch to the orange **b**'s dot, a hair below the fold at the top of unit **4,5.** Then sew straight down all the way to **c**. No need to backstitch there (though you can if you want to.) Here's what it looks like going through the machine.

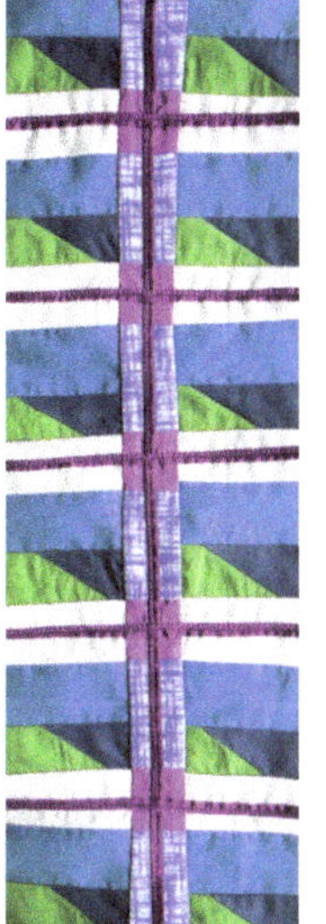

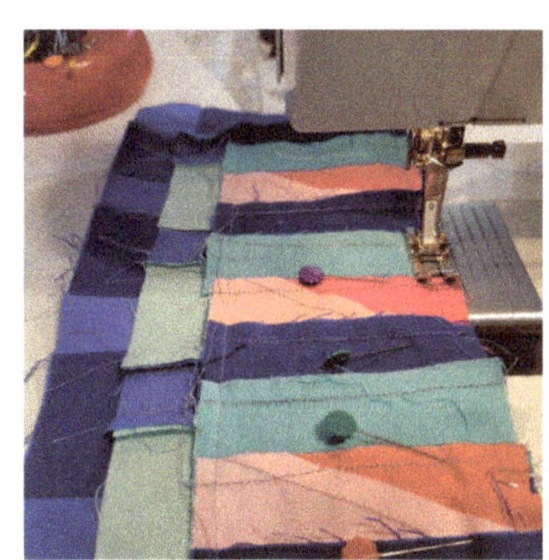

26 Press open. Here's the finished building! That flat roof was begging for a garden – I planted a giant strawberry on top, and the entrance to the treehouse, in the 'Nonsense Town' quilt on p. 10.

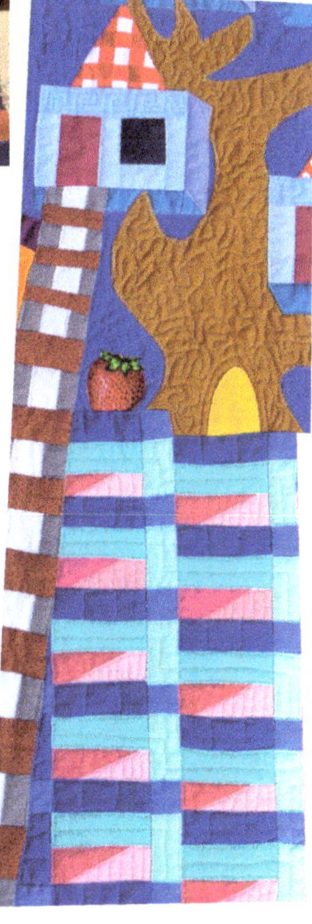

Design Option: Appliqué Folded Strips for Complexity and Texture

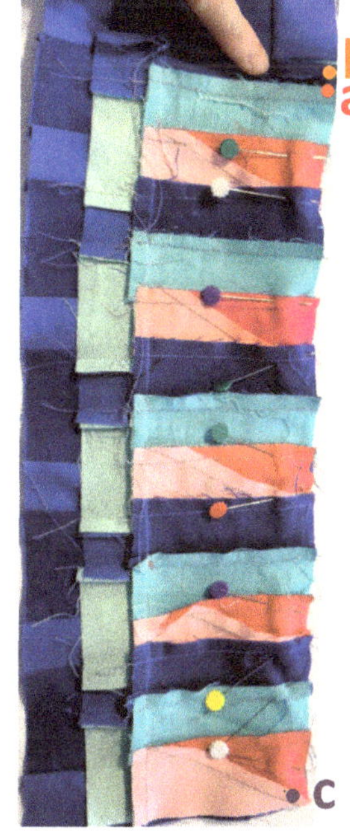

After finishing a version of the building in this chapter (without the side columns), I cut a bunch of dark purple strips to 1" wide. They don't have to be cut on the bias, because we're not curving them.

A Fold strips in half and press to create a crease down the middle. Then open it again.

B Fold side edges inward so they almost meet in the middle.

C Fold in half along the central crease.

D Finish your building, but don't turn outer edges under yet.

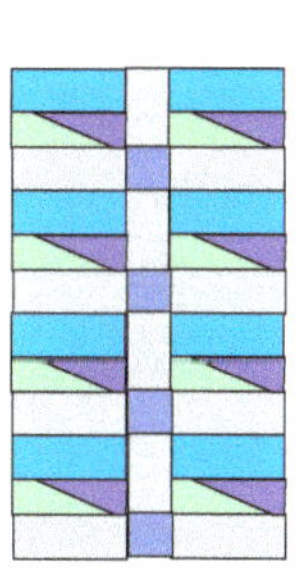

E Cut as many folded strips as you need for horizontals. Lengths should be full building width, raw edge to raw edge. Pin or glue in position. Sew along the top and bottom of each with a zigzag or decorative stitch. Ends are raw.

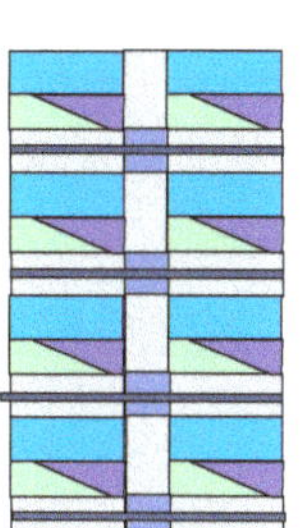

F Cut one more folded strip the full height of the building, raw edge to raw edge. Appliqué it down on both sides. Now all you have to do is turn the building's outside edges back, piecing or appliquéing it to another building.

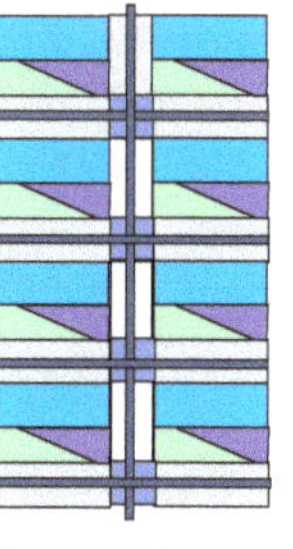

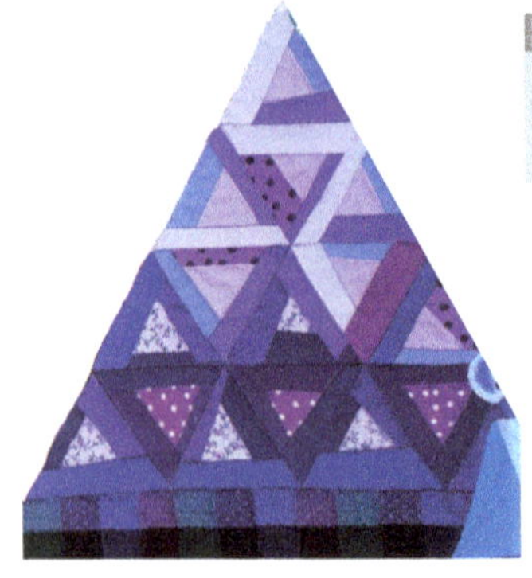

Pei Inspired Pyramid

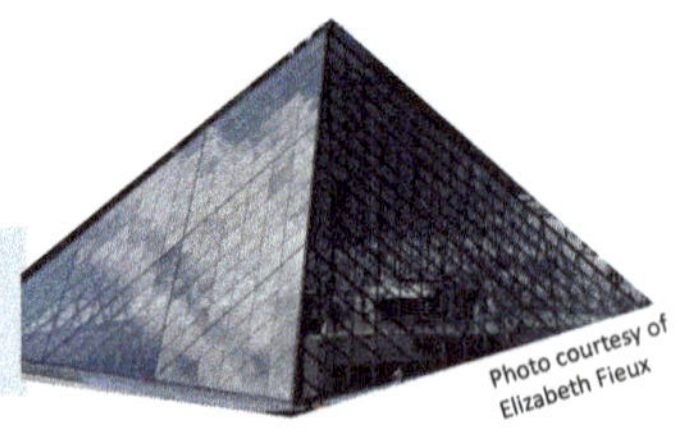

IM Pei's iconic Louvre pyramid is reflected by this structure. I put it in my 'Scrap City 2' quilt on p. 7. We'll use my improv paper piecing technique. Cut paper triangles, and do log cabin piecing on top. There's no need to mark the paper. For atmospheric perspective, I cut some logs and centers darker than others, and placed lighter ones higher in the pyramid.

As we piece on top of the paper, try to have your fabric pieces extend a little beyond the paper. This isn't seam allowance, and doesn't have to be perfectly consistent all the away around – it's a little extra wiggle room that will come in handy when we cut the triangles down to size.

1 You need sixteen 3.75" high equilateral paper triangles. **Either:** Print three copies of page 64 (do the size check). **Or,** draw them on lightweight paper with your triangular ruler, or a rotary ruler's 60 degree line.

2 Cut center fabric to 2.5" strips. Chop triangles from them, smaller than the paper triangles. Size needn't be precise, and you can use scissors. The first diagram shows approximate size difference between the paper and piece 1 triangles. It can vary.

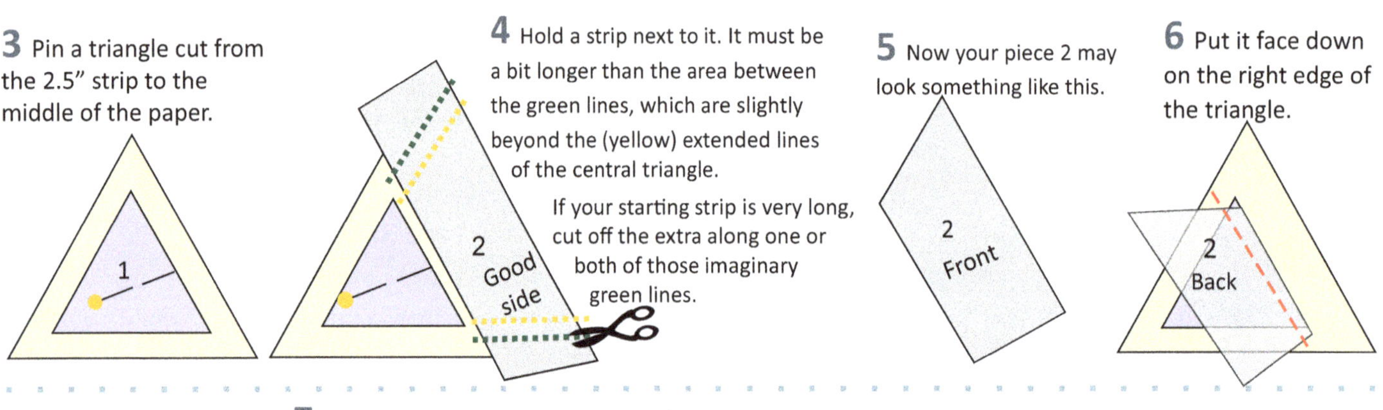

3 Pin a triangle cut from the 2.5" strip to the middle of the paper.

4 Hold a strip next to it. It must be a bit longer than the area between the green lines, which are slightly beyond the (yellow) extended lines of the central triangle.

If your starting strip is very long, cut off the extra along one or both of those imaginary green lines.

5 Now your piece 2 may look something like this.

6 Put it face down on the right edge of the triangle.

7 Test fold it open, leaving about 1/4" down, until it covers the paper between the two blue dotted extension lines of the central triangle. When it works, finger-press a crease into piece 2, (the red dotted line in figure 6), and shut it again.

8 Sew down the crease on the top piece (black dotted line below).

9 Press open. It's okay if the fabric extends beyond the paper triangle.

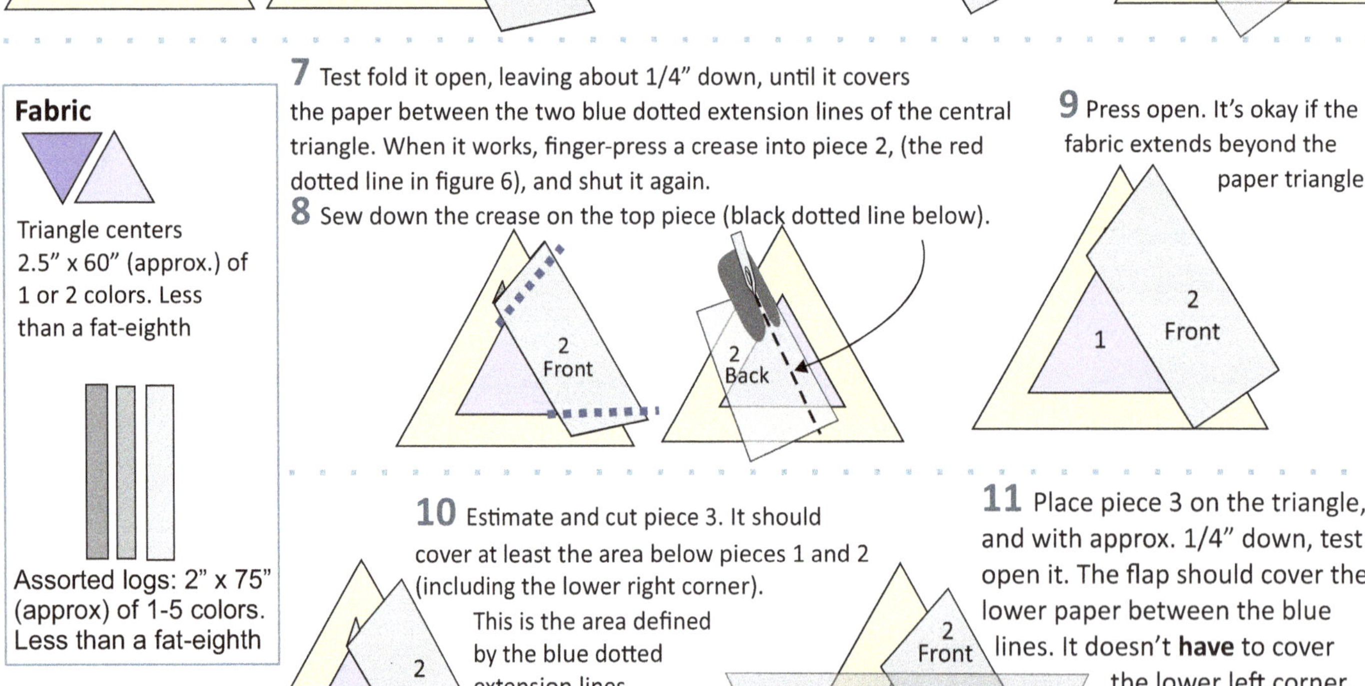

Fabric

Triangle centers 2.5" x 60" (approx.) of 1 or 2 colors. Less than a fat-eighth

Assorted logs: 2" x 75" (approx) of 1-5 colors. Less than a fat-eighth

10 Estimate and cut piece 3. It should cover at least the area below pieces 1 and 2 (including the lower right corner).

This is the area defined by the blue dotted extension lines.

11 Place piece 3 on the triangle, and with approx. 1/4" down, test open it. The flap should cover the lower paper between the blue lines. It doesn't **have** to cover the lower left corner, but it's okay if it does. When it works, sew on the crease (red).

(continued)

12 Press piece 3 open.

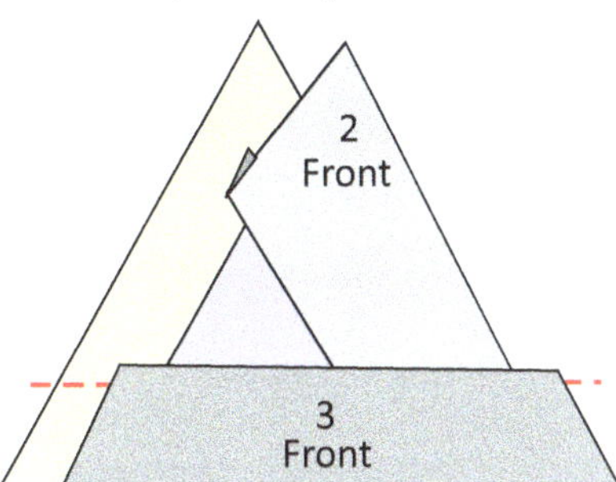

13 Audition piece 4. Test-open to make sure that, with 1/4" folded down, it will cover all the paper on the left, including both the upper and lower left corners. (Even if piece 3 covers that lower left corner, you need piece 4 on top of it to do the same.) When you find a position that works, finger-press a crease into piece 4 that works.

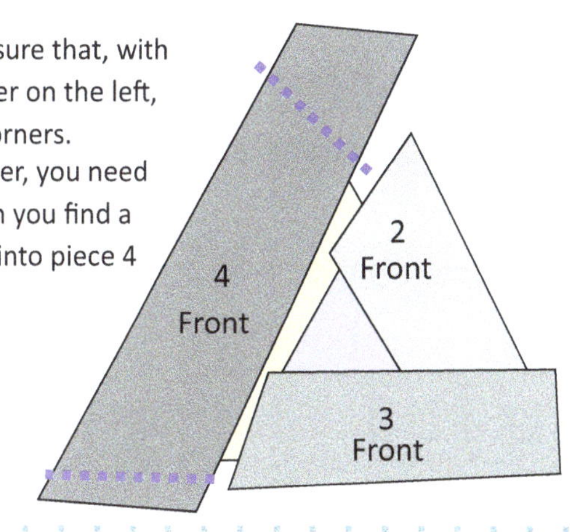

14 Sew on the crease that worked.

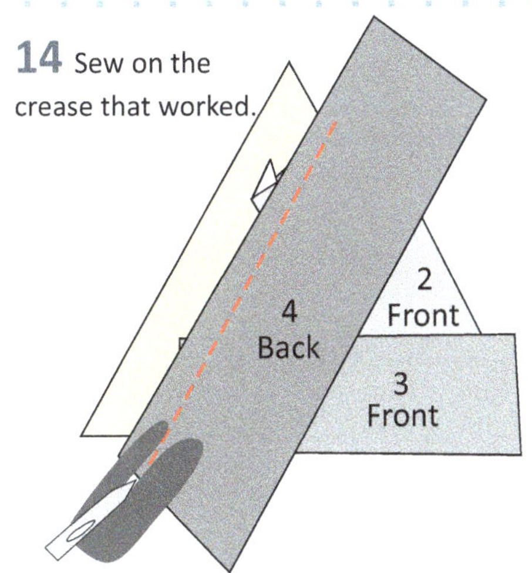

15 Trim the triangle back to 3.75" high, by either cutting along the outlines of the paper on the back, or using an equilateral triangle template (if you have one) and a rotary cutter on the front.

(Put tape 3.75" down from template's tip to help you cut multiples quickly and safely.) If your template has a blunt tip, measure only 3.5" down from the tip to where you place the tape.

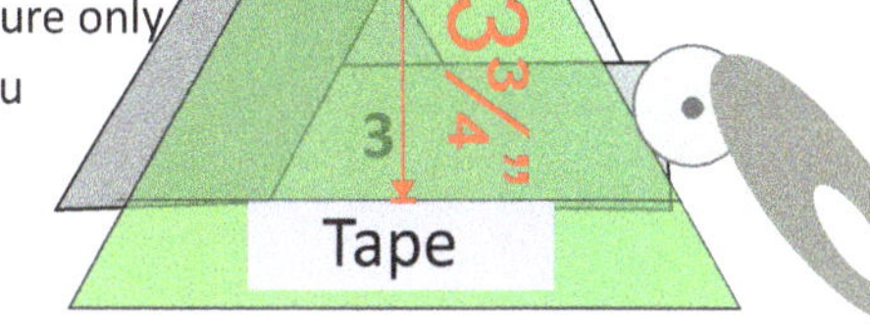

16 Arrange in rows as shown below. For atmospheric perspective, put lightest-colored triangles towards the top.

17 Mark the right edge of each row with a safety pin, because it's very easy to get confused. Starting at the bottom, row **A**, flip triangle 1 onto 2, and sew down the seam, no backstitching required. Open up and press seam. We can start by pressing all seam allowances in this row to the right. Alternate seam pressing direction with each row, as shown.

18 When each row is together, remove the safety pins. Flip row **B** face down on row one, match and pin tips of triangles together, then pin between tips. Sew across, removing pins before the presser foot reaches them. Add row **C** to the top of **B** next, and finally the top piece. I like to press all the seam allowances downward, toward the wider rows.

The last step is to press the sides and maybe the bottom inward 1/4". Because of the odd shape, this building will probably have to be appliquéd to other buildings.

Small safety pin helps keep track of the far right edge of each row.

Row C
3 triangles
Press seam allowances right

Row B
5 triangles
Press seam allowances left

Row A
7 triangles
Press seam allowances right

Three full size 3 3/4" high equilateral triangles (check height on your printout)

3¾"

3¾"

3¾"

Pei Triangle Tower

This building was inspired by another triangle-heavy IM Pei building, the Bank of China Tower in Hong Kong. Its sides feature triangles and other polygons. In my loose interpretation, I sewed one side of dark pink equilateral triangles to light pink strips.

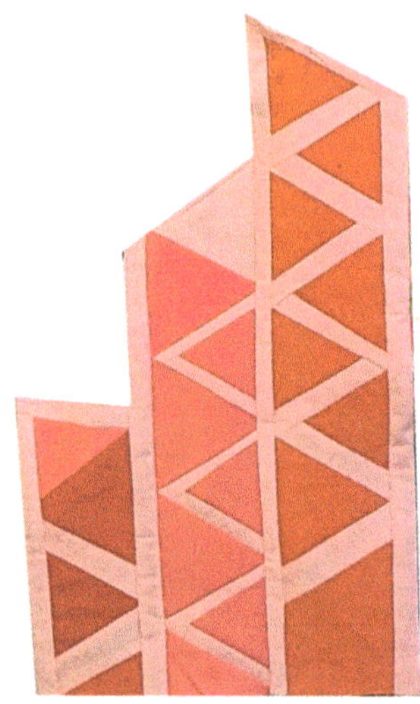

1 Start by making 7 equilateral triangles. (I like to start with a 3.75" high strip, then cut across it at 60" angles to create 7 complete triangles; PLUS a polygon as the ground floor.) These are the same size as the triangles in the previous project, on the left side of this page, so you can use the same template if you like.

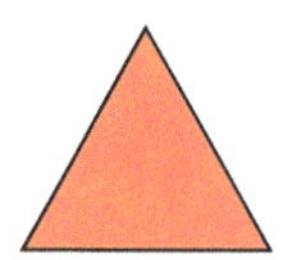

2 Sew a 1.5" strip to one side and cut the two sides along the dotted line, so you now have a larger triangle.

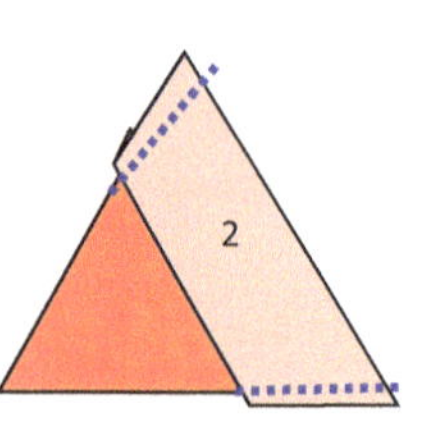

3 Join triangles as shown. That's one tower. Add a long vertical strip to each from the same 1.5" strip.

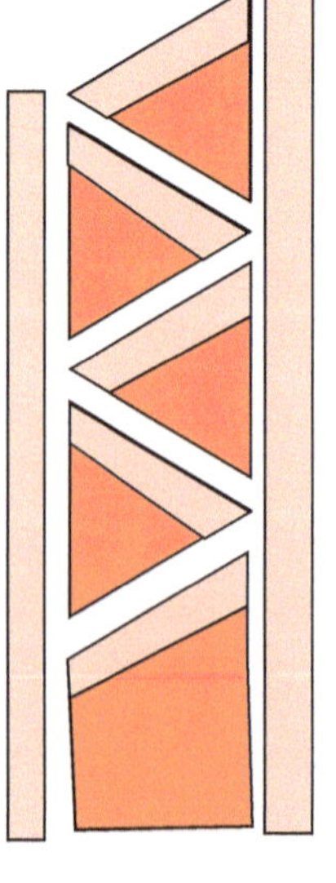

4 For more towers, I used a slightly smaller triangle size, and then went with darker, even smaller triangles for the shortest tower. This structure wound up in 'Nonsense Town,' p. 10.

See also Rivka Hamdani's unique version of this tower, using floral fabric, on p. 11.

Towering Irregular Triangles (and other shapes)

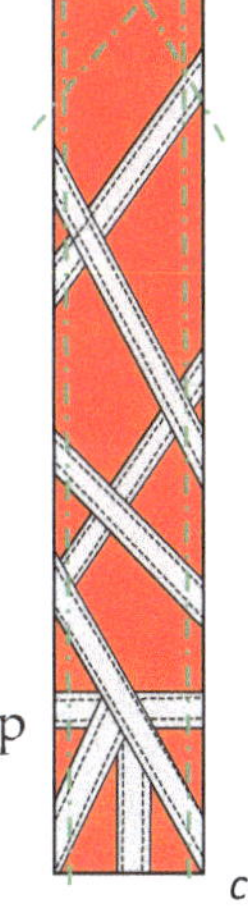

53 W. 53rd Street, NYC.

On the far left is my photo of 53 W. 53rd St. in NYC. Completed in 2020, it's super-tall (1050 feet), and super-luxury (up to $65 million per condo!) It also houses gallery space for the Museum of Modern Art. The thick surface lines, forming irregular triangles aren't just artistic – they're a "diagrid,"concrete-and-rebar girders that carry the building's weight. The random lines liven up a grid of rectangular windows. The building was designed by Jean Nouvel, but I've seen others like it (like IM Pei's Bank of China Tower in Hong Kong.)

I've made two versions so far – one with bias appliqué (left), and one with pieced inserts (next page). Appliqué was so much easier than piecing! Here's how I did it.

1 Cut a rectangle from a geometric print, 5.5" x 20". Press well, ideally with starch. Pin to tear-away stabilizer, or a piece of thin paper, a little larger than the building, to prevent stitching from bunching up the background.

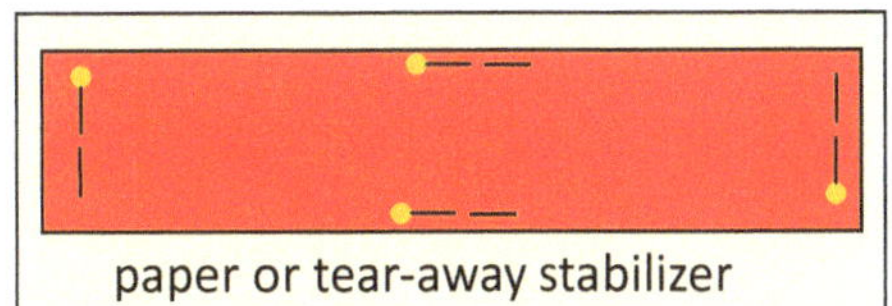

2 Cut about 65" of 1" strips. I cut mine on a 45 degree angle to make it bias; but since these aren't curves, you could cut them on the straight-of-grain. Fold long edges to the back 1/4" and press well; steam or starch helps.

3 Pin pieces 1 and 2 in position, with edges sticking out a little past the building's edges.

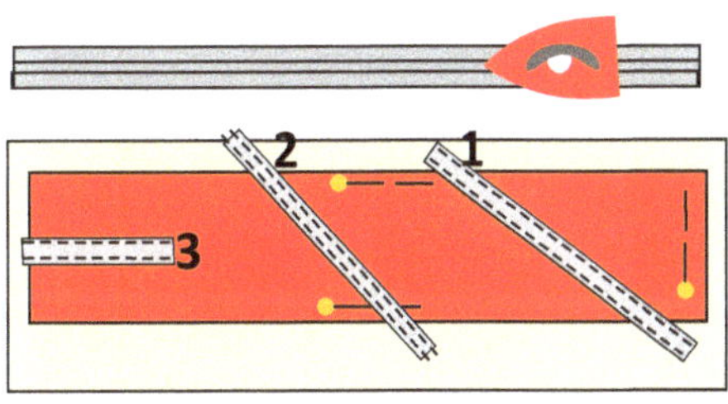

Finished size: 19" x 5"

Building fabric
Fat-quarter or quarter-yard

Girders.
1" x 65" total.
Can be cut from 1/4 yard, a fat-quarter, or a 2.5" strip.

4 Use girder-matching thread and ideally, a zipper foot. (Second best: An open-toe appliqué foot, with which my lines are a little wobblier). Line up the right edge of the zipper foot with the right turned edge of the strip. Sew with a straight stitch JUST inside the edge, about 1/8". After the first edge, turn everything to sew the other edge from the opposite direction.

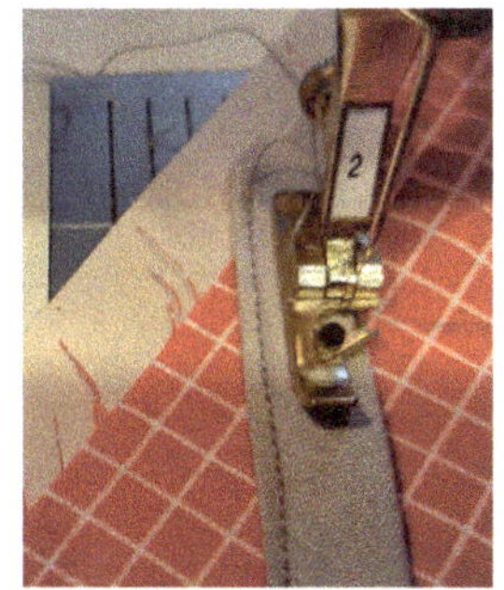

5 Add piece 4 (crossing the two earlier pieces). Keep going in order shown, or make up your own order. if a small hill forms in your strip ahead of the presser foot, ease it away, using fingers (carefully) to push excess under the presser foot a little bit at a time. Here's the view when adding piece 7, and then piece 8.

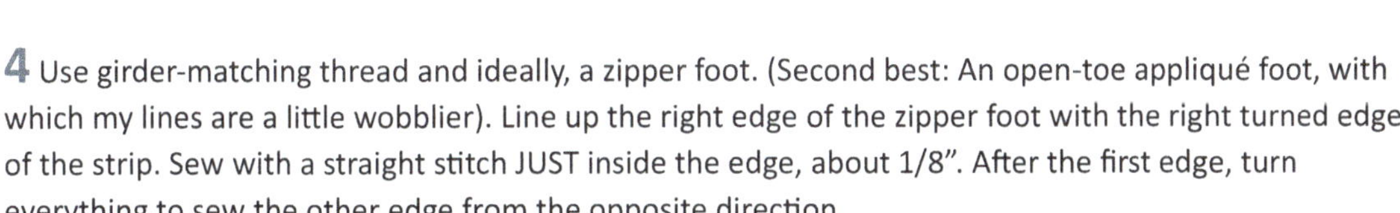

6 Remove paper/stabilizer from back. Trim girder ends even with the building's raw edges.

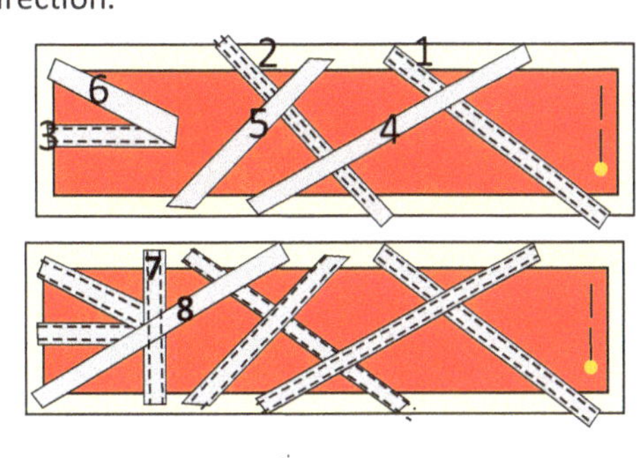

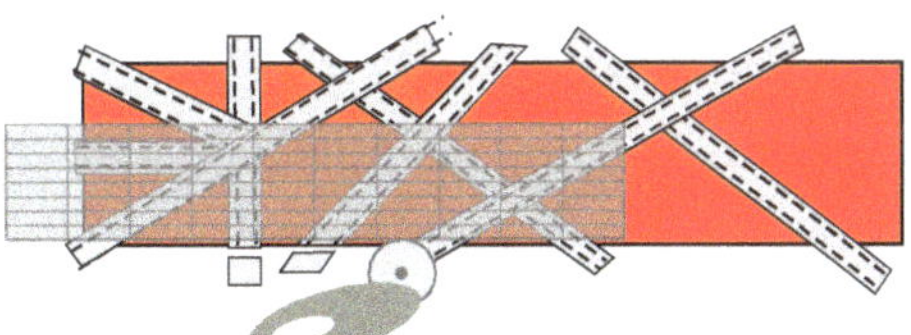

7 Turn sides 1/4" inward, and turn top edges back at a sharp, asymmetrical angle. (Green lines are fold lines.)

continued

Piece it?

How about piecing the building on the previous page instead of appliqué? I tried it here (with admittedly hideous scrap fabric.) I started with a 20" x 6" brown rectangle, and 1.25" blue strips. I made a long angled cut (1), inserted a blue strip, and sewed the sides to it. Then I made cut 2, and stitched in another strip – and so forth. I usually enjoy piecing more than appliqué, and this was a lot of fun – but it was also much trickier to keep the strips (or any geometric pattern on the fabric) lined up. Look at how the pieces of strip 2 misaligned after I broke them apart by adding strips 3 and 6! If you like this wonkier look, and enjoy doing it this way, go for it!

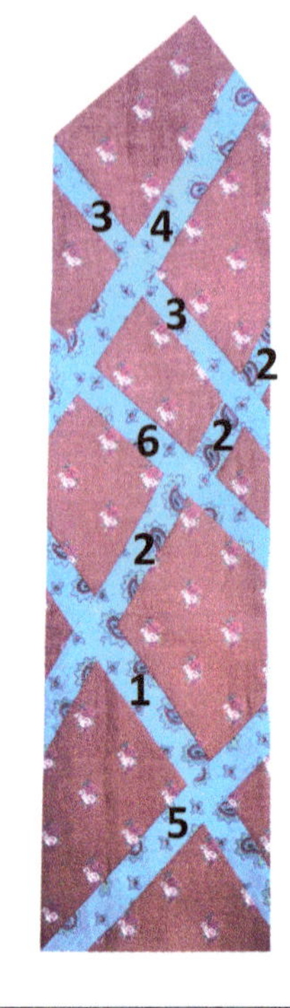

Straight Line Criss Cross

Straight Line Criss Cross The blue building is my version of Chicago's Hancock tower. Each orange strip is cut on the straight-of-grain (No curves, so it doesn't have to be bias-cut.) The building was cut in two steps, like method 2 above. Cuts were made straight across with a rotary cutter and ruler (Make one cut, insert the straight-cut strip; make the opposite cut, and insert the second straight-cut strip.) The wider your inserts, the less likely the building will shrink as you add them.

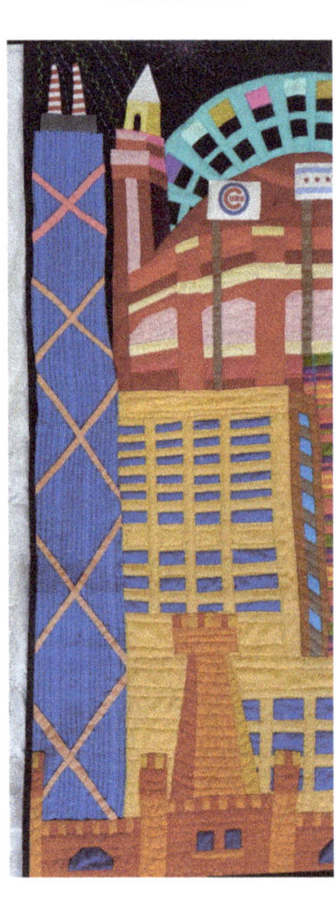

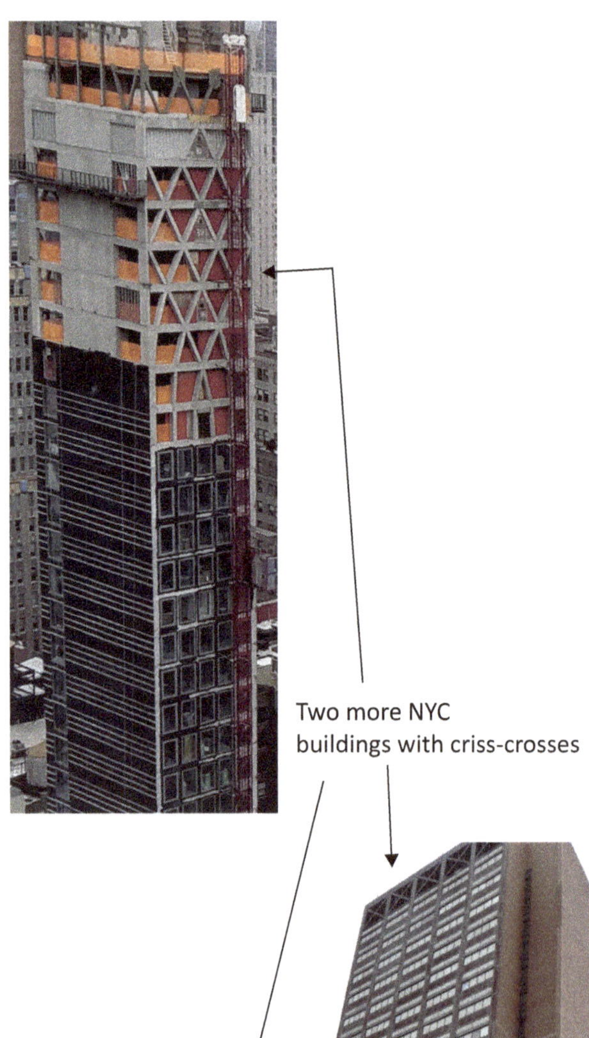

Two more NYC buildings with criss-crosses

Isosceles Triangle Inspiration

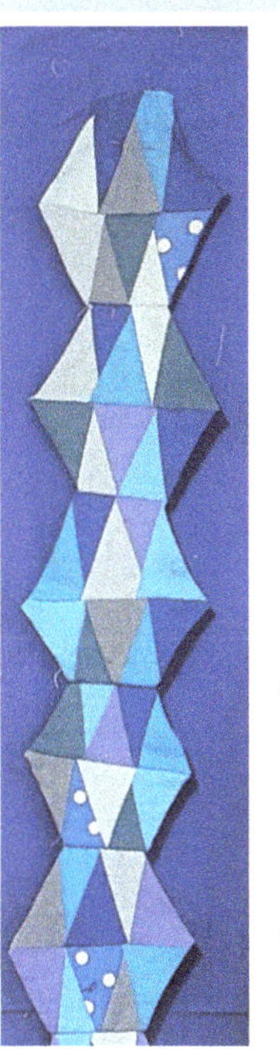
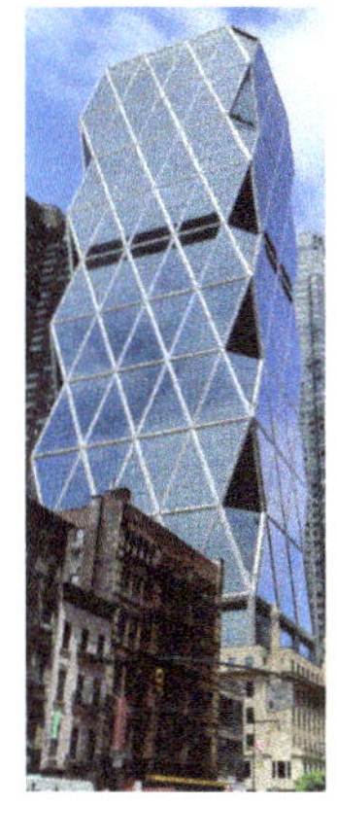

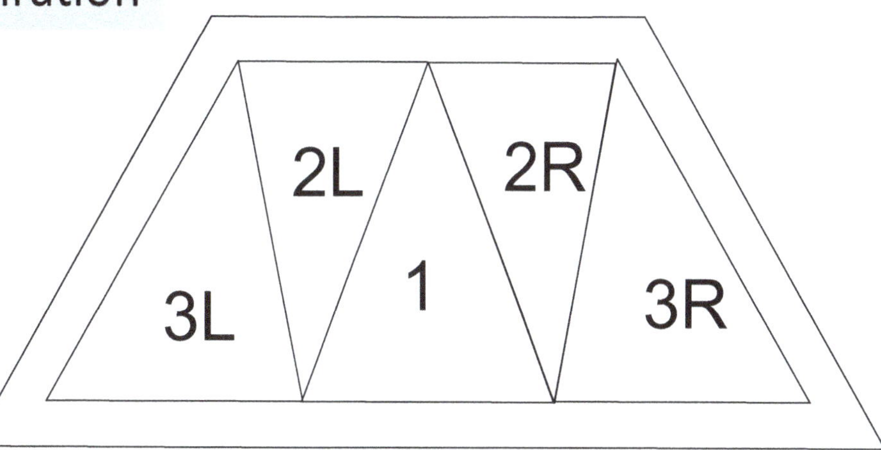

The Hearst Tower in NYC is a wowzer, a pillar of steel and glass isosceles triangles. I've tried many ways to capture it* and here's one – FPP, foundation paper piecing.

I used 8 shades of one hue (blue), most solids, one a polka dot. You only need a little of each.

Print out this page, cut out each half-hexagon just beyond its outer black lines, and sew on the inside, with fabric on the blank side, as in regular foundation paper piecing pattern (FPP). Or, improv stitch-and-flip triangles on top of each half-hexagon. Or, use the inner triangle pieces as cutting templates (adding 1/4" seam allowance to each).

Make as many pairs of halves as you want floors. As you finish each half, lay it in position. Avoid same fabrics touching (unless it's just their tips, not bases). For FPP: After each section is pieced, trim everything to outer lines; remove paper, and sew units into pairs, widest bases together. Stack those pairs and sew. When it's time to turn edges 1/4" under, you may have to rip a few stitches at "innie" seam ends – sorry about that!

*A different approach is used in my book "Quilted New York." There I use just one iscosceles triangle template, and conventionally piece a tower.

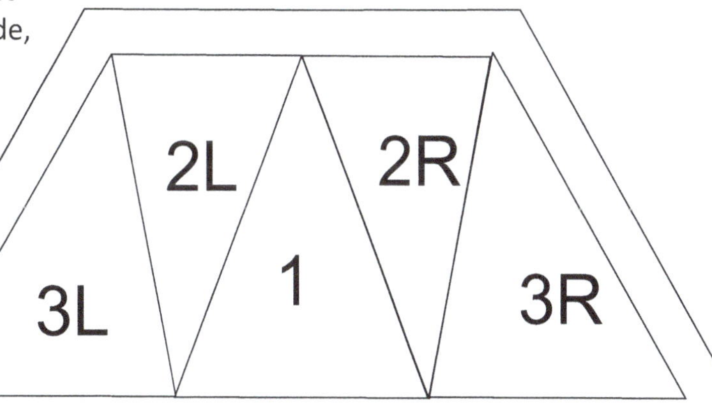

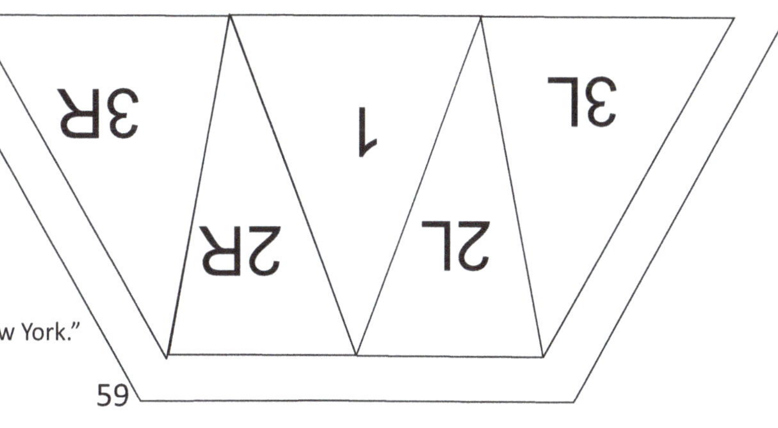

From Starry Wall to Glass Ceiling

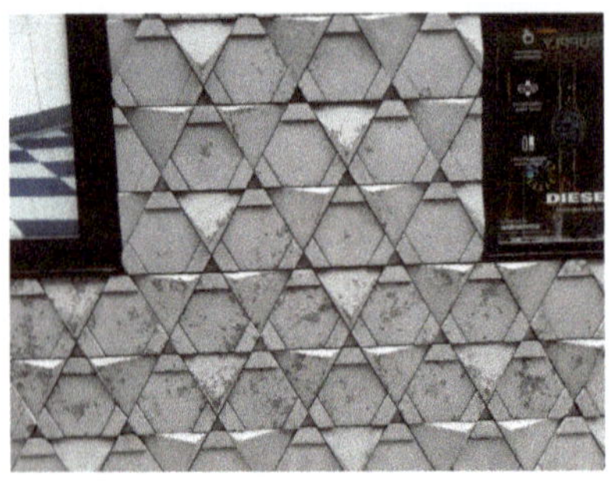

Inspiration doesn't just come from buildings – it comes from walls, sidewalks, streets, signs, grates and everything else.

I found this fascinating tile wall on several NYC buildings. It's full of 3-D texture, with protruding bumps and angles, plus tessellated hexagons, triangles and half hexagons.

Back home, I traced the photo to try to understand its construction. I initially thought it was made up of triangles – but I couldn't make that work, as you can see in this early attempt.

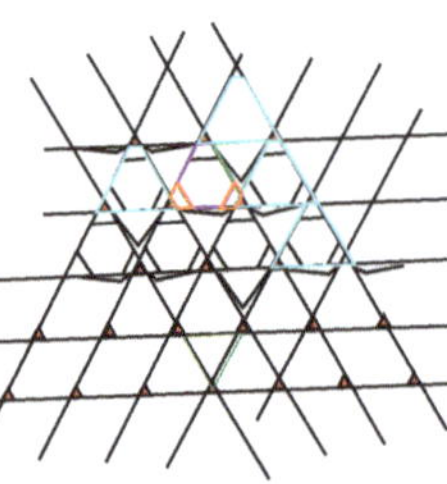

Eventually, I figured out that the basic unit was this diamond. I made it into a foundation paper piecing pattern. Full size patterns are on the next page.

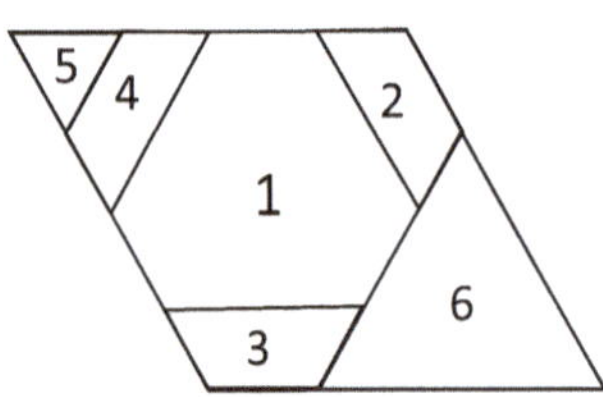

I foundation paper pieced 9 of the diamonds, and joined them. Pieces 2, 3 and 4 use the same (khaki) fabric here.

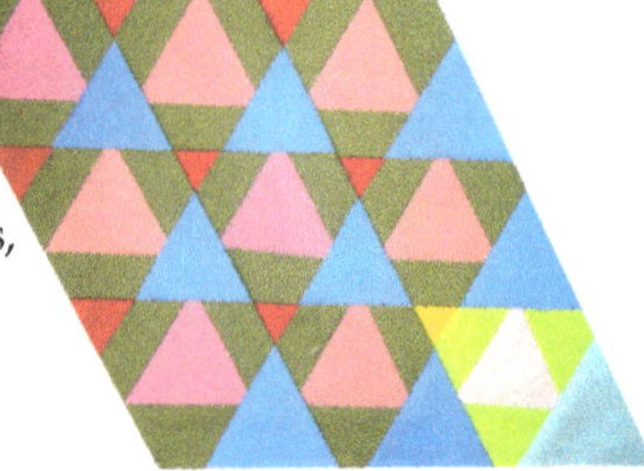

It became the ceiling of a slanted abstract modern building. Here's the finished building. I improvised a strip of sharp triangles as the base. The jagged triangles on bottom remind me of the Oculus Transportation Hub at the World Trade Center, and the roof looks something like the new Seattle Public Library! (The broccoli represents a fantasy rooftop garden!) See it in position in my Nonsense Town quilt, p. 10.

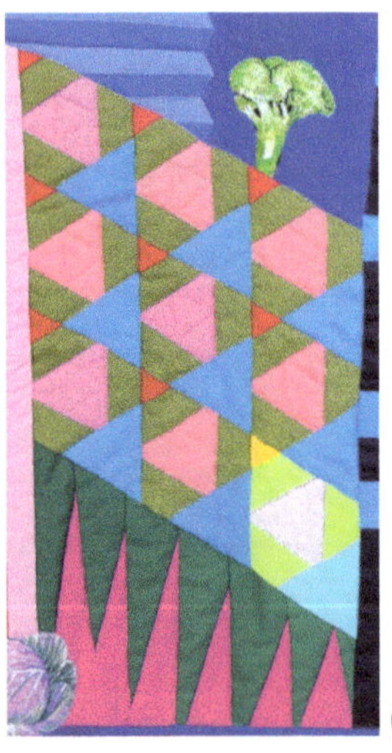

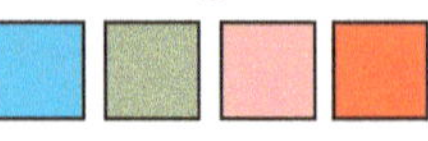

Finished size: 7.5" x 10"

Fabric

Fat-eighth of these, to make eight diamonds

Plus scraps of these, to make one diamond:

1 Print out two copies of the patterns on p. 61, and one copy of p. 62. Do the size checks in red.

2 Cut out each pattern just a little beyond its outer black seam allowance lines (1/8" is fine, needn't be precise.)

3 If you've never foundation paper pieced, find a simple tutorial online. You'll place oversized fabric pieces on the blank side of the paper, and sew directly on the printed side's inside lines. Fabrics' outer edges should reach to or extend a bit beyond the paper on all sides.

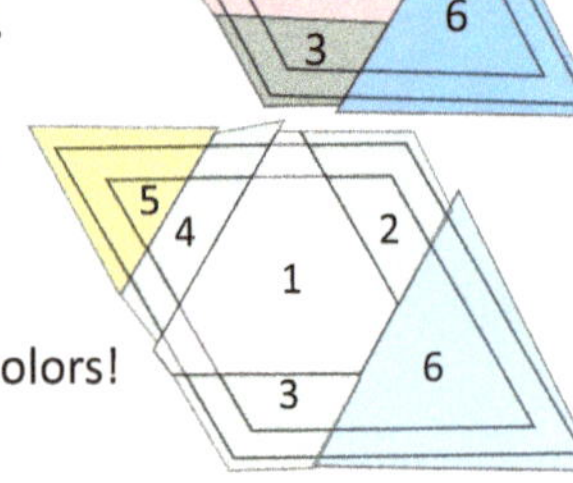

4 Pin piece 1 to the middle of the pattern, and add pieces around it. You'll need at least four different fabrics. (This is the view from the front fabric side, if fabric was transparent!) For fun, I made a sunspot – one block with lighter colors!

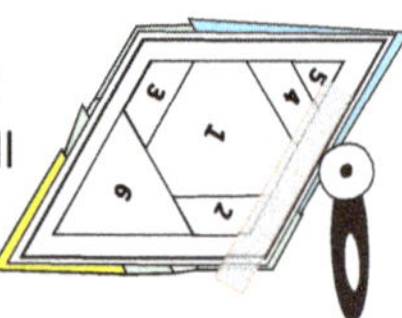

5 Trim excess paper and fabric from the back, cutting on the pattern outline. Don't rip out the paper yet! The printed lines will be helpful for alignment.

6 Arrange blocks in three rows. I put the light block on the lower right, but yours can go anywhere you like.

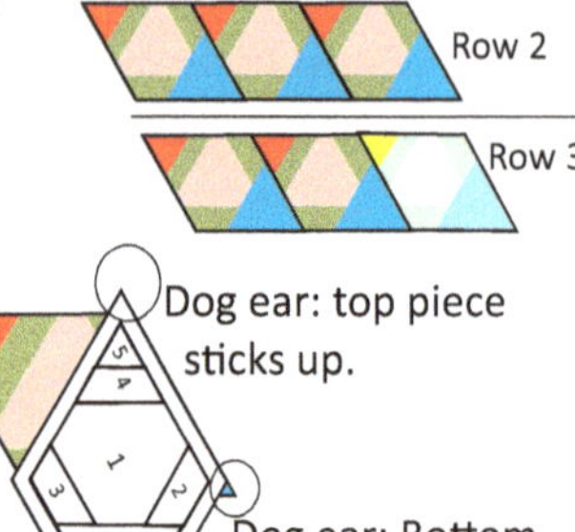

7 Sew each 3-diamond row together. Starting on left bottom, flip second piece onto the first. It will looks like this, with two dog ears. Sew beginning to end, and press seam allowances open. Continue like this to complete each row.

8 Flip middle row face down on bottom row. Pin vertically through the top printed corners of the top diamonds, to align rows.

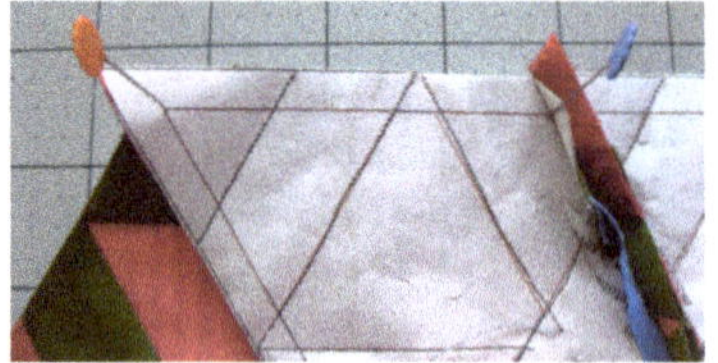

9 Place more pins flat. Remove vertical pins. Sew across the edge, permanently stitching the seam allowances open.

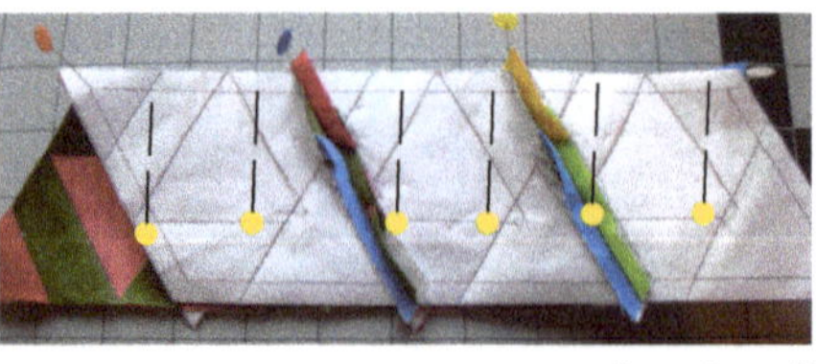

(continued)

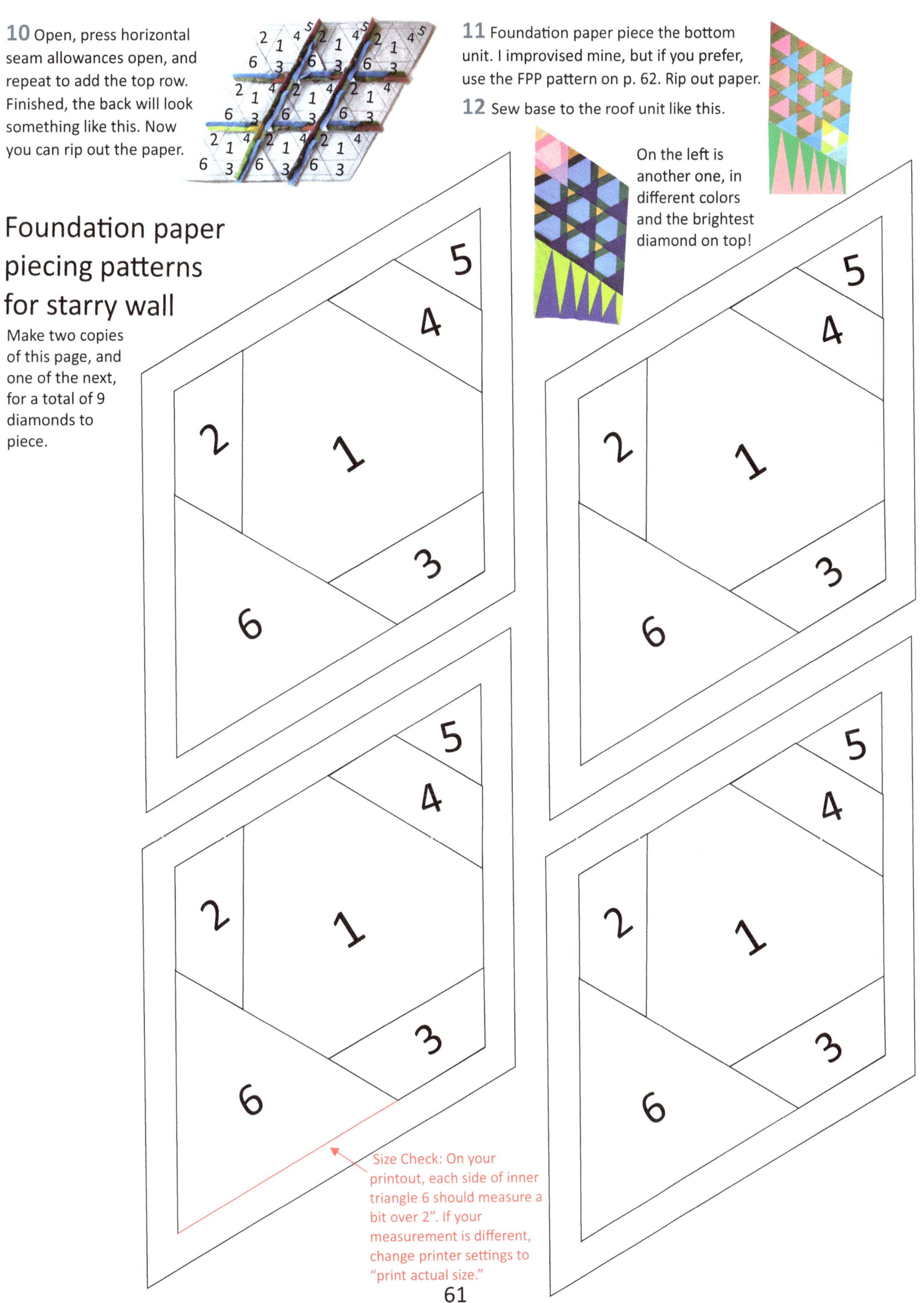

10 Open, press horizontal seam allowances open, and repeat to add the top row. Finished, the back will look something like this. Now you can rip out the paper.

Foundation paper piecing patterns for starry wall

Make two copies of this page, and one of the next, for a total of 9 diamonds to piece.

11 Foundation paper piece the bottom unit. I improvised mine, but if you prefer, use the FPP pattern on p. 62. Rip out paper.

12 Sew base to the roof unit like this.

On the left is another one, in different colors and the brightest diamond on top!

Size Check: On your printout, each side of inner triangle 6 should measure a bit over 2". If your measurement is different, change printer settings to "print actual size."

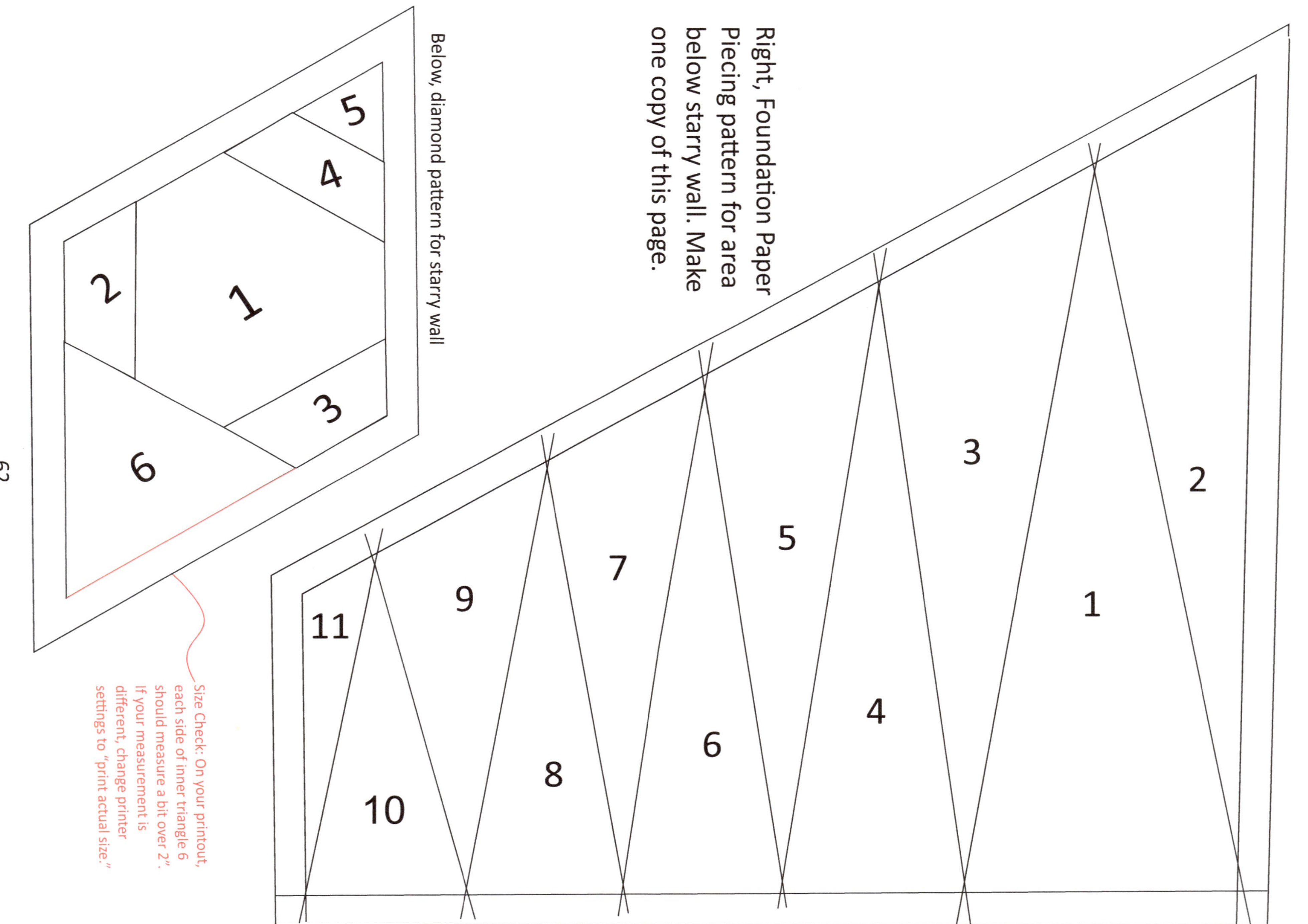

Right, Foundation Paper Piecing pattern for area below starry wall. Make one copy of this page.
Below, diamond pattern for starry wall
2
1
3
4
5
6
7
8
9
10
11
5
4
1
3
2
6
Size Check: On your printout, each side of inner triangle 6 should measure a bit over 2". If your measurement is different, change printer settings to "print actual size."

Curve It, Like Gehry

I made the fantasy building in the lower right corner *before* I saw Frank Gehry's 8 Spruce St. in NYC, below left, with its wild stainless steel ripples. Gehry's style is called "Deconstructivist," ("unpredictability and controlled chaos"); or "Postmodernism" ("playful"). What a coincidence! Playful controlled chaos is what improv quilters like me live for! Another example below: Ellipse Tower in Jersey City, with ripples formed by balconies and windows (not designed by Gehry). This page features an easy improv curve piecing technique.

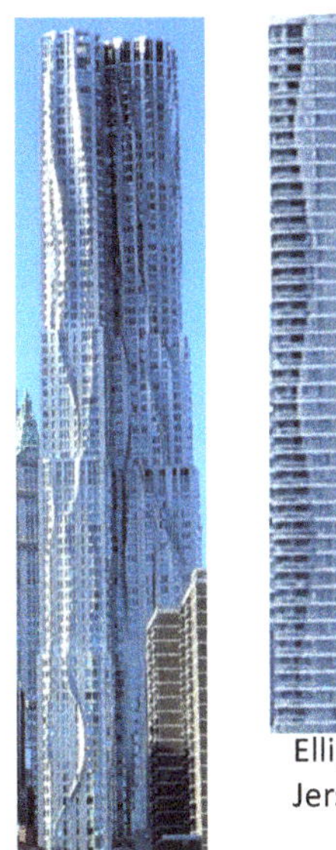

Ellipse Tower, Jersey City, NJ

8 Spruce Street, by Frank Gehry

Design Option 1, right
Make 3 or 4 different "blocks" using steps 1-9. Stack, with the lightest and shortest toward the top. Piece and/or appliqué together. Can also serve as a river.

1 Cut three strips 3"(or more) x 15".

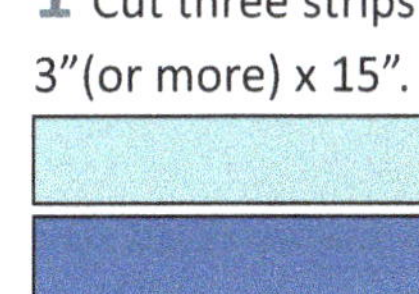

2 Overlap bottom two strips about 2". Fold and finger-press a crease in the top (light) one, on top of the dark strip's bottom edge.

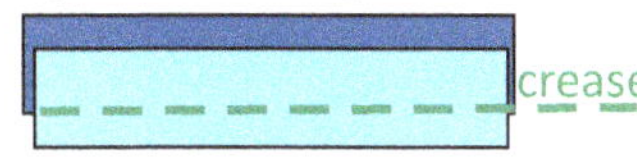

3 Cut a gentle curve in the area between the crease on bottom, and the highest edge of the top (light) strip.

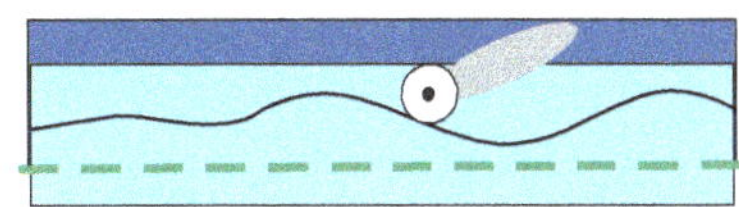

4 We'll only use the largest top and bottom pieces. (Not the two narrower pieces.)

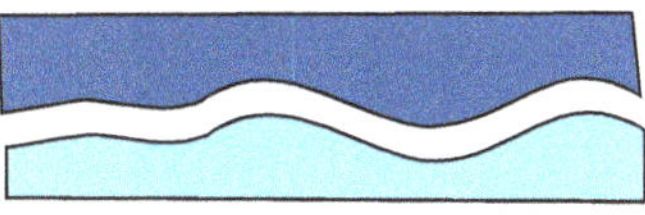

5 Don't pin! Place top piece at an angle so where you start is 1/4" in from the right edge on both levels. Take a few stitches. Stop, needle down. Bring top piece's raw edge even with the bottom piece's raw edge again, *just in front of the presser foot.* (Sometimes it matches for several inches; sometimes much less). Do a few more stitches. Plant needle. Adjust strips to match edges again. Sew to the end like this, stopping often.

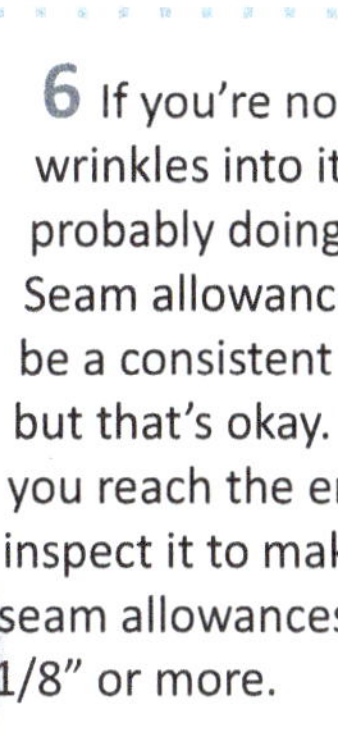

6 If you're not sewing wrinkles into it, you're probably doing it right! Seam allowance won't be a consistent 1/4", but that's okay. When you reach the end, inspect it to make sure seam allowances are 1/8" or more.

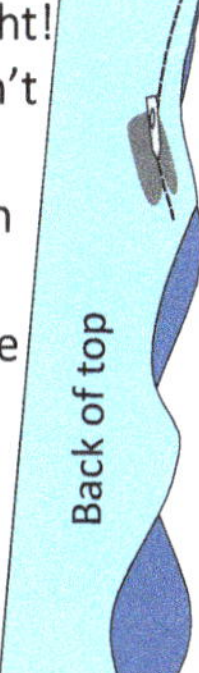

7 Open pieces. They'll tell you which direction to press seam allowances (They usually want to go toward whichever piece was on top). Press well, with lots of water/steam. It will flatten!

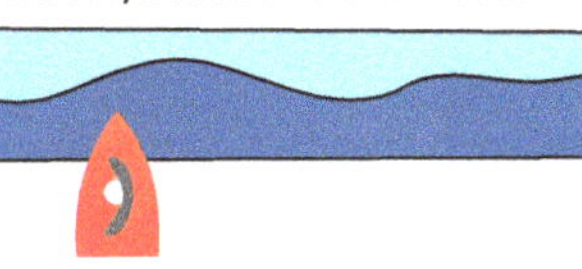

8 Place the set on top of a third strip, with about 2" of overlap. Finger-press a crease into the middle strip, where the bottom of the new strip falls. Cut another gentle curve between the crease and the top edge of the middle strip.

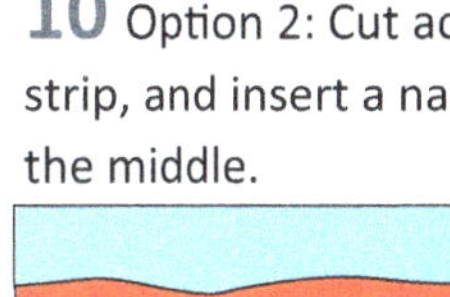

9 Sew together as in step 5. Press. It looks like this. You can add a fourth strip the same way as before. Then make some shorter ones. Stack vertically, as in option 1 on the left. Or...

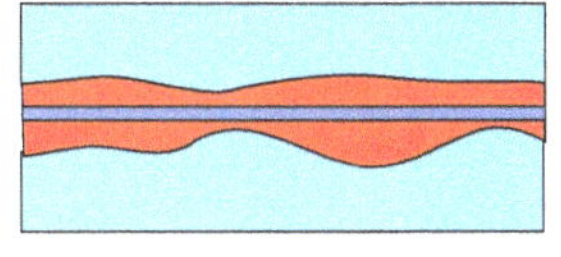

10 Option 2: Cut across the middle strip, and insert a narrow straight strip in the middle.

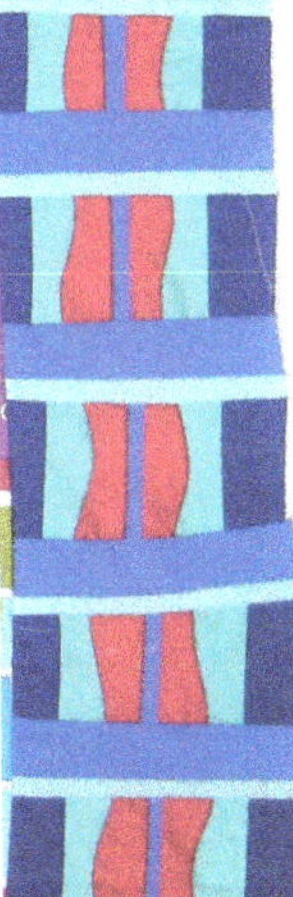

11 Option 3: Make horizontal cuts. For perspective, cut each section shorter as you go upward.

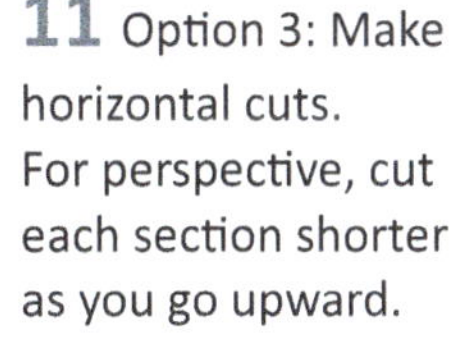

12 Inset horizontal strips. Option: Make those strips shorter as they rise, too.

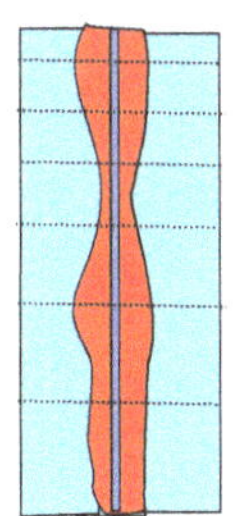

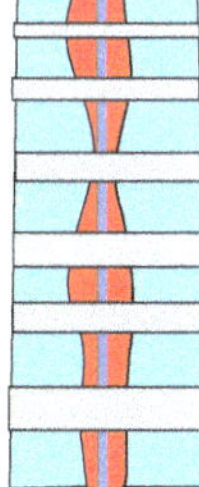

Right, this building was made with gradually shorter sections moving up (from step 11), but same-height insertions (from step 12). It's in 'Scrap City 1' on p. 7.

Pieced or Appliquéd Curves

The easiest route to curves is **fusible raw-edge appliqué**. Press web behind fabric, and cut out any curvy shape. Zigzag over raw edges. I do this for sharp curves. But for gentle curves, like in the buildings below, I use two other methods, both requiring bias-cut strips, both producing turned edges.

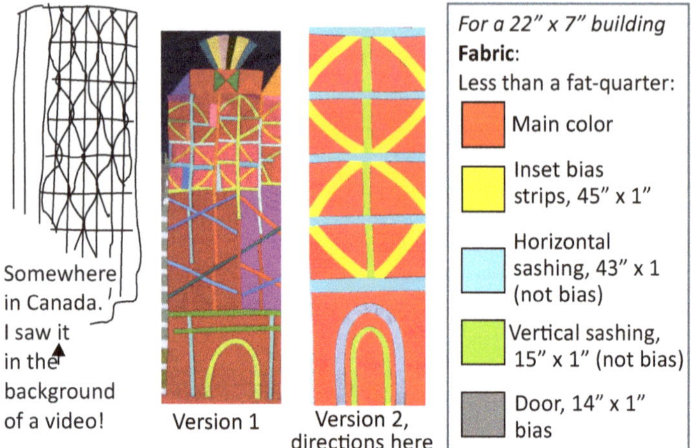

Somewhere in Canada. I saw it in the background of a video!

Version 1

Version 2, directions here

For a 22" x 7" building
Fabric:
Less than a fat-quarter:

Main color

Inset bias strips, 45" x 1"

Horizontal sashing, 43" x 1 (not bias)

Vertical sashing, 15" x 1" (not bias)

Door, 14" x 1" bias

Pieced bias-cut curves

This is how I made the tops of versions 1 and 2 above. It's a disciplined variation of the improv method on the previous page.

1 Cut eight 4" x 4" squares in the main color.

2 Take one. Fold and press it from one corner to the opposite corner. Repeat in the other direction. Unfold. On one crease, measure 1/2" out from the central intersection, and mark a dot there.

3 Cut a curve starting at a corner, through the 1/2" mark (or close), and traveling to the opposite corner. Now you have two pieces, one with an outward curve, one with an inward curve.

4 Cut eight 5.25" x 1.25" bias strips (yellow). (See step 15 for image of bias-cutting.) Press one in half to crease its center (blue line). Pin it to the outward curve side, matching its center with the underlying half-square's central crease.

6 Sew 1/4" from the raw edges (black dotted line). Clip into seam allowance every 1/2" or so, stopping just before the seam.

7 Press strip open, using steam. Press seam allowances under the strip.

8 Place inward half-square face-down on the strip. Match centers. Pin. Line up the rest of the top piece's curved edge with the underlying piece's curved edge, and pin more.

9 Sew 1/4" from the edge. Clip. Press seam allowances back under the strip.

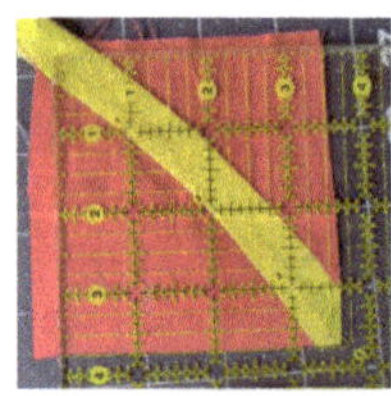

10 Unit is probably wonky. Trim it square. The largest square I could cut was 3.5" x 3.5", so that's what I did; you may need a different size.

11 Repeat steps 2-10 to make eight units. Lay out pieces like this.

12 Cut four vertical sashing strips (green) to 1" x 3.5" (or the same height as your squares.) It doesn't have to be bias-cut. Lay it in position. Sew each of the four rows of three pieces together.

13 Cut three horizontal (blue) strips 7" x 1.25" (or the width of your finished rows if it's not 7".) Sew then between levels.

14 Doorway: Cut a main color square the same width as your building, 7" x 7" here.

Continue with the directions below.

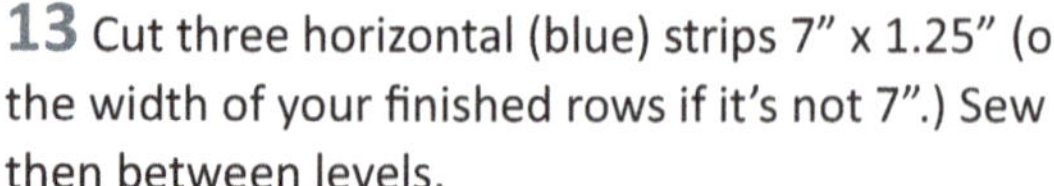

Appliquéd bias-cut curves

This technique can be used for many situations. On the right, light grey bias strips create curved floor separations. Below, we'll use it to make our building's arched doorway.

15 Cut a 17" x 1" strip at 45 degrees to the fabric's straight-of grain. Starch and press dry.

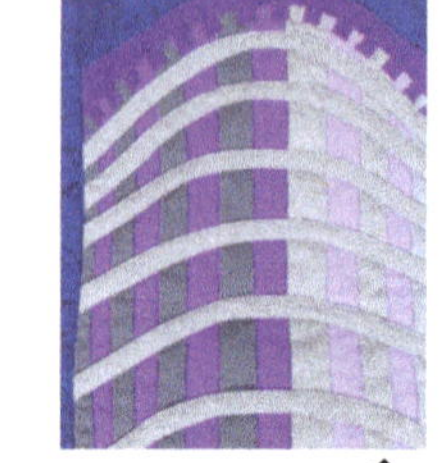

16 Press long edges in to the middle of the back. (If you have a bias tape maker, use it.

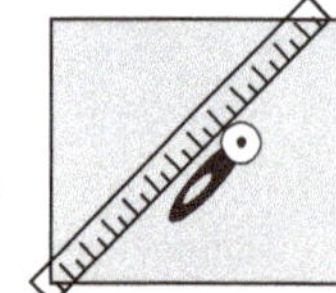

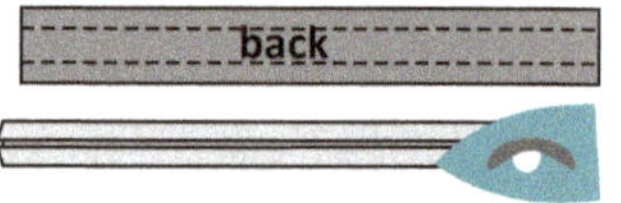

17 Curve the strip. Use steam and press the way you want it. Convincing it to bend correctly takes time.

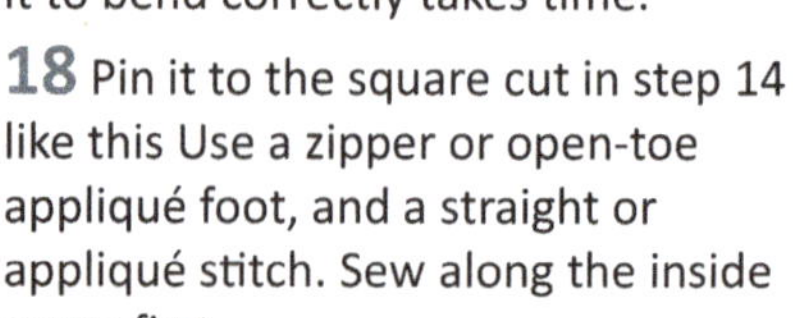

18 Pin it to the square cut in step 14 like this Use a zipper or open-toe appliqué foot, and a straight or appliqué stitch. Sew along the inside curve first.

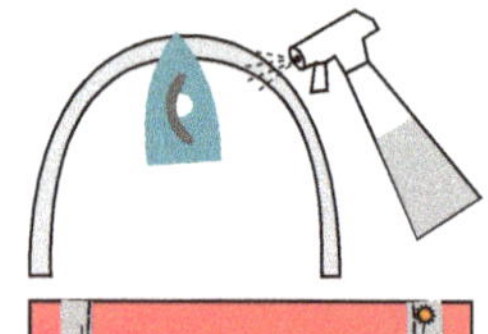

In the photo, we start on the left end. The zipper foot sits on the bias strip; the needle is on the foot's right, stitching just inside the right folded edge of the strip. Remove pins before foot reaches them.

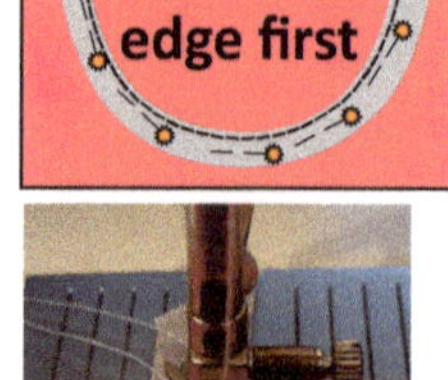

In the next photo, foot approaches the sharpest part of the curve. Use a finger or awl to help ease any excess fabric under the foot.

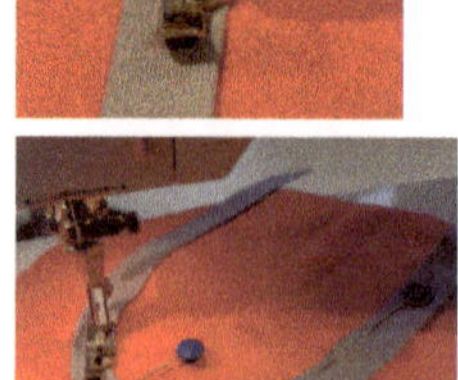

19 After the inside edge, sew outer edge, starting at the right-hand end of the strip, as in the last photo. Do more easing at curve's sharpest part.

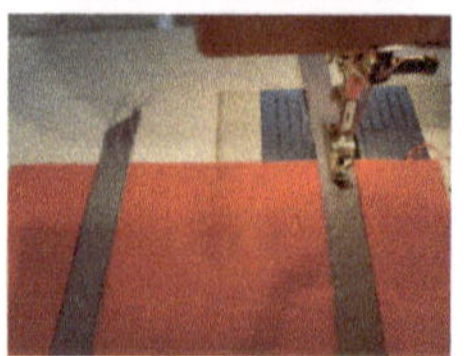

20 Sew the doorway square below the rest of the building. The building should look like "Version 2' on top of this page.

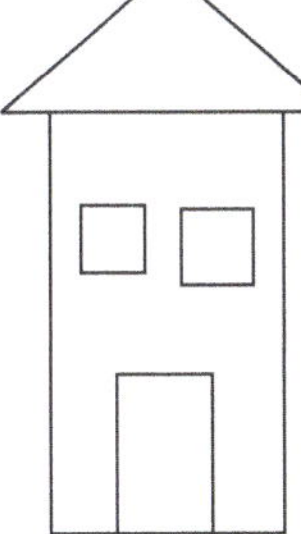

Introduction to Artist's Perspective

Flat View: This is how most people draw, including me, from kindergarten right through senior citizenhood. It's charming on quilts – see traditional schoolhouse quilts! But for a 3-D illusion, you will enjoy adding perspective to some buildings. All of them don't need it – doing this for just a few buildings can pack a powerful visual punch!

One Point Perspective

Looking straight at one wall of a building. The vanishing point is where diagonal side lines meet. It's also where the viewer's eye meets the horizon. Things get smaller as they get further away.

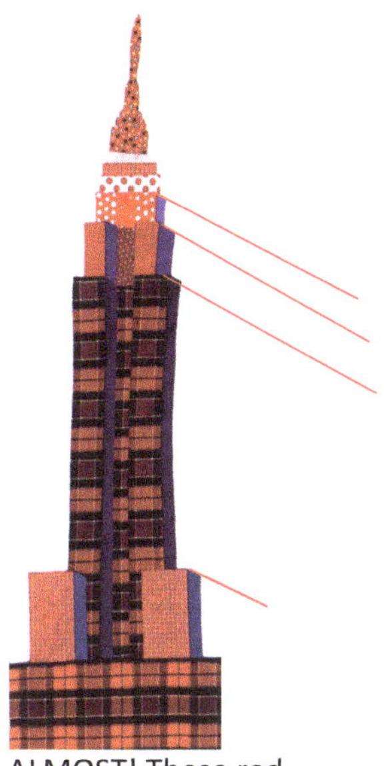

ALMOST! These red perspective lines extending the diagonals on the right side of this building would never REALLY meet, but that's okay. They **hint** that they'll meet eventually!

Two Point Perspective

When you stand directly in front of a building's corner.

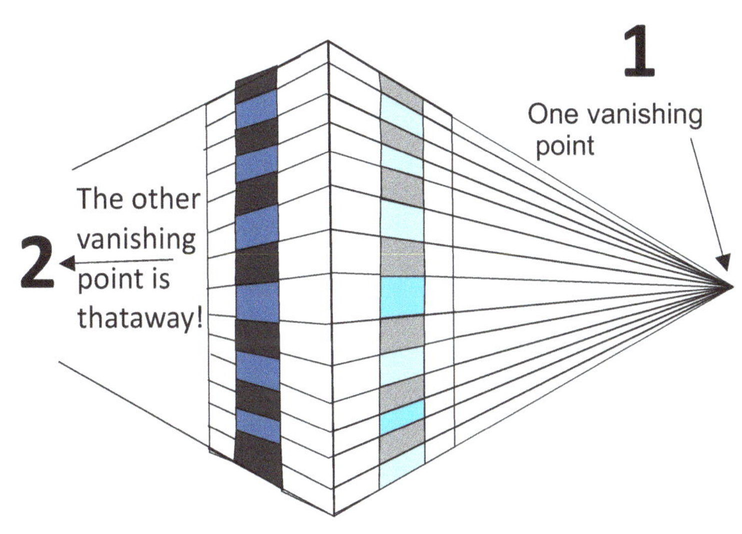

For both 1 and 2 point perspective: All vertical lines are at a 90 degree angle from the bottom.

90

ALMOST! Printed stripes, if extended, wouldn't REALLY meet – but they give that impression, which is enough!

Three Point Perspective

The new point is above or below the building. Not all "vertical" lines are 90 degrees from the ground. Each may be different. With this ground floor view, the up and-down lines would meet at a third vanishing point somewhere in the sky – possibly above your quilt!

Vanishing point #3 is above

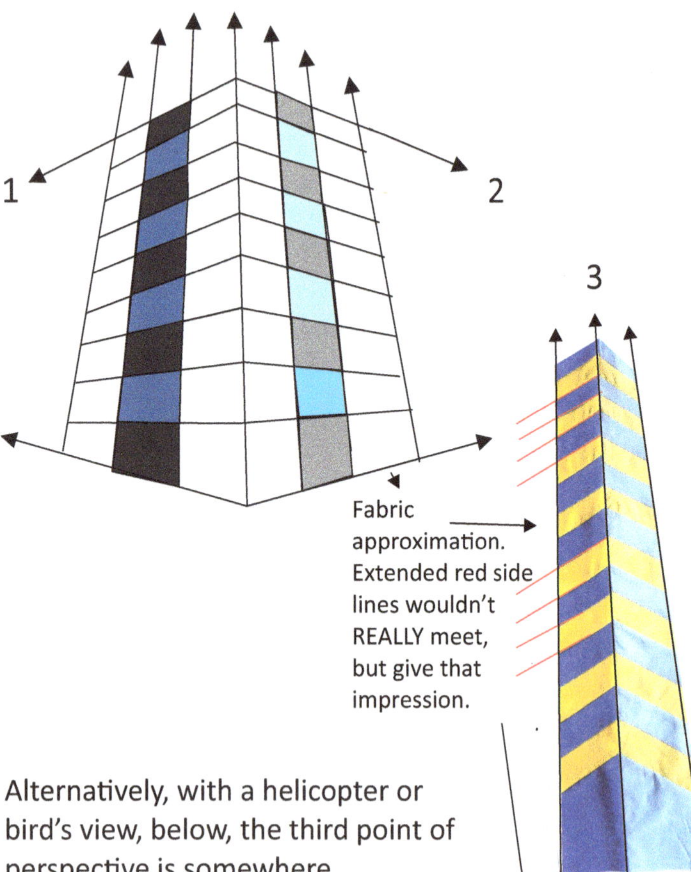

Alternatively, with a helicopter or bird's view, below, the third point of perspective is somewhere underground, which may mean it's off the bottom of your quilt.

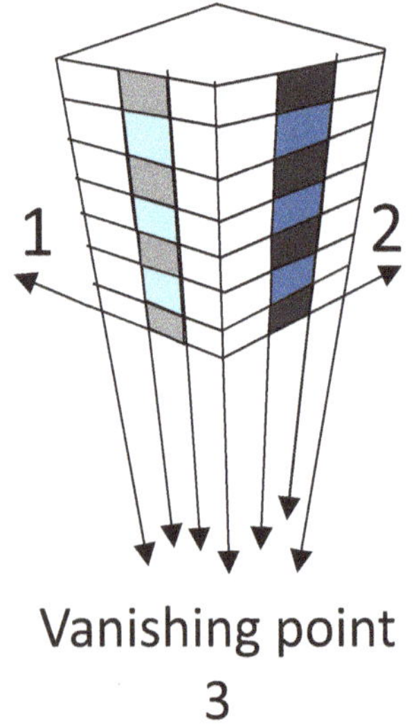

Things tend to get lighter, more faded, and more blue the further they are from the viewer.

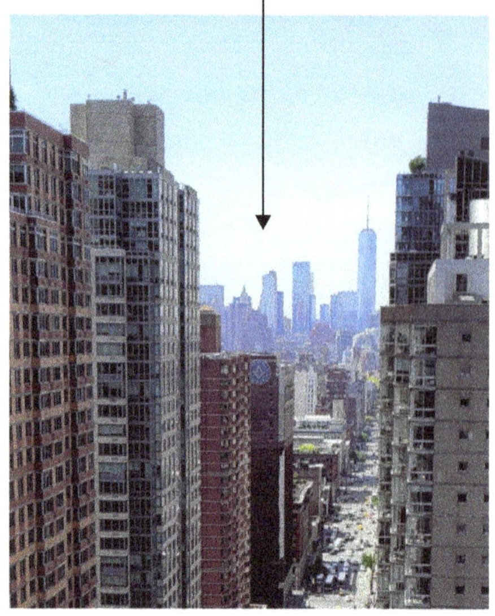

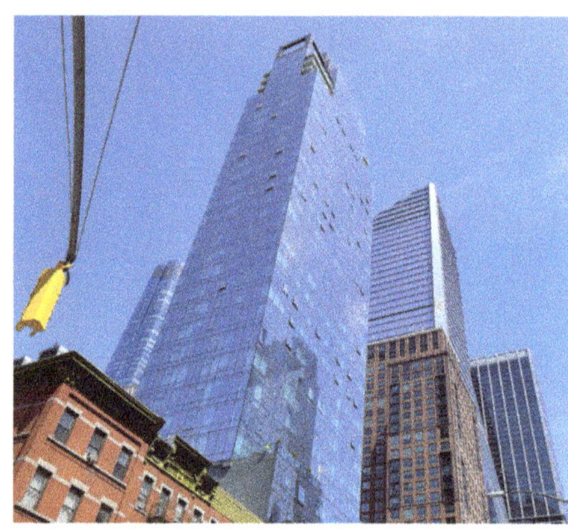

Contrast between light and dark sides enhances all kinds of perspective. But notice also that reflections and shadows can mess with the illusion!

Three-point perspective in fabric

The yellow-and-blue buildings are pieced (not made from striped fabric). The stripes narrow as they rise (above) or descend (far left). The red side lines give an impression that they'll converge off to the sides at a first and second vanishing point. But they wouldn't REALLY converge – to make that happen, each stripe would need its own template – that's way too much work for me! But it's extremely easy in fabric to make the up-and-down lines (black) genuinely aim at a single vanishing point above or below the building (and maybe the quilt). See the strategy for creating different versions of this building, starting on p. 74.

Piece-on Perspective

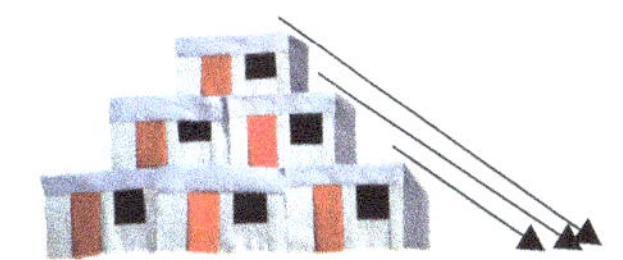

Sometimes, all you need to create perspective is a little triangle or 4-sided polygon on one side – the dark grey sides in the photo above and the diagram on the right. Its top edge, line A, will be on an angle, pointing to the quilt's vanishing point. The bottom line, B, can be straight across or angled to the vanishing point. The illusion will be vastly strengthened if you use a much darker or lighter fabric on the side, to contrast with the front.

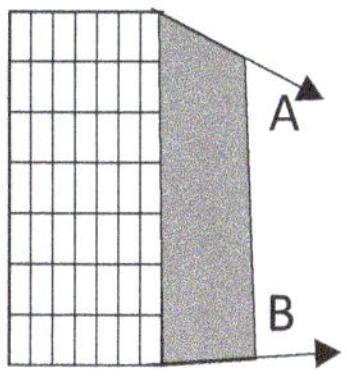

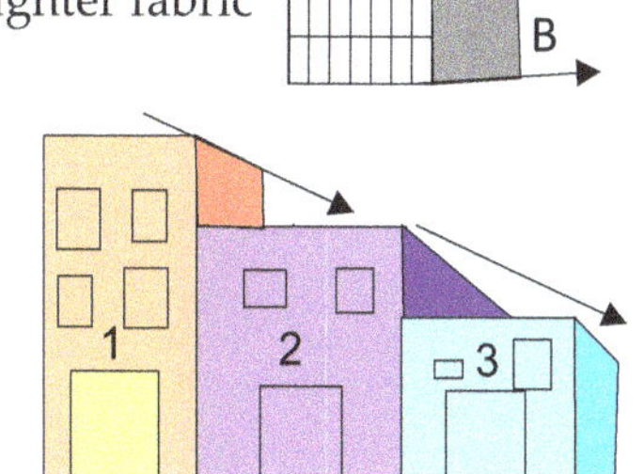

If the building is adjacent to others, you may not need an entire wall, just a small four-sided shape (dark orange on far right) or a triangle (dark purple).

There are many ways to add sides like these. This method below allows you to fold all edges back neatly and efficiently. It's almost the same as the technique described in for creating buildings with uneven outlines, with a few key differences.

The Fold-Sew-Fold Trick

1 Piece 1 is any building you've made with even edges, facing front. (Pieced or one-piece). Piece 2, darker, will become its side in perspective. Cut piece 2 to the same height as 1. All edges are raw. (For buildings with uneven edges, see p. 68.)

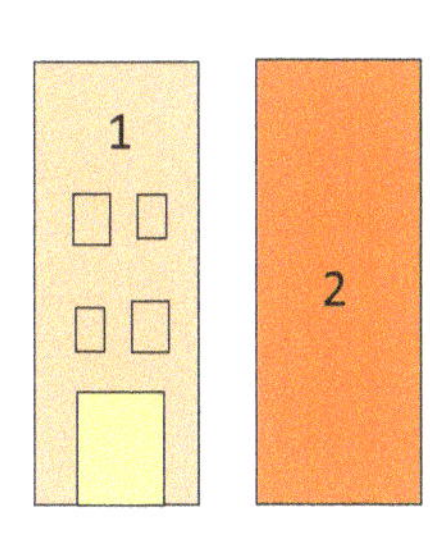

2 Press 1's top edge back 1/4", flat across (fold is the green line). **Don't** do this to 2. Now the perspective side – piece 2 – is 1/4" taller than piece 1.

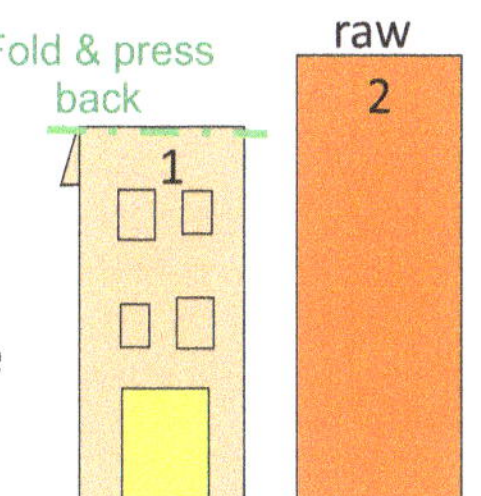

3 Flip piece 1, good side down, onto 2, good side up. Piece 2's top raw edge is peeking out 1/4" above 1's top fold. We will sew them together, sealing the flap.

But to sew, the seam must be on the RIGHT edge. So rotate the bottom end of the seam at **a** to the upper right. You're still looking at the back of piece 1.

4 Hold back threads at **a**. No need for backstitching here – there's no flap. Sew towards the dot by the **b**. Have an awl ready to help the flap to go under the presser foot, staying shut. Sew to the end of the fold, at **b**. Try not to oversew onto 2. (If you do, don't worry). Backstitch to **c**. Cut threads.

(Backstitching seals the seam tight, and prevents thread ends from sticking out on the finished piece.)

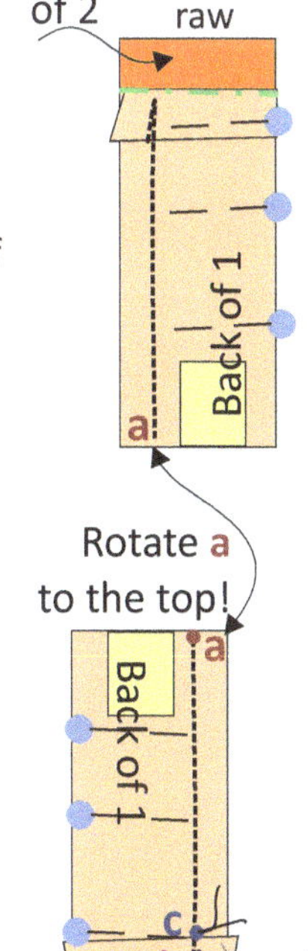

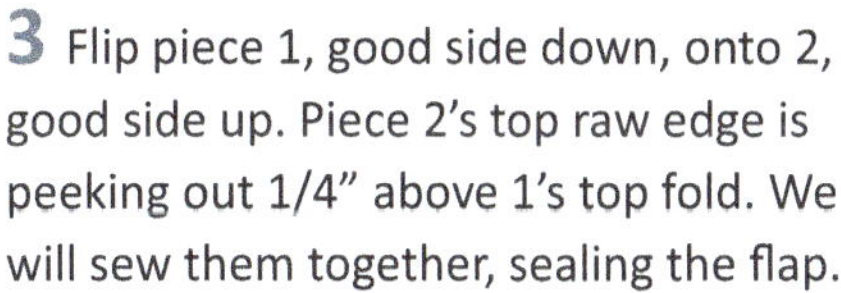

5 Open. Press seam allowance LEFT, behind piece 1. (WITH PERSPECTIVE, WE PRESS TO THE SHORTER LEVEL!!! That's different from what we did in Part III.)

6 Fold and press top raw edge of piece 2 on an angle (green line).

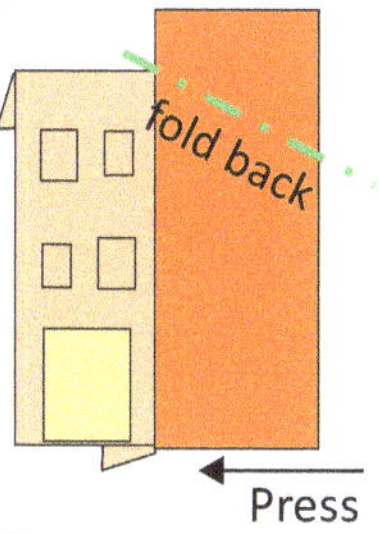

7 The building looks like this. Both top edges are folded back. There's probably a tiny triangle of the seam allowance still peeking out on top (circled), fold that back, glue and press.

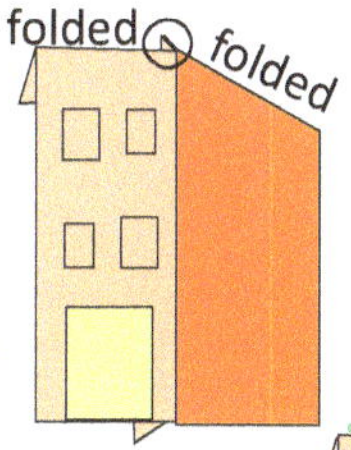

8 If you choose to appliqué this building to your quilt (and not piece it to other buildings) you will also need to fold left and right edges inward 1/4".

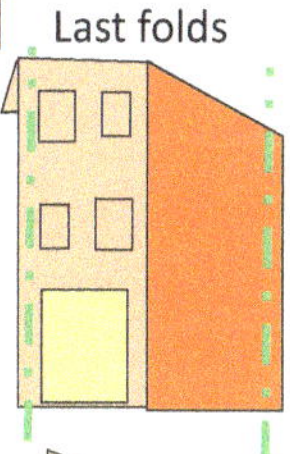

9 Or, appliqué another building, hiding some of the side wall. It can be set back or brought forward.

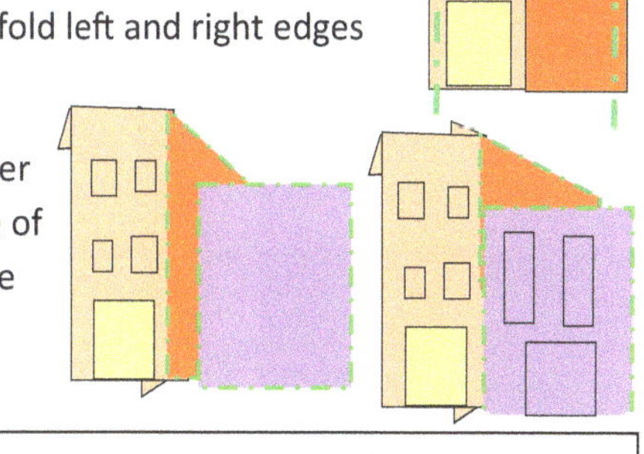

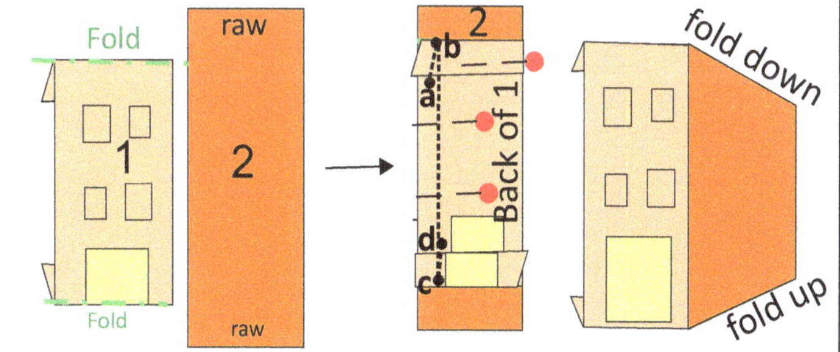

To fine-tune a higher vanishing point, press both top AND bottom edges of a building back 1/4" (on piece 1 below). Flip and center 1 onto 2. Sew, backstitching at BOTH ends (sew **a** to **b** to **c** to **d**, keeping stitches on piece 1). Then fold top AND bottom edges of piece 2 on an angle. Stairs can also be made this way – see p. 86.

Add Perspective to a Building with Uneven Edges

Ideally, you should add perspective while piecing the building. But the creative process isn't linear, and often I decide to do it after I thought the building was finished. On the right is my piece inspired by Chicago's Wrigley Building. It looked boring, so I added a perspective side. Here's how.

Before:

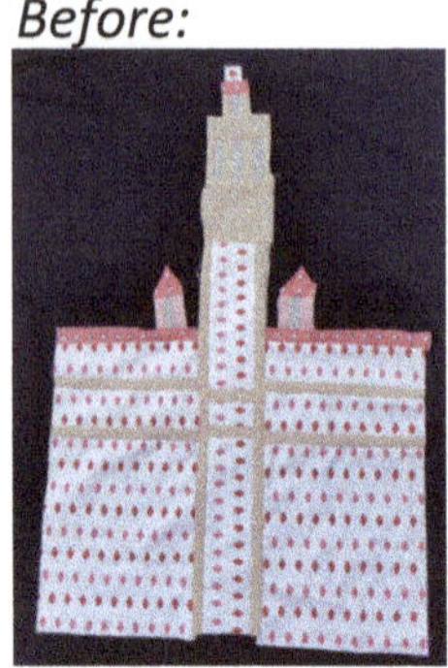

– Place the building on a large piece of paper.

– Pick an approximate vanishing point for the building (and maybe the entire quilt). Here, I decided it would be to the lower right.

– With a ruler, extend major horizontal lines on an angle, towards your vanishing point.

– Use them as guidelines, to draw in side pieces (outlined in black).

– Estimate and cut pieces from fabric. Combine piecing with appliqué to join the new pieces.

– You may have to rip some seams to add the new side. I had to rip stitches at the right/base of the tower, and completely remove the little gable on the right. After giving each a new side, I sewed everything back together.

– Remember: with 1 and 2 pt. perspective, all verticals remain 90 degrees from the ground!

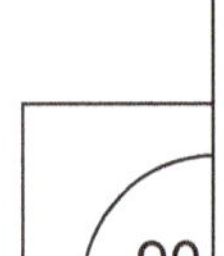

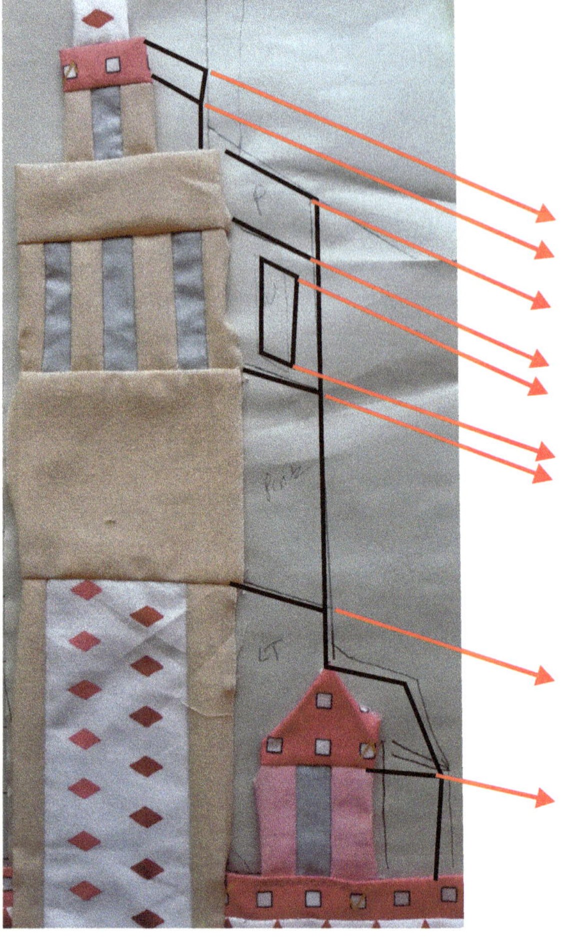

When you get confused

Don't blame yourself; feel free to blame me; but the truth is, artist's perspective can be **incredibly** complicated. There are many books about it, some easier to follow than others, and I bet your public library, like mine, has both kinds. Along with browsing those:

– Look at more photos of the building (or similar buildings). Trace and draw them, as many times as it takes to understand where the main lines are pointing.

– Go to Youtube and enter, "How to draw in perspective." There are many terrific videos. Be specific with search terms like, "How to draw stairs in perspective".

– Zoom with an artist. I call my daughter, an artist, and beg for insight and mercy. I send her a photo of my dilemma.

Also notice:

– The new side is darker than the front, which adds power to perspective.

– That cute diamond print saved me from having to piece zillions of identical windows!

After:

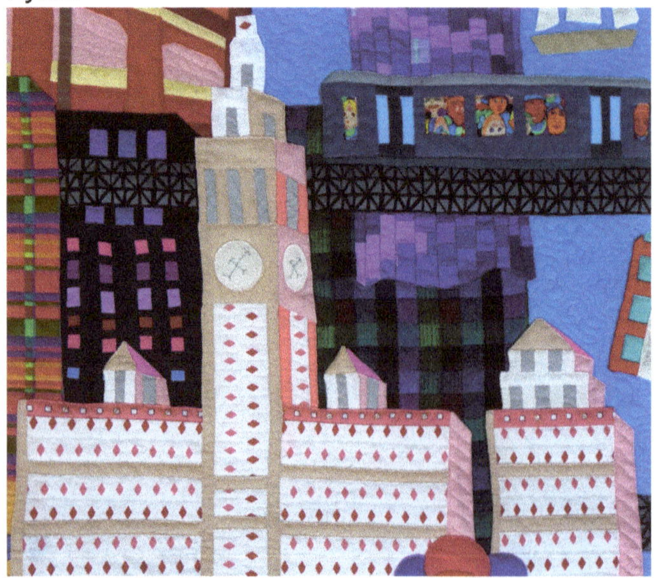

Two-Point Perspective Buildings from Printed Stripes

Cut same-size pieces at the same angle (60 degrees works well)

L = Left   R = Right

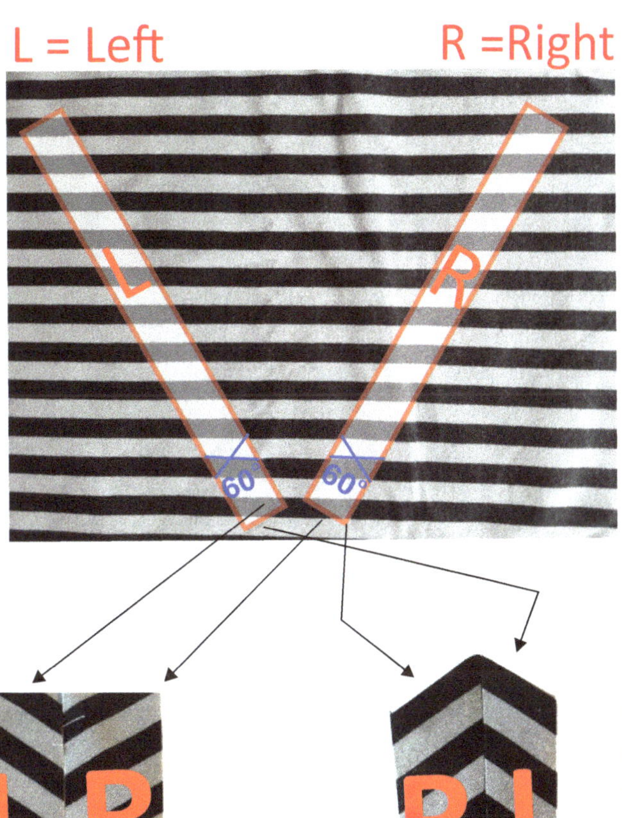

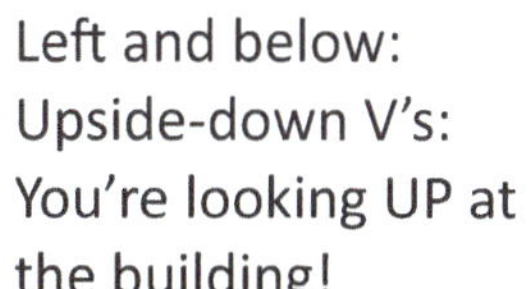

Upright V: You're looking DOWN at the building!

Real world. Looking down. See the upright V's?

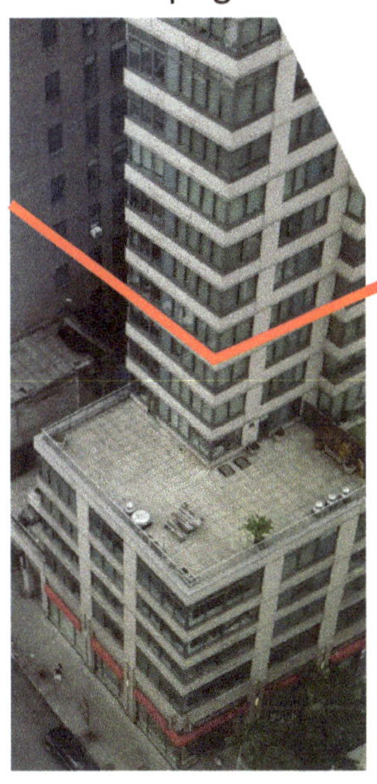

Left and below: Upside-down V's: You're looking UP at the building!

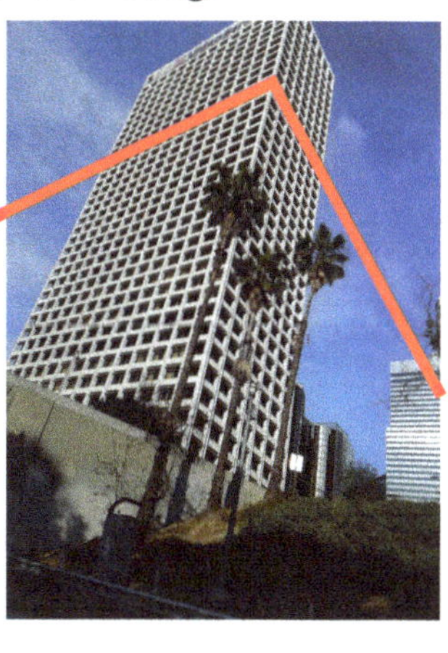

Right: Put a diagonal stripe on one side of any building. Use the Fold-Sew-Fold trick on p. 67. When diagonal stripes flow upward to the building, as on the right, the viewer seems to be looking up at the building. If diagonals flow down to the building, you're looking at the building from above. This approximates 1-point perspective.

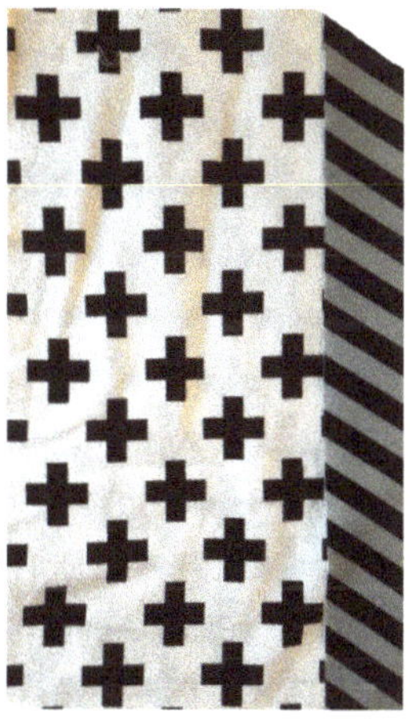

Make Your Own Striped Fabric, and Play With It!

Here we create striped fabric. Then we cut left and right sections at opposite angles, and a middle section straight across. This works especially well to create roundish skyscrapers. (This can also be done with a printed stripe.)

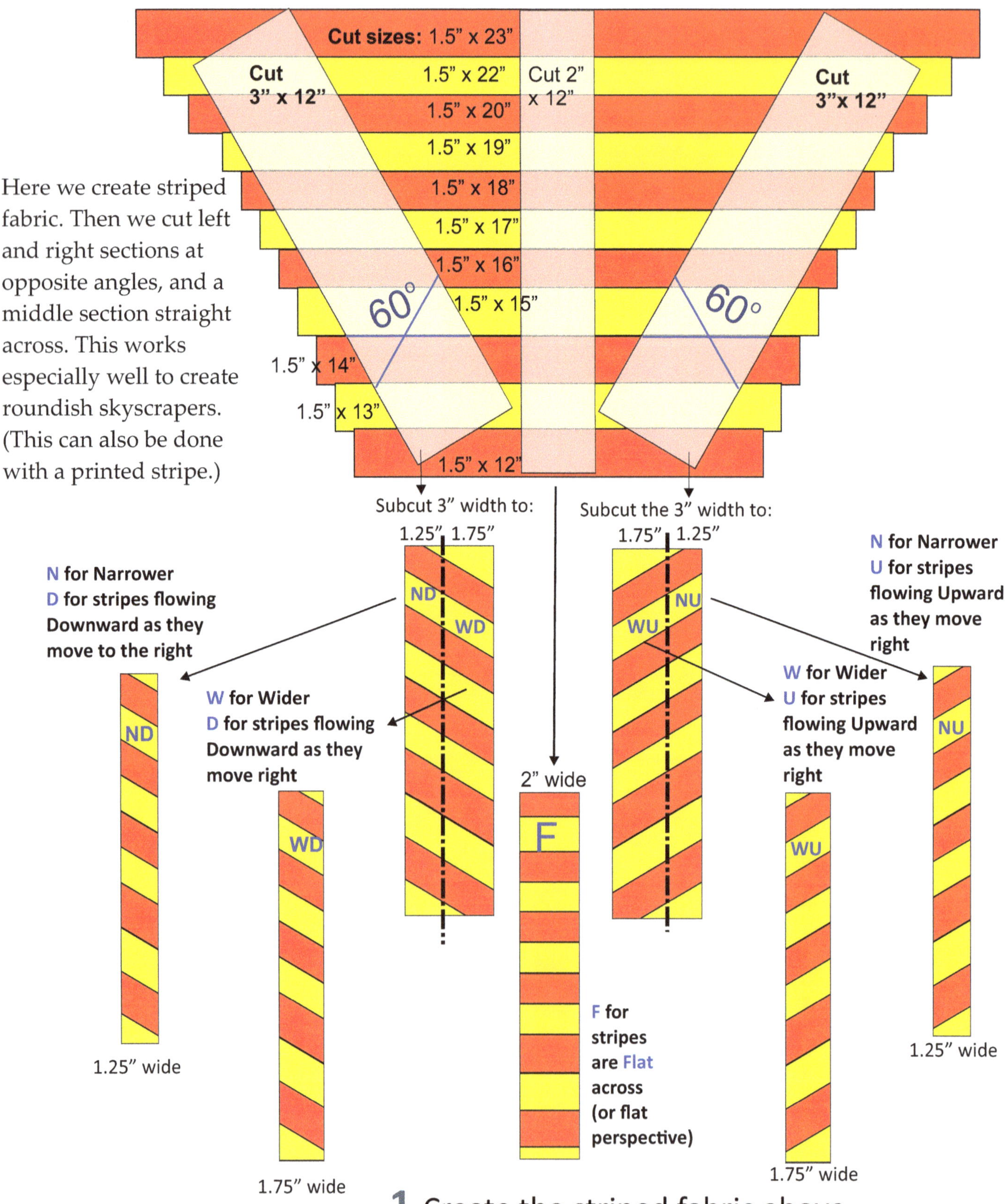

1 Create the striped fabric above.

2 Cut the five pieces shown above.

3 Arrange strips like this. F is the building's front wall. The stripes create an upside-down V, so we're looking UP at the building. Narrow strips on the outside support the illusion that N pieces are furthest. To reinforce that, plan to fold most of the NU and ND strips back, leaving only 1/2" showing. (Do this later).

Don't try matching the central strip's stripes to those on the sides. Evenly-spaced stripes cut flat across ("F") will **never** align perfectly with the same stripes cut at a diagonal. Blame geometry!

4 Consider adding solid vertical strips between the striped segments (dark red, right).

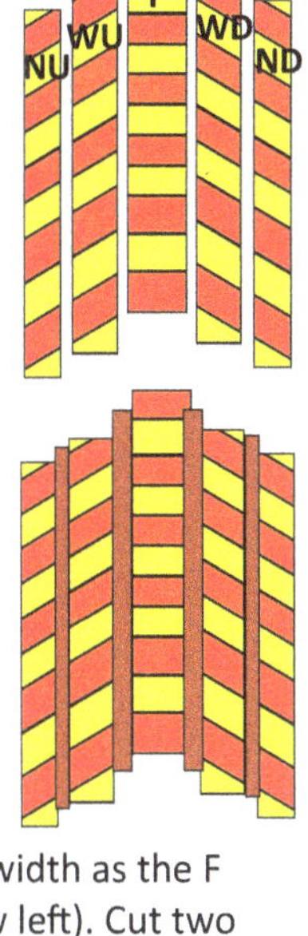

5 Cut a (grey) rectangle to serve as middle roof, same width as the F section (plus its two dark red side pieces, if it any, below left). Cut two more larger rectangles (grey) to serve as roof for the left and right sides.

6 Sew a roof piece atop each column. Trim side roofs' straight up and down (cut on the green lines) so they extend the lines of the segments below. Option: Add and trim three ground floor pieces the same way.

7 Sew the three vertical segments together. Press top edges back. Cut bottom edge straight across, or fold it into an upright V.

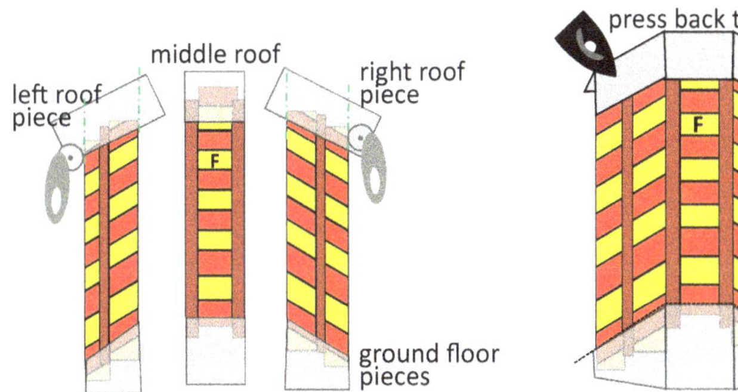

Option: Cut the middle F segment from a DIFFERENT striped fabric (printed or pieced). The building below, right, is made from two different striped fabrics.

Fabric #1

Fabric #2

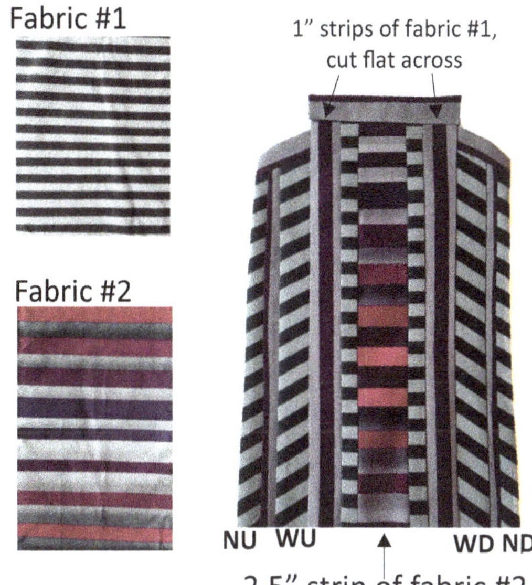

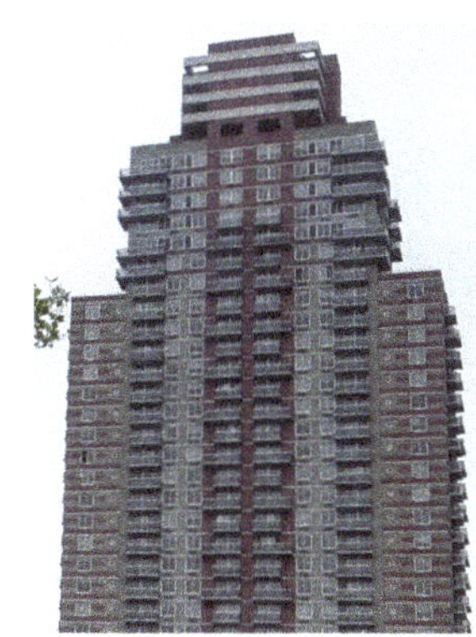

I found the building after I made it, in New York City! My version above is in the 'Nonsense Town' quilt on p. 10.

Alternate Dark and Light Strip Sets

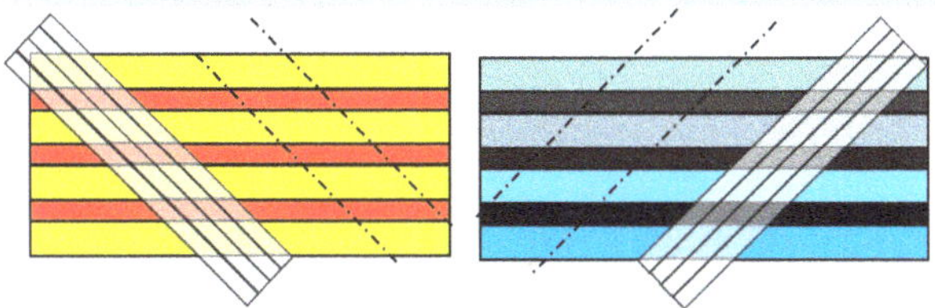

You might find two similar striped fabrics, one dark and one light. Or, you may find dark and light stripes within the SAME fabric! Or, create your own sets.

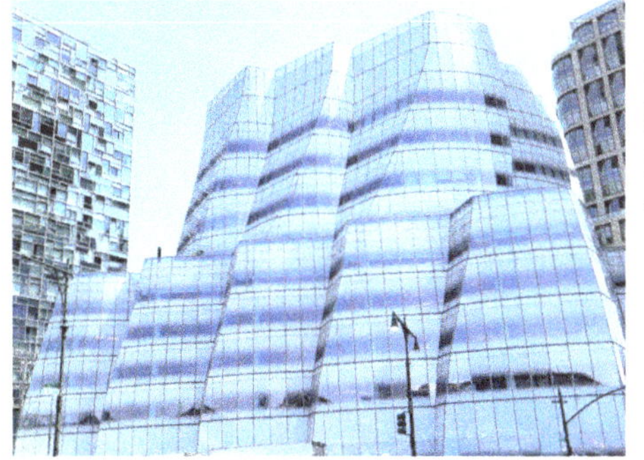

Frank Gehry's IAC building at 555 W. 18th in NYC looks like folded notepaper!

Two colorways of the same print, one light green and the other dark grey and black.

Four fabrics make a folded building:

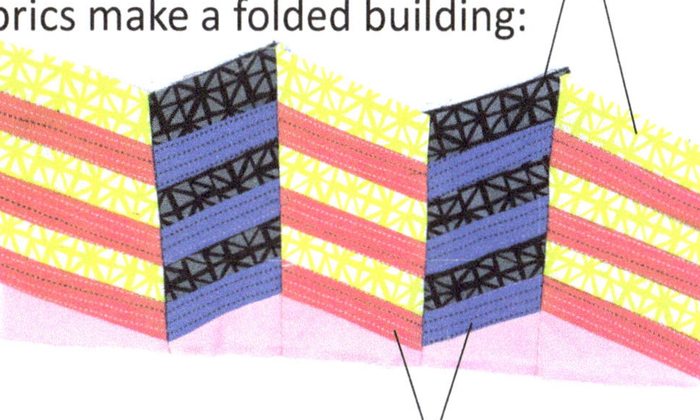

Two colorways of another print, one deep pink and the other dark blue.

Scrappy, Sparkly Two-Point Perspective Tower

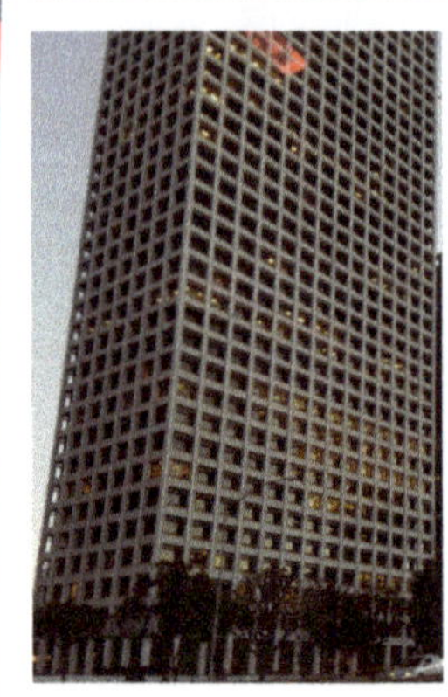

The building on the far left was an early step into artist's perspective. I put it in my first New York quilt (on the cover), where most other buildings were flat. Whenever I show this quilt, viewers remark on this building first.

The left side is lighter. That alone creates depth. What takes more time to notice are the exceptions – a few dark pieces on the light side, and vice-versa. They give the building sparkle; and paradoxically, create MORE realism. In real buildings, night or day, pattern of light and dark in the windows are often random, like in the photo.

With these directions, you'll wind up with ten colorful rows of three windows, on two sides. Window rows alternate with dark or light "building" strips. I used grey, but you can choose any color.

1 Cut 18" x 2" strips from at least five light and five dark fabrics in assorted colors. Or, cut shorter strips from more than five – the more variety, the easier it will be to avoid repeating the same color next to itself. (If you would prefer to use a template to cut the pieces, use this red outline!

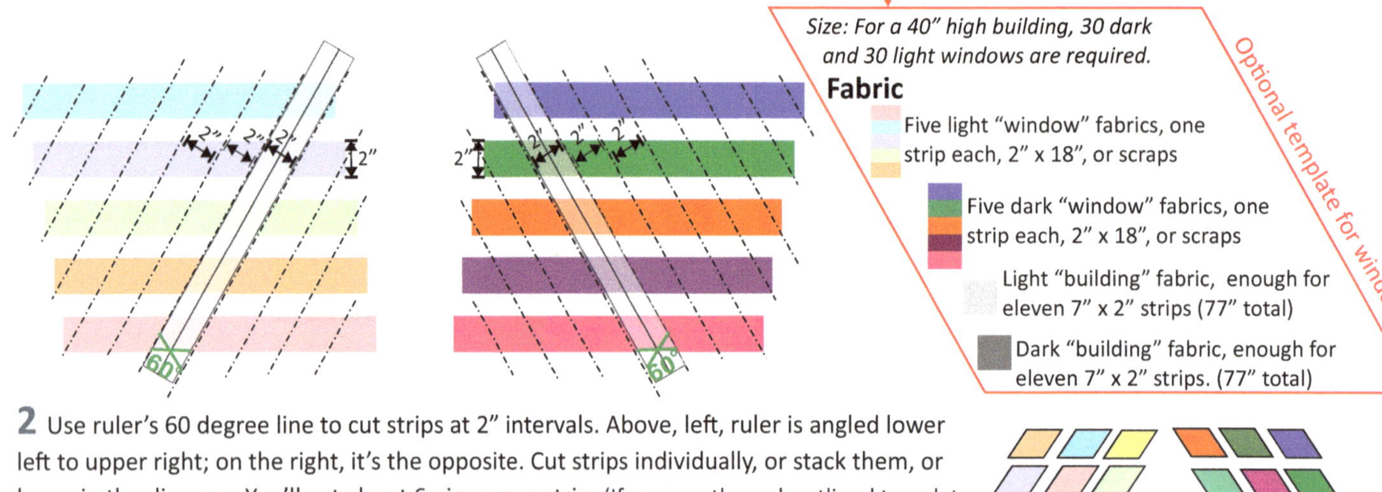

2 Use ruler's 60 degree line to cut strips at 2" intervals. Above, left, ruler is angled lower left to upper right; on the right, it's the opposite. Cut strips individually, or stack them, or lay as in the diagram. You'll cut about 6 pieces per strip. (If you use the red-outlined template instead, upper right, use the orientation shown to cut the darks; fhen flip it over to cut lights.

3 Arrange in each half into ten rows of three pieces, as on the right Place darks on one side, lights on the other.

4 **Somersault a few darks to the light side, and a few lights to the dark side** (like Darth Vader!) Except: With directional prints, you may not be able to flip or rotate them – for those, cut a few dark pieces to the light pieces' angles, and vice versa.

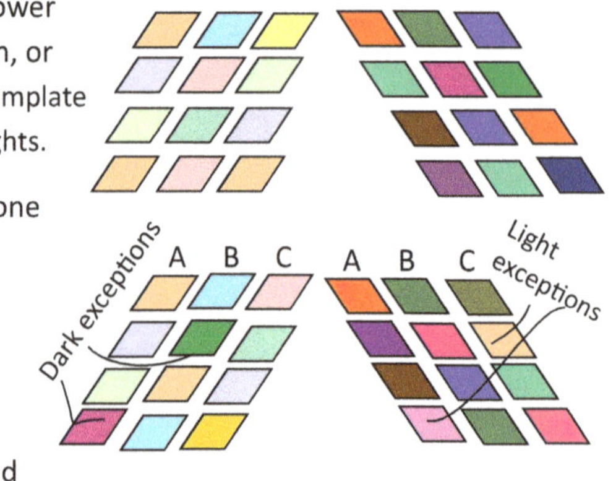

5 Sew into rows. On the top left of the previous diagram, starting with the peach and blue pieces in columns **A** and **B**, flip the second piece, **B** (blue), face down onto the first piece (peach) and match right edges. Here and for all left side pieces, the underneath piece's tip (peach, circled) extends a tiny bit above the front (blue) piece's top. In the lower corner, also circled, the front (blue) piece's tip extends a bit below the underneath piece. Pin. Sew.

6 Don't cut threads: keep going, chain sewing all the **A**'s to their neighboring **B**'s. Then cut thread and sew each **C** on top of each **B** the same way. Cut threads.

7 Do the same on the opposite side, but here the column **B** pieces that go on top have the tips that protrude, above piece **A** below them. And at the bottom end of the seam, piece **A** is longer.

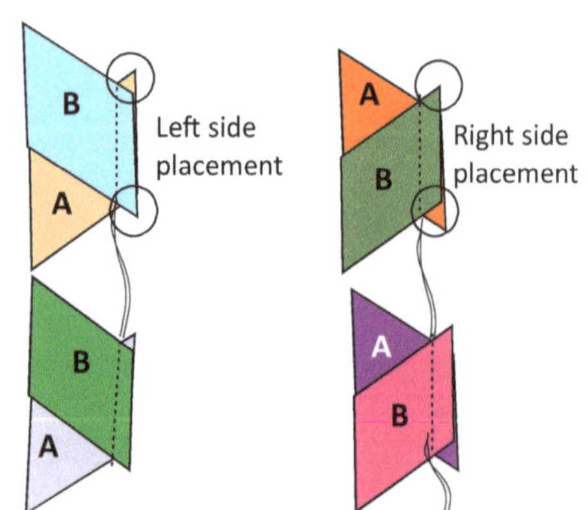

(continued)   72

8 When all rows are assembled, lay them out with space between them (Cut connecting threads if you chain-sewed.)

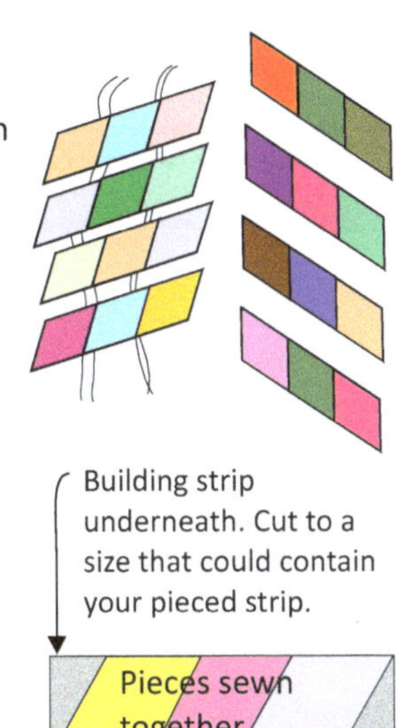

9 Create building strips. With rows of three pieces: Cut eleven light and eleven dark (grey) "building" rectangles to 7" x 2". (If using different numbers of pieces per row, cut spacer strips to the same dimensions as a rectangle holding your entire stitched strip. Trace the stitched strip, and use that to cut angles on the left and right edges of the building strips.)

Building strip underneath. Cut to a size that could contain your pieced strip.

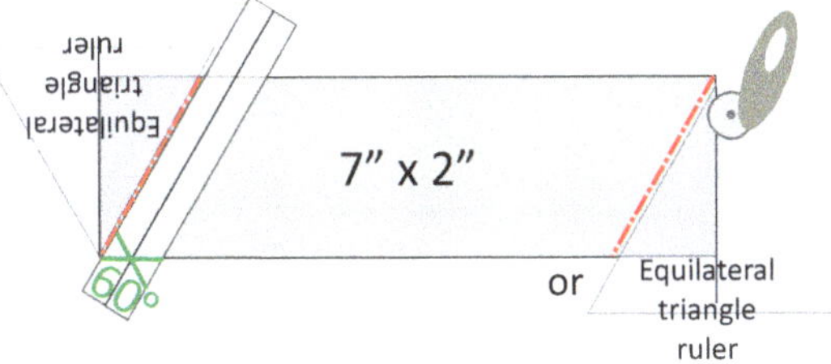

10 With 7" x 2" left side strips, use the 60 degree ruler line (**or** an equilateral triangle template) to cut a slice off, cutting from the strip's lower left corner up and to the right, as below. (With a triangle ruler, the strip's vertical side should line up with the vertical midline of the ruler).

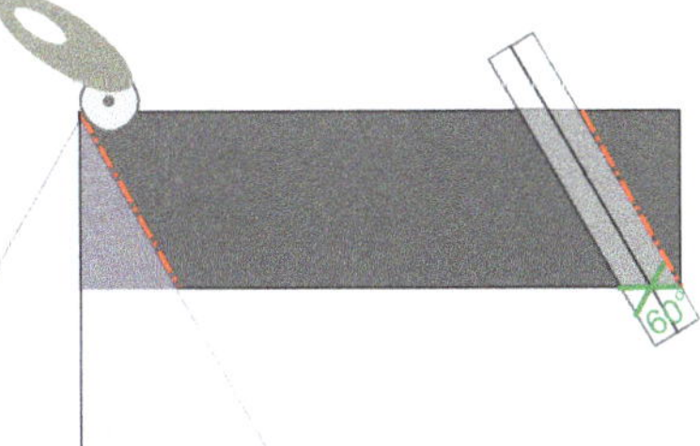

On the same strip's opposite end, cut at the same angle, with the cut going through the strip's upper right corner.

11 For the building's opposite side, angle cuts from the upper left to lower right.

12 Lay out pieces, alternating colorful with building strips. To join them, you can do the dog-ear method like in step 6, but a method I find even more reliable is to iron back the seam allowance, in advance, to test placement.

13 Press the top edge of a building strip 1/4" to the back. Place it on top of the lower edge of a colorful strip. Move it around until you figure out **exactly** where it needs to go to make the sides flow in a (fairly) straight line!

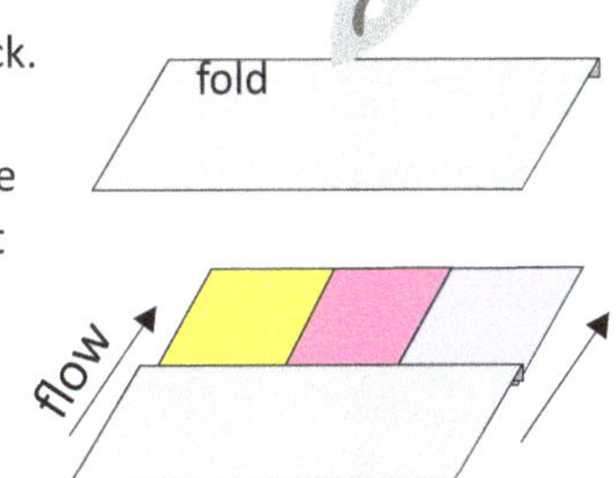

14 Pinching it in position, carefully place a pin to hold it. Place another pin above it, and remove the first pin. Sew the edge. (Dog ears at either end also help with placement, but pre-folding and testing like this works better for me.)

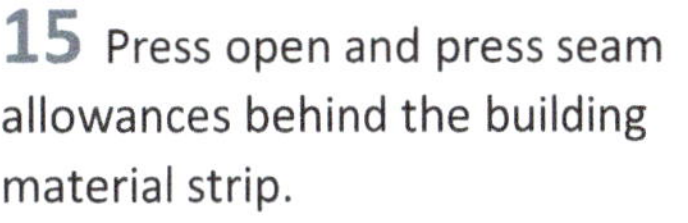

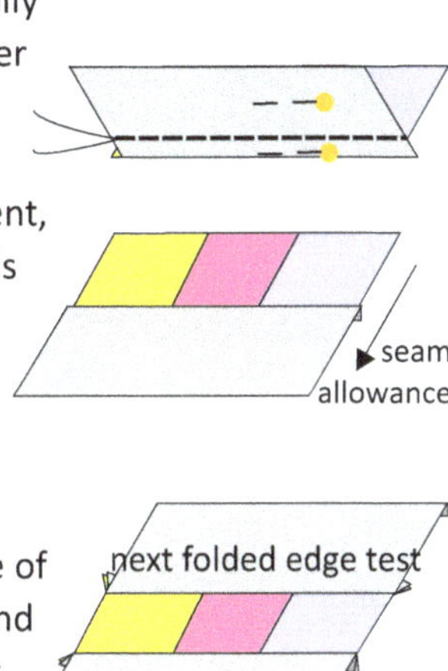

15 Press open and press seam allowances behind the building material strip.

16 Press under the bottom edge of the next building material strip, and place it on top of the row you just finished. Pin and sew as before.

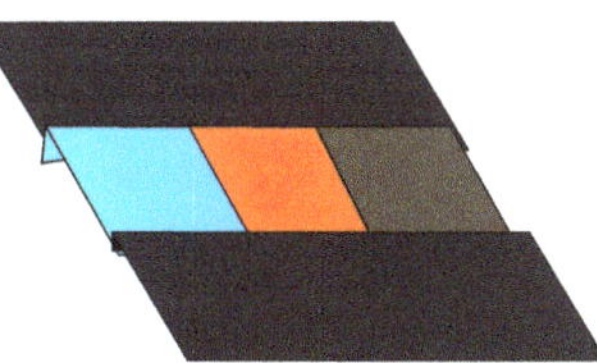

17 Keep going like this. Press all horizontal seam allowances away from the windows, and behind the building strips, to give the building a "lift" over the windows.

18 On the dark side, do it all in the opposite direction.

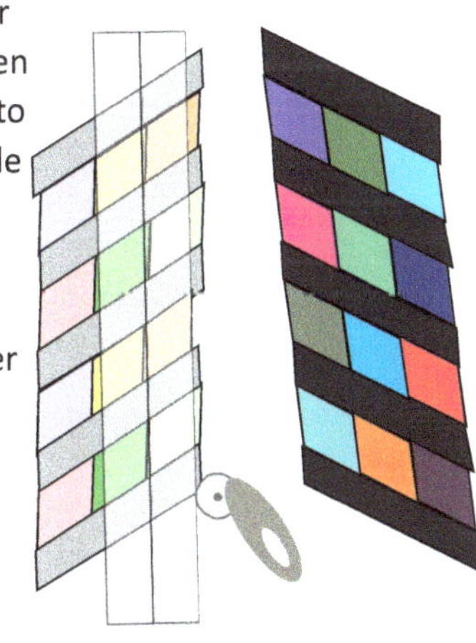

19 Join the two sides. If their middle edges are a little uneven (mine always are!) trim them to a straight line. If possible, angle the ruler in a way that makes the top a little narrower than the base – that will enhance artist's perspective (the further away, the smaller).

20 Sew the sides together. I match the floors up fairly well, but never perfectly (especially if I had to trim!) No one except you, me, and the quilt show judges will notice!

21 Fold back long side edges (If you fold at an angle, you can make the top narrower than the bottom, for 3-point perspective.) Fold top edges down. You can tuck the bottom behind another building, or create a ground floor from a light and dark rectangle, cut at a 60 degree angle, sewn to the bottom edge.

Three-Point Perspective Tower with Graduated Stripes

These buildings are an approximation of three-point perspective. They also have lots of design options. Don't use a printed stripe for this one; you'll be making your own stripes, which means you can make the stripes smaller as they rise, for a more impactful sense of perspective than you can get from a print with stripes that are all the same width.

1 Fabric: For a 20" by 6-8" wide building, you need a fat-quarter or quarter-yard of four fabrics, in two colors. Here the two colors are pink and blue. You need one dark and one light of each color. Cut each piece 4" x 22"

If you're using a print, and need a lighter shade, check the fabric back – you may find your lighter shade right there!

2 On cutting mat, stack darks strips on one side, lights on the other, all good side up. You decide which shade goes on which side. (Here, darks are on the left; you can reverse that to be consistent with other buildings on your quilt.) **Put the same color family on top of both stacks (blues here).**

3 Start on the bottom left corner of the left strip set, where you see the green markings. Measure 3.5" straight up from that corner.

4 Use the ruler's 60 degree line to cut upward from that spot, on an angle, to the strips' right edge. (The end should be at about 6" up straight from the lower right corner - it's at the tops of the red arrows). Cut across.

As you cut each pair, slide them away from the cutting area, but keep them in order. This first cut creates two potential ground floor pieces. (One will later become scrap.)

5 From here, we'll measure by **using the ruler's long horizontal lines to cut strips parallel to the previous cuts.** We're no longer measuring up the side.

The strips get progressively narrower, for 3 pt. perspective - because for a person on the ground, looking up at a skyscraper, the furthest floors seem thinner!

6 Measure and cut a line 2" above the first. Then do two cuts a little closer together, at 1.75" from the previous cut. Keep going using the measurements shown. Improv option: Estimate the distances, and just cut each strip a little bit narrower than the one before.

7 On the right stack, flip the direction of your ruler and repeat steps 3-6 at the opposite angle.

(continued)

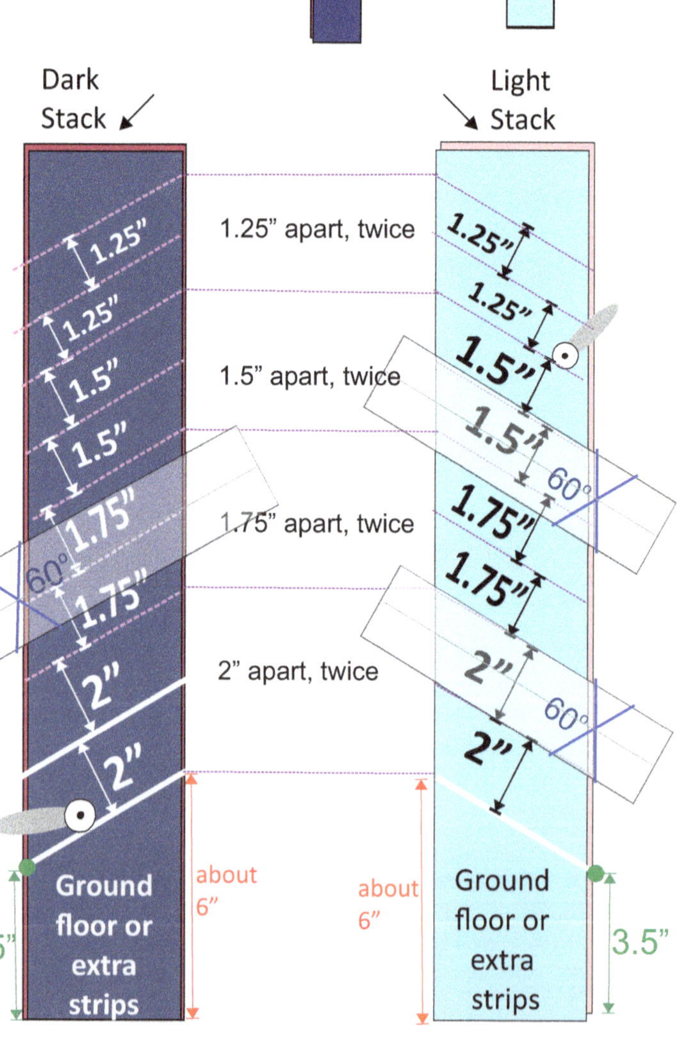

Join the Slices

8 Start with the left stack. On design surface, place the ground floor, in the color you want, on the far left. I chose BLUE, marked GF. Set aside the 2nd GF piece - it's scrap.

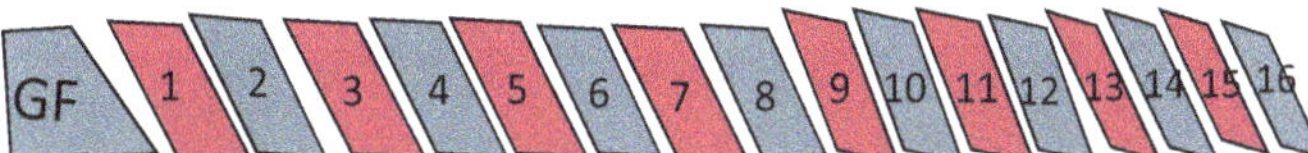

Peel remaining pieces apart and arrange from widest on the left, alternating colors, to narrowest on the far right, as above.

9 Chain sew into pairs: Flip piece 2, good side down, onto 1, which is good side up.

10 The top piece's (blue) tip should extend about 1/4" above piece 1. On bottom right, the back piece's tip (pink) should extend 1/4" below the top piece. (The solo extensions are called dog ears!) Pin and sew the first pair with a 1/4" seam allowance. Don't cut threads!

11 Send the next pair into the machine the same way – flip piece 4 onto 3 and sew. Continue like this, and only cut thread after the last pair (pieces 15 and 16).

12 Bring chain to the ironing board. Press each seam allowance down toward the lowest number (ie toward the widest pieces).

13 At the table, cut threads, and again arrange pairs by width. Chain-sew pairs into groups of four and press. Join those into groups of 8. Sew remaining seam, and add the ground floor. This side is complete. Press all seams downward.

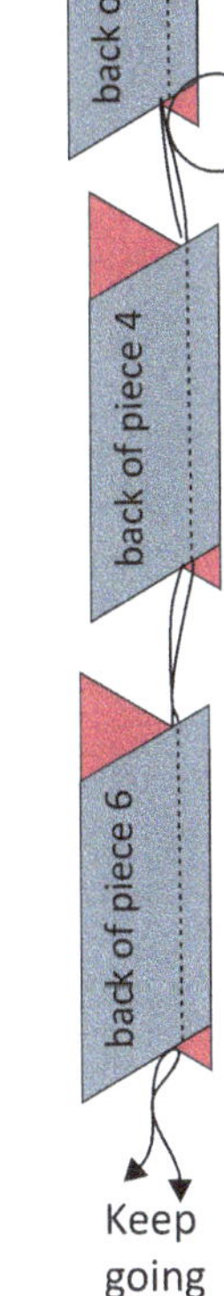

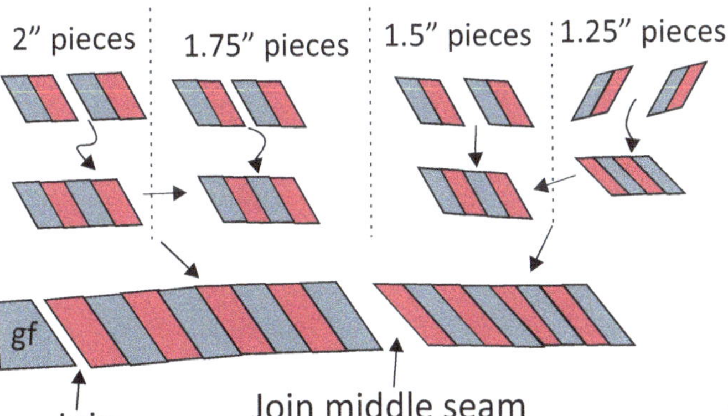

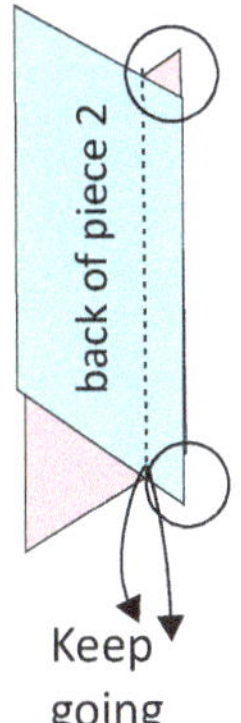

14 Arrange the right stack. You probably want a ground floor in the same color family as the other side - blue here. That makes piece 1 pink (as in the previous stack). (The light pink GF piece is now scrap).

15 Start as before, by flipping piece 2, face down, on piece 1.

This time, the underneath (pink) piece's tip extends above the front piece in the upper right corner.

Down below, the upper piece's (blue) corner extends beyond the piece underneath.

16 Chain sew all the pieces into pairs like this, then groups of four, and then one long piece, like in Steps 10 - 13. But press all seam allowances UPWARD on this stack!

17 The central edges probably won't be perfectly straight. Trim straight as shown. If lots of trimming is required, angle the ruler so more comes off from the top than the bottom. By making the top narrower, you're emphasizing a third vanishing point in the sky!

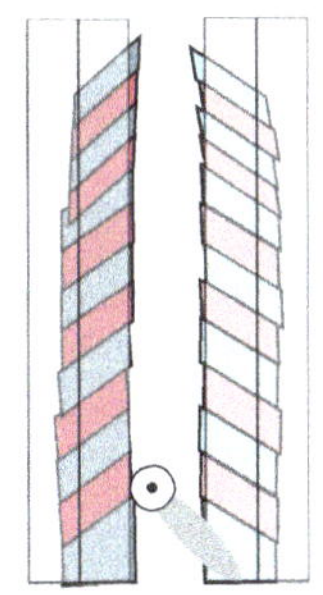

Fastest Finish

Read ahead to check out all the design options. The fastest finish (though not necessarily the easiest) is to pin and sew the left strip set to the right one, and sew down the middle. The not-easy part is matching every seam. I don't achieve perfection, but close is good.

If you stop here, the building will have a nice approximation of three-point perspective, with vanishing points on both sides, and pieces that become more slender as they rise.

The last step for this option is to turn all remaining outside edges to the back. You can fold them back 1/4", top to bottom, or, as you'll read on the next pages, you can fold back more at the top, to create even stronger 3-point perspective.

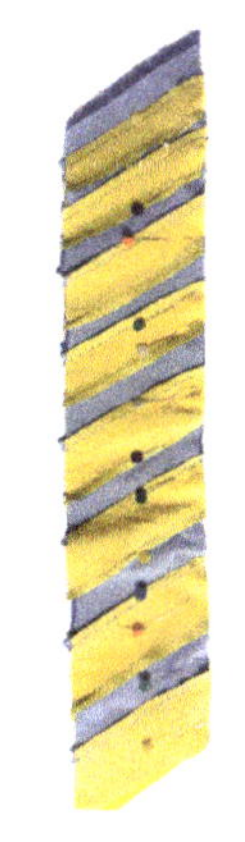

(continued)

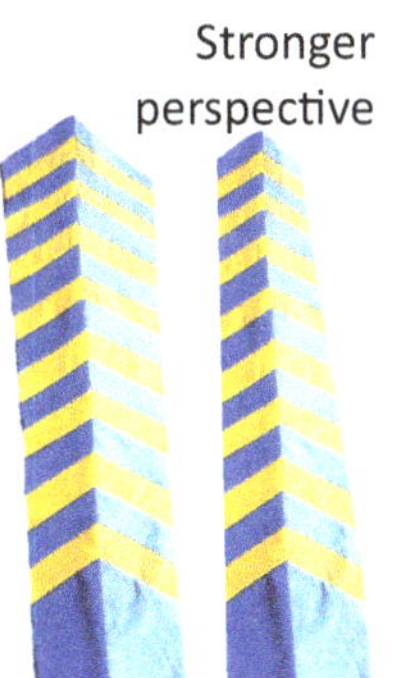

Stronger perspective

Option: Add a Stylish Band

Give the building a rounder look, (and avoid matching seams) by inserting a plain strip between halves. Measure the height of one side down its middle seam. Then either:

— **Insert a rectangular middle band.** Cut a strip - at least 1" wide by your building at its highest Attach halves to it. Or,

— **Insert a strip that narrows at the top.** Cut the strip a little narrower at the top. I suggest you keep the top of the strip no less than 1". At the bottom, you could grow it up to 2".

Narrowing, as explained earlier, emphasizes the third point of perspective above the building. But whether you do this or not, you'll have a few more opportunities to enhance the perspective.

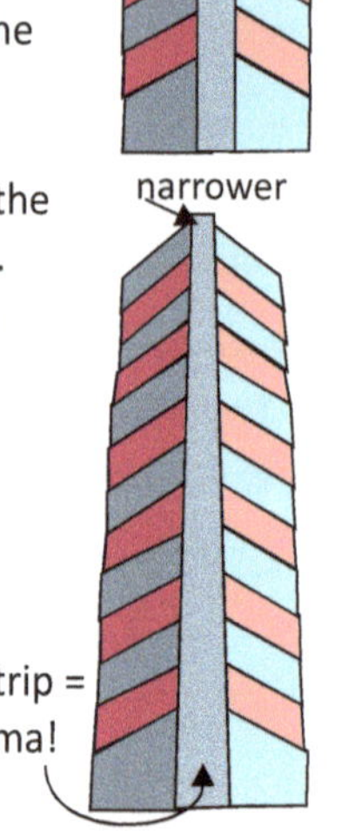

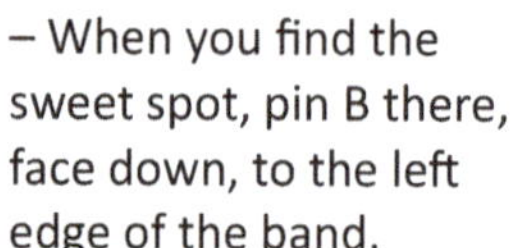

Option: Split the Sides

In this variation, split each side and insert bands there. (The building can have a central band, or not.)

With perspective, we want column A's wider than the B's, because the B's are further back. To accomplish this:

— Cut each side a little more than halfway out from its central seam (or from the seam on one side of a central band). This is a straight cut, and if you used the measurements here, cut it 2" out from the central seam.

— Measure the building's height through the center. I use the ground floor color - blue here. Cut two strips in that color to 1" wide by the height. One strip should be dark, one light.

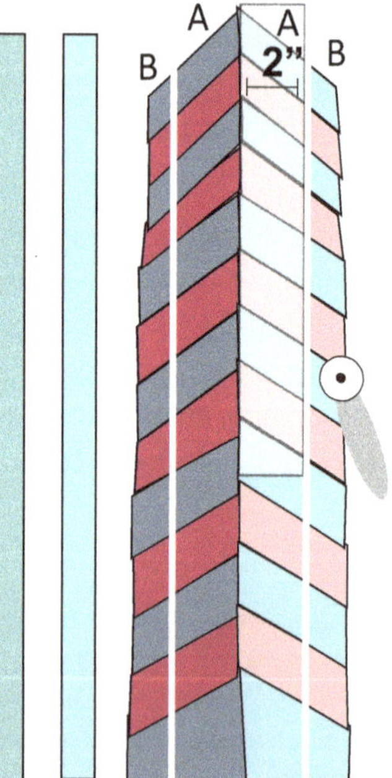

— On the left, stitch the new strip to column A's left edge. The strip starts a bit above the upper left corner of A. Press seam allowance under the new strip.

— Press the far left edge of the unpieced strip 1/4" to the back, where you see the green dotted line. That creates a flap.

— Slide the B piece 1/4" under the flap (up to about B's 1/4" yellow dotted line).

— Move B up and down small amounts, until the Part B diagonal seams look like they flow in a straight line to the same seams on A.

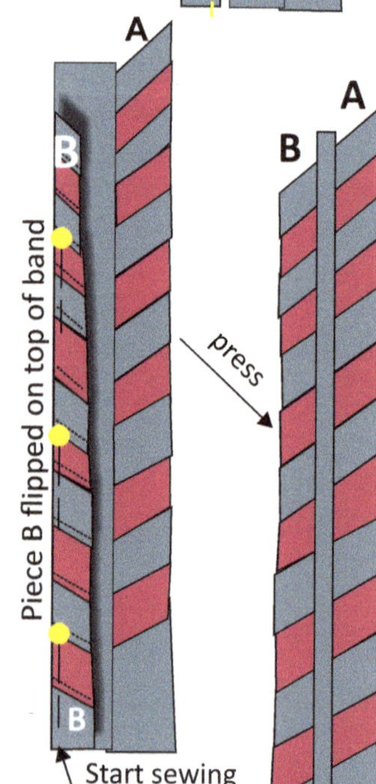

— When you find the sweet spot, pin B there, face down, to the left edge of the band.
— Pin through the seam allowance, sharp points down.
— Sew from the base so you can keep B's seam allowances turned correctly, removing pins as you approach them.
— Press vertical seam allowances right, under unpieced strip.
— Result is on far right.

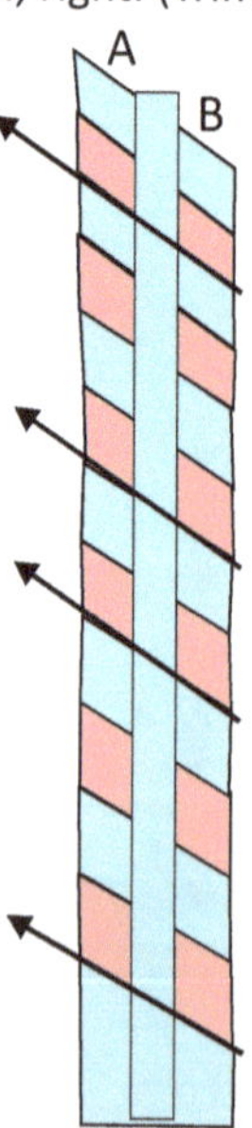

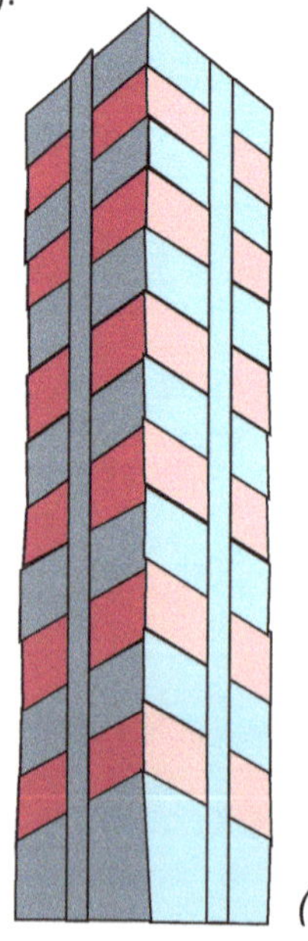

— Do the same on the opposite side (below left). You'll wind up with something like the building below, right. (Trim tops even).

(continued)

But Wait! There's More (Choices)!

Regardless of whether you inserted bands or not, the way to
finish the building and prepare it for appliqué is to press the top
edges down 1/4", the bottom edges up (if they're not at the
base of the quilt or being stitched to something else); and the
two outside edges back 1/4", for the entire length. Option: Fold
the sides back on a slant, as in the second diagram, so the top is
noticeably narrower than the bottom – this gives the building
an extra jolt of three-point perspective, since the two side lines
would hypothetically meet high above.

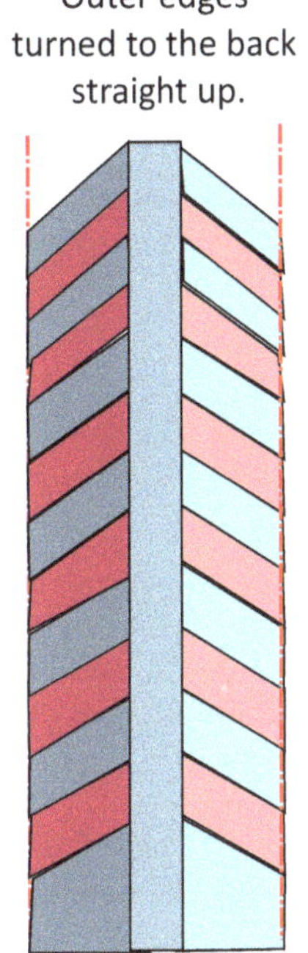

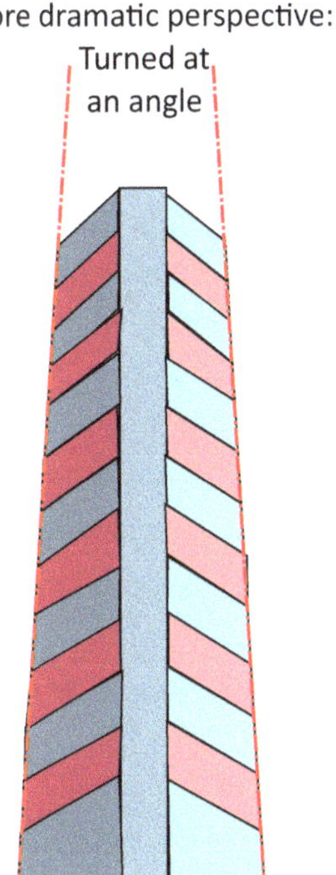

For sidewalk-level perspective, turn/cut the bottom edges of the
ground floor upward, so they form a gentle upright "V". If
there's a central strip, fold straight across that part, as shown.
This "V" (or "U") places the viewer on the sidewalk, at eye level,
looking down to the bottom of the ground floor, and then
looking waayyyy up to the distant top of the skyscraper!

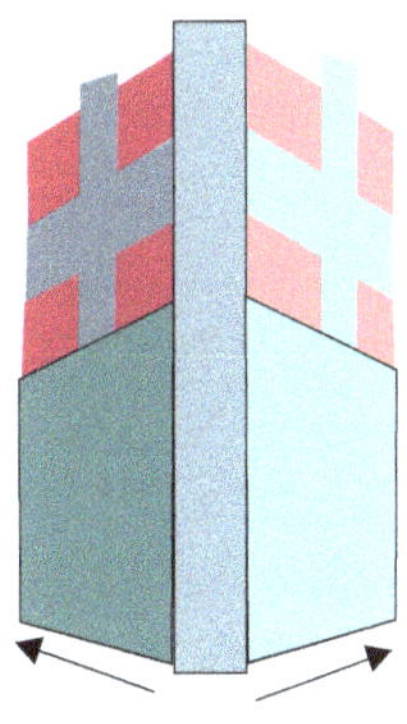

Make a Building Portrait

Every building presents an exciting challenge – how to capture what's intriguing, while having a good time. I avoid precision reproduction of photos. Mostly I try to express an essence, simplify, piece, with a little raw edge appliqué for small or curved details. When you have a building in mind:

1 **Take or look** at LOTS of pictures of it, if possible.

2 **Trace** photos, to help you understand it better. (Unless there may be copyright issues – see next page.)

3 **Draw your own version, and SIMPLIFY**. If the building has 32 windows with 9 panes each, boil it down to 12 windows and 2 panes – or just one geometric print!

4 **Don't design from the windows-out**. If you start by cutting windows from fabric, then surround them, then add more, the building might grow and overtake the quilt. Instead...

5 **Make a paper mockup** of your simplification. Draw the outline on a large piece of paper, to the size and outline you want. From there, design INWARD: Draw in windows, doors and other features. Simplify more as needed. I find it helpful to cut all the shapes out of construction paper.

The left photo below, left is a Library of Congress photo of the Chicago Theatre. In the middle is my first construction paper version. The right shows the finished piece

For the paper mockup, I looked at lots online photos, drew and cut approximate pieces, and taped units together. From that, I learned that I needed to make it smaller.

The mockup also confirmed that I would need to do fusible raw edge appliqué for the lettering and swirls – they were way too tiny for me to turn edges.

The finished fabric version (far right) is smaller and simpler.

6 A **'flexible curve'** (from sewing or art supply store) helps draft buildings with curves. Mine is blue, and I used it on packing paper (below, left), to draw the upper curve of the baseball stadium. I used that mockup to draft six internal sections, which I traced onto lightweight lined white paper.

I created each section separately (with a combination of regular and foundation piecing on top of the lined paper). Then I sewed the six sections together (putting strips of khaki in-between).

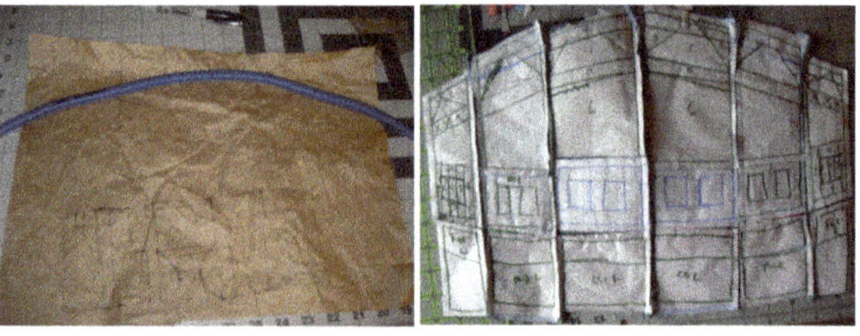

The final step was turning top, sides, and bottom edges under. Here's the finished piece.

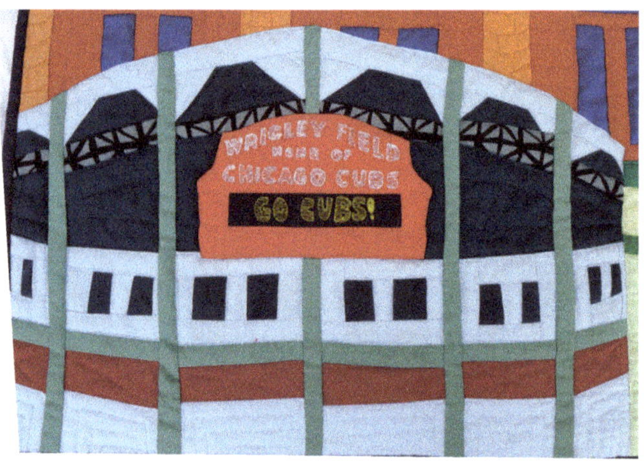

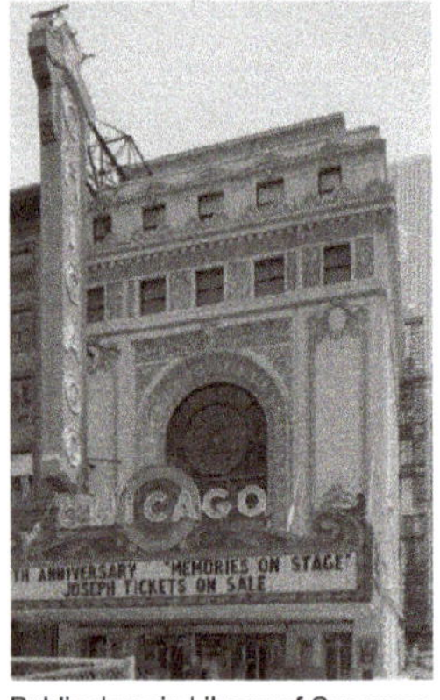

Public domain Library of Congress photo. Historic American Buildings Survey.https://www.loc.gov/pictures/item/il0807.photos.334935p/

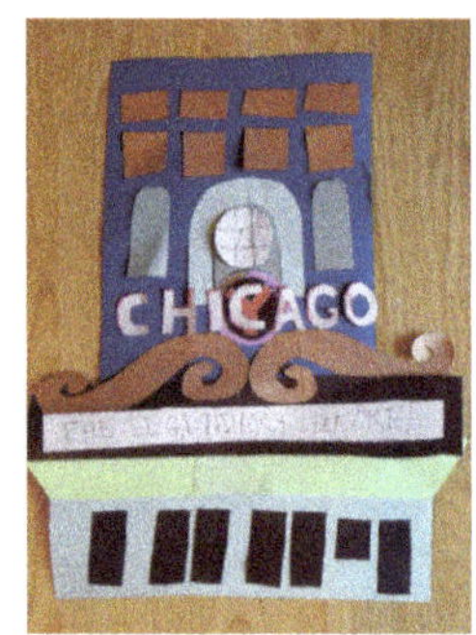

First paper version

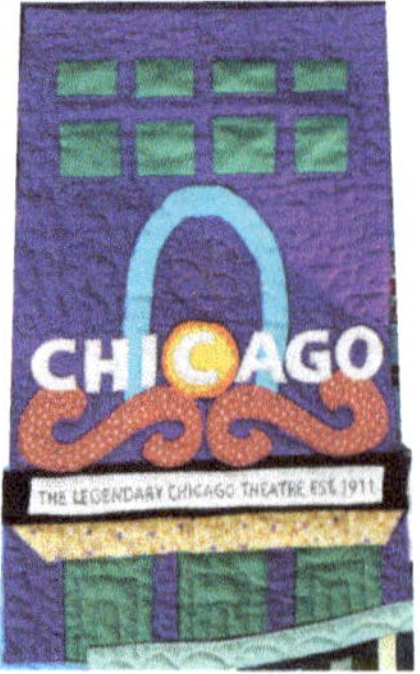

Finished in fabric. Smaller and simpler.

Using Photos

Photos are a huge help. But I use them carefully. Making a close copy of a specific photograph, without the photographer's permission, could be unethical and a copyright violation.

The vast majority of photos on the web are copyrighted, **even if they don't say so explicitly**. If you want to trace and replicate a photo that doesn't have a clear copyright statement (or isn't marked "public domain") contact the photographer and/or website to request permission. If you are not sure what the copyright restrictions are, contact them.

BEST: Take your own photos. Whenever we drive through cities, I constantly take photos (when I'm in the passenger seat. DO NOT DO THIS WHILE AT THE WHEEL! Seriously. The police will give you an expensive ticket, and way worse, you might cause an accident.)

Once safely parked, take more photos than you think you need, from a variety of angles. Figure out how to widen the angle on your phone camera. Include neighboring buildings. You'll be SO glad you did! These photos will be terrific sources of ideas for you, and you can use them without copyright concerns.

ALSO BEST: Use friends' photos, with their permission. When friends post their pictures of buildings of social media, and I see one I love, I write to them to ask if I can download and possibly use their photo in the future. I label the photo with their name so I don't forget where it came from!

Also, there are reliable sites like Shutterfly, where you pay a modest fee for permission to use the photo.

Some sites say they share copyright-free photos, but I've been told by a lawyer that some photos on these sites shouldn't be there and/or that commercial use may still be forbidden. I avoid relying on them.

If you're making something that there are zillions of pictures of (the Eiffel Tower), you still should be careful not to make an exact copy or tracing of any unique photo that might be copyrighted, unless you receive permission.

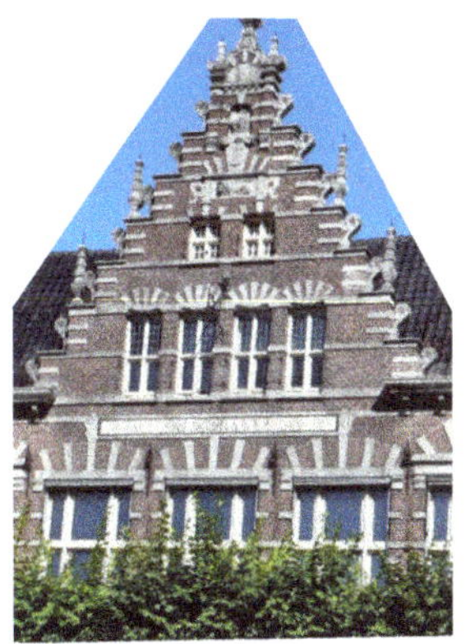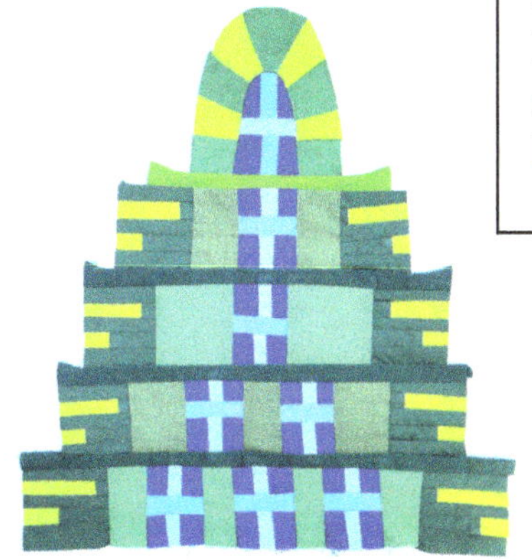

Left, my friend Gail Solomon took this picture of a building in Holland, and gave me permission to use it. My vastly simplified version is on the right.

All About Windows, Easiest to Modernist

Architects say windows are the eyes to a building's soul. In fabric, it becomes a whimsical soul – as in the not-quite-identical windows in a Harvard University dorm, right. (That's Dunster House, on a pillow, which I made at the request of a proud 89-year-old alumnus.) Slightly wonky windows brought it from preppy to lovable! My favorite window-making methods include:

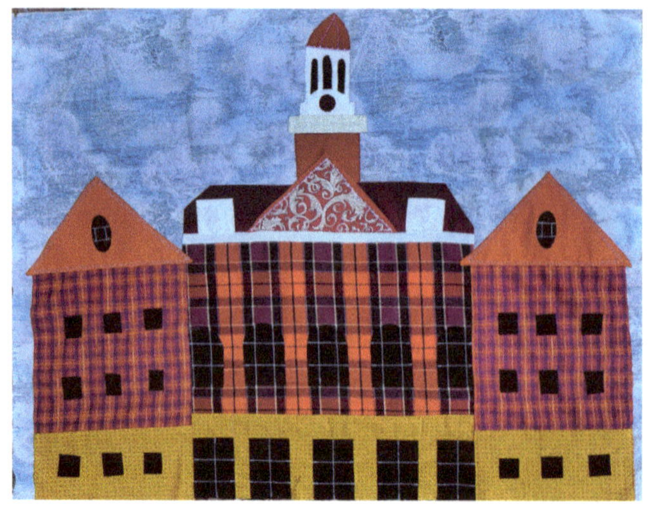

1 Traditional piecing If you press the seam allowances away from each window, it creates a bit of dimension, pushing the windows down. The windows in the townhouse on p. 35 are done this way. Using a geometric print in that project also solved the problem of how to make narrow panes!

2 Raw-edge fusible appliqué I did this for the doors and arched, round and oval windows in Dunster House above. Put fusible web to the back of fabric, and cut out. Press in place, and cover raw edges with a zigzag stitch. Now or later, you can embroider the panes, as I did with white thread. If you do this during the quilting phase, you'll be pushing the entire window downward, for some nice realistic dimension.

3 Turned-edge appliqué If windows are rectangular or square, press sides 1/4" to the back, and sew in place with an zigzagging or straight stitch.

If windows are arched or circular, draft a pattern. An arched window is a half-circle or half-oval on top of a square or rectangle. Draw this by tracing something circular, like a thread spool, then adding a square or rectangle below it.

Once you like the pattern, trace it onto freezer paper or glue it onto cardstock, and cut it out.

Place (with cardstock) or press (with freezer paper) the template onto fabric. Cut the fabric 1/4" larger than the template, all around.

Turn and press all the fabric's raw edges smoothly around the template. Starch or sizing sprayed directly, or into a little dish and applied with a paintbrush, will help keep the edges creased. Peel out the paper, press again, then appliqué the arched

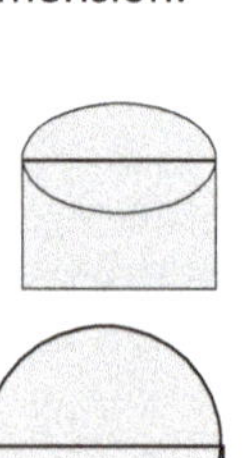
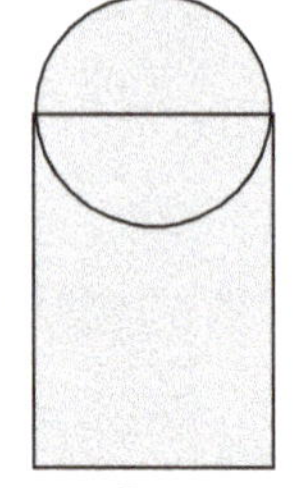
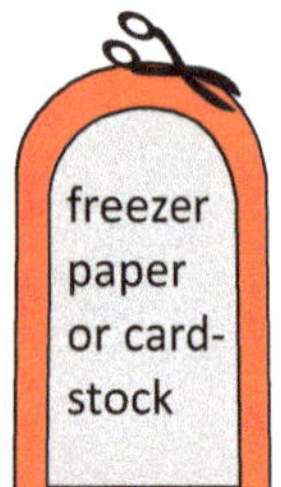

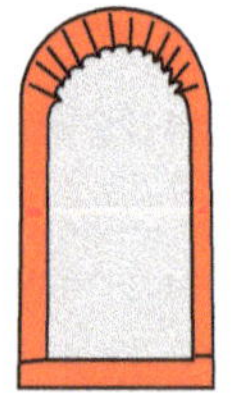

4 Modern slashed panes, right. The most fun! Cut a bunch of squares or rectangles. Slice in half one way (here, horizontally), and insert a narrow strip (no less than 1"). Slice the opposite way, and insert a different strip. (For variety, I threw in a couple of log cabin blocks.)

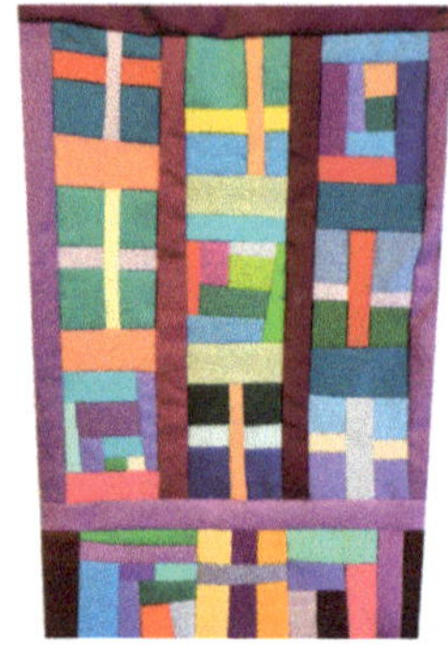

5 Squares in the corner piecing Easy way to make arched windows. It's how I made them in this castle, with only straight-line sewing. See p. 82.

6 Foundation paper piecing. Not the easiest method, but if you enjoy it, you can make windows that look curved with only straight line sewing. See p. 83.

7 Attic windows Fun for its 3D effect. See p. 45.

Less Painful Panes

Instead of piecing tiny panes, use a geometric print (p. 45). Or embroider them. I hand-stitched panes with embroidery floss in this green house pillow. But in the plaid building on top of the page, I machine-quilted the panes in contrasting thread, as a finishing step.

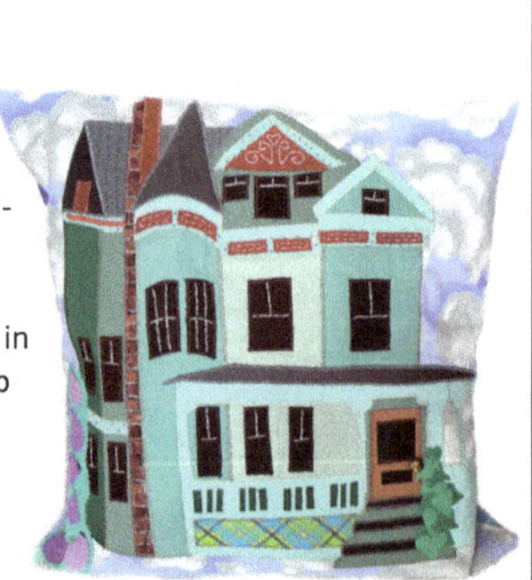

Reverse Appliqué Doors, Windows & Arches

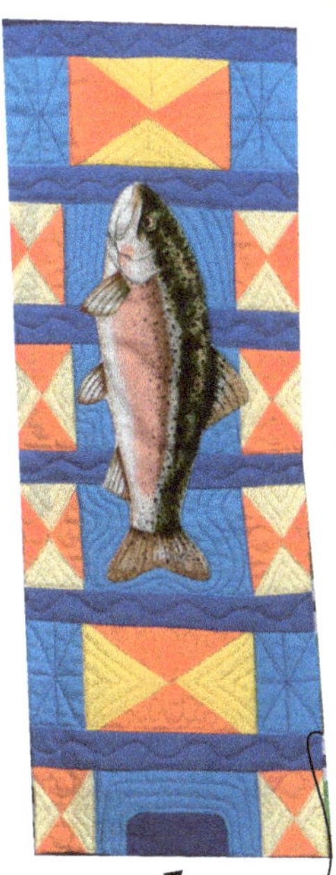

With reverse appliqué, you can add curved doors or windows at the last minute, even in an otherwise finished building. You need freezer paper, ironing fluid (like starch), and a small brush, Q-tip, or any size finger. You will also need a rounded shape – I used a cellphone corner!
(A fishy appliqué is optional!)

1 Here's what the finished bottom level of the building looked like before I installed a doorway.

2 Cut freezer paper about the size of the doorway, just within its outer seams.

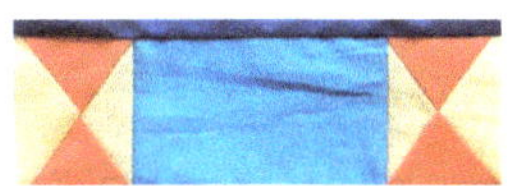

3 Fold in half and crease the center line. Waxy side is inside.

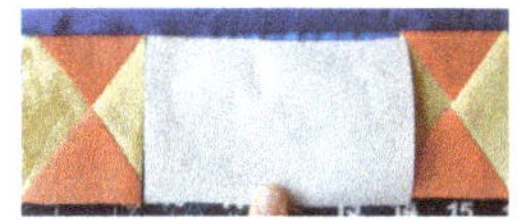

4 Draw a half-arch coming from the fold. That's my phone corner! Or use a half-circle or oval for a rounder arch.

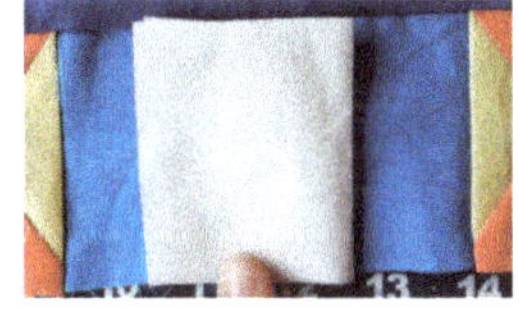

5 Cut it out through both layers of the paper.

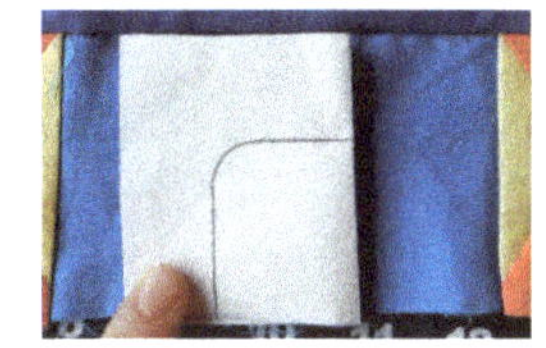

6 Center remaining freezer paper pattern on back of the doorway fabric. Press in place with hot iron.

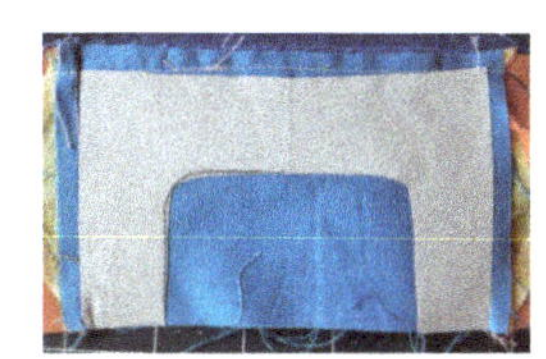

7 Cut away all fabric 1/4" in from the inside paper edge.

8 At the most curved areas – here the two upper corners – clip straight in towards (but not quite touching) the paper, 2 or 3 times. (If your arch is rounder, make clips all along the curved areas.)

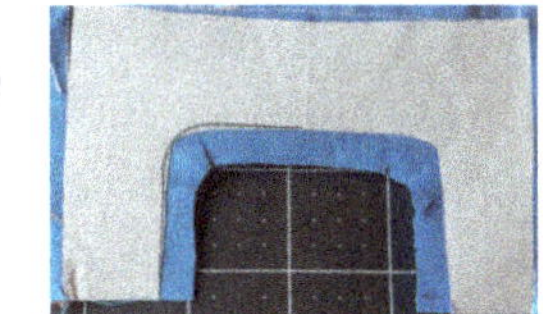

9 Spray some starch, sizing, etc. into a shallow bowl or lid. Paint the exposed inner area with the liquid (using a brush, Q-tip, or finger). Give it a half-minute to spread (while you wash your brush or finger!)

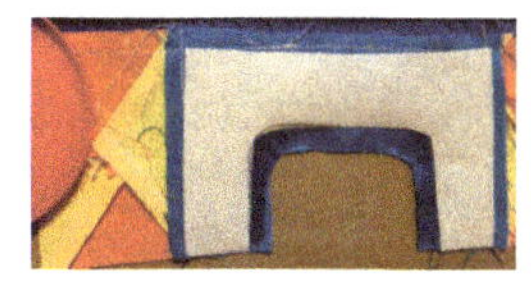

10 Press inner seam allowance to the back, as smoothly as possible. Check from the front.

OPTION: In corners, where you couldn't press much back, drip some "Fray Check". But first test the liquid on a scrap of the same fabric, to make sure it doesn't show when dry.

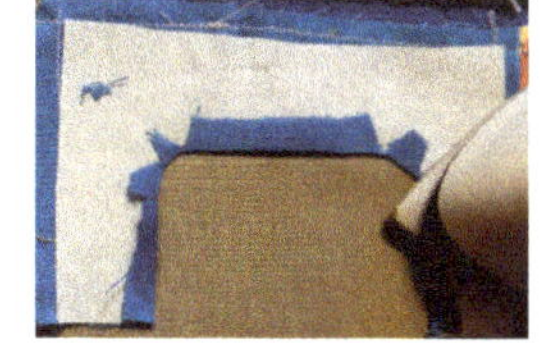

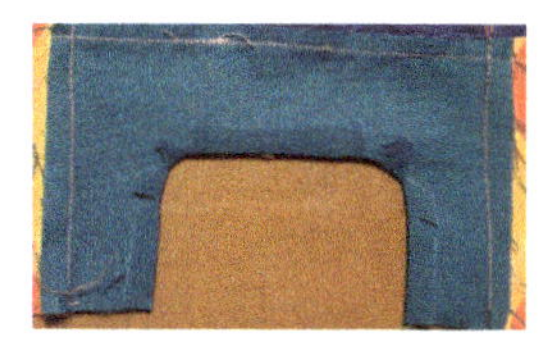

11 Remove template, and put it on your inside-the-building fabric, dark navy here. Cut a rectangle of this inside fabric just a little bigger than the template's outer edges.

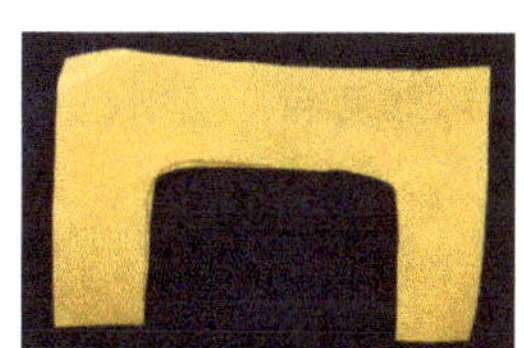

12 On the back of the arched doorway unit, apply a little gluestick to the back seam allowance.

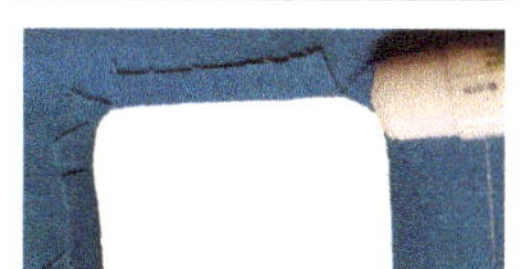

13 Place arched unit on top of the inside-the-building rectangle. Good sides of both are up. Press to dry glue.

14 Trim extra inside fabric extending more than 1" from the doorway outline, and anything extending below the building.

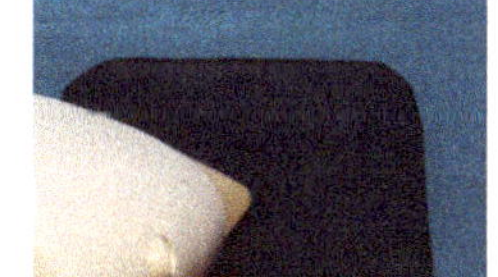

15 Press well from the front.

16 Topstitch with a plain or decorative zigzag.

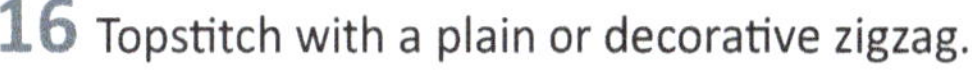

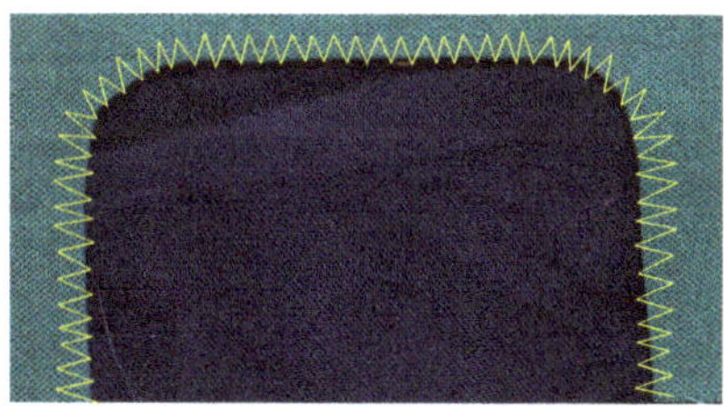

Arched Windows from Straight Lines

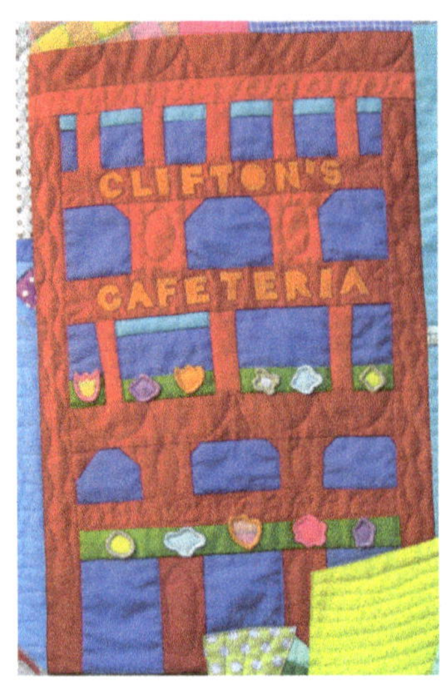

The kitschy interior of Los Angeles' 1931 Clifton's Cafeteria boasts a 40-foot walk-in redwood tree; a running stream; and taxidermy galore (lion, moose, bison). The outside has rectangular, arched, oval and scalloped windows – it looks like a box of chocolates. Walt Disney supposedly lunched there, and it inspired faux environments at Disneyland.

Arched windows are a challenge for curve-averse piecers like me. So for the version on the near left, I most often use a low-stress improv squares-in-the-corner method. For curvier-looking faux-arches, I do foundation paper piecing, on the next page, which is also straight line sewing!

Squares in the Corners

White is the window glass/room color. Light grey is the "building" color (bricks, cement, etc.) Dark grey is the back of the building color fabric. **The designs can be used at their actual sizes, or you can easily adapt this idea to any size arched window that you need.**

Smaller squares = gentler arch

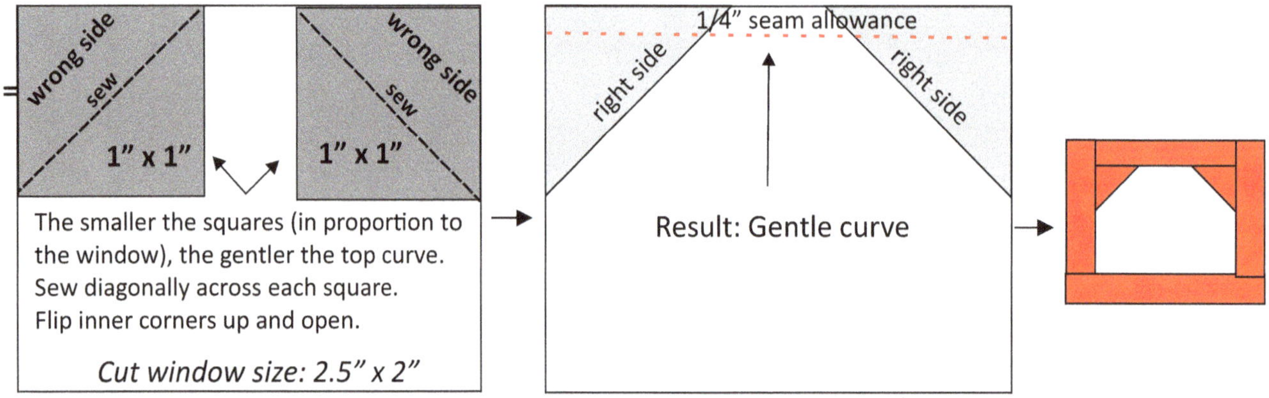

The smaller the squares (in proportion to the window), the gentler the top curve. Sew diagonally across each square. Flip inner corners up and open.

Cut window size: 2.5" x 2"

Larger squares = Steeper arch

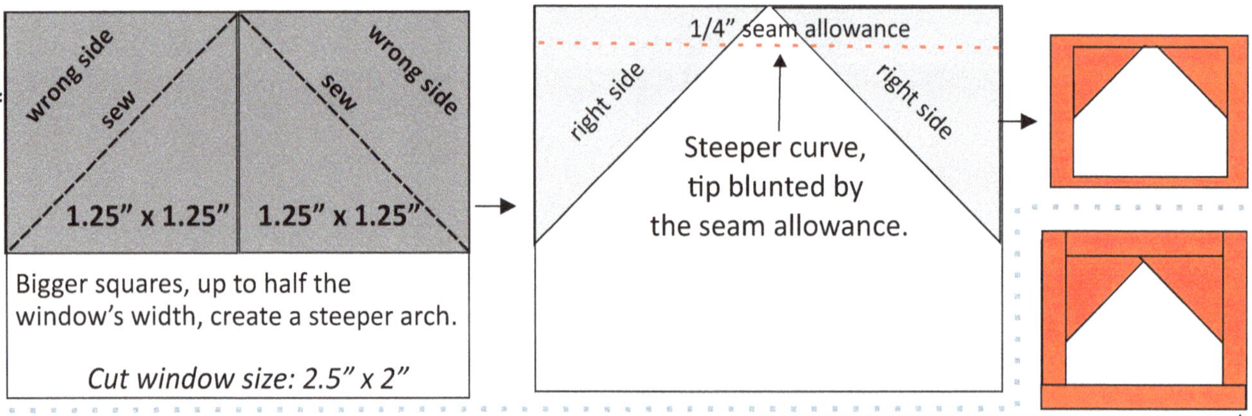

Bigger squares, up to half the window's width, create a steeper arch.

Cut window size: 2.5" x 2"

Largest squares = Pointed tip

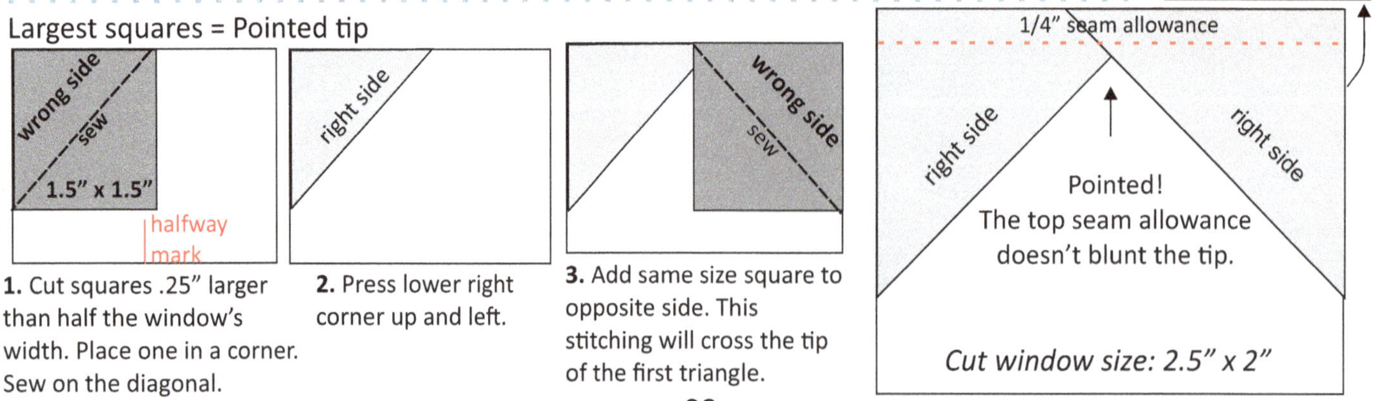

1. Cut squares .25" larger than half the window's width. Place one in a corner. Sew on the diagonal.

2. Press lower right corner up and left.

3. Add same size square to opposite side. This stitching will cross the tip of the first triangle.

Cut window size: 2.5" x 2"

4. Press up and enjoy!

Foundation Paper Pieced Arched Windows

For a curvier appearance, try foundation paper piecing (You can work from the back OR front with these ideas). Below left, mark two diagonals like these to create a flattish curve. Far right, two-part angles created rounder arches. Bottom of the page: Draft your own.

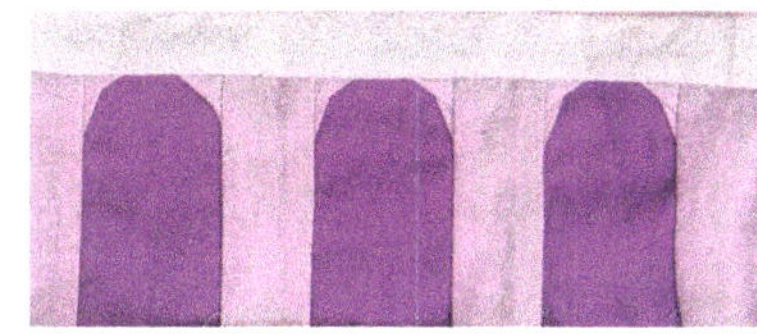

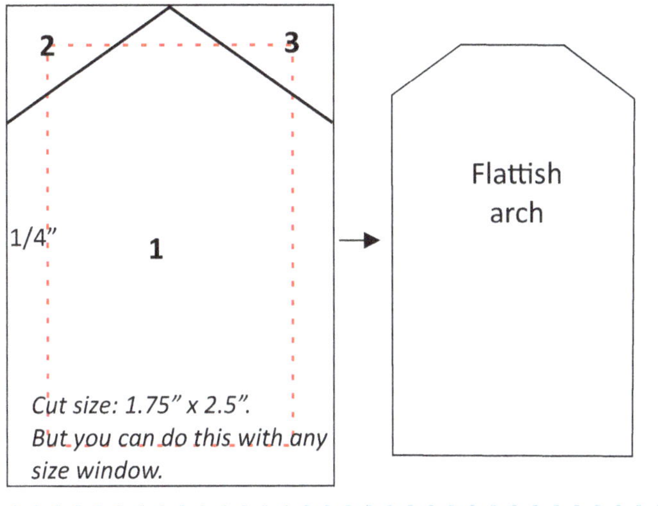

Cut size: 1.75" x 2.5". But you can do this with any size window.

Flattish arch

Rounder arch

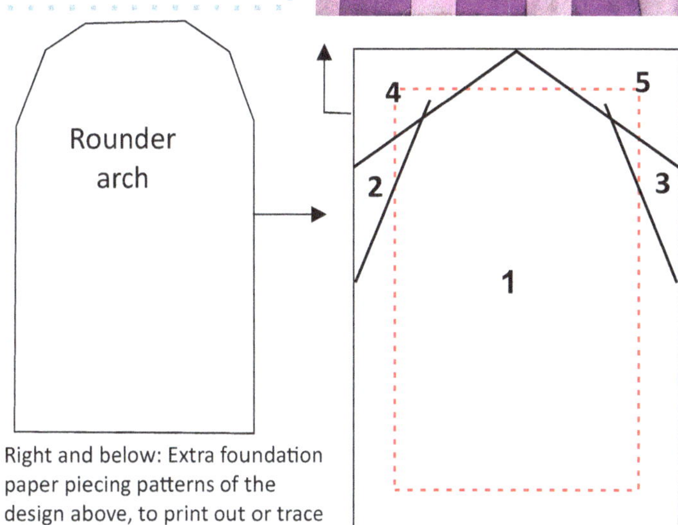

Right and below: Extra foundation paper piecing patterns of the design above, to print out or trace

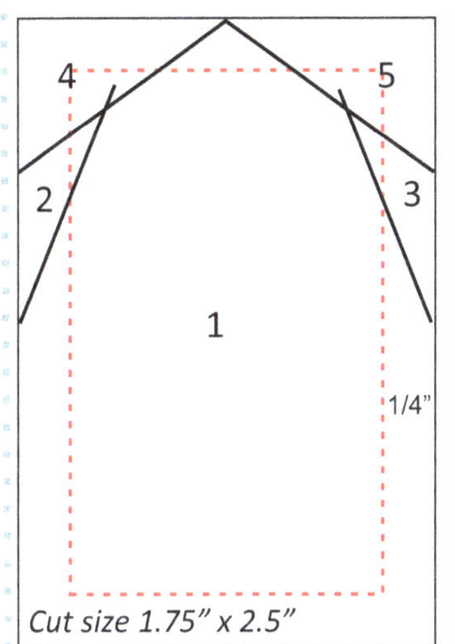

Cut size 1.75" x 2.5"

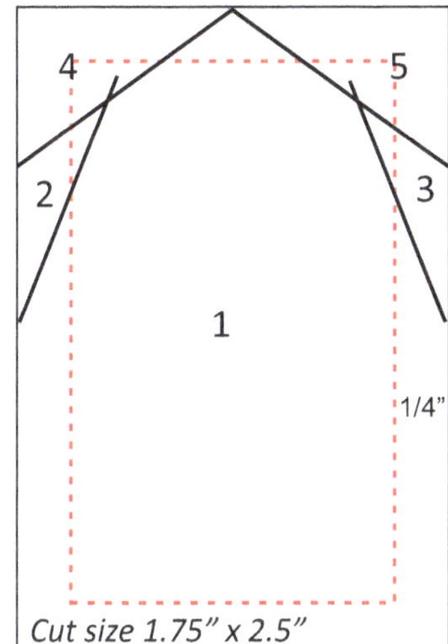

Cut size 1.75" x 2.5"

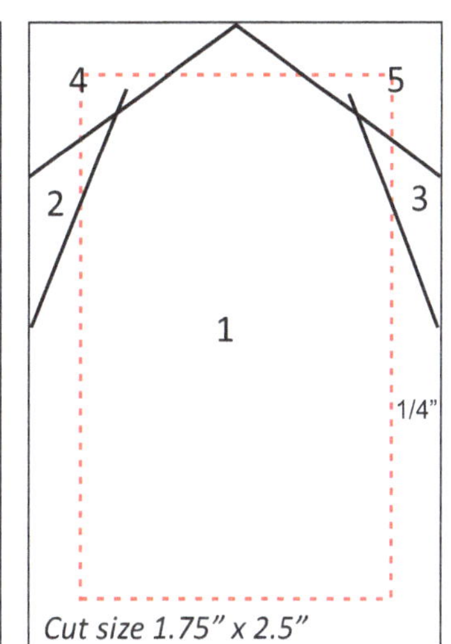

Cut size 1.75" x 2.5"

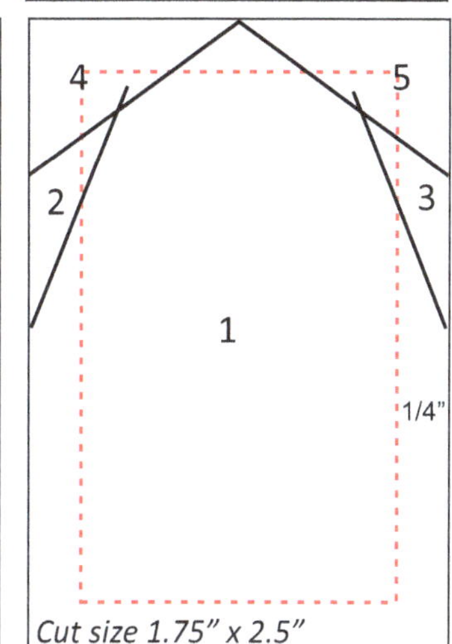

Cut size 1.75" x 2.5"

Draft Your Own Foundation Paper Piecing Pattern!

Cut paper to window size plus seam allowance. Draw 1/4" seam allowance (red). Fold in half to find top center (**z**).

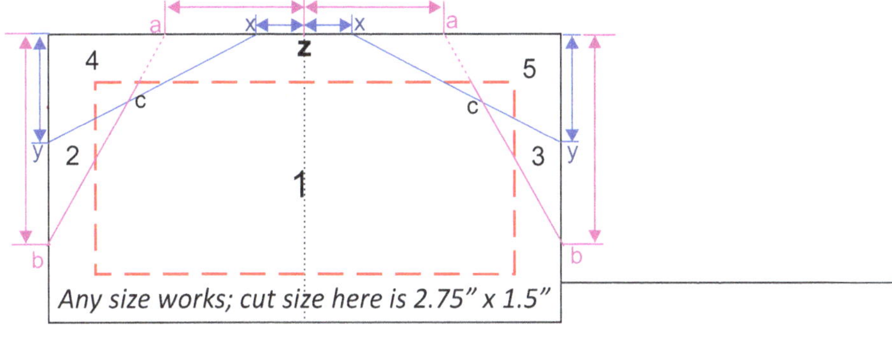

Any size works; cut size here is 2.75" x 1.5"

Below, extra foundation paper piecing pattern, drafted as on the left, for you to print out or trace.

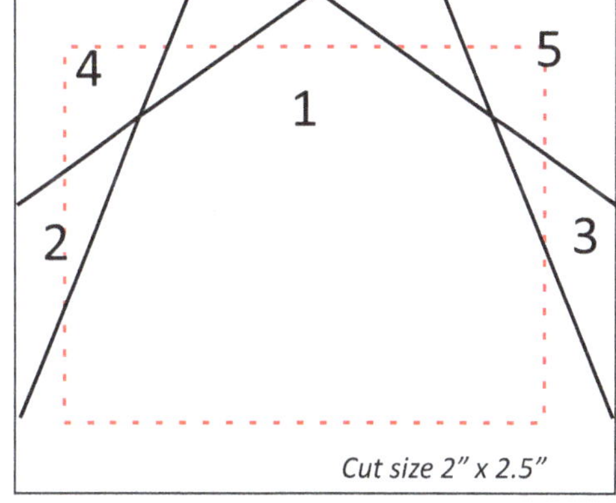

Cut size 2" x 2.5"

To make the flatter blue lines above, measure from **z** to the **x**'s, a short distance out on both sides; mark the **x**'s. Measure from the two top corners, down to a point high on each side (**y**'s). With a ruler, connect each **x** to its **y**.

For steep pink lines, mark further from **z**, at the two pink **a**'s. Measure and mark spots lower than **y** on both sides. These are the **b**'s. Connect each **a** to its **b**. Where lines cross (at **c**) must be beyond the 1/4" seam allowance.

Fiddling with the Roof: House of One Gable

This approach works well for designing any kind of roof.

1 Put a large piece of paper behind the top of the building.

2 Draw a line the length that you want the roof. (The red line in the diagram.)

3 For eaves – a roof wider than the building – add what you need to both side of your first line. (In the diagram, I extended the 8" black house's top line to the 10" red one.)

4 Draw the roof's side lines at whatever angle you like. They're blue here.

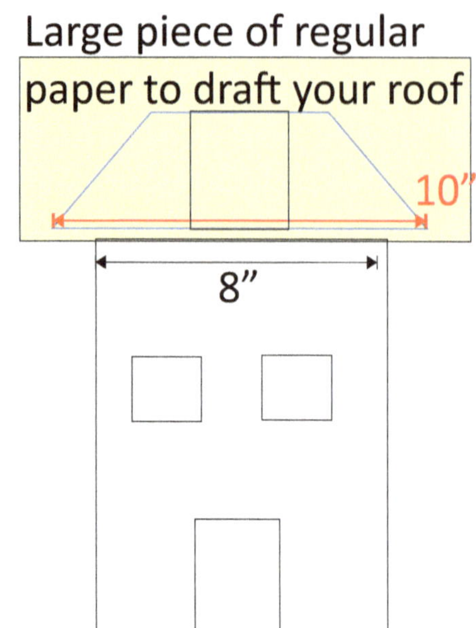

5 If you want a gable (attic window): Cut out your paper pattern. Work inward to subdivide the roof. I fold the paper in thirds to help me calculate equal subdivisions. Create 2, 3 or more equal sections; OR make the central section wider; or whatever you like!

6 From the drawing, estimate piece 1 (window glass) size. Build on it log cabin style, adding strips 2, 3, and 4 – each unit tells you what size the next one needs to be. For pieces that will wind up as side triangles – 5 and 6 in the drawing – cut them out as rectangles (outline in green) to the same height as the part you've finished.

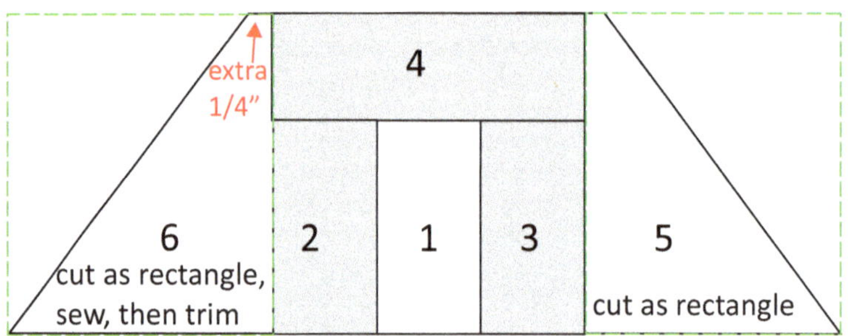

7 Sew together the middle unit (pieces 1-4 here). Sew the two size rectangles to your middle unit, and THEN trim those as shown, to a modified triangle, with an extra quarter-inch at the top.

8 If you feel it's done, fold two diagonal sides 1/4" to the back, and top 1/4" down. Or keep going to add more.

Roof Add-ons

Option A, Flat roof: Cut a rectangular strip the width of the unit below it, plus 3/4", and as high as you want it. Sew to the top. Trim sides, continuing the diagonal line of the lower pieces.

Option B, Triangle roof: Cut a triangle to the width of your rooftop plus .75" by desired height. Cut the two sides on a slant, continuing the diagonal lines of the lower area.

Option C, Curvy Roof: See next page.

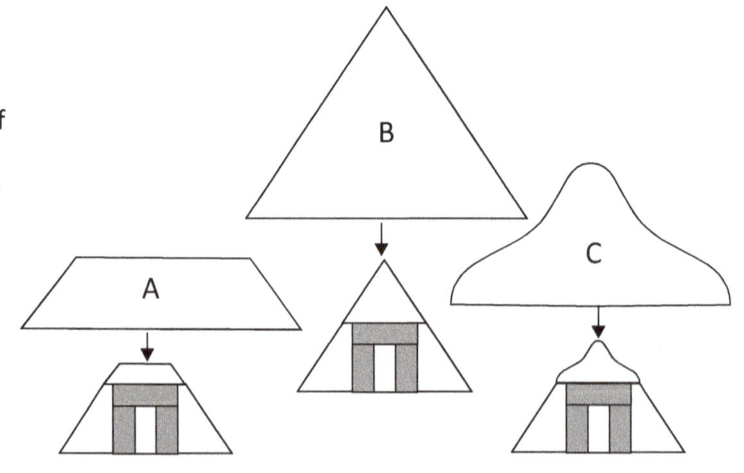

Curvy Roof with Freezer Paper Appliqué

1 Place freezer paper – cut bigger than you want the roof – under the building's top edge. Draw roof. If it's symmetrical (mirror image across its center line), decide which half of your drawing you like best, right or left!

2 Fold freezer paper so your favorite half is showing, and fold down the middle of the paper.

3 Cut out the pattern through both layers of paper.

4 With a hot iron, press the open pattern onto the back of the roof fabric.

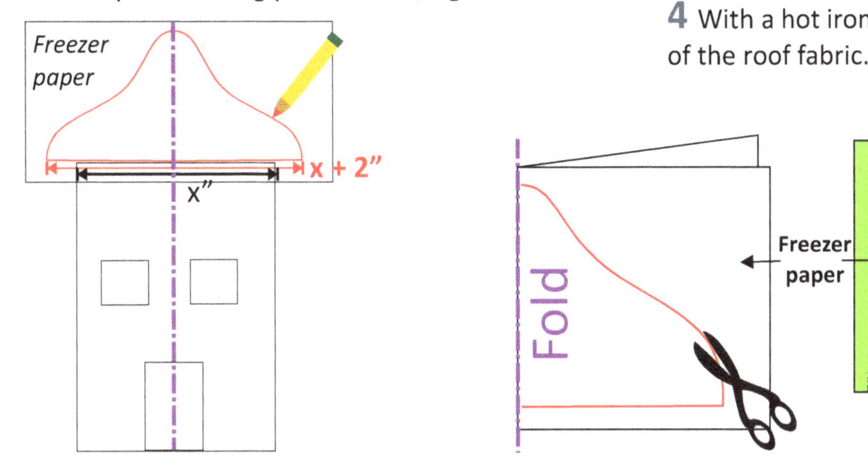

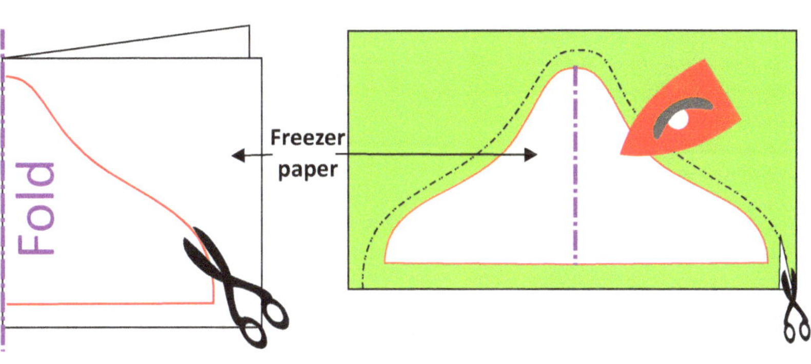

5 Cut out shape from fabric, 1/4" - 3/8" beyond the paper pattern. At inward curves, make 2 or 3 straight 1/8" clips into seam allowances. Stop a couple of threads before the paper.

6 Press top and side fabric edges inward. Starch helps. Don't press bottom edge up.

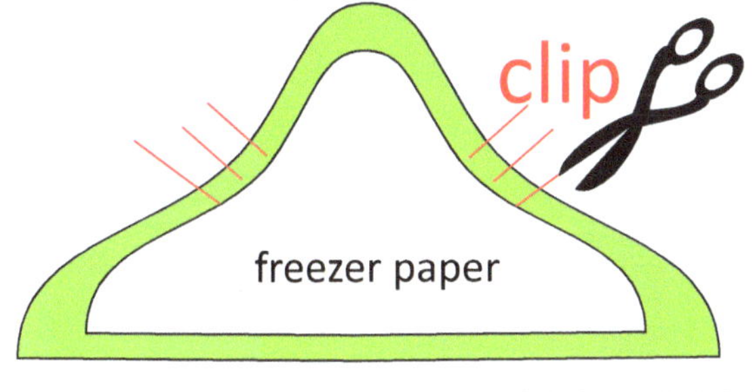

7 Sew from whichever side is narrowest, where you can see the flaps you'll be sealing. This probably means sewing from the back of the building, below right (But if you prefer to sew from the back of the roof, that's shown on the left. In that case, mark the start and end of the hidden roof flaps.) Backstitch at both ends, catching the flaps of the less-wide building. (Start sewing at **a**, backstitch to **b**, sew to **c**, end and cut threads at **d**.

8 Press seam allowances, as well as the roof, upward

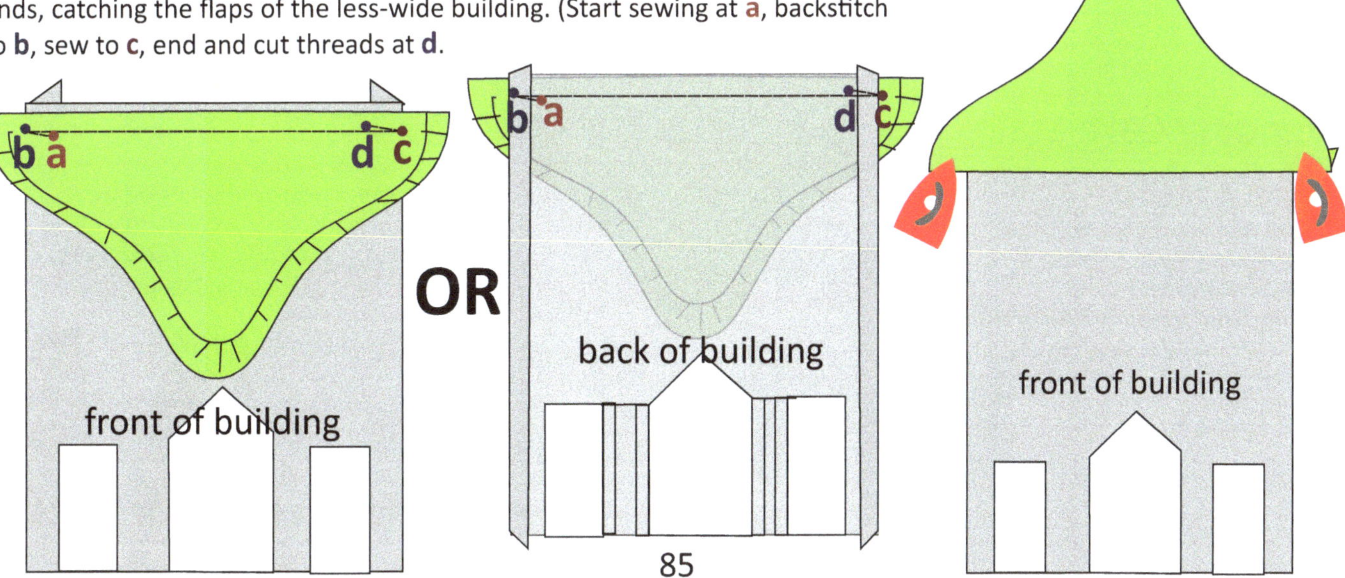

Stair (and Yurt) Theory

Perhaps the greatest challenge of portraying buildings is that you want to include all the details – but that would require countless microscopic pieces. This is especially true with stairs, which are tiny compared the rest of the building. Here are some ideas for making stairs without losing microscopic pieces of your mind!

Stairs have two units: The "top," which is stepped on; and the "drop", which goes straight down. Alternating dark and light values is the most powerful thing you can do to create the effect of stairs.

In daylight, the top – facing the sky – is usually the lightest. But that also depends on the sun's position, and/or the location of streetlights, flashlights, etc. Plus, you're the artist. So you can switch that around.

On the far right is a photo my friend Margaret took of our town's notoriously long staircase, enjoyed by local masochistic fitness buffs. My tracing is next to it, adding the vanishing point (blue dot) above the flight.

It's amazing how fast the tops dwindle, relative to drops. For the bottom four steps, you could see a penny on a stair top. But by the time you're looking halfway up the flight, the tops are slivers, and then nothing more than a shine. They're almost too tiny to draw – let alone piece!

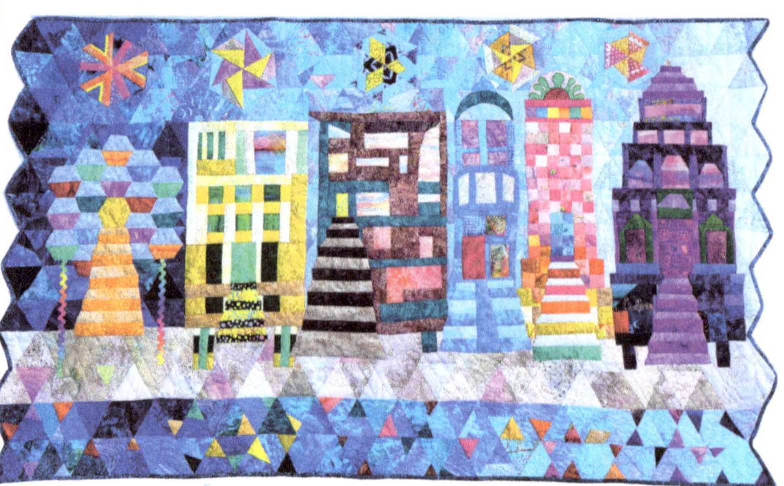
Below, *'Beach Houses,'* 2023, each with its own long stairs. 66" x 38"

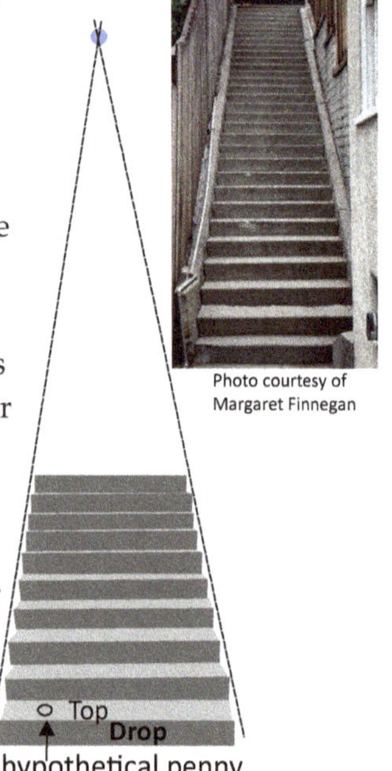
Photo courtesy of Margaret Finnegan

So you MUST simplify! Reduce the number as well as the size of stairs!

In my early version of the Chicago Art Institute below, I shamelessly consolidated its front stairs from 12+ to two. Stair tops are light pink, and drops are dark pink. I changed the proportions to make the top extra-wide, creating a landing. (The arched doorways were created with straight line foundation paper piecing, p. 83. The lions are raw edge fusible applique.) See the finished version on p.9.

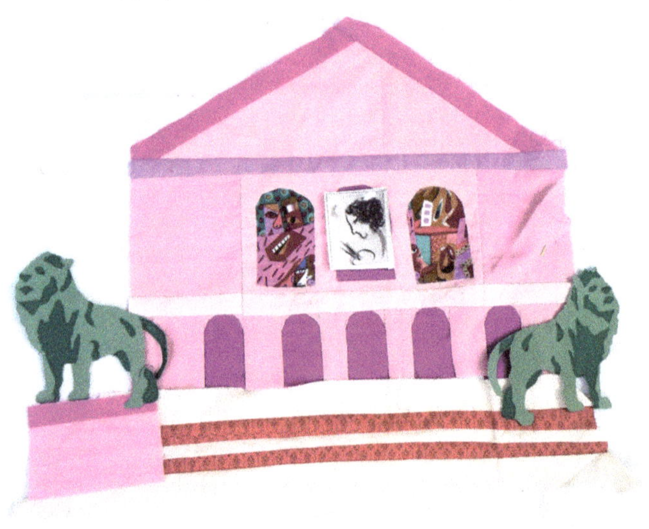

Wedding Cake Stairs

Cut each piece a half-inch narrower than the one below. (Use dimensions listed, or create your own.) Alternate dark and light strips. Press sides on each piece inward before sewing it to the next piece. See p. 33 for wedding cake piecing directions.

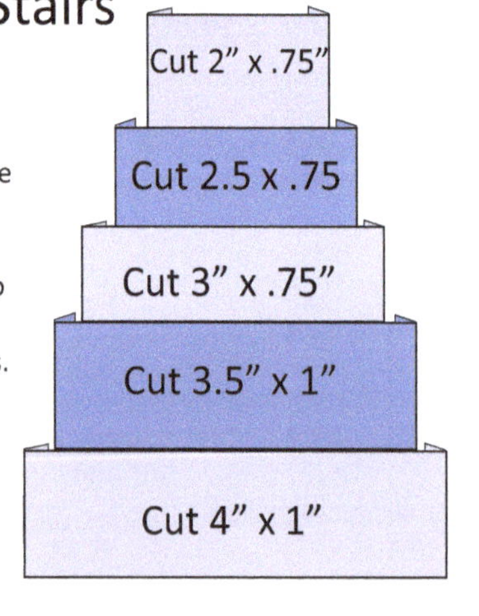

Sliced Cake Stairs

Cut stairs to the same sizes in the diagram on the left (or any sizes you want), but DON'T turn in side seams before sewing. Instead, find and press or mark centers on each strip. Piece together the traditional way (with no flaps or backstitching). Side edges will be raw. Press horizontal seam allowances downward. Trim sides on a diagonal, as shown.

Because each side edge is a straight line, it's easy to turn and press the entire edge under 1/4". Also turn the top and bottom edges, when you're ready to appliqué them in place.

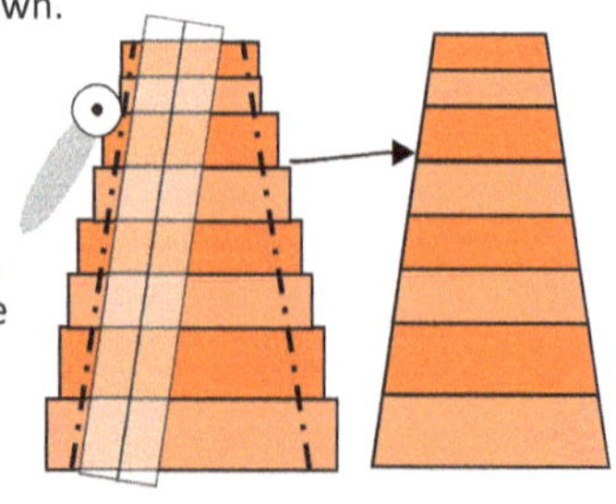

Foundation Paper Pieced Stairs

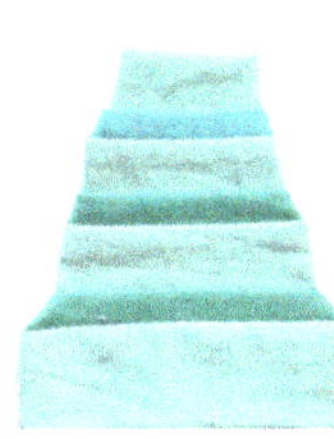

This makes convincing stairs, or can serve as a roof, pagoda, or yurt! Photo in the lower right corner of this page shows what I did with mine. The pattern below finishes at 3.5" x 3.5", but you can size it up. Don't shrink it, because piece 2 is sooo tiny already! You need scraps of two fabrics, a dark and a light.

1 Print out this page and check that pattern is 3.5" high.

2 Cut out pattern on the blue outline. This differs from most FPP, where the paper 1/4" seam allowance is kept in place during piecing. We need it gone **now**, to help us press sides inward later.

3 Cut color 1 (a drop) at least 1/4" bigger on all sides than the pattern piece. Pin piece 1 behind the paper's piece 1 area.

Cut piece 2 (a top) at least 1/2" bigger all around than the piece 2 area on paper. Place it face down along the bottom edge of piece 1. Sew on the line from the reverse side. Press piece 2 downward.

4 Continue working this way. Extra fabric should stick out out on the sides at LEAST 1/4". (More is okay)

5 When you've added all the stairs, the back looks like this.

6 Trim raw edges to about 1/4" beyond the paper. Use paper's edge to help press all raw edges back. Fold odd-number "drop" edges straight up-and-down, and "tops" at an angle (see photo below). Sometimes releasing a few stitches from seam ends helps.

7 Remove paper and press again. A glue stick helps persuade raw edges to stay turned.

Your stairway is ready for appliqué wherever you want it!

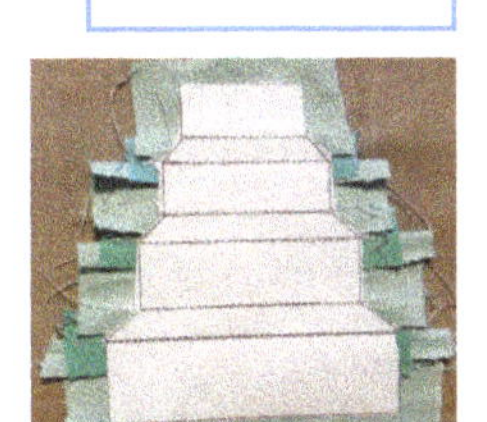

FULL SIZE PATTERN

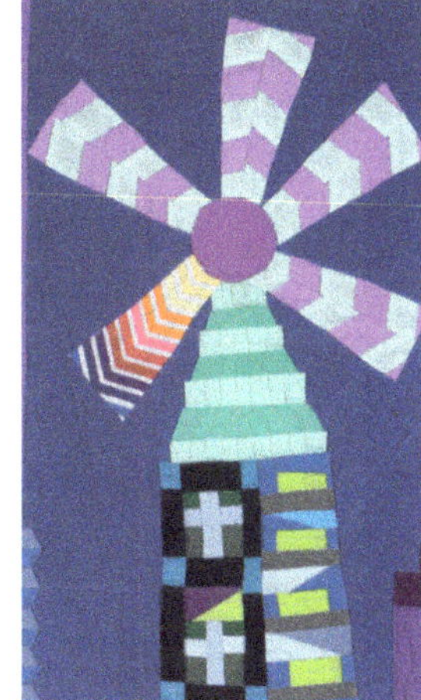

87

Intro to My Favorite Stairs:
Remember the Fold-Sew-Fold Trick?

Back on p. 67, I introduced the "Fold-Sew-Fold" trick as a way to add a side in perspective to a front-facing building. It worked like this.

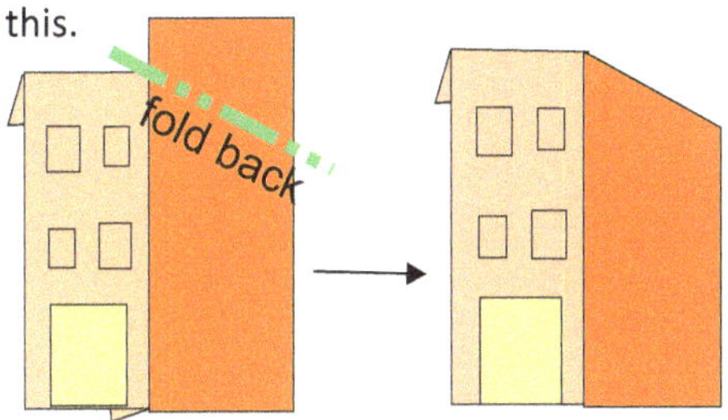

And we talked about doing the same thing on bottom, like this:

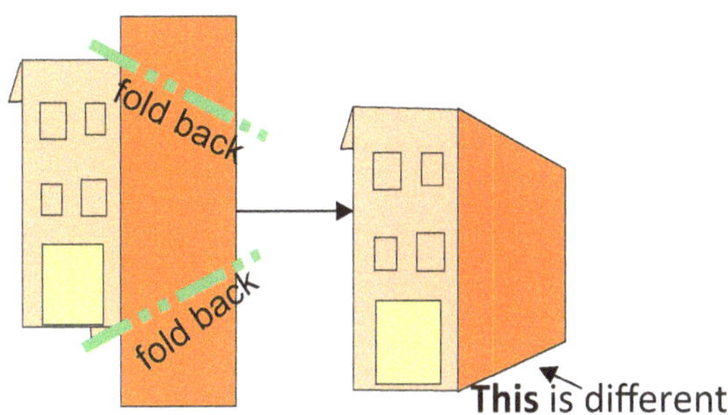

If you did this with a bunch of strips in a row, you'd get:

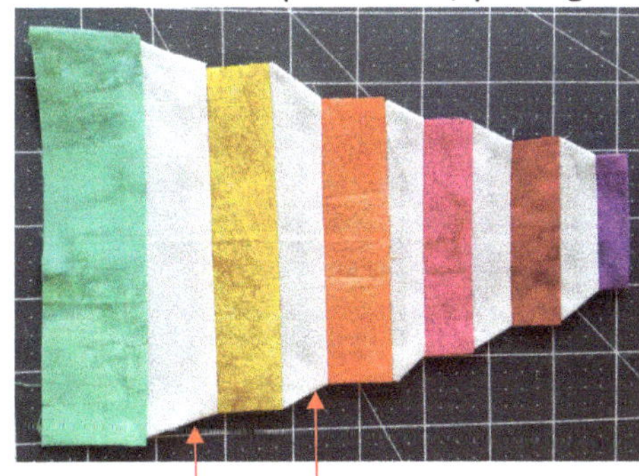

On the white strips, top AND bottom edges are now slanted toward a vanishing point. The colorful strips look like buildings facing forward, each with a white side on its right. OR...(turn the page!!!)

Here's how I wound up using this stairway – as the neck of a windmill, in 'Nonsense Town' on p. 10.

Stairway to Heavenly Perspective

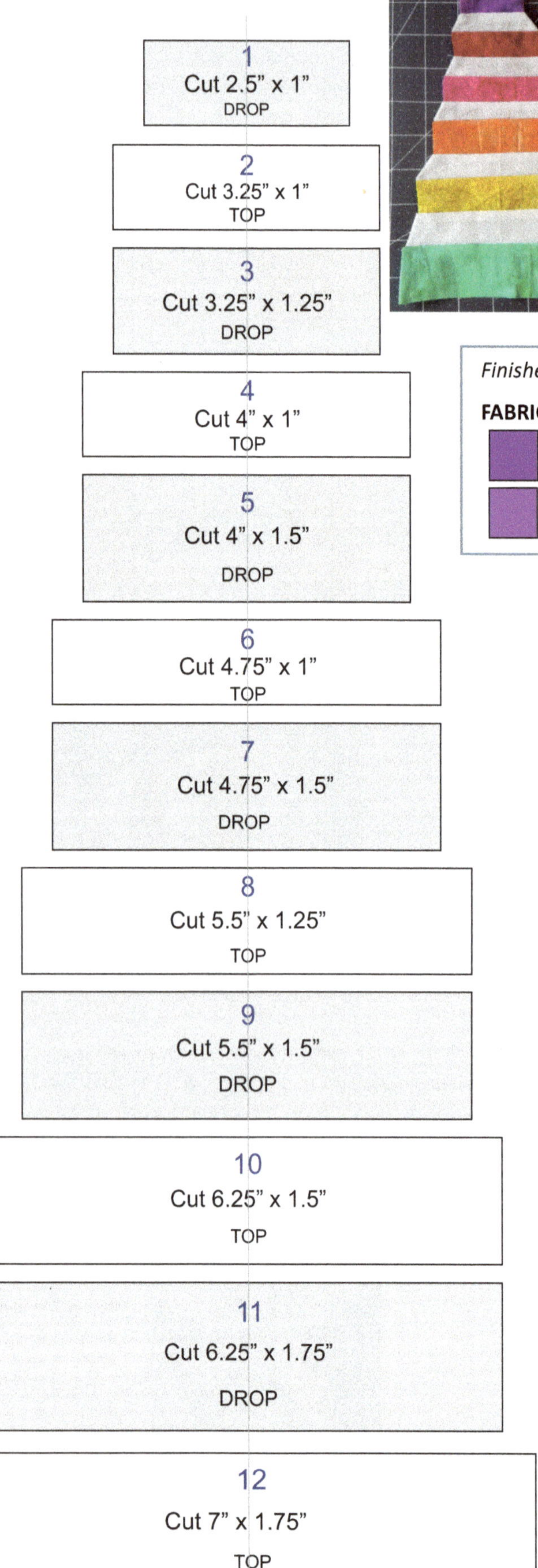

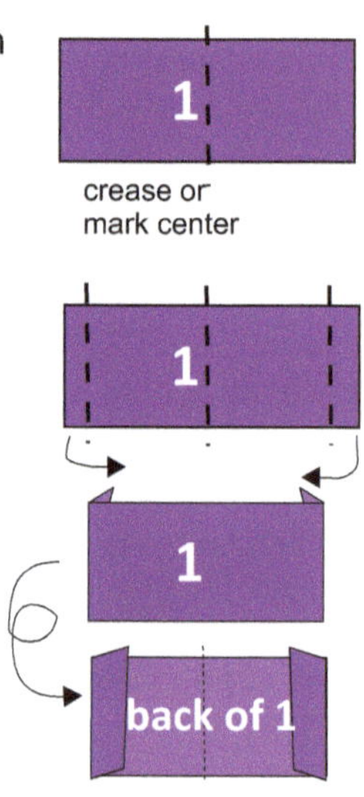

This stair-making method is the most fun, and perspective-wise, convincing. It uses the same fold-piece-fold trick shown earlier to create building sides. But here we do it sideways, and on two ends!

Choose at least 2 fabrics, with contrasting values. Odd number pieces are dark, and the D also stands for DROP. Even-numbered pieces will be TOPS, and face the sky, so they're light.

Finished stairway is approx. 9" x 7"

FABRIC: Less than a fat 1/8th of at least two colors (purple and gold here):

Fabric 1/Good side/Drop	Fabric 2/Good Side/Top
Fabric 1/Back/Drop	Fabric 2/Back/Top

---

1 Cut all pieces to the measurements in the left diagram.

2 On every piece, press short ends together to find and press a crease down the middle. If you can't see the crease, mark the top and bottom back.

3 On all the dark/drop pieces only: Fold both side edges inward 1/4", to the back.

4 Place the stack in order again. All the drops have their sides pressed in, and all the tops don't.

5 Place dark piece 1, good side down, onto piece 2, good side up. Align centers and top raw edges, as below. Pin. Here, and for all future pieces, we put the shorter piece on top, so we can sew with a clear view of the start and end.

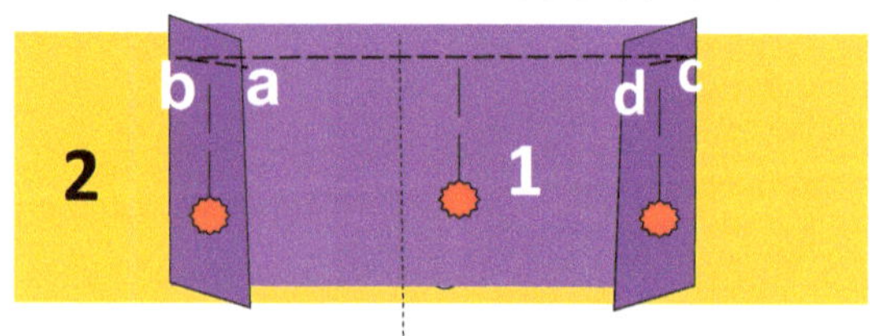

6 Rotate the seam to the right, and stitch. Bring up threads at **a**, just below the flap. Backstitch to just within the fold, to **b**. Sew down to **c**. Backstitch to **d** and cut threads. The backstitching secures the flap and make it easy to hide thread ends that will want to stick out of the finished edges.

Left diagram — cut pieces:

Piece	Cut	Type
1	Cut 2.5" x 1"	DROP
2	Cut 3.25" x 1"	TOP
3	Cut 3.25" x 1.25"	DROP
4	Cut 4" x 1"	TOP
5	Cut 4" x 1.5"	DROP
6	Cut 4.75" x 1"	TOP
7	Cut 4.75" x 1.5"	DROP
8	Cut 5.5" x 1.25"	TOP
9	Cut 5.5" x 1.5"	DROP
10	Cut 6.25" x 1.5"	TOP
11	Cut 6.25" x 1.75"	DROP
12	Cut 7" x 1.75"	TOP

(continued)

8 Press seam allowance down under piece 2. Also, press the extended areas of the seam allowance (on top of 2 on the far right and left), downward.

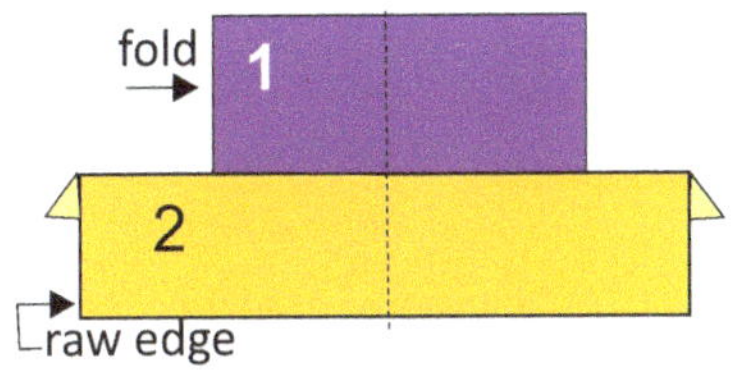

9 Take piece 3, a drop. Its side edges are pressed inward.

Place it face down on bottom of piece 2, matching centers and bottom edges. (You can see the good side of piece 1 peeping out from above, but I left that piece out of this diagram to simplify it!) Pin. Stitch across, starting at **a**, backstitching to **b**, sewing to **c,** and backstitching to **d**. Cut thread.

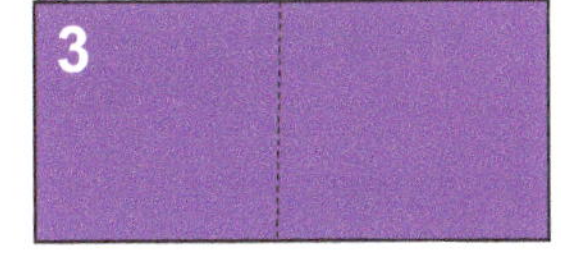

10 Press seam allowances down.

11 We'll do one more. Piece 4 is a top. Put the shorter unit (piece 3, attached to all its earlier pieces) good side down, centered on the top edge of 4.

Sew the bottom edge of 3 to the top edge of 4 as before, starting at **a**, backstitching to **b**, sewing to **c**, backstitching to **d**. Cut threads. Press seam allowances down. Keep going like this.

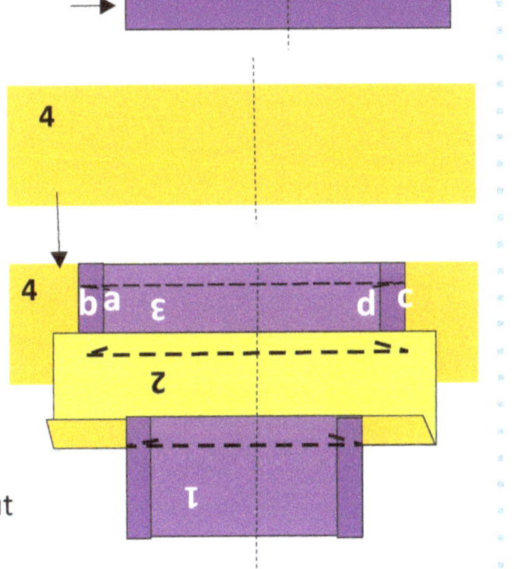

Eventually, it will look like this. The two outer edges of all the drops are folded in; the tops' outer edges are still raw.

12 Now comes the fun part, which will instantly throw it into a satisfying facsimile of 1-point perspective!
Fold each top's highest outer corners down and back. Fold between where the previous drop ends and the next drop starts. Green dotted lines show this. You'll be wrapping each top's corners around the lower corner of the previous drop.

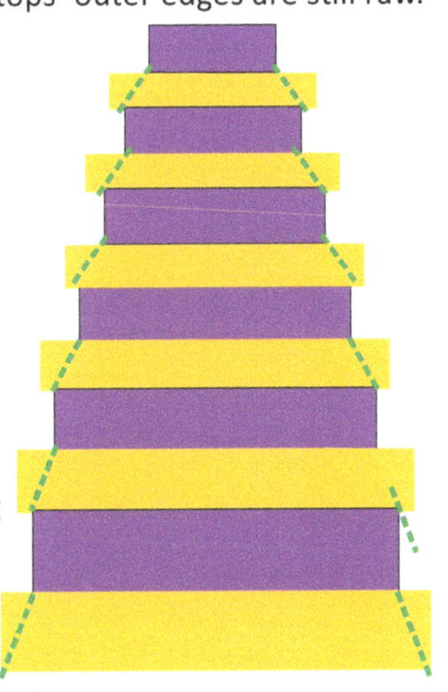

When you fold those corners back, the tops' tips may peek out from behind the drops.

There's an easy fix! At the ironing board, we'll "smush" (architectural term) those points back and out of the way. A bit of glue stick is a big help.

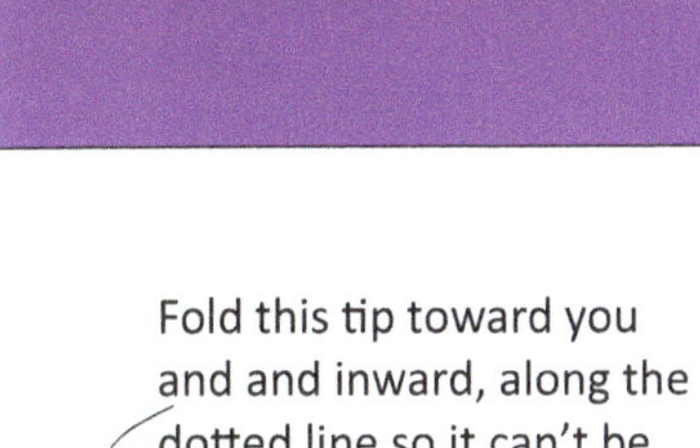

Fold this tip toward you and and inward, along the dotted line so it can't be seen from the front.

Folded, it might look something like this.

You may also want to press the underlying drop's tip (purple) to the left. Or leave it for now, and push it out of the way during appliqué.

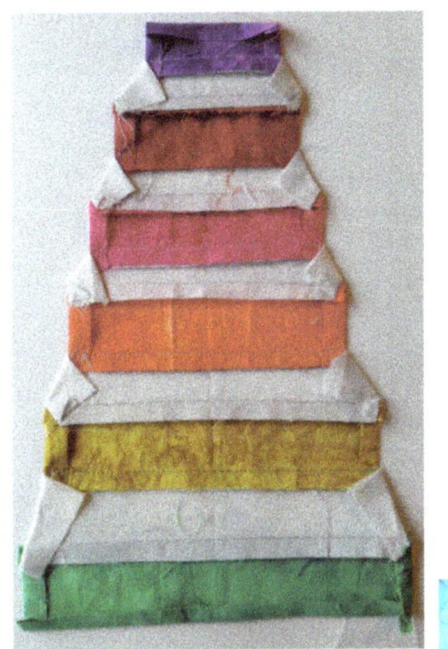

Here's the back of my rainbow stairs, with all edges and tips smushed to the back.

Check from the front that your stairway is ready for appliqué to any building...or maybe it's a stairway to heaven?

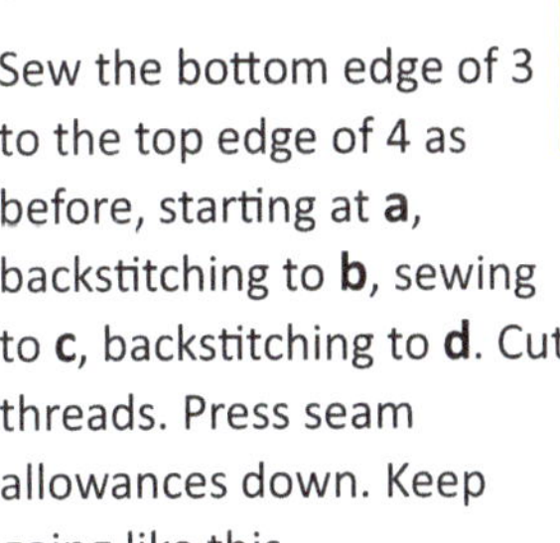

What to do with your stairs? They can be a pagoda style building. Or plop them on top of a building, just below the door, like I did with this beach house quilt! The building that received these stairs is on the right. The blue building got different stairs! See the entire quilt on p. 86.

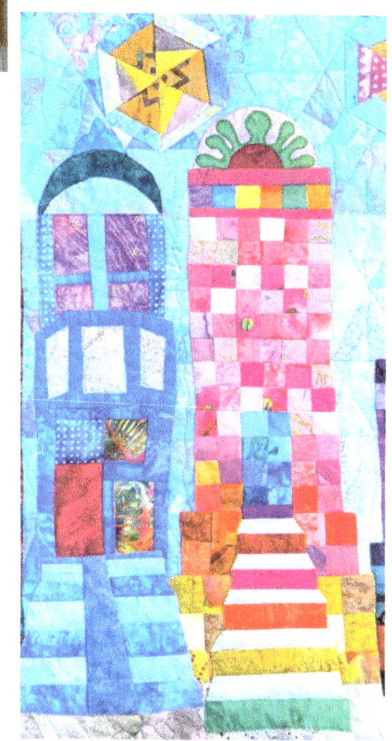

Stairs + Stripes = Step Pyramids

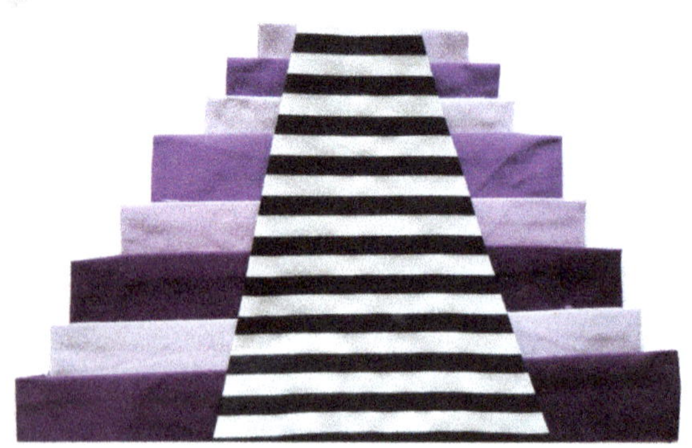

Idea #1 Make simple wedding cake stairs (bottom of p. 86). Then cut and appliqué a wedge of horizontally striped fabric to the middle. (This is a printed navy-and-white stripe. I cut it in a wedge, and turned its right and left edges inward before topstitching it in place.) Bottom and top edges are raw; turn them under last, along with the top and bottom edges of the central wedge. Below: Add a simple house on top and you've got a cousin of the Chichen Itza Temple of Kukulcan!

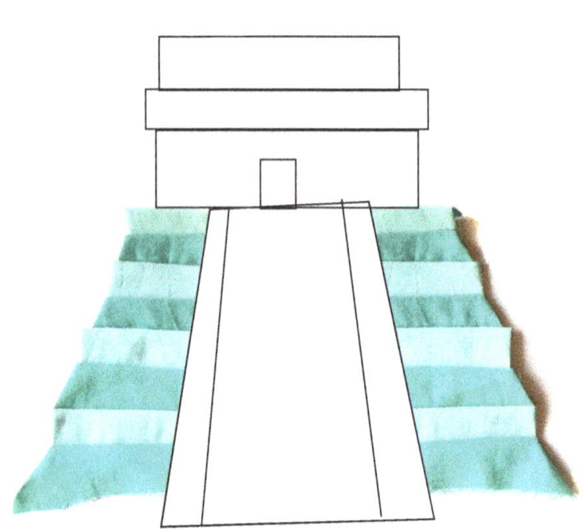

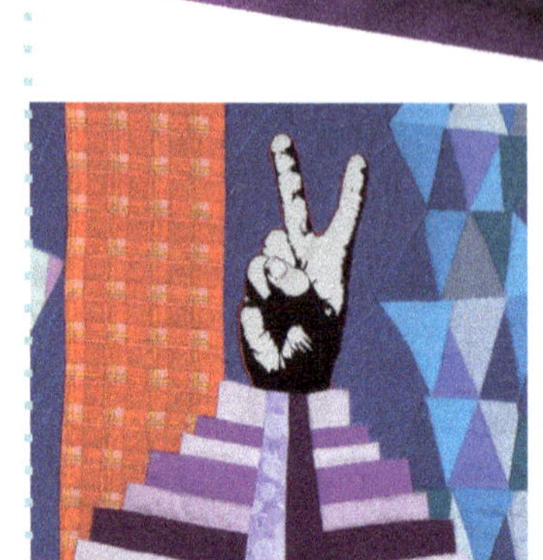

Idea #2 Cut a wedding cake stairway straight down through the middle. Cut two wedge shapes and stitch them together. Piece half the stairway to one side of the wedge pair, half to the other. Last, turn top and bottom edges inward on the same angle as the stairs. The photo shows how I used this construction in my 'Nonsense Town' quilt on p. 10

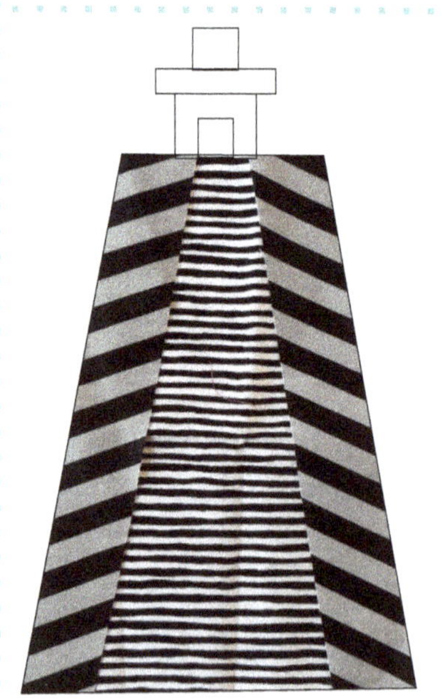

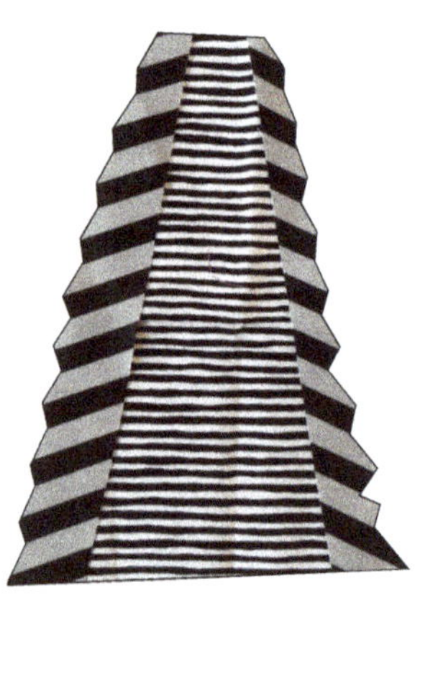

Idea #3 Instead of piecing a staircase, use two different printed stripes. On the upper right, you can cut out the stripes like stairs for a more interesting profile. I would put fusible web on the back of the side stripes before doing this fussy-cutting, and then raw edge appliqué the unit in place. I would not want to turn all those edges under.

Audition Arrangements

Here's how I think about arrangements.

Clusters or Columns A good approach when you only have a few buildings, say 3 - 5.

If I had these five different buildings, I'd first press the top edge of the shortest one – pink – to the back first

Then I'd sew it between the purple and red building. Sew that group to the top of the blue building. Last, add the green building to one side, and the triangle roof. See p. 43, and the next page, for details on putting clusters like these together.

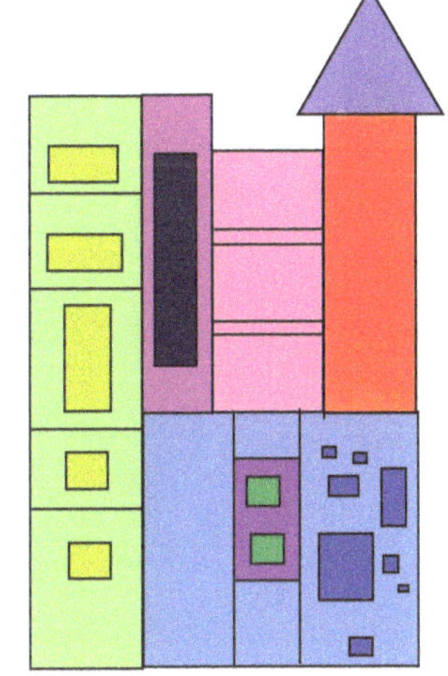

With more than three buildings, I start thinking in rows Some choices:

Rule of Thirds Place the tallest or most dominant building 1/3rd of the way across.

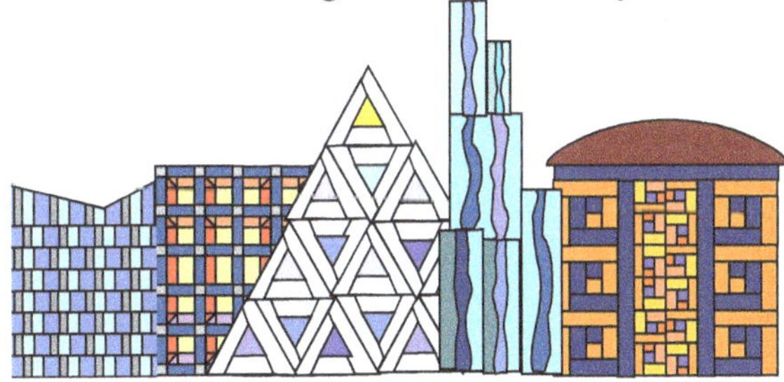

Tallest in the Middle The hypothetical quilt in the diagram below, right is an example; as is the quilt on the left, from my book 'Quilted New York'.

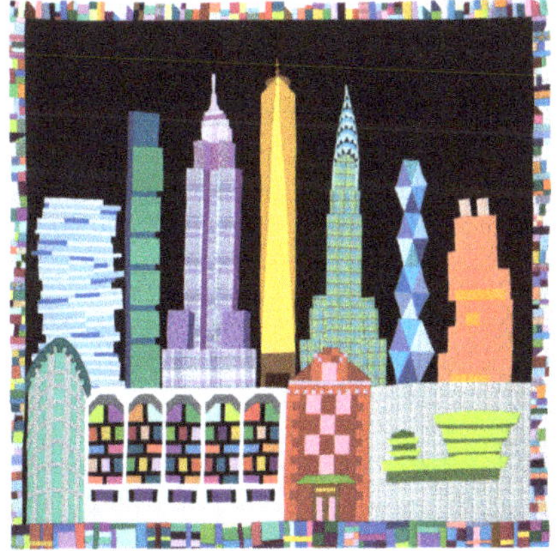

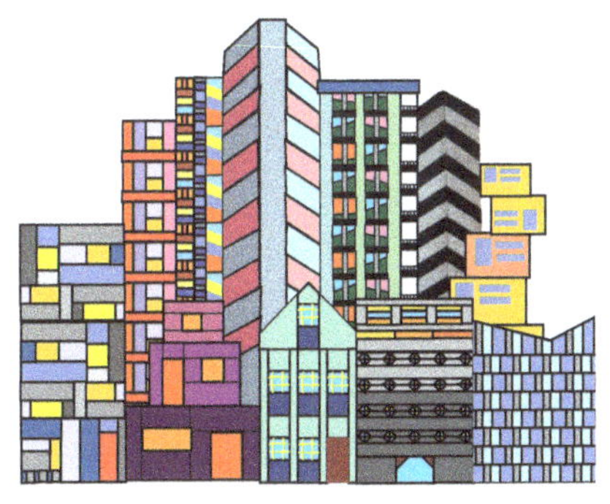

Row by Row Scrap City 2 (right; a larger view is on p.7) is made up of three rows, each with about 6 buildings. 'Nonsense Town' on p. 10 is constructed in two rows.

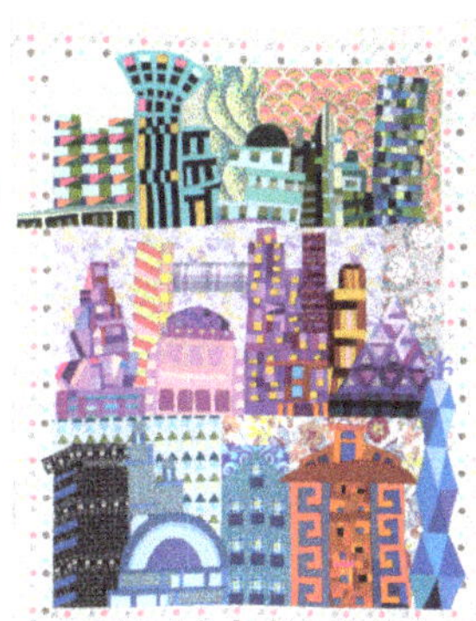

Scrap City 1 (p. 7) has a cluster of stacked buildings on the left; plus 4 more buildings in a row on the right. The two neighborhoods are bisected by a road. It serves as an almost-central focal point.

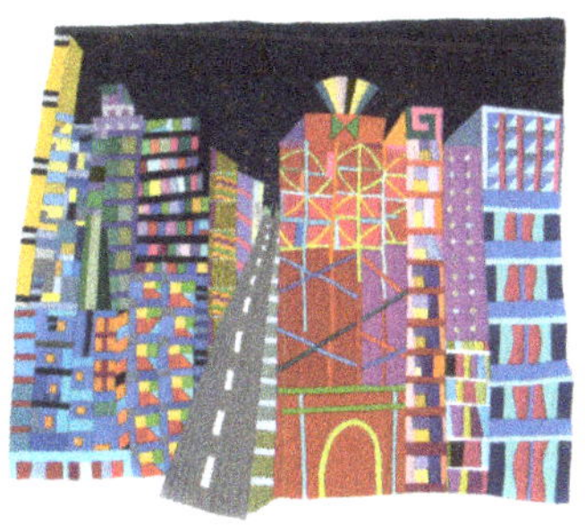

When auditioning arrangements, it's vital to stand back frequently, take a good look, and even snap photos. This will help you spot and avoid run-together buildings! This can happen when their colors are different but their values are similar. Take a picture of every arrangement that you like! (And some you don't – you might change your mind!)

Build Rows First

Most of my arrangements have some buildings stitched side by side, ie in horizontal rows. Smaller quilts may remain one row; for large quilts, I stack and layer rows. For the lowest/"front" row, I try to sew the buildings to each other, with no background involved at all.

1 **Front row first**: I usually put the shortest buildings along the bottom. In this hypothetical, all bottom edges are raw. The green and pink buildings both have straight sides, so we can easily piece them together. The pink building's sides were turned inward when the roof was added, so we may have to unfold its lower left seam. (A little water will dissolve any school glue). Press top edge of shorter green building back 1/4". Place it face-down along the left edge of taller building, and start sewing at **a**. Sew to **b**, stopping just before the fold. Backstitch to **c**. Cut threads. Press new vertical seam allowances under the higher building.

2 Next we want to add this odd-shaped building. Side edges should be turned under (on the triangle and pink buildings). Appliqué is the easiest way to join them. Use a zigzag in the area shown, starting and stopping with a few back and forth straight stitches. (Appliqué info is on p. 17.)

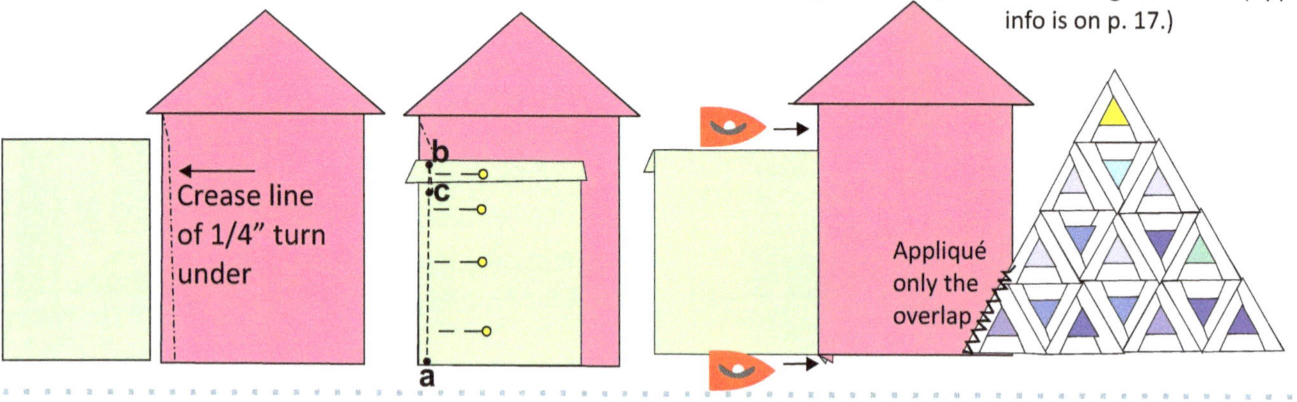

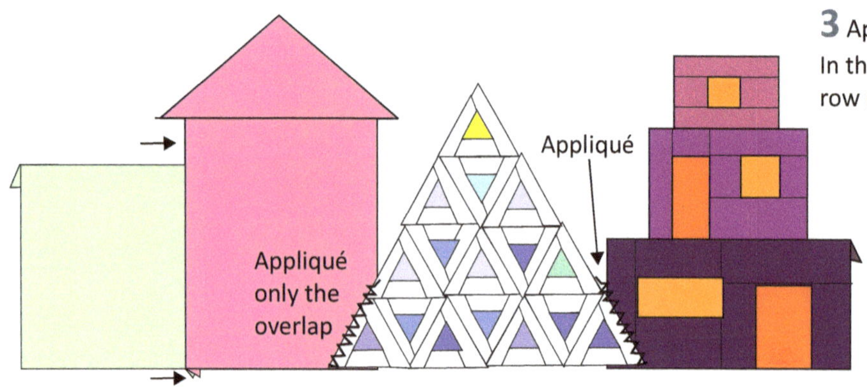

3 Appliqué or piece the next building on the right. In this case, applique is easier. Keep adding until the row (or cluster) is finished.

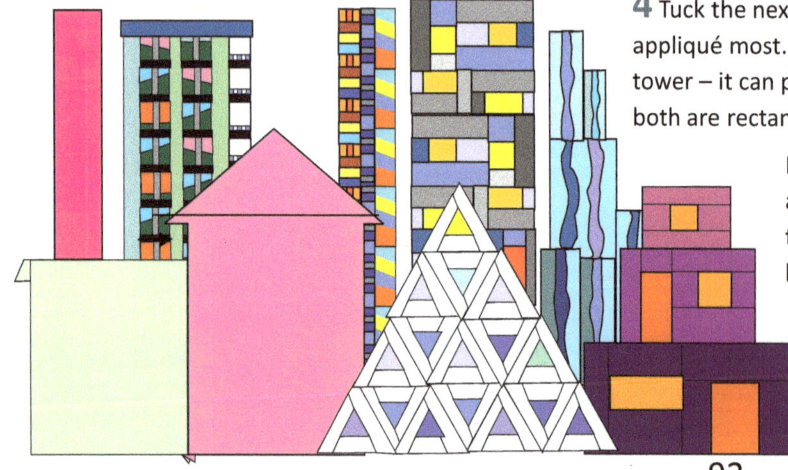

4 Tuck the next row's buildings behind the tops of the front. Baste, then appliqué most. You *may* be able to piece a few, like the far left magenta tower – it can probably be pieced on top of the green building, because both are rectangles and it's only behind one building.

But the rest of the buildings on the upper level need appliqué, because of their unusual shapes and/or because they're behind two buildings that have roofs at different levels. Invisible thread will hide these stitches.

So far, we've sewn together everything we could without involving background fabric. That's next. We'll appliqué the upper buildings (and some first row buildings) to the sky/background. I do this at the same time that I'm auditioning backgrounds. Read on!

Audition Background Fabrics, Secure Buildings

If you can easily piece or appliqué some buildings to others, without involving the background, do that first. In the diagram, you can piece all buildings in the front and middle row to each other. The top/yellow row's middle and top building can be pieced or appliquéd to the buildings below them. But before I sew anything to the background, I hold extensive background auditions!

Audition Before Stitching
Sky color makes a HUGE difference! I test backgrounds while arranging and joining buildings. I pin large fabric pieces to my design wall, pin buildings (some solo, some sewn together) on top. Race to the other side of the room; squint; take a photo; race back to the wall, unpin buildings, remove that background fabric, and pin up the next candidate. It's a workout!

So far, winners (in quilts on pp. 7-10) include dark blues (royal, navy) many times; white once; and black once. Prints can be delightful (Scrap City 2, p. 7). You won't know which background complements the scene until you try!

How Much Background Fabric?
It should reach at least 1″ below the lowest gap between or next to buildings. Here, that spot is on the lower right (next to and just below the **a**). If there's not enough fabric to go that low, I cut a sky fabric strip from the area that will later be trimmed away, beneath center buildings. I sew that strip to where you see a navy seam line (to the right of the letter **d**.) No one is going to notice it (imho).

Pin, Then Hand Baste
This prepares you to appliqué some buildings to each other, and most to the sky, with no batting or backing involved yet. (The alternative to hand-basting is just pinning, and that works for a small quilt– but when a large top is crumpled in the machine for appliqué, I would certainly stab myself with the pins!) So we'll do this in two stages, pinning and then hand-basting.

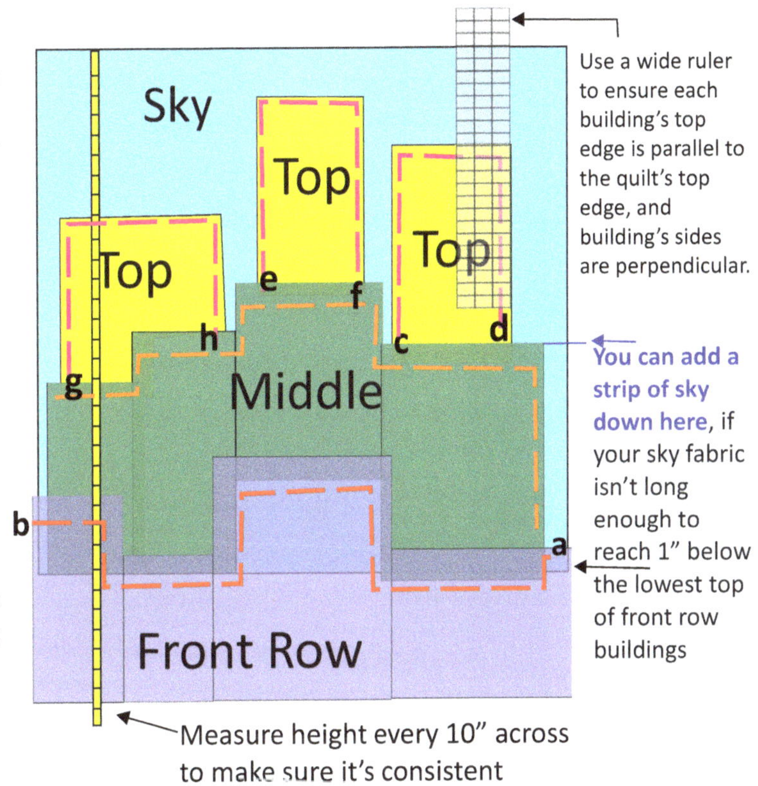

1 **Pin or tape background fabric to a floor or table.** It needn't be ultra taut, just flat with no wrinkles.

2 **Lay buildings (in rows, clusters, or solo) on the background.** Measure the height every 10″. The distance should remain the same all the way across. When it's good, lightly pin. If things are off-kilter, first try straightening the front row. If heights still aren't consistent, mark and trim extra off the sky/top. I avoid trimming buildings' bottom raw edges, but sometimes there's no choice. When you get each segment properly aligned, put a few pins in it.

3 **On highest buildings, use a wide (or square) ruler to set skyscrapers straight,** shown on the diagram's upper right. It's too easy to create a slightly leaning tower! Again, when it's right, pin it.

4 **Start thread basting from the bottom/front row.** Replace your occasional pins with generous thread-basting. Hand baste (red dotted line) about an inch below the tops of the front row buildings if there are buildings above/behind them. If there's nothing but sky behind a front row building, basting can come closer to the top edge.

5 **Baste middle row buildings next (orange dotted lines).** Again, if there's a building directly behind/above, baste an inch or so down from the middle row buildings' top folded edges. In areas where there will be nothing but background behind them, you can baste closer to the middle row buildings' top edge folds.

6 **The yellow/top buildings are basted last.** Since these aren't in front of anything (except sky), you can baste very close to its top folded edges. This basting is in magenta in the diagram.

(continued)

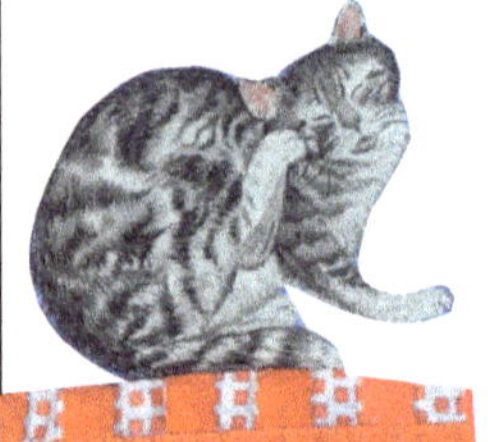

Adding Characters?

If you want to add fun novelty fabric characters to your scene – especially if you want to tuck their edges under buildings – do it just before the steps on this page. As explained on p. 14, I put fusible web on the back of the figures, then cut close around their edges. Press them where you want them. If their edges are raw, use a wide stitch (like a zigzag) that's tighter than for turned-edge appliqué, closer to a satin stitch.

But you don't HAVE to add them now– I've done it even after the quilt is quilted! In that case, of course, you can't tuck edges under buildings.

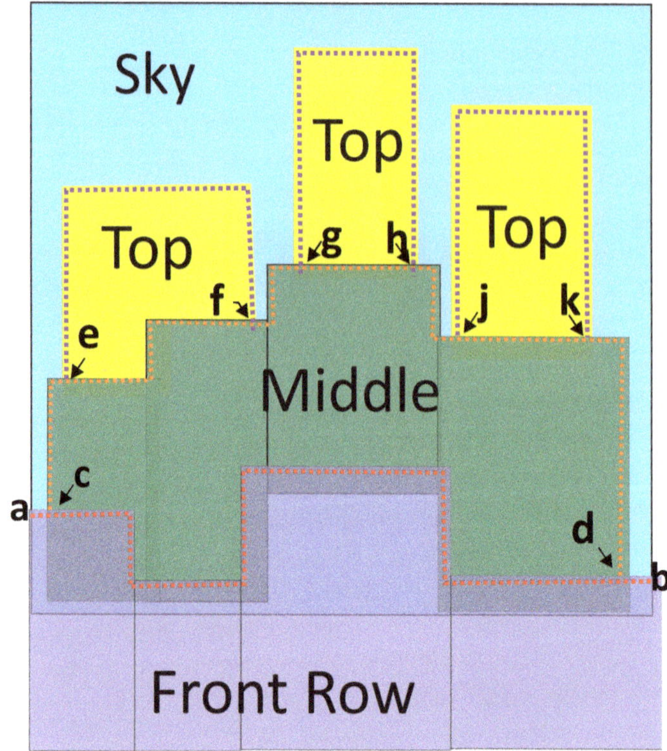

Machine Appliqué

Install an open toe foot and use whatever stitch you like best for turned edge appliqué (p. 17). Invisible thread is ideal, so you won't have to switch thread colors for each building.

We'll appliqué in reverse order of basting. Start with tops and sides of top (yellow) buildings.

On the far left at **e**: Use a finger to hold back the folded top edges of the green/middle row building (This is why you basted an inch down from the top). Start with a few tiny back-and-forth straight stitches in that about-to-be-hidden spot, where the **e** arrow points, on the yellow building's lower left corner. Take off, and do your appliqué stitch on the purple dotted line, up the side from **e**, across the top, down to **f**. There, again use a finger to hold back the green building's seam allowance, while you finish with back-and-forth straight stitches on the lower right corner of that yellow building. Clip threads. Let go of the flap. It will hopefully hide the ending stitches.

Repeat this procedure for the other top buildings; sew on the purple dotted lines, up and around, from **g** to end at **h**, then **j** to **k**. No need to sew across their horizontal bases.

Next go for the sides and tops of the buildings in the middle/green row. Sew from just below and left of **c**, all the way to the far right of (and below) **d**, this time on the orange dotted line.

In the front/blue row, appliqué from end **a**, to **b**, along the side and top folds (the red dotted line.)

Once everything is appliquéd, you may be able to cut away a substantial amount of sky fabric, most of the fabric behind the dark blue and green areas. I leave a seam allowance of an inch of sky fabric in place (rather than cutting back to 1/4"), to make the quilt a bit stronger and allow for some leeway if a building's position needs a last-minute adjustment.

Scavenge for Quilting Ideas!

Cities are full of quilting ideas! Photograph walls, sidewalks, grates, etc. They may be just what you need to inspire your designs.

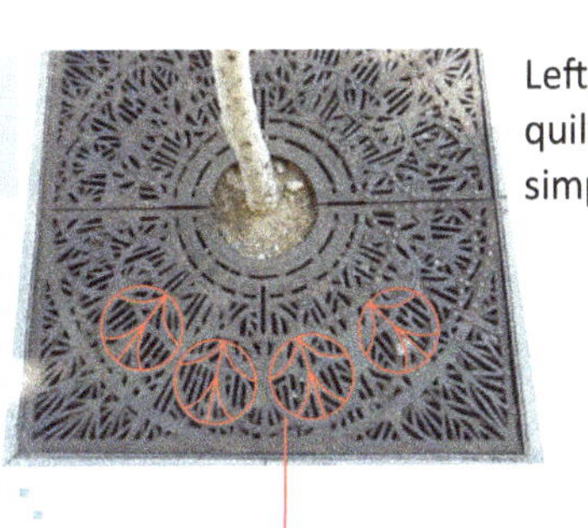

Left, This tree grate would make an awesome quilted sunrise (or sunset!) Trace and simplify the main lines.

Right, building is embellished with Art-Deco-inspired details!

Below, vertical rows of geometric quilting designs hint at more buildings in the background.

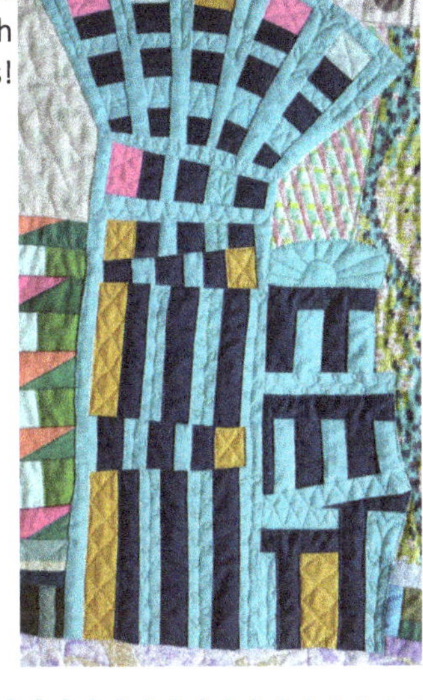

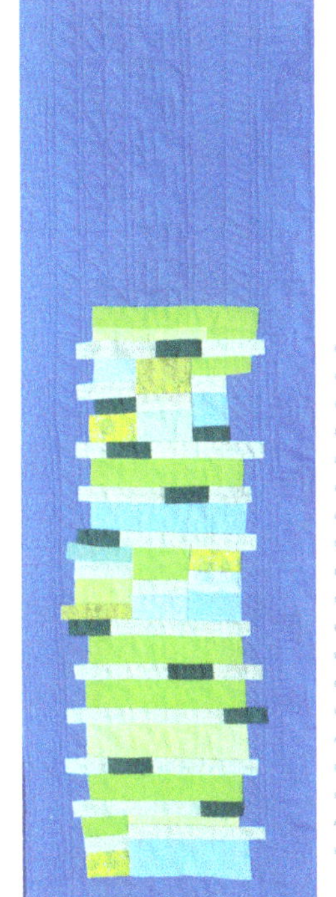

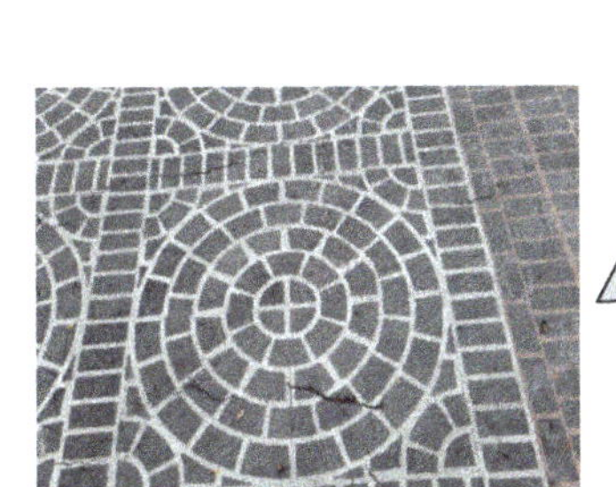

Cobbled street design would make a sleeker sunset than the one above! Along with paving stones, check out sewer grates for ideas!

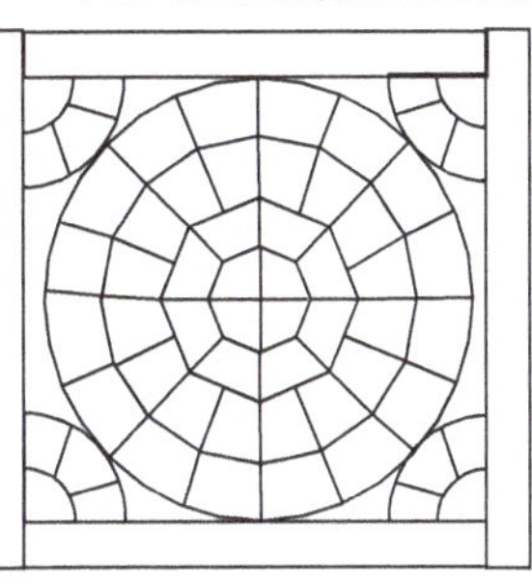

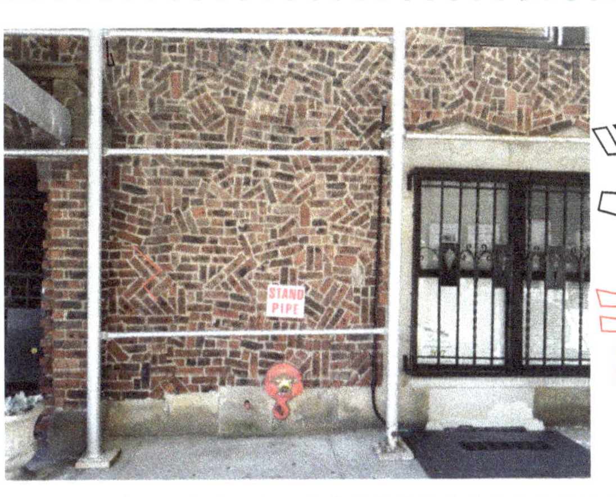

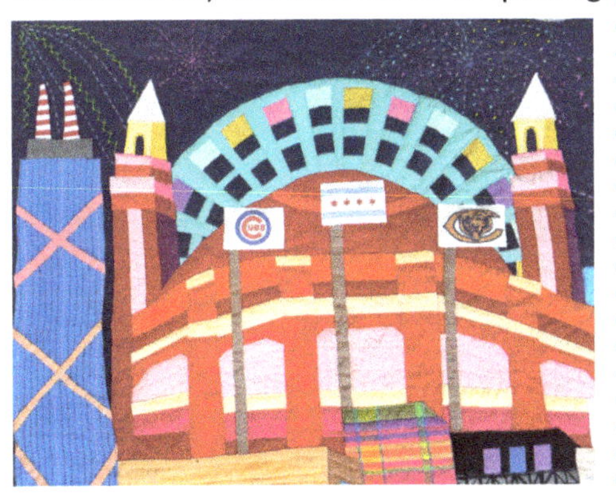

Stippling inspiration: I traced main lines of an exuberant brick wall on a NYC apartment building (left). Fun freemotion designs emerged!

The fireworks in the sky are hand-embroidered, and also serve as quilting!

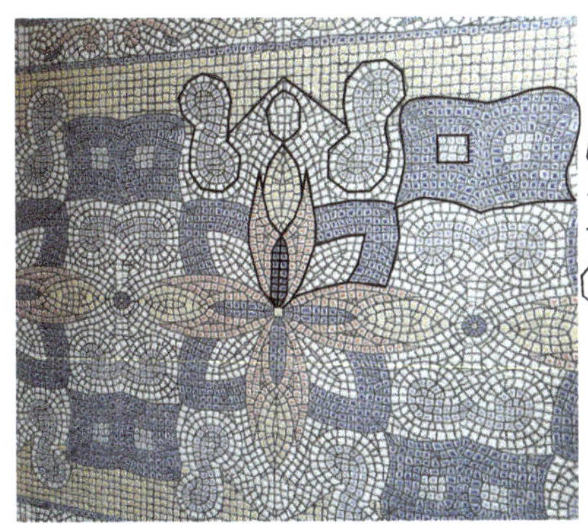

In the entrance of a tiny, dingy midtown NYC restaurant, I found this fantastic mosaic wall. To quilt this complex design, I'd have to draw it on my quilt first.

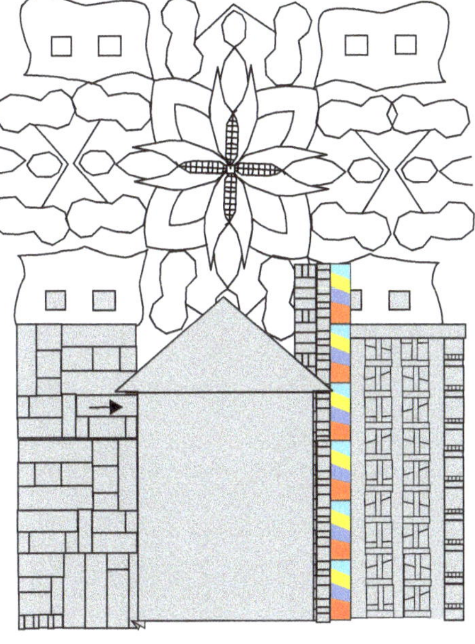

Quilt in a Vanishing Point

Quilting in a vanishing point (pp. 65-66) can add depth to a scene. It also creates guidelines for lots of city-inspired freemotion quilting designs like those on the previous page.

1 First do all the quilting along main building outlines, and WITHIN each building.

2 Mark equidistant dots all around the sky area. Every 2" is dense; I think every 4" is better if you want to add freemotion quilting designs inside each segment.

3 If the quilt doesn't already have a vanishing point, pick a spot. In the diagram, far right, I'm putting it to the left of the highest tower.

4 Draw one line (or two, 1/4" apart), from each edge mark to the vanishing point. A long clear ruler is very helpful; or use a yardstick. No need to mark the buildings if you won't sew these lines on top of them (I don't).

5 Fill in each segment with freemotion quilting. Or use them as guidelines to embroider in spaceships, fireworks, clouds, stars, etc! (See top of p. 7.)

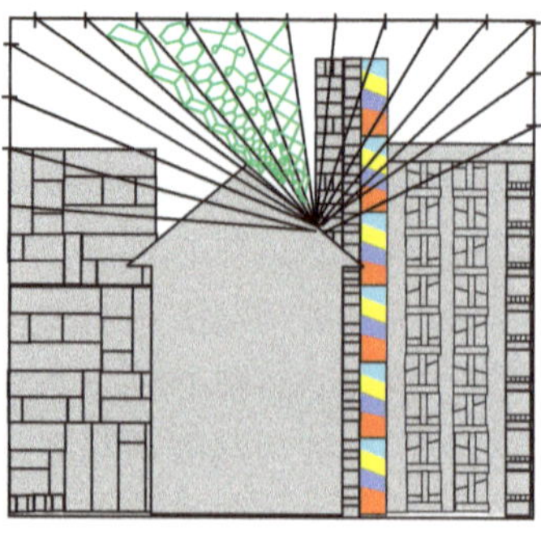

Another example:

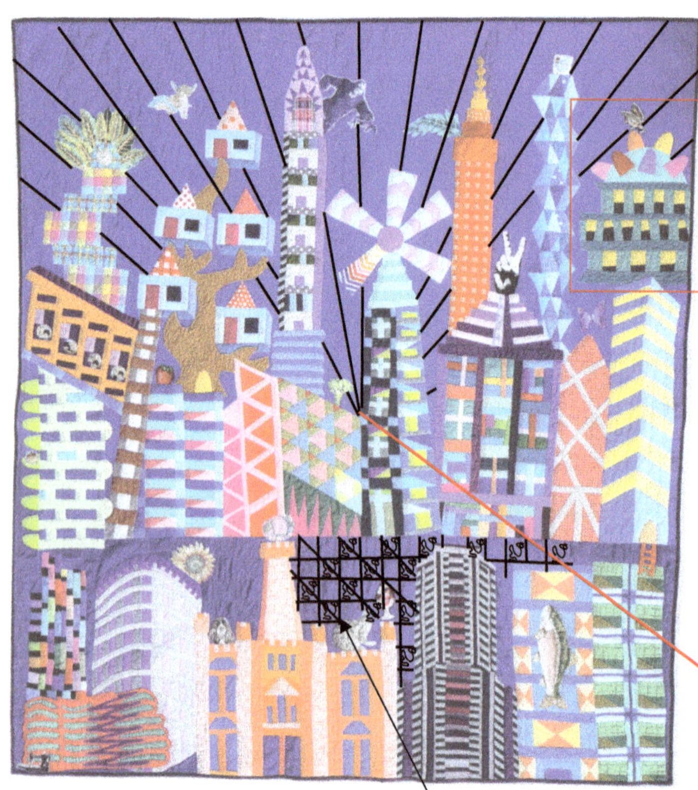

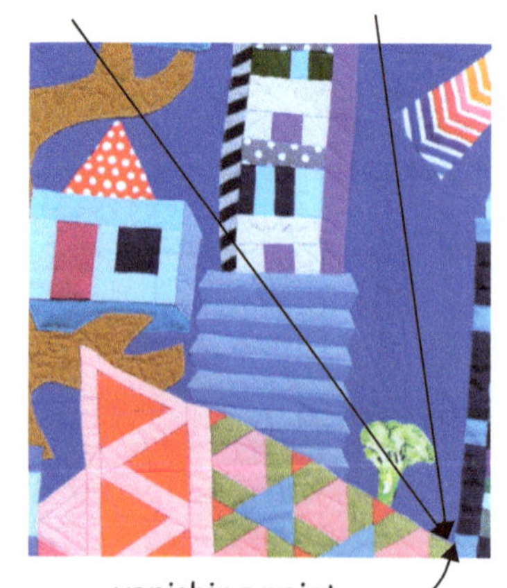

Near left, a closeup of the observatory (in the red box on the large quilt image on the far left), with background double lines and freemotion designs. The building itself is heavily quilted with whimsical designs.

In the 'Nonsense Town' quilt, p. 10, I sectioned off the sky with quilted double lines (1/4" apart, but in the diagram you only see single lines). All come from the quilt's edges, and aim at the quilt's vanishing point. That point is on the lower right of the broccoli in the big photo, left, and the closer view below, right. I filled each segment of sky with a different freemotion design.

In the quilt's bottom third (directly above), I ignored the vanishing point and instead quilted a straightforward grid of squares, plus one-way diagonals, in the sky. Every other square is filled with free-motion stippling. I did this everywhere that there's sky above the bottom building row. (The diagram only outlines a little of it).

Within each building, I quilted main lines in the ditch, like around windows and doors, and between levels. If there was still room on the building, I added decorative quilting.